The
Anatomy Murders

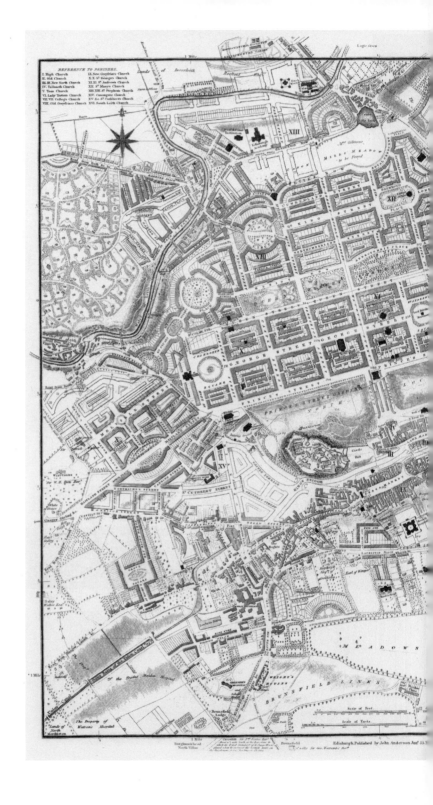

Edinburgh, Published by John Anderson Jun.ʳ 55 N.

Map of Edinburgh, 1830, by John Anderson Junior.
Reproduction by Carson Clark Gallery, Edinburgh.

The
Anatomy Murders

Being the True and Spectacular
History of Edinburgh's Notorious
BURKE AND HARE
and of the
MAN OF SCIENCE
Who Abetted Them in the
Commission *of* Their Most
HEINOUS CRIMES

Lisa Rosner

PENN

UNIVERSITY OF PENNSYLVANIA PRESS
Philadelphia

Published by
University of Pennsylvania Press
Philadelphia, Pennsylvania 19104-4112

Printed in the United States of America on acid-free paper
10 9 8 7 6 5 4 3

Library of Congress Cataloging-in-Publication Data
Rosner, Lisa
The anatomy murders : being the true and spectacular history of Edinburgh's notorious Burke and Hare, and of the man of science who abetted them in the commission of their most heinous crimes / Lisa Rosner.
Includes bibliographical references and index.
   p.   cm.
ISBN: 978-0-8122-4191-4 (alk. paper)
1. Burke, William, 1792–1829.   2. Hare, William, 1792?–1870?
3. Murder—Scotland—Edinburgh—Case studies.
4. Murder—Scotland—Edinburgh—History—19th century.
5. Edinburgh (Scotland)—History.
HV6535.G6R568 2010
364.152/309224134 22   2009018495

Contents

Introduction

The Burke and Hare Murders

THOUGH NEITHER WAS NATIVE TO THE CITY AND BOTH ARE long gone, William Burke and William Hare remain two of Edinburgh's most famous residents. Over a twelve-month period they killed sixteen people—three men, twelve women, and one child—in a murder spree which ended only with their arrest in November 1828. The motive was profit, for Edinburgh was a major center of medical education, and lecturers would pay high prices for "subjects," that is, cadavers for dissection. The means was a form of suffocation. Assisted by Hare's wife, Margaret, and Burke's companion, Helen M'Dougal, the two men enticed their victims to drink to insensibility, then lay on top of them, compressing the chest while holding the mouth and nostrils closed: "burking," it came to be called. The crimes were made possible in part by general conditions of the early nineteenth-century city, with its large mobile population and small police force. There were additional contributing circumstances: Margaret Hare ran a lodging house for transients in the busy immigrant district known as the West Port, and Dr. Robert Knox, the up-and-coming anatomist to whom the killers sold the cadavers, asked no questions. "Murder is no novel crime," wrote one contemporary journalist, "it has been done in the olden time as well as now; but murder perpetrated in such a manner, upon such a system with such an object or intent, and accompanied by such accessory circumstances, was never, we believe, heard of before." Its "deep tragical interest" made it "picturesquely horrifying," and it has retained its hold on the popular imagination ever since. Burke and Hare are famous among true-crime aficionados, forensic experts, and devotees of horror stories. They have been depicted in literature, on stage, and in film. And whenever questions are raised about the lucrative medical transplant industry, or the illicit harvesting of body parts, we are sure to hear the story of Burke and Hare.

These were the first serial killings to capture media attention, sixty years before Jack the Ripper. The early nineteenth century was marked by an enormous expansion in the popular press, and news of horrific murders sold sensationally. Edinburgh newspapers eagerly followed the story, providing daily and even twice-daily reports and commentary. These reports were reprinted and embellished in the periodical press from London, Manchester, and Dublin to New York, Boston, and the Ohio frontier. Full-length versions followed as soon as publishers could set the type. First off the press was Thomas Ireland's *West Port Murders*, a series of twenty-four-page pamphlets later combined in a single volume. It promised "An Authentic and Faithful History of the ATROCIOUS MURDERS COMMITTED BY BURKE AND HIS ASSOCIATES; Containing every authentic particular, and a full Disclosure of all the extraordinary circumstances connected with them . . . Illustrated by Portraits drawn from Life, and other highly interesting Copperplate Engravings of Plans, Views, &c." Ireland had not quite completed his print run when the publisher and bookseller Robert Buchanan issued his more upmarket book, *Trial of William Burke and Helen M'Dougal*. Advertised as the only "*authentic* edition" of the trial, it featured sworn testimony from the murderers' neighbors and associates as well as a corrected version of the proceedings. Buchanan published two other sets of documents relating to the murders over the next few months, reprinting local newspaper articles and pamphlets not available elsewhere. An avid reading public scooped them up, binding them together with lurid illustrations, broadsheets, and caricatures.

The murders became part of the lore of Edinburgh, a story steeped in the distinctive geography of the city, with its tall gray tenements "dispersed over a very irregular surface of ground," wrote Thomas Shepherd in his 1831 collection of engravings, *Modern Athens*, "and placed partly in valleys, and partly on the tops and sloping sides of hills." He compared the High Street, lying on the highest sloping ridge, to "the backbone of a herring," with Edinburgh Castle at its head on the west end, and Holyrood Palace on its tail to the east. The ribs were formed by "the numerous narrow lanes," called *wynds* or *closes*, running steeply down the hillside, and the Hares' house in Tanner's Close, southwest of the High Street, became notorious as the scene of most of the murders.

Scottish writers have always been drawn to Burke and Hare. Sir Walter Scott followed the affair as avidly as the rest of Edinburgh at the time and discussed it freely with his friends and legal associates. So did John Wilson, the literary force behind *Blackwood's Magazine* under his pen name of Christopher North. Known for its macabre tales and an important influence on Edgar Allan Poe, *Blackwood's* made cadavers and body snatchers staples of periodical fiction throughout the nineteenth century. Robert Louis Stevenson drew on the murders in his short story masterpiece "The Body Snatcher." The playwright and surgeon James Bridie took up the murders in his 1931 play *The Anatomist*; more recently, Burke and Hare had a cameo role in Ian Rankin's *Fleshmarket Close*. Modern visitors to Edinburgh will hear many Burke and Hare stories, some of which are even true. The rest—of cadavers hauled up secret passageways, of beautiful prostitutes dissected by their lovers—are gruesome and enthralling, easy enough to believe on a foggy November evening, passing under a bridge or climbing a dark stone stair.

The impact of the murders reverberated well outside of Scotland, for they coincided with political developments that ultimately transformed modern Britain. In 1828 the Tory establishment, which held power in Parliament, was under attack by Whig opposition leaders agitating for governmental reform. During precisely the period that Burke and Hare peddled their cadavers, a Whig-led parliamentary committee was investigating the way in which medical schools obtained bodies for dissection. The Select Committee on Anatomy, as it came to be known, made public the dangers inherent in the body trade. Once the murders came to light, committee members seized on Burke and Hare as the "true authors" of the reforms they proposed. The government, they claimed, was "responsible for the crime which it has fostered by its negligence, and even encouraged by a system of forbearance." Radical publishers Cowie and Strange issued *Murderers of the Close*, the first novel based on Burke and Hare, featuring engravings by the political caricaturist Robert Seymour, best known today as Charles Dickens's first illustrator (Figure 1). Within a few years the Whigs were in power, and the Tories had all but ceased to exist. In 1832 Parliament passed the Reform Act, which legislated an unprecedented increase in the number of male voters and gave representation to Britain's growing industrial centers. In the same year it passed the Anatomy Act, which legislated procedures by which medical schools could obtain dead bodies. In 1837 Queen Victoria ascended the throne, marking a new era in British history. The Burke and Hare murders became permanently enshrined as a symbol of the "bad old days" before Parliament's Great Reform, before enlightened legislation and modern progress.

Figure 1. Robert Seymour, "Burke Murdering Margery Campbell," from *Murderers of the Close*, reproduced courtesy of the Trustees of the National Library of Scotland. This artist's conception of the murder was based on testimony and cross-examination presented at the murder trial.

By 1861, when Alexander Leighton published *The Court of Cacus; or, the Story of Burke and Hare*, the bad old days seemed very bad indeed. Leighton had briefly studied medicine in Edinburgh in 1826, but he went on to be a lawyer's clerk and, later, a writer and editor of Scottish tales. He had connections in Edinburgh medical circles, and his book reflects the marked changes that had taken place in the medical profession. Three cholera epidemics had come and gone, killing thousands but transforming public health institutions. Educational reforms and licensing regulations had raised the status of physicians to the dignified professionals of the Victorian world. Louis Pasteur in France, Robert Koch in Prussia, and

Joseph Lister in Scotland had all begun their pathbreaking work on the germ theory, creating modern scientific medicine and permanently fusing the image of the healer with that of the scientist. Leighton and his readers expected doctors to be heroes; they looked back on earlier generations of doctors with some sympathy for their efforts, but distaste for their barbarous practices. And they viewed the behavior of the previous generation as shockingly unprofessional, from the invective used against rival practitioners to the methods used in obtaining cadavers for dissection.

The *Court of Cacus*, then, was in part an exposé of the medical practices of the 1820s, a delineation of the shadows that made subsequent advances shine all the brighter. Leighton disclosed some of the dirty little secrets of the pre–Anatomy Act medicine: the existence of professional body snatchers who roamed the graveyards of Edinburgh, the raucous competition among medical practitioners for fame and fortune. The true villains of his book were not Burke and Hare, nor were they the medical profession as a whole. Instead, Leighton put the blame on anatomy teachers who created the demand for bodies, vying to see who could most callously overstep the bounds of human decency in obtaining them. Villain-in-chief was Robert Knox, who had sworn to outdo his rival lecturers and chose possession of fresh cadavers as the means to do so. He was, according to Leighton, a "marked man," as befit the main character "in the great tragedy subsequently enacted." He was a brilliant surgeon, Leighton argued, but that was the problem: he was so concerned about being preeminent in his field that he was blind to all other considerations. His vanity and ambition, his "vindictive impatience of an intruder on his particular walk," as Leighton put it, brought about his downfall.

There were eyewitnesses still living in 1860, and Leighton interviewed some, but he also invented fictional eyewitnesses when it suited him, and whole sections of *The Court of Cacus* are simply made up. "Unfortunately for the cause of historical truth," wrote the physician Henry Lonsdale, Robert Knox's former assistant, Leighton "had dressed up his story so well, and introduced moral and pious reflections to suit the Scottish mind . . . that many mistook his work for a *bona fide* narrative of events!" Writing ten years after Leighton in 1870, and after Knox's death in 1862, Lonsdale's avowed goal was to set the record straight. He did so by presenting Knox as a supremely talented scientist like Lister or Charles Darwin. Admired by his students, venerated by his patients, Knox could have had a brilliant career, had it not been blighted by his unwitting association with evil men. Oddly, though Lonsdale wrote so vehemently against Leighton, he repeated many of the same Burke and Hare legends found in *The Court of Cacus*. His later status as Knox's colleague and defender gave them a spurious air of authenticity, though Lonsdale was only twelve years old, still living at home in Carlisle, at the time the murders took place.

Leighton's and Lonsdale's books became the basis of the most influential work on the murders, William Roughead's *Burke and Hare*, published as a volume in the Notable Trials series in 1921. Roughead was trained as an Edinburgh lawyer, though he never practiced, preferring to devote himself to writing on true crime. His introductory essay gave an insightful and entertaining overview of the crimes, for Roughead was an excellent storyteller. The rest of the volume provided a reprint of Buchanan's 1829 edition of the trial, as well as the later supplementary publications. Roughead brought to the murders the sensibility of the detective-story genre. Though the Burke and Hare story is not a whodunit in the usual sense, the nineteenth-century versions had left a raft of unanswered questions for readers brought up on Wilkie Collins and Arthur Conan Doyle. What was the psychology of the crime? Were Margaret Hare and Helen M'Dougal guilty, as well as the two men? What had Knox and his assistants known, and when did they know it? Was there a cover-up on the part of the judicial authorities? Roughead sifted the evidence, examined contemporary publications, analyzed legal documents. He also added an ironic style, and an early twentieth-century relish of Victorian indiscretions, so if a salacious anecdote suited him he did not look too closely at its provenance. In this way some of the least reliable details from nineteenth-century publications became firmly embedded in the Burke and Hare saga.

Within a few years of Roughead's *Burke and Hare*, Sinclair Lewis's *Arrowsmith* provided a compelling portrait of a new type of physician-scientist, a researcher rather than a clinician. During the 1930s, as new vaccines and medications appeared to tame one deadly epidemic after another, films like William Dieterle's *The Story of Louis Pasteur* and *Dr. Ehrlich's Magic Bullet* glorified the efforts of medical researchers. In somber counterpoint were movie versions of Burke and Hare, which juxtaposed the evil of the killings with the good to which doctors might turn the murdered cadavers. Robert Wise's 1945 horror classic *The Body Snatcher*, starring Boris Karloff and Bela Lugosi, depicted a surgeon dissecting a woman he knows has been murdered so that a crippled young girl may walk again. Dylan Thomas's 1953 screenplay *The Doctor and the Devils* was the basis for the gritty 1985 film with Timothy Dalton and Jonathan Pryce; it, too, confronted viewers with questions about the costs of medical progress. Even as we draw the line at murder, do we ignore other dubious practices? Black market sale of body parts? Medical experimentation on human subjects without their knowledge? Miracles of modern medicine routinely available to the rich, but not to the poor?

These questions are still with us, and they ensure the continued fame of Burke and Hare. But precisely because they are still with us, it is time to take a new look at the facts of the original case. A murder cannot be considered solved if its investigation is based on hearsay; a cautionary tale loses its bite if it is based on rumor and anecdote. As a historian I am drawn to these sixteen murders for what they reveal about medicine, but I stay with them because I am also fascinated by what previous accounts have left out. For the past 180 years writers have relied on contemporary published sources, but a wealth of unpublished materials in Edinburgh's incomparable libraries has been largely unexplored. I use these letters, account books, police reports, and medical notebooks to recapture the voices of the historical actors in this drama—murderers, victims, doctors—and to retrace the paths which led to their often disastrous decisions. I also use them to uncover additional actors, such as policemen, journalists, and Edinburgh intellectuals, all of whom had roles to play as the drama unfolded. This historical detective work provides a new, vivid perspective on the story, one startling in its immediacy and interest.

In addition to the strange partnership of Burke and Hare and the medical profession, and the grisly murders themselves, this book is about the intersections of the disparate worlds of nineteenth-century Edinburgh—between lecturers and students, doctors and patients, between the upper and lower strata of society—which made the murders possible and shaped their aftermath. The chapters travel, cadaver by cadaver, through that fateful twelve-month period. We traverse the geography of the city and its variegated social and economic life, from the habits of its lower classes to the recreations of its gentry, from the demands of its doctors to the political aspirations of its legal elite. What emerges is a city, a profession, and a crime on the edge of modernity, suddenly confronting innovation in murder as well as in the arts and sciences. "Thus the march of crime has far outstripped 'the march of intellect,'" according to one commentator; "with all the pretended illumination, the present age must be characterized by some deeper and fouler blots than have attached to any that precede it." Its "brighter spots" were counterbalanced by its "darker shades and more appalling obscurations." We will search out those shadows as we explore the worlds of Burke and Hare.

Chapter 1

The Corpus Delicti

Margaret Docherty or Campbell

THE CORPUS DELICTI—LITERALLY, THE CORPSE THAT FORMED the material evidence for the charge of murder—was discovered on Saturday, November 1, 1828. In life, it had belonged to Madgy or Margery or Margaret Docherty, also known by her married name, Campbell, who thereby acquired the sad distinction of initiating the murder investigation into Burke and Hare. Because testimony concerning her death figured prominently in the later trial, we know more about her than any of the other victims. Madgy Docherty, as we will call her, was a small woman between forty and fifty years old, originally from Donegal in Ireland but lately residing in Glasgow. She had few belongings besides her clothes, a "petticoat, a red short-gown, striped, a long printed gown, short-sleeved and open before, and sewed with white cotton thread before" (Figure 2). Anyone seeing an older woman dressed in that fashion would know her for a recent immigrant, and in fact she was a talkative body who told everyone her business: her husband's name was Campbell, but hers was Docherty, and she had come to Edinburgh on October 30 in search of her son, Michael Campbell. He had arrived for the harvest and had been boarding for two months with a family in the Pleasance, a former county road now lined with lodging houses. But the landlady, Mary Stewart, told Docherty that her son had left the previous Monday; they had missed each other by three days. Docherty stayed overnight, and in the morning went out to find one

MRS CAMPBELL OR DOCHERTY.
MURDERED BY WM BURKE.

Figure 2. Artist's conception of Margaret Docherty. Reproduced from a contemporary print, courtesy of the Library of the Royal College of Physicians of Edinburgh.

of her son's friends, working at a shop at the foot of St. Mary's Wynd. The term *wynd* meant a lane leading off a main street, and St. Mary's Wynd was a bustling thoroughfare whose picturesque combination of fashionable shops and boisterous street life attracted artists and visitors. Tourists might follow it until they reached the High Street, heading uphill to the garrison at Edinburgh Castle or downhill to the royal residence at Holyrood Palace. Neither of these was Madgy Docherty's destination. She had no money and had not breakfasted; nor would she tell where she was going, saying only "that she did not know where her son was, and she was leaving town." Her road lay west on the main route for the migratory Irish, running parallel but far below the High Street: along the Cowgate to the Grassmarket and on through the West Port of Edinburgh to the Glasgow Road (Figure 3).

There had once been an actual West "Port," or gate, at the western end of the city, but by 1828 the name referred to the long street, also known as Wester Portsburgh, that was the main point of entry and egress for western Scotland and Ireland. Grocers, spirit dealers, and small shopkeepers of all descriptions—even a bookseller and circulating library—fronted the street, while "closes," narrow enclosed courtyards, led to clusters of tenements just behind. Thomas Shepherd's *Modern Athens* presents striking views of these tenements, exulting that "one of these 'stacks of houses'" contained "no less than ten storeys, or 'flats'; and it is a fact that many of these flats are inhabited by distinct families, whilst one flight of stairs communicates to the whole." Many of the stories had been further divided, either by landlords or tenants, so that each of the rooms on a floor might be occupied by "distinct families," with an extra straw pallet tucked here or there to be rented out at threepence a night. Until the eighteenth century these tene-

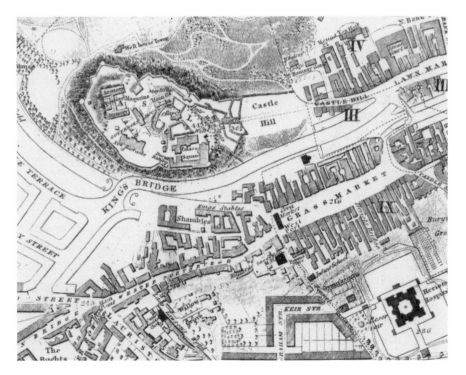

Figure 3. Map of the West Port district. The Hares' house in Tanner's Close and Burke's and M'Dougal's house just to the east were on the north side of Wester Portsburgh, approximately above the "TSB" in "PORTSBURGH" on the map.

ments had housed the Scots nobility and their retinue. But from the 1770s Edinburgh had embarked on an ambitious series of civic improvements. North and South Bridges, far above Madgy Docherty's head as she walked along the Cowgate, had been completed in 1788, demolishing one of the most populated sections of the old medieval city while furthering urban expansion beyond the old city walls. Edinburgh's New Town was laid out by city planners and private investors in honey-colored stone along elegant Georgian avenues and crescents; as each new section was completed, the wealthier classes abandoned the narrow, crowded Old Town tenements for larger, more modern residences along York Place and Charlotte Square. The North and South Bridges grew congested from the carriages rumbling through the Old Town, and plans were under way for a new route, the modern George IV Bridge. The city had burst its medieval boundaries to the east and south as well, with well-maintained coach roads leading to the fashionable seaside resort of Portabello, or to gentlemen's estates in the Pentland Hills.

There were many among the upper classes whose business or profession still brought them to the Old Town: lawyers attending the courts in Parliament Close, professors and students in the newly completed quadrangle of Edinburgh University, doctors heading to the Royal Infirmary and Surgeon's Square. In the evenings, though, the Old Town was left to those who could afford nothing better, separated from the city's expansion not just by bridges but by indicators of poverty, such as higher infant mortality and lower literacy. A kind of spotlight shone upon this economic disparity every evening. "The Old Town, the immense houses of which, towering one above another, are seen from the splendid line of Princes-street" wrote one foreign visitor, "is particularly brilliant at night. This Old Town glitters every day of the week with numberless ranges and clusters of lights, as other cities do only on great festive occasions. Yet all this splendid array of lights is the consequence of poverty and wretchedness. All these high houses are filled with crowded inhabitants from cellar to roof, and every room has its separate family. All these poor people are at work till very late at night, light glimmers from the window of every crowded and comfortless room; whilst in the houses of the rich, whole suites of rooms lie unoccupied, and consequently dark."

Yet we should not think of the Old Town as the depths of misery and depravity, or Madgy Docherty as a sheep among wolves. Her route underneath the stilts formed by the bridges followed the path of the city's industrial base, including tanneries, breweries, saltworks, linen factories, and paper mills. She passed by the fish, meat, and poultry markets, the en- trepot of the increasingly commercialized agriculture of the region, where hundreds of animals were driven or carried from the surrounding coun- tryside, slaughtered, and sold. On October 31, especially, the roads would have been as noisy and lively as a country fair, for the next day, Novem- ber 1, was All Hallows, the day of Edinburgh's annual livestock market, when the Cowgate and Grassmarket filled with sheep, cattle, horses, and their human attendants, and the city overflowed with dealers in agricul- tural products and their customers. Madgy Docherty had made her way from Glasgow and no doubt felt able to make the trip back again. The migratory Irish in Scotland depended on seasonal work, like the harvest that had attracted Michael Campbell, and as with other migrant work- ers, formed their own communities, which retained country traditions of hospitality and mutual assistance. Even a newcomer might find someone from her village or a friend of a friend to give her a bed for the night or something to eat. Indeed, anyone making the trip from Edinburgh to Glasgow on foot depended on such acts of generosity. There are ways in which all long-distance travelers increase the likelihood of encountering generosity, such as recognizing the differing value, in different situations, of using Scots or Irish names. Docherty seems to have called herself Mrs. Campbell, a Scots name, when speaking to the Scotswoman Mrs. Stewart in the lodging house in the Pleasance. By the time she got to the Irish immigrant district in the West Port, she used her Irish name, Mrs. Do- cherty. The strategy, if that is what it was, worked perfectly. On entering a grocery store to ask for charity, she was fortunate enough to meet a fellow countryman, whose name, he said—what a coincidence!—was Docherty as well. He was a shoemaker, who had been in Edinburgh some years, and he invited her back to his room, in a tenement not far away. She might stay for a fortnight, he told her, which would give her time to locate her son; at any event she should stay the night to celebrate Halloween. They returned to his room, where his wife, Nelly, made Madgy Docherty breakfast and helped her do some washing.

The man's name was not, in fact, Docherty, but rather William Burke, and though he was indeed from Ireland, he was not related to his new guest. Nelly's legal name was Helen M'Dougal, for she and Burke were not formally married, but they had lived for ten years as man and wife and she was known to friends and relations as "Mrs. Burke." Their "house"—as even one-room flats were called—was in a tenement near the tanneries on the north side of Wester Portsburgh, in an unnamed alley between Weaver's and Grindlay's Closes. When anyone entered from the main street, there was first one step down, explained a neighbor, Ann Conway, and then a passage, with her own room being "the first door that meets you going in." Across the passageway from Ann Conway and her husband, on the left side, was a one-room lodging house, run by another neighbor, Janet

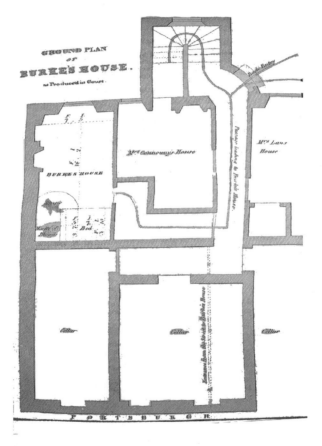

Figure 4. Map showing the location of Burke's and M'Dougal's residence, produced for the trial. Reproduced in *West Port Murders*. The building could be entered either directly from the main street, Wester Portsburgh, or through the back entry connecting up to neighboring yards and streets.

Law. Burke and M'Dougal lived farther along the passage on the right-hand side. A door there from the main passage led down another corridor, between ten and fifteen feet long, which turned to the right and led to a second doorway. Commentators later noted that the two doors separating Burke's dwelling from the main entry-way provided an unusual degree of privacy for an Old Town tenement. So too did its one window looking out on a little-used courtyard. A room sixteen feet by seven was the main living quarters for the couple, as well as any guests they might have. At the time of Docherty's arrival these included Ann Gray, one of Helen's relatives, along with her husband, James, an ex-soldier, and their young child, who had been lodging there for about two weeks (Figure 4).

The neighbor, Ann Conway, saw Docherty "supping porridge and milk" by the fire on the afternoon of Friday, October 31. That evening Conway saw her again. Docherty, "somewhat the worse for drink," had been left alone by her hosts, and she followed Conway into the passage. She spoke of going back to St. Mary's Wynd, "to see a person who had promised to fetch her word about her son," but Conway persuaded her to stay inside, telling her that she'd never find her way back through the tangle of streets and houses. Besides, as she had been drinking, "the police would take her up." Docherty agreed to remain in the building, but somewhat to Conway's annoyance, she insisted on lingering in Conway's room. She was puzzled as to why the woman referred to her host as "Docherty"; "I told her his name was Burke," she said, "[but] she would not allow me to say so; she said it was Docherty." Helen M'Dougal had told Conway, "they had got a stranger, a friend of her husband's, a highland woman"; however, Docherty was from Ireland, as everyone could tell from listening to her. Indeed, she fell into conversation with Conway's husband, who had been in the army in Ireland, and they spent some time discussing people he had known in Donegal.

Ann Gray had also been inconvenienced by Madgy Docherty's arrival. She had been home for most of the day, but in the evening Burke had told her to leave with her family, supposedly because he disapproved of Mrs. Gray's quarreling with her husband. She wasn't quarreling, she had told him: she had just been checking on her child. But Burke was determined that they leave. He had arranged for them to stay with his friends, William and Margaret Hare, who had a lodging house in a nearby tenement just to the west, in Tanner's Close. The Grays agreed, but they had the strong sense that they were being got out of the way, perhaps because they were not Irish. "I thought it was Halloween night," Ann Gray said, "[and] they did not wish me amongst them."

In the evening the Grays took supper with the Hares, who then returned, with Helen M'Dougal, to find the Burkes' new guest with Ann Conway. They all shared a bottle of spirits, and "were merry, dancing, and drinking," according to Janet Law. As it grew late, Ann Conway asked Madgy Docherty to leave, because she had to get up at 3 A.M. to get the fire started and make porridge for her husband, a laborer who started work at 4:30 A.M. But Docherty, she said, "bade me not be cruel to strangers"— she evidently felt safe with the Conways—and refused to go until Burke returned. It was probably after 10 P.M. when Ann Conway saw him going by in the passage, and was able to rid herself of her neighbors and their guest.

She was not, however, to get much sleep that night. The merry party continued for a while in Burke's room, as Docherty sang and Margaret Hare and Helen M'Dougal danced, but sometime before 11 P.M. a fight broke out between Burke and Hare. Hugh Alston, a grocer, had his shop directly above Burke's room, with his own home directly above that. He heard two men quarreling, and a female voice calling "Murder!" Alston worried about fire in the building; and he went downstairs and stood in the passageway. He heard more quarreling, but no blows, and though he heard again a woman's strong voice "crying murder," it did not sound as if she herself was in danger. Then there were strangling sounds, and the woman's voice, still strong, called for the police to come, there was "murder here." With that Alston went for the police, but found none: Halloween was a traditionally raucous night, and they were either making their rounds or enjoying the fun. When Alston returned, all was quiet, and he went back home. Burke and Hare had started fighting, Burke later explained to his neighbors, with Hare getting the better of it. Madgy Docherty, seeing her new friend apparently being choked, was the one calling "Murder" and "Police." "It was just a fit of drink like," Burke said, but the woman was "quiet enough now."

None of this was out of the ordinary. Halloween was a festive night in the West Port, and this was one of the more respectable of the tenements. Burke's lodging was certainly not one of those disorderly houses watched by the local police and frequented by thieves and prostitutes. It was "one of the neatest and snuggest little places I ever saw," later declared Christopher North in *Blackwood's Magazine*, describing the "walls well plastered and washed—a good wood floor—respectable fire-place." The "character of the whole flat," he concluded, "was that of comfort and cheerfulness to a degree seldom seen in the dwellings of the poor." Nor was the drinking, or even the fighting, cause for concern. Burke and Hare were known to drink heavily, but so did most men and many women in all classes of society: a dram of spirits was a cheap and easy pleasure for the poor, as good Scotch whiskey was for the rich, both being much more healthful than the water. And fights between Burke and Hare were common, as were quarrels between husbands and wives. It was fire Hugh Alston had been worried about, not assault: the female voice calling "Murder" had clearly not been strangled, and there was no sign of the escalating rage that commonly preceded a homicide. At 3 A.M., the Conways awoke to a quiet house and ate their breakfast in peace.

By that time, Madgy Docherty had been dead perhaps three hours. Drunk and dizzy, she had lain down, or been pushed, onto the bed just after she had intervened in the fight between Burke and Hare. Burke positioned himself on top of her to compress her lungs, and Hare covered her mouth and nose with his hands. Her face became livid, and blood-flecked saliva came from her mouth as her heart pumped hard in a fruitless effort to send the diminishing supply of oxygen through her body. There was no real struggle—Burke, though small, was solidly built, and he and Hare had done this sort of thing before. Once she was dead, they stripped her body and put it under "a quantity of straw lying at one end of the bed."

Burke had already begun his preparations earlier that evening for reaping the benefits of the planned murder, preparations that would later ensure that he, rather than his associate Hare, went to the gallows. David Paterson, doorkeeper and assistant in the anatomical establishment belonging to Dr. Robert Knox, had been attending a "beef-steak supper" and was therefore not at his home at 6 Wester Portsburgh when Burke had come by around 10 P.M. This was probably the errand that had delayed Burke's joining the Halloween party in Ann Conway's room. By midnight, when Burke called again, Paterson had returned home, and he agreed to accompany Burke back to the tenement in search of "something for the Doctor." Paterson had done business with Burke and Hare before, and knew the "something" referred to a corpse suitable for dissection. They were, as far as he knew, grave robbers, also known as resurrectionists, those unpleasant, illegal, but necessary functionaries who dug up the recently interred and haunted cheap boardinghouses for the newly dead. Paterson "did not wish resurrectionists to be coming about his lodgings," but he asked no questions. "If I am to be catechised by you, where and how I get subjects," Burke had warned Paterson on a previous occasion, "I will inform the Doctor of it, and if he allows you to do so, I will bring no more to him, mind that."

Paterson's house—or, more properly speaking, his mother's house—was a mere two hundred yards and a quick walk from Burke's lodgings, but it was situated on the more salubrious south side of Wester Portsburgh, and its lower-middle-class propriety was a world away from the cheap lodging houses for transients. After wandering through Burke's corridors, Paterson remarked to Burke "that he "lived in a very strange and intricate situation," to which Burke answered that "it suited his purpose." Probably Burke, Hare, and the women—for both Helen M'Dougal and Margaret Hare were present—had hoped that Paterson would take away the body at once. But it was after midnight, and Paterson was not about to examine the body in darkness, or try to find a cart to transport it to Dr. Knox's dissecting rooms in Surgeon's Square, in Edinburgh's medical district. That was porter's work. Paterson later claimed that he was suspicious about this particular corpse, though if so, his reservation did not keep him from dispatching his fifteen-year-old sister, Elizabeth, with a message for Burke around 9 A.M. the next day, Saturday, November 1. She had never been to Burke's room before, and had to ask directions to the entryway from Janet Law. The message was for Burke to call on Paterson to discuss delivery of the corpse, but Burke had other pressing tasks before he could attend to it.

For the first question out of everyone's mouth on that Saturday morning seemed to be, "Where was Mrs. Docherty?" "What have you done with the little woman?" Janet Law inquired of Helen M'Dougal. In one of the series of ill-considered statements that led to her arrest, M'Dougal said "she had kicked the damned bitch of hell's backside out of the door, because she had been using too much freedom with William." Had she simply said that Docherty had gone back to St. Mary's Wynd to await word of her son she might have allayed suspicions; as it was she increased them. Burke also behaved oddly. He called his neighbors in to share a dram, apparently as a kind of apology for all the commotion the night before, but Ann

Conway could not help noticing that it gave Helen M'Dougal the opportunity, again, to explain how she had kicked Docherty out for being "ow'r friendly." Janet Law and Ann Conway also noted that Burke spilled spirits on the bed, straw, and even the ceiling, laughing and saying "he wanted it done so he could get more." Neither woman stayed long in the room, but instead soon returned to the morning's tasks.

Madgy Docherty's absence meant the Grays could return to lodging in Burke's room, but Ann Gray felt uneasy. As she smoked her pipe after breakfast, she still felt she was being kept away from something. Burke wouldn't let her near the bed, even though it was where she kept her own belongings. "Keep out there," he swore at her when she tried to get her child's stockings from the straw pallet; what was she doing there "with a lighted pipe?" when she took potatoes from their storage place under the bed. Nor would he leave the Grays alone in the room. Whenever he went out he left Helen M'Dougal lying on the bed, and a neighbor, seventeen-year-old John Brogan, sitting in the chair near the straw. All occupants passed an uncomfortable day, with Ann Gray, in particular, keeping an eye on the bed and straw, and Burke, M'Dougal, or young Brogan keeping an eye on the Grays. But Burke could not wait around: he had to get the body out of his room, the sooner the better, or no amount of spilled liquor would disguise its presence.

Burke went to find John M'Culloch, a porter in Alison's Close off the Cowgate. He knew M'Culloch from previous deliveries and arranged for him to transport a new package. M'Culloch was not in any doubt that he was transporting a dead body, though it was wrapped in a sheet and placed in a tea box: when he went to "lift the box, there was something like hair" that he felt. He tucked the hair inside the box, and pushed down, hard, to close the lid; then he roped the box and carried it, with Burke, to Dr. Knox's dissecting rooms. One of Dr. Knox's staff received it about 6:30 P.M., but he gave no payment. Burke, Hare, M'Culloch, and the two women went next to Dr. Knox's residence in the genteel southern suburb of Newington for their money, but because Knox, too, did not care to have resurrectionists at his home, they were directed to wait at a public house at the top of the Cowgate. They had thus traveled across town for no purpose, and the women had left before Paterson arrived at the pub bearing 5s for M'Culloch, and £2 7s each for Burke and Hare. Another £5, they were told, would be forthcoming on Monday.

By then, from their point of view, the damage had been done. Earlier that evening, Ann Gray's vigilance had paid off. Helen M'Dougal had gone out, and soon after John Brogan left as well. Finding herself and her husband alone, Ann Gray went straight to the straw near the bed. "I was looking on purpose," she said later. "I thought there was something that was not right; because [Burke] was throwing about the whisky. And . . . the first thing I got, on lifting up the straw, was the woman's right arm." Her clothing was entirely gone, and when James Gray lifted up her head by the hair, they could see blood "about the mouth and on the one side of her head" with her face turned toward the wall.

The Grays knew that dead bodies, stripped and bloody, do not just turn up under straw mattresses. They quickly packed their belongings and left. On the way out they ran into Helen M'Dougal, just returning from the Newington jaunt, and James Gray asked her straight out what was going on. She fell to her knees, begging him not to inform on them, offering him a few shillings until Monday and following it with an incredible offer of £10 per week. If the Grays had thought that there might be a reasonable explanation for the late Madgy Docherty's appearance under the straw, this offer of, for them, all the riches of the Indies effectively eliminated it. "God forbid that I should be worth money for dead people," Ann Gray replied; how could M'Dougal bring such disgrace upon their family? "My God, I cannot help it," M'Dougal replied. "You surely can help it," said Ann Gray, "or you would not stay in the house." The Grays hurried out the door, only to run into Margaret Hare. "What are you making a noise about?" she asked, and when told the reason, suggested that the whole matter could be cleared up with a few drinks in a local tavern. But the Grays refused and headed to the police station a few blocks away at Fountainbridge.

When John Fisher, a criminal officer, arrived at the police station at 7 P.M., he listened carefully to James Gray's story. Taking a patrolman, John Findlay, as well as Gray, he proceeded to the tenement, where he met Burke and his wife. Leaving M'Dougal outside with Findlay, Fisher went with Burke and Gray back into their room. Fisher asked Burke "What had become of his lodgers?" There was one of them, Burke replied, indicating Gray, or at least, he said, there was a former lodger, for he had turned the Grays out of his house for bad conduct. "What had become of the little woman that had been there on the Friday, the day before," Fisher asked patiently. "She was away," Burke replied, she had left about seven that morning. William Hare could vouch for it, and there were "a number more" witnesses to attest to it.

Fisher looked around the room, noted the blood near the bed, and went back outside to talk to Helen M'Dougal, who wasted no time in incriminating herself further. How had the blood got on the bed, he asked her. "A woman had lain in there," she replied, "about a fortnight before that time, and the bed had not been washed since." Fisher did not point out to her that fresh blood could not be mistaken for two-week-old bloodstains, but simply inquired after the "little woman" who had spent the night. "She could find her," she said, "she knew her perfectly well." In fact, she had seen her that night, and Docherty "had apologized to her for her bad conduct the night previous." And what time had Docherty left the house? "Seven o'clock at night," M'Dougal replied. Fisher may have believed the Grays, or he may have inclined toward believing Burke that their story was "all personal spite." But given the blood and the disparity between Burke's and M'Dougal's accounts, he was justified in insisting that the couple accompany him to the police station for questioning.

Fisher returned to their rooms later that night with the police surgeon, Alexander Black, asking the neighbors additional questions and searching more carefully. They found a striped bed gown—identical, as he was later told, to the one Docherty had been seen wearing the night before—and more fresh blood under the bed. Fisher interviewed the neighbors, learning all about Docherty's visit, the Halloween party, and its aftermath. A servant girl who lived nearby "informed them that she had seen Burke and his wife, Hare and his wife, and the porter M'Culloch, going up the stair." M'Culloch carried a tea box "with the top stuffed with straw," and she "laid her hand upon it and found it soft." Her testimony led Officer Fisher to the carter John M'Culloch. "There was still no tidings of the body," Fisher said later, but there was an obvious place to look. Cadavers were commodities in Edinburgh, essential raw materials for the teaching of anatomy. And so "it was suggested that the dissecting rooms should be searched." The next morning, Sunday, November 2, sometime before 8 A.M., two police officers visited Number 10 Surgeon's Square, the venue for the anatomy and operative surgery classes given by Dr. Robert Knox, Fellow of the Royal College of Surgeons of Edinburgh. David Paterson was there, in his capacity as porter and assistant, and the police inquired whether any bodies had been delivered recently. If Paterson had had no suspicions before, he certainly did now, and he brought out the tea-chest which had been delivered the previous night. On opening it, they found a body of a woman, whom Gray identified as Madgy Docherty. Other people who had seen her at the Halloween party later confirmed the identification. At 8 A.M., therefore, the police superintendent, Captain James Steuart, arrived at Tanner's Close. He arrested William and Margaret Hare and took them to the Police Office. John Brogan was taken into custody as well, though later released. On Monday, the chief sheriff's officer in Edinburgh, Sheriff-Substitute George Tait, questioned all four of the suspects. Their testimony careened wildly between obvious falsehood and downright stupidity, so that it was quite clear to Archibald Scott, the procurator fiscal—the official charged with determining whether a crime had been committed—that there were grounds for a murder investigation.

But were the grounds sufficient for a charge of murder to stand up in court? Sir William Rae, lord advocate—the highest legal officer in Scotland—was afraid they were not. A murder case under Scots law would require a jury trial, and he "had reason to know," he later wrote, "how scrupulous a Scottish Jury uniformly is, in finding a verdict of guilty, where a capital punishment is to follow." There was, in the first place, no clear evidence that a murder had even been committed. Madgy Docherty had been alive, and now she was dead, but though both the police surgeon and two forensic experts examined her body, they could find no incontestable physical evidence of murder. Suffocation was indicated, but it would have been consistent with the medical evidence for Docherty to have suffocated from too much drink or her own vomit. All four of the prisoners were examined repeatedly over the course of November, but however wild or inconsistent their tales, they could not be prevailed upon to confess. Helen M'Dougal refused to speak at all. Burke and Hare maintained that they had no knowledge of how the "little old woman" had ended up dead. A month passed and no new evidence had come to light. In the hands of any able defense counsel, all four prisoners would walk out of court free men and women. And Rae could be sure that excellent lawyers would come forward to defend the prisoners, because Edinburgh's own version of the political clash between Tory government and Whig opposition took place in the courtroom. Since the lord advocate, who headed the prosecution, as well as virtually all the judges, were appointed by the Tory administration, Whig lawyers made it a point to act as defense counsel in all capital cases. Without an airtight case against the murderers, Tories would lose, and Whigs would win.

Besides, rumors were circulating. By Monday, November 3 the Edinburgh Courant reported the murder, and its account was reprinted the same day in a penny broadside. Suddenly it seemed as if half of Edinburgh had missing persons to report—old wives, pensioned soldiers, former servants who seemed to have disappeared without a trace. A well-known street person, Jamie Wilson, who was generally highly visible, had not been seen for over a month. A local woman, Janet Brown, reported the odd disappearance of her friend, Mary Paterson, the previous spring. Rae began "to dread," as he noted, that Madgy Docherty's death had not been an isolated instance. Under those circumstances, it was clear to him "that he should, for the sake of the public interest, have it ascertained what crimes of this revolting description had really been committed,—who were concerned in them,—or if other gangs remained, whose practices might continue to endanger human life." What he needed, as with all gangs, was an informer. The women were not satisfactory for this: Helen M'Dougal would not speak, and Margaret Hare could not give evidence against her husband. Burke was thirty-six years of age, while Hare gave his age as twenty-one, and might be presumed to be more impressionable. Moreover a stronger case could be made against Burke than Hare. And so William Hare was approached, and offered immunity from prosecution if he would turn Crown's evidence against Burke.

Hare could have chosen to remain silent, and the prosecution might never have found enough hard evidence to indict either him or Burke. But the year was 1828; Dr. Joseph Bell, the model for Sherlock Holmes, would not be born for another nine years; and the detective-story genre, which familiarized even the most law-abiding citizen with terms like "alibi" and "self-incrimination," was in its infancy. None of the prisoners were criminal masterminds, though some later accounts made them out to be; their murders were brutal and stupid, and they had made no contingency plans for what to say if questioned. Perhaps they had counted on never being questioned, or, more likely, had simply avoided thinking about it. On December 1, 1828, Hare made a full declaration "of the facts relative to the case of Docherty, and to such other crimes of a similar nature, committed by Burke, of which he was cognisant." William Burke and Helen M'Dougal were tried for murder at the High Court of Justiciary on Wednesday, December 24, 1828, with William and Margaret Hare the chief witnesses against them. The senior defense counsel was Henry Cockburn, a prominent Whig who would later become lord advocate, and whose *Memorials of Our Time* paints a vivid picture of contemporary Edinburgh. The charge against M'Dougal was found "not proven," that distinctively Scots verdict that counts as an acquittal while reserving judgment about guilt or innocence. Burke was found guilty as charged and sentenced to death.

By that time news of the most shocking murders anyone could remember had spread throughout the world, creating a new verb—to burke—and the myth of a new, practically undetectable form of suffocation. Murders were rare in Edinburgh and could generally be traced to a fight gone wrong or one jealous rage too many. The occasional sensational trial suggested murder occurred only within reassuringly small subsets of the population: as a result of a fatal duel, among young gentlemen, or a knife fight in a brothel, among prostitutes and their clients. But Burke and Hare made no distinctions; one person's cadaver was just like another's, and so anyone, anytime, could end up burked on a dissecting table. "Puir folk thocht o' themselves in the fate o' the sixteen corpses," as Christopher North put it, but the well-to-do also feared "to quit their houses after dark . . . since, by the above method of Burking, a person may be deprived of his existence before he has the power to resist the attack made on him, or be able to call out for assistance." A man might come to town on his lawful business, a woman might stop for the night in respectable lodgings, but all their prudence could not guarantee their safety. People feared that anyone could become a murder victim, for there was literally a price placed upon every head. Anyone, as long as the existing demand for cadavers continued.

How had this dreadful system of burking come into being? demanded the law officers, the public, and the world. And so William Burke, imprisoned in the condemned cell in the Edinburgh jail and awaiting execution, was persuaded by his religious advisers to make a full statement, to relieve his own conscience and reassure the public. He gave his official confession—the most authoritative account of the sixteen murders still extant—to the judicial authorities on January 3, 1829.

It had all started, he explained, some fourteen months before . . .

Chapter 2

The Anatomy Wars

Donald, the "Old Pensioner"

THE FIRST CORPSE IN THE SERIES WAS NOT MURDERED, William Burke said, but instead died of natural causes in late November 1827, less than a year before the final victim met her demise. That first body had belonged to a man named Donald, who succumbed to dropsy, the morbid overabundance of fluid in the tissues. Burke described him as an "old pensioner," but he died shortly before his quarterly pension was due, owing £4 to his landlord, William Hare. Later accounts described the Hares' lodging house in Tanner's Close in the direst terms—"a dirty, low, wretched close . . . which . . . opens off the West Port, from which it descends a few steps"—but Christopher North wrote in *Blackwood's Magazine* that all such highly colored descriptions were "prodigious nonsense." The building was freestanding, and from the outside, North said, looked "like a minister's manse." True, Hare's house was at the bottom of the close—"and I presume that one house must always be at the bottom of a close"—but the flat above "was inhabited, and two of his apartments are large and roomy," well fitted with at least seven beds, "with excellent fireplaces and windows." At one end the conjunction of the outer staircase and the outside wall formed "a small inner apartment or closet, the window of which looks only upon a pig-stye and dead wall." This inner apartment was about ten feet by five feet, rather like the box bedrooms that can still be found in old-fashioned Edinburgh flats, and perhaps a month before

Donald's death it had come to be occupied by William Burke and Helen M'Dougal. Burke had known Margaret Hare from previous visits to Edinburgh. He had run into her again at the beginning of November, and, over a dram, confided to her that he "had an intention to go to the west country to endeavour to get employment as a cobbler," a recently acquired skill. She "suggested that they had a small room in their house," which would allow him to "follow his trade of a cobbler in Edinburgh." It was a good suggestion, for the constant traffic in the West Port ensured shoemakers a thriving business. In this way Burke and M'Dougal set up housekeeping in the rooms opening off Tanner's Close, as "sensible, and what might be called . . . respectable" a couple as might be met with in the West Port.

It was to the older, more experienced Burke that Hare turned with his dilemma over the disposal of Donald's body. It was a day or two after the death, and Hare had already made arrangements for the cadaver to be buried at the expense of the parish, but after observing it in his rooms, decomposing and taking up space for twenty-four hours or more, Hare "proposed that his body should be sold to the doctors," with Burke to get a share of the price. "It would be impossible to do it," replied Burke, for the carpenter "would be coming in with the coffin immediately." But once the coffin was delivered, and the corpse duly placed in it with the lid nailed down, the carpenter left. Hare took a chisel, opened the coffin, and he and Burke hid the body in one of the beds. They took tanner's bark from behind the house, packed it tightly, and put it in the coffin, covering it with a sheet; they then nailed down the lid again, "and the coffin was carried away for interment." Perhaps this marks the association of the two men with that helpful carter, M'Culloch, who apparently never asked awkward questions, for it is hard to see how a two-day-old body under the bed in a crowded lodging house could have passed unnoticed, or how any porter could have remained so completely incurious about the sound of the coffin's contents, the tanner's bark sliding heavily against the inside of the coffin as it was hoisted up and carried out of the close. Hare "did not appear to have been concerned in any thing of the kind before," Burke later said, and we can believe him, for if Burke and Hare had been versed in the law, they would have known that concealment was not really necessary. A corpse is not considered property under Scottish or English law, and Hare's obligation to the parish was only to see that it was properly disposed of. Had Burke and Hare been true resurrectionists, and dug the body out of a churchyard, they would have been guilty of the crime of "violation of sepulchers," liable for fine and imprisonment. As it had never been interred, the two men were legally free to sell it.

But neither Burke nor Hare was versed in the law, and they behaved throughout as though they were dealing in illicit goods. Later that afternoon they went to the main university buildings just off South Bridge. They were looking specifically for Dr. Monro, that is, Alexander Monro *tertius* (as he was known), professor of anatomy and medicine, because, as Burke explained, they "did not know there was any other way of disposing of a dead body." Monro was featured in broadsides describing the execution of condemned criminals, for one of his perquisites as professor of anatomy was acquiring their bodies for dissection; perhaps that is how Burke had heard of him. At the college they met a young man, "like a student," and asked him if there were any of Dr. Monro's men about. The young man "asked them what they wanted with Dr. Monro," and they explained "they

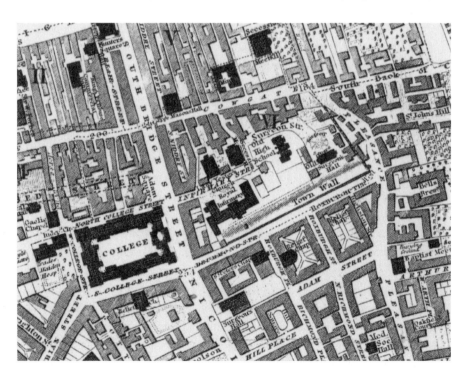

Figure 5. Map of Edinburgh University and the medical district. Robert Knox's dissecting rooms were in Surgeon's Square, just east of the Royal Infirmary.

had a subject to dispose of." But late afternoon was no time to find Professor Monro in his anatomical theater, because the light was too poor: he generally prepared his specimens in the morning, lectured from 1 to 3 P.M., and then returned to dine in his elegant home on George Square. Dr. Robert Knox, on the other hand, was known to be in his anatomical establishment at all hours, offering an "Annual Course of Lectures on the Anatomy and Physiology of the Human Body," at 11 A.M. and 6 P.M. His course of "Demonstrations on the Surgical Anatomy of all the Surgical Regions of the Body," offered Tuesdays and Thursdays at 3, might have just let out. His dissecting rooms were right across South Bridge, behind the Royal Infirmary in Surgeon's Square, and perhaps Burke's and Hare's young man had come from them. At any rate he knew the address well enough, for he "referred them to Dr. Knox, No. 10 Surgeon Square" (Figure 5).

Dr. Knox was not available when Burke and Hare arrived. Instead, they spoke to three young gentlemen, whom they took to be the doctor's assistants, later identified as Alexander Miller, William Fergusson, and Thomas Wharton Jones. Burke and Hare explained again that they were offering a subject for sale. Come back after dark, the gentlemen told them, even offering to find a porter to carry the body. But Burke and Hare had given false names—"John" and "William"—and did not want anyone "to know exactly where their houses were." Instead, they "went home and put the body in to a sack, and carried it to Surgeon Square" themselves. Unsure what to do next—where did bodies go in a doctor's establishment?—they laid the cadaver down on the ground outside the cellar while they notified the gentlemen that they had returned. They were bidden "to bring the body to the room, which they did; and they took the body out of the sack, and laid it on the dissecting table." The body was still dressed in a shirt, which Burke and Hare removed at the gentlemen's request. They had expected questions about that shirt, but none came, not even when Dr. Knox himself arrived, having presumably been sent for at his home at 4 Newington Place. He merely "looked at the body, and proposed they should get £7 10s," asking "no questions as to how the body had been obtained." His assistant Jones paid Burke and Hare their fee, adding, as he did so, that the surgeons "would be glad to see them again when they had any other body to dispose of." Hare took the larger share of £4 5s—Donald had been his lodger, after all—and gave Burke £3 5s. Perhaps they looked at each other incredulously as the door closed behind them, unable to believe their good fortune: a corpse, which had been treated like contraband in the West Port, apparently could be sold almost on the open market in Surgeon's Square. We can assume that they went home and celebrated by sharing more than one dram with the two women, and perhaps the whole lodging house: a mere evening's work had turned Donald's remains from a dead weight into a liquid asset.

Within Number 10 Surgeon's Square, Jones, Miller, and Fergusson, and perhaps Knox himself, must also have felt they had cause for celebration, and perhaps they, too, broke out the whiskey. A fresh cadaver, that essential basis of all anatomical theory and practice, had, almost literally, knocked on their door and asked to be dissected. They had not had to sneak out at night to steal a maggoty corpse from a heavily guarded cemetery, or cut down the body of a convicted criminal before it could be turned over to Professor Monro, whose university position gave him a monopoly on all legally executed cadavers. Instead they had purchased a fresh dropsical corpse, in superb condition, for the same price as they might have paid for an old subject packed in brine and shipped from Dublin. They would be glad, very glad indeed, to see the two men again whenever they had any other bodies to sell.

Burke and Hare did not know it, but they had entered a war zone, where battles raged over student fees and professional recognition, and ill-gotten cadavers littered the field. Anatomists in Edinburgh were engaged in a battle over professional reputation. Professor Alexander Monro held the most privileged position within Edinburgh University, as he had for many years. The territorial dominance of the Monro clan had begun a century earlier, when John Monro, a farsighted surgeon with political influence in Edinburgh's Town Council, had arranged for his son, Alexander, to become the professor of anatomy and medicine. As the first of the Alexander Monros to hold that position, he was generally known as *primus*. The professorial chair became a kind of family property, to which his grandson and great-grandson—Alexander Monro *secundus* and *tertius* respectively—succeeded in due course. Over the next hundred years the Town Council had ample opportunity to congratulate themselves for their good judgment, as Edinburgh University emerged as the premier institution for medical education in the English-speaking world. Five hundred or more students arrived in October for the start of classes, spending 3 guineas per course and anywhere from £100 to £500 for each year they resided in the city. Anatomy and physiology, taught by the succession of Professors Monro, was the moneymaker par excellence, attracting more students than any other course for most of the eighteenth century.

Yet however advantageous these developments for the city of Edinburgh, the university medical professors, and of course the Monro family, their virtual monopoly on anatomical teaching did not go unchallenged. Both the Alexander Monros *primus* and *secundus* were excellent anatomists, and their lecture course remained the cornerstone of Edinburgh medical education, attended by nearly all the students, with the most ardent taking it again and again. But in 1798 Monro *secundus* retired, and his son, Alexander Monro *tertius*, succeeded him as professor. This third Alexander Monro was a competent lecturer but nothing more, according to Robert Christison, first his student and later his colleague, who pointed out that "a lecturer who seldom shows himself in his dissecting room will scarcely be looked up to as an anatomist." To the reform-minded parliamentary commissioners appointed to investigate the Scottish universities in 1826, Monro *tertius* was the embodiment of supernumerary privilege, refusing to allow any change to the curriculum if it interfered with his privileges, offering dissection only grudgingly, and charging a guinea per student to insure that few attended. In this latter point he was successful. As the numbers of students flocking to Edinburgh rose exponentially in the early years of the nineteenth century, as one influential medical practitioner after another proclaimed the importance, the centrality, of hands-on anatomical experience to their profession, the percentage of students attending the university anatomy course dropped precipitously. By the 1820s barely a third of the approximately five hundred medical students arriving in Edinburgh each year bothered to attend Monro's lectures.

The other two-thirds did not dispense with anatomy entirely; it would have been professional suicide to do so, when every civil or military examination, when every prospective partner or well-educated patient, would be sure to question them in minute detail on the "number of vertebra. . . . What bone supports the tibia. . . . What muscles are inserted into the patella. . . . The branches of the arch of the aorta? . . . The contents of the abdomen? . . . The course & division of the carotid artery?" Instead, in ever-increasing numbers, they turned to outside lecturers. Fellows of the Royal College of Surgeons, which issued licenses for surgeons independent of the university, were happy to encourage this trend. In 1828, the Royal

College issued new requirements for licentiates, requiring students to produce certificates "from a Professor or Teacher of Anatomy recognized by the College, that he has actually been engaged in the dissection of a human body." Assuming these requirements were adhered to—and there is every reason to believe they were—then the students so conspicuously absent from the courses of Monro *tertius*—including at least a hundred licentiates per year—were all attending private anatomical classes.

These private classes were taught by a generation of younger, more modern surgeons, many of whom were fresh from military experience in the Napoleonic wars more valuable than anything they had learned in lectures. They returned to Edinburgh after 1815 convinced that the time was right for an assault on Monro and the rest of the medical establishment. One of these was Robert Knox, whose dissecting rooms were in an especially advantageous position on Surgeon's Square, between the buildings of the Royal College of Surgeons and the Royal Medical Society, the main student society. He had, however, many rivals. James Syme and Robert Liston taught surgery as well as anatomy, contending with Knox for patronage from the Royal College of Surgeons and with each other for preeminence in operative technique. John and Alexander Lizars combined their anatomical lectures with the family engraving business to produce incomparably detailed illustrations of the human body. John William Turner offered lectures in surgery at 9 Surgeon's Square, while a few doors away, at number 4, the brothers John Aitken and Thomas Johnstone Aitken offered courses in anatomy, materia medica, and pharmacy.

These men did not make common cause. Indeed, they often loathed one another. For they were competitors, not just for students, but also for future university positions, each hoping to acquire a professorial chair when its incumbent died. Rare as it was for an outsider to gain a position at the university, it was not impossible, and many private lecturers believed that correct configuration of influence and ability might do it. It was necessary, therefore, to make a name as a brilliant—no, the most brilliant—lecturer in a given area of expertise, with the most students, the best publications, and the greatest scientific reputation. The result was that medical Edinburgh seethed with fierce rivalries, manifested in ways that would be considered highly unprofessional today. They took every opportunity to criticize each other as well as Monro, in person and in print. With each attack, they believed, they demonstrated their own superiority over entrenched interests, and how frustrating it seemed that they were simply ignored by Monro, "who," according to one commentator, "himself a good anatomist of the old school, with family honours not distinguished from a professional inheritance, could afford to view the new men with an easy if not proud disregard."

All these anatomists relied on Edinburgh body snatchers, whose job it was to ensure that lecturers in anatomy and surgery were kept supplied with sufficient "subjects" for their teaching and research. The most notorious of these resurrectionists was Andrew Lees, a tall, pale-faced man in his late thirties living in Scott's Close off the Cowgate. His lawful occupations were plowman and bricklayer, and he could fall back on them whenever he had to leave the city to avoid the police. His close associates were John Spouse, a laborer living in Bell's Wynd off the High Street, and James Hewit, a painter in Carubber's Close. All these were unremarkable Old Town addresses, the usual lodgings for plowmen, laborers, and painters. A fourth body snatcher, John McQuilkan, may have been drawn into the trade by his proximity to the medical district, for he was a porter at the west end of Drummond Street near the Royal Infirmary. For much of 1828, though, he was temporarily unavailable. He had been arrested near a disturbed grave in Liberton churchyard and charged with the crime of violation of sepulchres. The arresting officer had found nearby "a bag a small piece of rope and a shovel." On being confronted with them McQuilkan declared "he never saw any of these articles before & he knew nothing about them." Witnesses testified that he had been seen carrying them, though, and he was convicted and sentenced to six months in jail. His ineptness suggests that McQuilkan was new at the trade. Successful body snatchers could raise a corpse a month, and though exhuming bodies was technically not stealing—for Scottish law, like English, did not consider cadavers as property—it was generally an activity associated with habitual criminals, "thieves by habit and repute."

All these exercises in cadaver procurement were necessarily kept secret, but they coincided with the highly public hearings of the parliamentary committee appointed to investigate the means of "preventing the unlawful Disinterment of Human Bodies, and for Regulating Schools of Anatomy" which, in one of the ironies of history, were ongoing during the precise period of the Burke and Hare murders. The Select Committee on Anatomy, as it came to be known, had its origin in a loose coalition of reform politicians clustered around the utilitarian philosopher Jeremy Bentham along with prominent members of the London medical profession. Henry Warburton, the member of Parliament who first proposed and later chaired the Select Committee, was influenced both by Bentham and by his own affiliation with the University College London and its anatomical school. The conclusions the Select Committee would reach were clear from the start, for Warburton and his allies were determined to push reform of the dissection laws through Parliament. The substance of their Anatomy Bill, first presented to Parliament in 1829, had been in the works for much of the preceding decade, and Bentham had been in close contact with Sir Robert Peel, the secretary of state for the Home Office. When the committee collected evidence, they chose their witnesses carefully, admitting only those who agreed with their views, or whose testimony clearly pointed to the need for reform. Warburton himself wrote the report to support the policies he wished to see implemented. "It is the opinion of almost all the witnesses," he wrote, "that the adoption in this country of a plan, similar in most respects to that which prevails in France, would afford a simple and adequate remedy for the existing ills." In France, the public authorities regulated dissection. All those who died in a hospital received the last rites, and, if unclaimed at that point, were transported to a "dead room" for twenty-four hours. If, at that point, relatives or friends had not claimed the body, it was taken by a duly appointed public official, "at an earlier hour, in a covered carriage, so constructed as not to attract notice," and brought to the anatomical schools. It was this practice that procured so many cadavers for dissection that students from around the world flocked to Paris for instruction. Witnesses to the Select Committee, Warburton went on, recommended transplanting that system to Britain, so that "the bodies of those who die in workhouses, hospitals, and other charitable institutions, should, if not claimed by next of kin within a certain time after death, be given up, under proper regulations, to the Anatomist." In exchange for the cadavers, "the Anatomist," under this system, "should be required, under adequate securities, or a system of effective superintendence, to cause to be administered, at his own expense, to the bodies which he dissects, religious solemnities and the usual rites of burial."

That this would be an efficient use of human raw material that would otherwise go to waste—literally—was undeniable. It was equally undeniable that it would put the burden of sustaining medical science—literally—

on the cadavers of the poor. The assumption that this was the least the poor could do in exchange for their admission to a public charity, or confinement to a public prison, permeates the language surrounding these and similar proposals. "No one can object to such a disposal of the bodies of those who die in prisons," wrote Thomas Southwood Smith, in an influential article entitled "The Use of the Dead to the Living." He argued that no one "can reasonably object to a disposal of the bodies of those who die in poor-houses. These persons are pensioners upon the public bounty: they owe the public a debt: they have been supported by the public during life: if, therefore, after death they can be made useful to the public, it is a prejudice, not a reason—it is an act of injustice, not the observance of a duty, which would prevent them from becoming so." It was not their poverty which made them eligible for what Smith referred to as a public service, he was careful to note, "but because they are friendless: because, that is, no persons survive them who take such an interest in their fate as to be rendered unhappy by this disposal of their remains."

The Edinburgh medical establishment jumped at the suggestion that they be allocated the cadavers of those who had died in a public charity, without friends to pay for their burial. The Royal College of Physicians of Edinburgh, which numbered among its Fellows the entire Edinburgh University medical faculty, suggested that material for dissection might come from "the bodies of persons found dead on the roads and streets, in rivers and canals, or the sea shore, in almshouses and elsewhere . . . as also the bodies of foreigners, strangers and others, dying at inns, lodging-houses and public institutions, in the absence of friends, and without visible means of defraying funeral expenses." The Royal College of Surgeons clarified their own views with their succinct request for the bodies "of the worthless, and those who die without friends." Indeed, an article in the *Edinburgh Medical and Surgical Review* suggested that the Select Committee was too liberal in its definition of "friends," for "so much latitude is allowed to claimants," protested the author, "that any person whatever, though nowise related to the deceased, may claim his body, provided he is willing to defray the expences of the funeral." This would limit the supply of cadavers to anatomists in what the author considered a most unjustifiable way, "if not by other means, by the establishment of friendly societies for the purpose of burying the friendless poor." Unclaimed cadavers should be legislated into public property, these pronouncements imply, so that they may become the property of the anatomical lecturers who had most use for them. They were thus disinterested intermediaries by which "the poor," they argued, would ultimately benefit, for Warburton's report echoed medical writers in arguing that anatomy, if not practiced on the dead, "must be learned by mangling the living," and the living thus mangled were far more likely to be poor than rich. The rich will always hire experienced practitioners, Warburton noted, while "it is on the poor that the inexperienced commence their practice." For that reason the poor "will be the most benefitted by promoting" the study of anatomy, "and the principal sufferers by discouraging it."

These arguments, however true to the existing conditions of medical practice, were so self-serving on the part of their proponents that they outraged radical politicians like Henry Hunt and William Cobbett. If maintenance by the public coffers during life was a criterion for dissection after death, said Hunt, then surely the first dissected should be those supported at the greatest expense, like the royal family. "I would recommend, in the first place that the bodies of all our kings be dissected, instead of expending seven or eight hundred thousand pounds of the public money for their interment. Next, I would dissect all our hereditary legislators. After that, the bishops, with a host of those priests and vicars who feed themselves, and not their flocks. . . . Were there a law passed to this effect, I would willingly consent that my body should be given 'for the promotion of science.'" Let the anatomists have all the "placemen and pensioners," Cobbett cried during a political rally, "if they must have subjects, as they call them, for the benefit of science. . . . What so reasonable, as to have the bodies of men who have been subsisting at the public expense, and done nothing in exchange for their sustenance? If these men would give up their bodies, there would be some little reason in pensions. . . . They might then say, 'Why, true, we have done you no service while we have been living, but you shall have our carcases when we are dead.'" Cobbett was equally scathing over the argument that the friendless and worthless, in effect, deserved dissection. "Gentlemen," he said, "let us not, because we may not now be in that situation ourselves, let us not imagine that the poor . . . have not their feelings, as well as we have. . . . Think of the feelings of the father of a family, or any other man, knowing that he was going to die, and contemplating at the same time that his body was to be taken, and chopped up." As for the argument that it was necessary for science, that was nonsense, said Cobbett. "Science! Why, who is science for? Not for poor people. Then if it be necessary for the purposes of science, let them have the bodies of the rich, for whose benefit science is cultivated."

There is every evidence that Hunt's and Cobbett's views struck a responsive chord. The idea that medical men had a vested interest in their patients' demise has been a constant factor in the reluctance of nonprivileged groups to trust the medical establishment from the 1800s to the present. One witness to the Select Committee reported a rumor which had spread in Dublin "that children were kidnapped for the purpose of dissection," and "were to be sent over either to Scotland or England by the steam vessels." Irish immigrants in both England and Scotland refused to bring their children to hospitals to be vaccinated through the 1840s. Workhouse inmates sent horror-stricken petitions to Parliament, begging for protection against being dissected after death, purely because they had been "unfortunate and destitute" in life. "As a child in the mid-1950s in London's Notting Hill," notes the historian Ruth Richardson, "I can clearly remember the local belief that the chimney of a nearby hospital (an old workhouse infirmary) belched the smoke of human fuel. In my school playground small children nodded knowingly, and told each other that those who went in there never came out." The suspicion of body part harvesting from the poor to give to the rich has become a staple news item, found frequently in urban legend, fiction, and film.

In the 1820s, anyone wishing to point a finger at the mutilation of the dead poor for the living rich could bring up the issue of false teeth, for it was common practice for grave robbers and, it was rumored, surgeons to sell the teeth from cadavers to manufacturers of false teeth for the gentry. Suspicion of that activity led to the arrest of the Glasgow anatomy lecturer Granville Sharp Pattison, together with two of his students, in 1819 "for the crime of violation of sepulchres." The police had investigated a complaint of a disinterred body, Pattison told the Select Committee, "and there was a skull without teeth found in my dissecting rooms." He "was dragged away by the police," he said indignantly, "carried through the populace, pelted with stones; I was then indicted, and tried like a common criminal in Edinburgh, a man sitting on each side of me with a drawn bayonet." How, then, could a parliamentary commission seriously consider passing a law to appropriate, not just the teeth, but the bodies of the men "who had laboured," Cobbett pointed out, "and who, very likely, had been brought to death's door by excessive labour . . . and that for the benefit of those who had brought them into this condition."

Yet neither Hunt nor Cobbett confronted the practical evils inherent in the existing system, which left the poor with protection neither against poorly trained surgeons in life nor against body snatchers after death. Until the early years of the nineteenth century, the most energetic body snatchers were the anatomy lecturers themselves, who led their coterie of students in nocturnal raids on local churchyards. Stories were still told of the great John Hunter scouring London for human and animal remains, like medical students from Vesalius onwards. In Glasgow, "every public teacher had what he called his private party," Pattison explained; "this consisted generally of eight students, and those young gentlemen went out themselves and exhumed the body." There was simply no other way to obtain cadavers, and "I suppose the whole time I studied in Glasgow," Pattison continued, "that there was not probably a single student," who "had an opportunity of making any dissections" if he did not belong to an anatomy lecturer's private party. Robert Christison, professor of medical jurisprudence and forensic expert, recounted stories years later of lecturers and students rowing along the isolated churchyards on the banks of the Forth.

But for the most part the old days of personal enterprise, when medical professionals themselves crept round to local graveyards and dug up corpses, was well nigh over except for the occasional student prank. It was "most abhorrent to the feelings," Patisson admitted; moreover, it was dangerous. Graveyards were too well guarded, either by the town watch or by voluntary associations of bereaved relatives. Either set of guardians was likely to be armed, and to shoot first and ask questions later. Pattison recalled students "very frequently" being "shot at, when engaged in the process of exhumating," and at many of the Edinburgh churchyards placards were posted, "giving notice of watchmen being stationed at night with firearms." So when Andrew Ewart, engaged in watching the churchyard at Liberton, mistakenly shot and killed his friend and fellow watcher Henry Pennycook, the defense argued that he was not guilty, for "in making his rounds on a dark night, he came suddenly on a man skulking round the church; he saw that he was armed," and believed him to be a resurrectionist, "there to procure dead bodies by force." The prosecution countered by arguing that even had the dead man "been in the act of raising a dead body from the grave," it would not have been sufficient grounds for shooting him; moreover it was necessary to put an end "to the belief that lethal weapons might be resorted to by individuals at their own discretion, to prevent or to punish whatever was disagreeable to their feelings." Yet "the people of Scotland had been hitherto allowed to believe," replied the defense, "that it was lawful to protect the graves of their departed friends in this manner." Though this belief was not true, the defense admitted, Ewart had acted "in the discharge, as he thought, of a sacred and imperative duty." The jury found Ewart guilty, but "earnestly recommended him to mercy," among other reasons because they were convinced that "he conceived himself justified in using firearms for the protection of the church." His death sentence was later commuted to one year's imprisonment; it might have been lighter still if the dead man had actually been digging up graves.

For those reasons, by the 1820s the amateur body snatchers had been replaced by professionals for whom the ready money was worth the risk. One of these, identified only as "A.B.," testified anonymously before the Select Committee. He thought there were about "forty or fifty men" in London "that have the name of raising subjects." For the most part, though, they used body-snatching as a cover "for thieving. . . . They are nothing but petty common thieves. . . . They get a subject or two, and call themselves resurrectionmen." In Edinburgh, Andrew Lees was "a bad character and associates with thieves," according to police reports. He was later indicted on a housebreaking charge involving a gang of boys, aged thirteen to sixteen. The boys were arrested, tried, and sentenced, but Lees stayed beyond the city limits for six months and, when he finally surfaced, denied any involvement. The police officer in the case testified, regretfully, that he "did not know of [Lees] being punished for stealing," and in fact he was never convicted on any charge. James Gow, "a well known Resurrectionist," according to Procurator Fiscal Archibald Scott, also turned up in police records. Aged about thirty at the time of his first arrest in 1827, he had a checkered criminal career, including arrests for counterfeiting and for theft, before turning to body snatching.

All these resurrection men preferred the graves of the poor: they were less likely to be guarded, and they might yield more subjects. "When I go to work," reported A.B., "I like to get those of poor people buried from the workhouses, because, instead of working for one subject, you may get three or four; I do not think during the time I have been in the habit of working for the schools, I got half a dozen of wealthier people." For that reason, proponents of the Anatomy Bill argued, their plan was not as inequitable as it seemed. Some might argue that it was not just, admitted Warburton, that the "bodies to be chosen" for dissection, according to the proposed plan, "would, necessarily, be those of the poor only." To which it may be replied, that under the existing system, "the bodies exhumated are principally those of the poor."

Cobbett was not impressed by these arguments in favor of what he called the Dead Body Bill. Proponents claimed, he said, "if we don't do this—if we don't sell the dead bodies of the poor, they will be taken out of the graves, and sold by other people. There will be smuggling; there will be an illicit and contraband trade. If we don't establish a regular trade in dead bodies, we shall have a contraband one." But is it so impossible to make a law to protect cadavers? demanded Cobbett. "What! our omnipotent parliament could not do this? . . . They who passed a law to protect the bodies of pheasant, hares, and partridges—wild animals, which are here one hour and twenty miles off the next—could not they pass a law to prevent fellows violating the sacredness of the grave?"

Cobbett's point was that members of Parliament were ready enough to pass laws protecting their pleasures—game for hunting—while claiming to be incapable of protecting the bodies of the poor, and it was well taken. Yet the analogy is not exact. Yes, Parliament had passed game laws, as indeed they had passed laws preventing violation of sepulchres. Both were liable to be broken. But there were not, for pheasant and hare as there were for cadavers, a set of purchasers in every major city, forming a closed caste and impossible to police, ready to pay poachers whatever the market would bear. A comparison to modern international laws protecting African ivory or snow tiger pelts would be more pertinent. For the Select Committee investigations made clear that there existed a national trade in cadavers of the poor, extending from London prison ships to Dublin potter's fields, from Manchester hospitals to Edinburgh boardinghouses. It is likely, indeed, that every source of supply mentioned in testimony to the Select Committee, from hospitals to penitentiaries and not forgetting the poor who died on the canals or the turnpikes, was already being mined by anatomists throughout the country. No set of laws could protect every graveyard, every hospital mortuary, every winter shelter along the rivers and highways. The existing punishment for violation of sepulchres was six months in prison, and what kind of deterrent was that, when set beside an incentive of £10 or £12 per cadaver?

Robert Knox's own account book for his dissecting rooms shows how extensive was the trade in dead bodies. Though his accounts for the fateful year 1827–1828 have never been found, we do have careful records kept by his chief assistant, William Fergusson, for the period 1829 through 1832. Fergusson noted all income and expenditures relating to the dissecting rooms. We learn from them that Knox had a fairly steady supply of cadavers from the Edinburgh resurrectionists, including Andrew Lees, James Hewit, and James Gow, all of whom also turn up in police records for the same period. They called quite openly at Knox's dissection rooms, and Fergusson paid them with notes drawn on the Royal Bank of Scotland, where they went, again quite openly, to transfer their bank notes to cash. However unsavory the Edinburgh body snatchers, they appear to have been trustworthy purveyors of cadavers. Knox's account books capture their businesslike air by referring to them as "Lees & Co."

The Edinburgh body snatchers formed only part of Knox's extraordinarily ambitious body-purchasing network. They supplied him with approximately fifteen cadavers each year, probably more than they conveyed to any other Edinburgh anatomist. But he also had agents in Glasgow, Ireland, and Manchester. His Glasgow suppliers were reasonably consistent, providing a steady stream of another fifteen cadavers throughout the year, packed in trunks and sent by canal to Edinburgh. Occasionally these trunks were opened by the sheriff—their contents having begun to decompose—and their contents confiscated. It is possible that these cadavers came originally from Ireland, since "It was universally known," according to one witness to the Select Committee, "that all the bodies" interred in the pauper's burial ground in Dublin, Bully's Acre, "were taken up a few hours after they were interred." Knox's agent in Ireland sent him about ten bodies, most in the fall: he started out in Dublin, then went to Cork and Sligo, dispatching cadavers back to Edinburgh as he went. From Ireland, the same man went to Manchester, where he shipped an additional seven to ten cadavers for the spring. The long-distance traffic in cadavers throughout Britain must have been like smuggling, an illicit but fairly steady business venture for those willing to run the risk of engaging in it, periodically disrupted by the police but continuing nonetheless.

Did Knox know he was dealing with an illicit trade? Indeed he must have, for he paid out small sums of money to the wives of Lees, Hewit, and Gow when they were incarcerated or in hiding out of town. It was commonly assumed that cadavers were stolen, not just from burial grounds, but from lodging houses and apartments before interment: Thomas Halls, one of the Bow Street magistrates in London, had "no doubt that is done." That was the understanding of Thomas Giordani Wright, who had studied with Knox in the winter of 1825–1826. Uninterred bodies were not unusual in dissecting rooms, he wrote in Knox's defense. "I myself dissected a decapitated head which had not been dead to all appearances above a day or two and had assuredly not been buried, without surprize being expressed by anyone present; and I know that a traffic is carried on by the body snatchers in purchasing the poor immediately after death, nor do they scruple to steal these during the night if they cannot prevail in any other way." Does it "consist with your knowledge," David Paterson was asked at Burke's and M'Dougal's trial, "that there are people in town that sell dead bodies that have not been interred?" "I have heard it," Paterson responded. "I have known gentlemen that have attended poor patients that have died, and then they afterwards gave in a note of their place of abode to Dr. Knox." What had Knox done with it? He had, according to Paterson, given the note to Burke and Hare, though no cadavers were brought in as a result. What, we may wonder, did Knox imagine his "resurrectionists" would do? Purchase the bodies or steal them?

Knox, then, like all the other anatomical lecturers, knew perfectly well that he was flouting the police and supporting the desecration of human cadavers by body snatchers. These men knock in the coffin lid, explained Thomas Wright, "and a rope is fastened round the neck of the corpse by which it is dragged from its resting place. . . . It is then disfigured about the face to prevent recognition, the teeth are generally broken out as perquisites of these human wolves, and the stiff carcass is tied with ropes and beat into shape for package in a small box or trunk." The cadavers so obtained might then be smuggled, again in defiance of the law, for hundreds of miles. By 1828, these practices had led to a public outcry throughout Britain, resulting in a series of popular demonstrations in which anatomical theaters had to be protected by the police. Still, neither Knox nor his Edinburgh colleagues paid attention to the outrage thus provoked. The efforts of the chief medical institutions were directed at removing restraints from the body trade, not better regulating it. Certainly they did not attempt to address public concerns. The Royal College of Physicians asked the Select Committee to propose "the abolition or restriction of the power assumed by various petty officers, to break open boxes and packages in which it is alleged dead bodies are conveyed from one place to another, and also unnecessary intrusion into premises in which for the purposes of professional education, dead bodies are usually or frequently contained." The Royal College of Surgeons likewise spoke out against the "officious, and, it is believed, sometimes unwarranted interference of magistrates and public officers, where bodies have been detected, or suspected to be concealed. . . . These interferences have usually only the effect of obstructing the progress of medical education, and of unnecessarily exasperating popular feeling and prejudice. Were the powers of magistrates and public officers defined and limited to cases in which application is officially made to them by relations or connections, and their officious and unwarranted interference prevented and discountenanced, this obstacle might, it is conceived, be in a great measure removed." In other words, the Colleges were asking that all oversight by public authorities, all external inquiry into how they obtained, transported, and utilized their bodies, simply be removed.

Who, then, would regulate the body trade? the public might reasonably inquire. It was not as though anatomical lecturers could be trusted to police themselves. In fact Edinburgh medical practitioners were usually treated very gently by the judicial authorities in their investigations, and not pressed to answer questions if by doing so they would incriminate themselves. "With regard in particular to the class of offenses concerned with the present state of the laws relative to the supply of dead bodies for the instruction of medical practitioners," noted Sheriff-Substitute George Tait, "in ordinary circumstances, it had been the practice . . . to deal with them with a little more reserve than with ordinary crimes, and not to compel the lecturers to give information with regard to their supply." When Professor Alexander Monro had a shipment of Dublin cadavers confiscated and buried by customs officials, the lord advocate, Sir William Rae, sent a private letter to the head of the Scottish customs office hoping "that it may be in his power quietly to give such directions as may prevent as far as possible any unnecessary impediments being thrown in the way of the conveyance of dead subjects." Anatomists were, then, already being treated as a privileged group. Even the body snatchers benefited from this gentle treatment, for there were remarkably few prosecutions for violation of sepulchres through most of the 1820s.

The result was not only the Burke and Hare murders but also a series of body-snatching incidents which demonstrated how ready were the anatomists to work with their suppliers in deceiving the public. Within weeks of Burke's celebrated murder trial, anatomical lecturers in Surgeon's Square had returned to obtaining their cadavers through the usual, illegal channels, despite the greater "risk of the public feeling being outraged and of the clamour both against the Lecturers and the public authorities." In February 1829, James Hewit and James Gow came to the residence of the anatomist John Lizars in Surgeon's Square, asking for money for a spade and other implements, in order to procure a body. As Gow later testified, Lizars refused to give them any money, so Hewit and Gow continued on to the next anatomist on the square, John Aitken. His brother and fellow surgeon, Thomas Johnstone Aitken, met them at the door and declared "that he would take the body but would not advance a penny." Two days later, about 7 P.M., Hewit and Gow, together with two associates, George Cameron and John Kerr, returned to Dr. Aitken's house with the body of a female subject wrapped in a bag. On Aitken's request they brought it into a back room, where they removed it from the bag and, placing it into "a black leather trunk studded with brass nails," they carried it to his premises in Surgeon's Square. For this they received "an order on the Royal Bank for £10, which Hewit presented at that bank the same day and got that sum and it was divided among the four." Gow "did not hear the Dr ask any questions as to where the body had been got," nor did he ask why he and Hewit had returned with two additional companions. By the next night two more men, Lees and Spouse, had joined the group in conveying a child's body to Aitken, for which they received £2. Gow's share was 5 shillings. On the third night, Saturday, February 21, the resurrectionists brought the body of a man, covered in a bag, into town "and conveyed it to Mr. Lizars house in York Place and the body was placed into a cellar." Lizars paid £12 for the subject, and Gow received £1 as his share, bringing his total up to £3, 15 shillings, much more than he would ever earn for a week's work as a laborer. For their part, the two dissecting establishments had acquired three cadavers between them, among the few they had had all winter.

At no point did any of the anatomists inquire where the bodies had come from, acting throughout as though the "subjects" turning up in their dissecting rooms were completely divorced from the spark of humanity previously inhabiting them. Precisely how the bodies had been obtained, and whom they had belonged to, was unnecessary information. Indeed, where they could, they left the business of accepting the bodies to their doorkeepers and assistants. Like David Paterson in Knox's establishment, Lancelot Donelly in Lizars's appeared to have standing instructions to be on the lookout for cadavers, as did George Stewart Campbell, the skeleton maker in High School Yards. None took any more responsibility for investigating the provenance of the cadavers than Knox's assistants William Fergusson, Alexander Miller, or Thomas Wharton Jones.

Then the trouble started. The three bodies delivered to the anatomists in February 1829 had come from the churchyard of Lasswade, and family members of the deceased went to the police (Figure 6). The subsequent investigation confirmed what had been long known to the authorities, that resurrectionists located available bodies through informants. In Lasswade, as in many other parishes, noted Archibald Scott, the procurator fiscal, "a number of the inhabitants club together and watch by rotation the graves of deceased members and their relations in order to prevent their being carried off for surgical dissection." For the most part this system worked well, "as regular notices are sent to those whose lot it is to attend, but should it happen, as it occasionally does, that no member or relation has been interred within a prescribed period, then these watching cease, and the Churchyard is left unprotected." This was exactly what the "needy resurrectionist" was looking for, "in order for to pounce on his unhallowed prey, nor are there wanting, near to Churchyards, beings who share in the profits, by communicating when these opportunities occur." In Lasswade, the opportunity was communicated through Helen Miller, a widow living with her father, John Begbie, a laborer. Her sister was married to George Cameron, who also listed his occupation as "laborer," but was known as a resurrectionist: indeed, his father-in-law would not let him in the house "as he does not approve of his way of living by which he means his lifting dead bodies." For that reason Helen Miller usually visited her sister in Edinburgh. One evening at the end of January she came to see James Hewit, telling him "that two bodies were lying in Lasswade churchyard, which, from there being no Watch, could be carried away." One of the bodies had belonged to her cousin, John Braid, "who had met his death owing to a fall from a Cart of Hay" about three weeks previously. We may note that the initiative in this case came from Miller; perhaps a cousin's cadaver did not seem to her to merit special protection, or perhaps as a poor widow, living with her father, she had to take her opportunities for ready cash as she could find them. Both temptation and opportunity to sell the cadavers of relations would be greater among the poor than the rich, another sign of the vulnerability of a poor man's corpse under the existing system.

Hewit discussed this opportunity with Gow, for at least two men were needed to exhume a corpse. "He had some times got good information from her," he told Gow, but "she has at other times come into town with false information . . . for the purpose of getting a belly full of drink." This time she seemed to be telling the truth, and insisted that Hewit and Gow come that night to see the graves. They had no equipment, and it was at this point that Hewit and Gow had applied to the two anatomists, Lizars and Thomas Johnstone Aitken, but when they refused advance payment Helen Miller promised them the use of her father's spade.

Figure 6. Contemporary engraving of the village of Lasswade, whose graveyard was a source of supply for Edinburgh body snatchers. From James Grant, *Old and New Edinburgh*, reproduced by West Port Books, Edinburgh.

Hewit and Gow set out about 9 P.M. on Wednesday, February 18, from the High Street in Edinburgh, arriving in Lasswade about 11 P.M. Miller met them there and took them to the churchyard, describing where they could find her cousin's grave; in addition, she said, there was "a body of an old woman"—Joan Swan—"who had been buried at the expence of the parish, not above one or two feet below the surface of the earth." Gow and Hewit located both graves, inserting a stick to see how deep they were buried; and having reconnoitered, they walked Miller part of the way home before returning to Edinburgh.

The next day they picked up two more associates, John Kerr, a laborer, and John Burnett, who described himself as a "medical student" though Lizars referred to him as a "resurrectionist." The four men left Edinburgh about 10 P.M., but on arriving at Miller's house, where she was to give them a spade, found it locked. They located one in a neighboring yard, and, "as they thought it rather early to commence operations," Gow explained, waited until after midnight to begin digging up the body of the old woman. One man dug while the others stood watch; then, having extracted the body, they filled up the grave, throwing the spade over the churchyard wall when they were done. They hid the body in a quarry while they went to see Dr. Aitken; as we have seen, it was finally turned over to him at about 7 P.M.

The next night, Friday, February 20, a ball was being held in Lasswade, "which as might be expected," noted Archibald Scott in his report, "attracted more or less the attention of the inhabitants but more so the younger part, those most likely to attend to the duties of the Churchyard, as a son can attend for a father, and so on. This circumstance therefore gave additional scope for the resurrectionists' exertions, nor were they slow in availing themselves of the opportunity." About 10 P.M., Gow, Hewit, Kerr, and Burnett left Edinburgh for Lasswade, with the intention of digging up Braid's body. They had previously purchased their own spade, and once again made their way to the churchyard about midnight. They extracted Braid's body, then "commenced to another grave"—Alexander Kerr's, about five years old when he had died—when there was a sudden confluence of additional resurrectionists. "Spouse and Lees came from the Eastward" into the churchyard, said Gow, "and Cameron and Barclay from the Westward; and they said that they expected to find them there." The original party of two, first expanded to four, had now become eight. Lees and Spouse dug up two more graves, but with no success: the only body they found "was so old that they did not carry it away, and it was left in the grave." By this time they had been in the churchyard, Gow thought, about three or four hours, and perhaps local people were starting to stir, for the body snatchers quickly left for Edinburgh without filling the graves back up. As a result, the violation of the four graves was discovered "early on the following morning," Archibald Scott explained, including that of the old woman "in an exceeding putrid state." To make matters worse, the resur-rectionists—"as they wished to demonstrate their disappointment at the Loss, and to confirm their reckless heed of humane principle," wrote Scott, had left "detached portions of the body . . . scattered about, which is said to have presented a most shocking spectacle, and to add to the detestation of the affair, the graves of those they had disinterred, were left uncovered, which is somewhat singular, the general practice being to leave the graves as nearly in the same state as when the bodies are first buried." In the meantime, the men had hidden the bodies until night, when they brought the child's body to Aitken, and then returned with a cart to get Braid's body and deliver it to Lizars. Lizars later testified that he had examined the corpse and "ascertained that it had died a natural death," but it is not clear how he could have "ascertained" any such thing: Braid's body was a month old, and his fall from the cart had left him with a broken back.

Eight resurrectionists and three cadavers could hardly move silently and undetected from Lasswade to Surgeon's Square. By the night of Satur-day, Febuary 21, John Braid's sister and friends had obtained a warrant to search the Aitkens' rooms. Perhaps Helen Miller, accused by her neighbors of complicity, had given them information to lead them to Aitken, or per-haps they had some other source. They did not find the cadaver in Aitken's rooms, reported James McKenzie, the sheriff-officer, but when the search was completed, Thomas Aitken requested the chief witness, Braid's sister Mrs. Morrison, to search the rest of the house "so that she might be the more convinced the body of her brother was not there." Dr. Aitken must not have realized that she could have any connection with the other ca-davers, but she, and the officer, noticed the bodies of an old woman and a child, which Mrs. Morrison "instantly conceived to be those taken away at the same time with her brother." Since she was not competent to be a witness for the other bodies, believed to be Joan Swan and Alexander Kerr, the matter had to wait until Monday, when the Aitkens' rooms were again searched. This time the body of a woman was found "secreted in a trunk," but the child's body was nowhere to be found. The sheriff-officer procured a warrant to search John Lizars's rooms, where the body of a male subject was found, but Braid's sister said it was not her brother, and Lizars, like Aitken, refused to answer any questions on the grounds he might incriminate himself. Sheriff-Officer James McKenzie was dispatched to Lasswade to ascertain the facts and return with competent witnesses for the other bodies, but in the meantime the surgeons took their own steps to obstruct justice. When Officer McKenzie went back to the Aitkens' establishment with the witnesses for Joan Swan, he was "under the impression the body would be in the same state as when I left it yesterday," he wrote in his report, "but I was somewhat surprised at now finding a number of students dissecting it, who I instantly required to desist as those who accompanied me were confident she was one of those taken from Lasswade on Friday last." He "then cited Dr. Aitken and Mr. Thos Aitken to attend at the Sheriff's Office immediately," but they, too, refused to answer any questions, as did their assistants and household servants. McKenzie persuaded Thomas Aitken to cooperate to the extent that he promised "that not only the woman's body but the child's also would be given up to me, at the rooms at 1/2 past 5," but "at the time appointed, neither the Dr. nor his brother appeared." John Aitken offered no explanation for his behavior, other than "'he had nothing to do with his brother's promises'—'he would neither assist nor resist in the matter, do as I pleased.'" McKenzie had the body of Joan Swan placed in a coffin and made arrangements for her to be reinterred the following day, then returned to the investigation in Surgeon's Square.

Young Alexander Kerr's body was never recovered, despite another thorough search of Aitken's rooms. "Before searching the premises, I called on Dr. Aitken," reported the indefatigably polite McKenzie, "who, as on the occasion of Braid, declined to interfere in the matter whatever saying, he would 'neither assist, nor resist.'" Thomas Aitken accompanied the policemen while McKenzie and two assistants "made a most minute search for the body in question . . . but without obtaining the least clue as to where it was now secreted." What McKenzie did see were "the remains of a Dog, which I saw on the dissecting table, and [from] the freshness of the detached pieces which appeared to have belonged to it, I therefore conjecture it to have been put there instead of the child." But he could not find Kerr's body: "that it was not in [Aitken's] rooms at the making my search at this time, I am most certain, not a 'hole or bone' in the whole building, but was rummaged."

The level of obtuseness displayed by the anatomists enraged the solicitor general, John Hope, known for his hot temper. "I am wholly at a loss to understand the principle on which this precognition has been conducted," he wrote in fury on hearing that the Aitkens, Lizars, and their assistants had refused to answer any questions about the matter. "On the part of the Lecturers themselves this conduct is equally inexcusable and short-sighted—I hold that any man is bound to give evidence when examined. . . . The outrage on public Decency in the present case was most scandalous and it is perfectly intolerable that when the bodies are traced . . . immediately to the rooms of different Lecturers these Gentlemen who at the same time are clamorous for the protection of the Police should refuse to give any information by which the public authorities may know the Parties who have committed this offense with such an utter disregard of the feelings of the Neighbourhood." Perhaps the medical men shared that utter disregard? Or else they felt that "such an inquiry is a mere farce and that these Lecturers are at perfect liberty to do what they chose & to laugh at the public authorities?" But Hope would not "acquiesce in any such notion," for to do so was "to allow these Gentlemen to become the administrators of the public Law of the land and it is instantly necessary that notions of such an extraordinary description should be most promptly & strongly checked." To that end Hope directed that his strongly worded letter be read to the anatomists, and that they be made to understand "that in every such case they must be prepared either to give the information required of them or to stand their Trial for the offense in which they are more or less implicated." John Aitken still refused to testify, but John Lizars and Thomas Aitken agreed to answer questions. After spending a night in jail, so did John Hislop, medical student and assistant to another Surgeon's Square anatomist, John William Turner.

What had happened to Braid's body was not pretty. John Lizars had received it on Saturday, as Gow had testified. By Monday, though, he had sent it off to Turner, "having learned that Dr. Turner was in want of a subject"—and presumably having learned as well that the police were in search of this particular cadaver. Turner kept the corpse only four hours, for when he, too, learned "that a search was making in different dissection rooms," he removed it "to other premises in Surgeon's Square where it remained a day or two." But by now Braid's corpse had become a hot potato, and Turner ended by sending it to George Ballingall, professor of military surgery—though he, too, told the police that it was merely because Ballingall had complained that he was "in want of a subject." Ballingall was most happy to cooperate with the police, but of course he had nothing to hide: he had merely accepted a body from a colleague and was not implicated in its exhumation. He was afraid, he informed the police, that the body might be hard to identify, as it was "somewhat disfigured in consequence of surgical operations which had been performed on the face." Surely Ballingall had marred the face deliberately, unless we prefer to believe that he could not connect the unexpected gift of a cadaver with the police searching Surgeon's Square. Ironically, considering how much the medical men had done to obfuscate the evidence, the body was finally determined to be Braid's through anatomical science. It had apparently been partly dissected even before it reached Surgeon's Square, for Lizars had "observed that it had been opened in the head, chest, & belly and sewed up again, apparently by a professional person, from which he concluded that it had been examined privately," before interment. Ballingall subsequently reported the same features on his cadaver: "it had been opened," he said, "at the head, chest, and abdomen." Braid's cadaver, or what was left of it, was returned to his family and reinterred.

The case never came to trial. Lees, Spouse, and Hewit stayed outside of Edinburgh, where they could not be apprehended. Gow, whose testimony provided most of the evidence for the case, was exempted from prosecution because of it. Fume as he might, John Hope never had the opportunity to try the anatomists for reset of theft. The consequence was that there were no consequences: that is, the illicit trade in cadavers continued just as before. Even Gow, who had had so close a call, returned to bodysnatching, because the high prices to be had in the body trade were so enticing. When Gow heard of the corpse of Barbara Rodger lying in a room in Old Assembly Close, he arranged for the caretaker to leave the passage door unlocked so he could steal it. Unfortunately for Gow, the door remained locked when he arrived with several associates early one morning. One of the men "began to think of the impropriety" of the theft, for breaking open a locked door would turn the crime into housebreaking with intent to steal, a serious offense. But Gow declared "that she, meaning the dead body of the woman, should be his by right or by wrong that morning and forced open the door with his back." The noise alarmed the neighbors, who called the police, and though Gow and the others got away, they were soon apprehended. It is clear that Gow was working for one of the Edinburgh anatomists on this attempted theft, for he had picked up a bag from Surgeon's Square before starting on his way. Gow's wife received a shilling from Robert Knox on March 22, 1830; perhaps she asked for money from the other anatomists as well. By that time James Gow had been tried and found guilty of housebreaking. His last body-snatching attempt had thus led to his fourth arrest in four years, and his third conviction. On April 13 he was transported to the colonies for seven years. There is no record of what became of his wife.

The collaboration between anatomists and body snatchers was a dark chapter in the history of medicine, whitewashed in its own day as somehow necessary to teaching and practice. "Tried in reference to the invariable and the necessary practice of the profession," wrote defense counsel Henry Cockburn, "our anatomists were spotlessly correct." But it is hard to see what could be "spotlessly correct" in the appropriation of John Braid, Alexander Kerr, Joan Swan, or Barbara Rodger, and we may well agree with Solicitor General John Hope, who wrote of "the incalculable danger" of the anatomists "allowing the persons who supply them with dead bodies to suppose that the Lecturers are to be no check upon the way & manner in which the bodies are supplied." The anatomists, he said, "ought now to feel that the more impunity and the more irresponsibility which they endeavour to extend to persons engaged in such a traffic, the more their own character truly becomes implicated in the conduct of such persons." The less responsibility on the part of the anatomists, "the greater is the risk of enormities being perpetrated and the more audacious the more careless of all decency and the more blackguard will the persons furnishing them with bodies become." Ultimately, "the greater will be the risk of the public feeling being outraged and of the clamour both against the Lecturers and the public authorities becoming greater."

The solicitor general's warning was not mere hindsight. Thoughtful commentators had realized for some time that the high market price paid for the dead could be dangerous to the still living. In its letter to the Select Committee on Anatomy, written well before any murders had come to light, the Royal College of Physicians of Edinburgh urged that purchasing cadavers be made legal, so that anatomists need no longer fear police investigation. They warned, though, that any legalization of the sale of cadavers "should of course be understood to apply only to the case of individuals selling during their lifetime the right and disposal of their own bodies after death, and receiving the money themselves. For if the sale of relations, connections, or others were authorized, the College think that a greater inducement than the law ought to sanction, would be thereby held out, among the numerous needy and profligate individuals, in the lower ranks of Society, to the neglect of sick persons, and might even lead to the actual commission of murder."

But in November 1827, there was no question of murder, just a fine fresh dropsical cadaver offered by an apparently new firm of purveyors with the nondescript names "John" and "William." Perhaps they were just starting out in the trade, Robert Knox may have mused, for they were willing to accept rather less than the usual price; perhaps they wished to undercut the competition, or perhaps as Irishmen they had connections unavailable to the Scots resurrectionists. But their business practices were no concern of his. We should therefore not be as surprised as Burke and Hare that Knox's only response to their first delivery was to examine Donald's body, and propose that they should get £7 10s. And it was "getting that high price," Burke said, that "made them try the murdering for subjects."

Chapter 3

Burking Invented

Joseph the Miller, Abigail Simpson

WHO WAS THE FIRST MURDER VICTIM? ACCORDING TO BURKE, it was Abigail Simpson, from the nearby village of Gilmerton, who came to lodge in Hare's house. She sold salt and camstone, a kind of limestone popular for whitening windowsills and stairs. After drinking for much of the night with Hare, she lay, insensible, "on her back in the bed," and Hare "then said that they would try and smother her in order to dispose of her body to the doctors." According to Hare, the first murder was Joseph, a miller, also one of his lodgers, who was "very ill, lying in bed, and could not speak sometimes." Hare and his wife were "uneasy" that rumors of "fever in the house" would keep away other lodgers; moreover, Joseph was apparently close to death, and so Burke and Hare "agreed that they should suffocate him for the same purpose." Sir Walter Scott, who took an active interest in murder cases as both lawyer and novelist, was inclined toward Hare's version of events. "For there was an additional motive to reconcile them to the deed in the miller's case," he noted, "the fear that the apprehension entertained through the fever would discredit the house, and the consideration that there was, as they might think, less crime in killing a man who was to die at any rate. . . . It is a step in the history of the crime."

To the psychology of the murders we may add considerations of method. In Joseph's case, Burke "got a small pillow and laid it across Joseph's mouth, and Hare lay across the body to keep down the arms and legs." It seems likely that they soon decided that it was dangerous to use a pillow. We do not know whether it was a feather pillow, that favorite device of later detective stories, or whether Burke and Hare were concerned that it might provide a chain of evidence that could link them to the corpse. But there was little reason for Burke to carry pillows around the lodging house—that was surely Margaret Hare's responsibility—and if other lodgers drew a connection between Burke's pillow toting and a subsequent dead body, it would cause far more "uneasiness" than any fever. So it seems likely that Joseph was killed first, with the aid of the pillow, but that afterward the two men employed the method Burke described in Abigail Simpson's death: "Hare clapped his hand on her mouth and nose," and Burke "laid himself across her body, in order to prevent her making any disturbance."

This was the method that, a year later, would become known as "burking," after its most famous practitioner. It was an ingenious method, practically undetectable until the era of modern forensics. Burke's weight on the victim's rib cage prevented the diaphragm and lungs from expanding, while Hare's covering the nose and mouth prevented even the slightest air flow into the lungs. As the *Caledonian Mercury* explained to its readers, clearly relishing the anatomical detail, "At every inspiration, the ribs of the chest or thorax are dilated by muscular action to an extent of about one-fifth larger than immediately after expiration and, in cases of a full or strong inspiration, to nearly one-third. A partial vacuum is thus produced, and the atmospheric air rushes in by the trachea to fill the cavity in the diaphragm, the recipient of the air inspired, and to oxygeneate the blood." Without that vacuum produced by the expansion of the diaphragm and rib cage, air could not be drawn into the body. "In murder upon scientific principles, therefore," the *Caledonian Mercury* went on, "the first point is to compress the ribs of the thorax, so as to prevent this dilatation; and if the compression be powerful, it will of itself be sufficient to destroy life in a few minutes, without the application of pressure to the throat at all, and without leaving on the body any external marks of violence." Nor need the compression be long continued, "for independently of the necessity of respiration to the support of life, the blood, for want of oxygen, instantly becomes poisoned, and this of itself would occasion immediate death." Burke's account confirms this, for, he said, once they had "kept the mouth and nose shut a very few minutes," while compressing the chest, the victims "could make no resistance, but would convulse and make a rumbling noise in their bellies for some time." Once all crying, or other signs of resistance ceased, he and Hare would let up on the victims, leaving "them to die of themselves; but their bodies would often move afterwards, and for some time they would have long breathings before life went away." "Even a full grown bull might be destroyed in this way in a very short space of time," thundered the *Caledonian Mercury*, but this is sheer hyperbole, as will become clear to anyone who tries to form a mental picture of killing a full grown bull by lying across its chest. In fact burking is rare as a form of adult murder, because the human rib cage is too sturdy to be easily compressed: any conscious victim will struggle enough so that strangulation, or a blunt instrument, will be the method of choice for the determined murderer. For that reason nearly all the victims in the Burke and Hare murders were elderly, infirm, or very, very drunk, as we will see.

Once dead, neither the miller Joseph nor Abigail Simpson would have presented forensic evidence that would suggest, much less prove, murder. Death by compression of the chest presents much the same appearance as by suffocation. The police surgeon who testified for the prosecution, Alexander Black, had to admit that such suffocation could proceed from accidental causes. "Have you ever seen a case of suffocation separate from strangling?" Henry Cockburn, M'Dougal's defense counsel, asked Black during cross-examination. "I have known many cases of drink, of people lying on the street, brought in in that way," Black replied. "Were the symptoms here like those you have seen in suffocation from drinking?" Cockburn continued. "Yes," responded Black, "I must say that in a number of those cases they had all the appearance—very much swollen and black." "Were the eyes swollen?" asked Cockburn. "Yes," responded Black. Bloodshot eyes, and congestion of the face with blood, may vary considerably from one victim to another, and may also be found in deaths from natural causes. What this meant is that Burke and Hare had hit upon a murder method that was apparently undetectable. Their practice of leaving their victims "to die of themselves" meant that any slight marks of fingernails on the face or bruising on the chest could be plausibly attributed to death throes of the victim, or postmortem trauma.

So ingenious did this method appear to contemporaries that the *Caledonian Mercury* suggested that Burke and Hare must have had some coaching in anatomy to come up with it. "WHO taught Burke," the writer asked, "a common Irish labourer of the very lowest class, to commit murder after a fashion, the science displayed in which is a subject of wonder and dismay to many of the most skilful [*sic*] anatomists in this city.?" Hare, perhaps, had taught Burke, but the writer strongly suggested that some surgeon—Knox, by implication—must have explained the anatomical principles to both men. Burke later went on record to declare that no one had taught him how to murder: he had not lain on the chest of the victim "to prevent the person from breathing," but rather "for the purpose of keeping down the person's arms and thighs, to prevent the person struggling." At the trial, Alexander Black gave evidence that he had had many opportunities of examining "persons strangled or suffocated." "In what manner?" asked James Moncreiff, defense counsel for Burke. "Probably putting soft substances on the mouth, pressing the lungs, and pressing the chest," Black replied.

If Joseph was the first murder, he was killed some time in January or early February 1828. According to Burke, he "had once been possessed of a good deal of money," and had connections with the Carron Ironworks, the oldest ironworks in Scotland. By the time he ended up in the West Port, he seems to have become an itinerant worker. Burke gave the date of Abigail Simpson's murder with unusual precision, stating it was February 12, 1828. She had come to Edinburgh the previous day, and "was decoyed in by Hare and his wife." Contemporaries considered "tenderness and hospitality" to be "the universal characteristics of the Irish," together with "a certain easy politeness towards strangers." Even the poorest "offer what they have, without embarrassment, to the most fashionably dressed visitor; and although they never forget the respectful address, 'your honour,' yet they always appear to consider him what he really is—their guest and equal." This generous hospitality, this easy politeness, too, became hallmarks of the murders. Abigail Simpson drank sociably until it was too late, and she was too drunk, to go home, so she stayed all night, laughing and drinking still more. She received a pension from a gentleman in town, she told her new friends; and she and Hare carried on a running joke about his marrying her daughter at Gilmerton, clearly not realizing he was already married to the landlady of the lodging house. By the early hours of the morning Simpson was sick to her stomach and vomited up much of what she had consumed, but "they then gave her some porter and whisky, and made her so drunk that she fell asleep on the bed." It is possible that alcohol poisoning alone could have killed her, but the three "perps"—for Margaret Hare was certainly involved—had no intention of finding out.

Both Joseph's and Abigail Simpson's bodies were delivered to "Dr. Knox's young men" at Surgeon's Square within twenty-four hours, by which time they were "cold and stiff," though when Knox came in later he approved their "being so fresh." Burke explained, "He and Hare always told some story of their having purchased the subjects from some relation or other person who had the means of disposing of them, about different parts of the town." This must have seemed plausible enough. The first cadaver they sold, Donald, died of a dropsy, or edema, with the obvious symptom of fluid filling bodily tissues to the bursting point, while Joseph would have had symptoms of a wasting fever. Abigail Simpson must have reeked of alcohol and vomit once she arrived at Surgeon's Square, carried there by a porter dispatched by Knox's assistant Miller. Alexander Miller had been previously apprenticed to George Bell, an Edinburgh surgeon, who "was in the habit of having his apprentices constantly engaged in attending upon the poor." This was common among Edinburgh surgeons, who often gave their apprentices "a more particular charge" of the "lower people" among their patients to provide them with opportunities for practice. Miller could have recognized—or been predisposed to find—dropsy, fever, and alcoholic stupor as frequent causes of death among the wynds of the Old Town, in contrast to the apoplexy, kidney stones, and gout which prevailed in the New. Neither he, nor any of the other assistants, nor Knox asked any further questions. Once he had received the bodies, Paterson would have placed them in a tub filled with either water or alcohol, depending on the use Knox intended them for. Either liquid would have drawn out the blood and removed any unusual lividity. Knox paid £10 for each body, and back at Tanner's Close the money was divided in what became the customary proportions, with Hare receiving £6 and Burke £4, and Margaret Hare paid £1 out of Burke's allotment. M'Dougal received no money, and indeed Burke always claimed that she knew nothing about it. He "never durst let her know," he said, "he used to smuggle in drink, and get better victuals unknown to her," telling her only "that he bought dead bodies, and sold them to doctors." Any West Port neighbors who might ask awkward questions were told the same thing, "and that was the way they got the name of resurrection-men." At first they seem to have been unsure about what to do with leftover clothes. No mention was made of Joseph's, but Hare took

Mrs. Simpson's "drab mantle" and "white-grounded cotton shawl" with "blue spots" to dispose of in the canal. If he did throw them away, doing so, like using the pillow, was a mistake from inexperience. Selling or keeping the murder victim's possessions would have been the more usual practice according to police reports, and no more likely to betray the murderers than throwing perfectly good clothes into the canal. Indeed, we may note that Burke and Hare seem to have given astonishingly little thought to covering their tracks. There is no sign that Joseph, or Abigail Simpson, or later victims, were screened to ensure that they were alone in the world, so that their disappearance would raise no questions. "They often said to one another that no person could find them out, no one being present at the murders but themselves two," Burke said. Their sole criterion was "if lodgers would drink," and drink to insensibility, in the lodging house, rather than publicly in a tavern. If so "they were disposed of in that manner."

Encountering Burke, M'Dougal, and the Hares with their first victims is to come upon them after they had stepped out upon a particularly slippery slope. Before Joseph and Mrs. Simpson, a step to the right or left might have taken them down some other, less dangerous path; afterward, as Burke remarked, they felt "they might as well be hanged for a sheep as a lamb." Despite the public outcry against them, there is no sign they were particularly depraved: they had no criminal record, and seemed to be getting by with the usual makeshifts of the working poor, a combination of seasonal agricultural labor and work at a variety of trades. There is no evidence to fit them into any sort of modern profile of serial killers, and there is no indication of sexual assault or sadism as a motive. The best answer we can come up with is that murdered corpses—*shots* for the doctor, as they came to refer to them—brought a great deal of money.

We can understand the dynamics of the murders more clearly if we take the time to consider the £10—approximately $400 in modern currency— Knox paid for Abigail Simpson's cadaver. To Knox, it was money well spent. The fees for two beginning anatomy students, attending his lectures at 3 guineas apiece, and two advanced students, at 2 guineas apiece, would more than cover its costs. Students who actually dissected their own cadavers paid an additional 3 guinea fee; more cadavers attracted more students, so that Knox may have cleared a profit for every £10 corpse he purchased. For the most part he seems to have plowed the money right back into his anatomical classroom and museum. But he might have chosen to spend it on clothing, furnishings, books, or his children's education without arousing any comment. For in the world of the professional middle classes, £10 came and went pretty freely; indeed, Edinburgh's highly developed consumer culture generally ensured that it went out more often than it came in. A body purchased for £10 that could yield both increased student fees and an enhanced professional reputation was a sound investment indeed.

In Burke's and Hare's world, £10 was a very different matter. William Burke had come to Edinburgh as a "navvy"—short for "navigator"—who supplied the hard labor to build the networks of roads and canals that transformed Lowland Scotland. He was born in Urney, County Tyrone, in Ireland. According to the information he gave when he entered the Calton

WILLIAM BURKE.

as he appeared at the Bar.

taken in Court.

Figure 7. Portrait of William Burke during the trial, drawn by the portrait painter George Andrew Lutenor, one of the jurors. Reproduced from *West Port Murders.*

Hill Jail, he was thirty-six in 1828, which would put his birth date in 1792. At five feet, five inches, he was of medium height, "complexion swarthy, with brown hair and blue eyes, and an oval face" (Figure 7). Gaelic was probably his native language, and his name may originally have been Liam de Búrca. We know nothing about his family, but he went to school long enough to be able to read and write English. All later commentators agreed that he was charming and well spoken, with the typical "natural vivacity" associated with Irishmen, "not at all ferocious in his general manner," as Henry Cockburn remarked, "sober, correct in all his other habits, and kind to his relations." He was the outgoing, gregarious member of the group, and as their operation expanded it would generally fall to him to scout for potential victims, strike up a conversation, win their confidence, and invite them home to drink. According to his own statement, Burke joined the Donegal militia in 1809, and served for seven years, "most of that time as an officer's servant." Though the militia records are complicated by the vagaries of bookkeeping, there is a "William Burke" on the Donegal militia roll for 1809–1815, listed as a private in Captain Irwin's company. Though raised a Catholic, he attended "Presbyterian, Episcopalian, and Methodist" churches while a soldier, either out of genuine interest or, like other young men, in pursuit of pretty girls. He was at the regimental hospital in Ballina, in County Mayo, several times during 1810–1811, and it may have been on one of those occasions that he met his wife, Margaret Coleman, for he notes that he was married at Ballina while still in the army. The couple subsequently had two children.

The demobilization of the military services, including the militia, in 1816 coincided with economic depression, and Burke, like many other Irishmen, left his wife and children to seek work in Scotland. Seasonal migrants had been arriving from Ireland for the harvest for close to a century, but this process was accelerated by the steamboats that, from the 1820s, shuttled between Glasgow and the Irish ports of Belfast, Londonderry, and Dublin, the trip taking fifteen, twenty, and twenty-four hours, respectively. From six thousand to eight thousand laborers, most of them young men between sixteen and thirty-six, arrived for the harvest each August, generally remaining through October. They paid from 2 to 3 shillings each for the privilege of crowding onto the upper decks, exposed to the weather and "huddled together and mixed up with horned cattle, pigs, sheep, and lambs." On one ship from Londonderry, reported a Glasgow newspaper, "not merely were the main and quarter decks, the paddle boxes and the gateways crowded, but the very shrouds and the top of the cook's galley were occupied." Passengers were mildly requested to "cease forcing themselves on board after the deck is covered for, although they may manage to 'stick in the rigging' this fine weather, a bad night might occur, when some of them might be suffocated by the crushing that will unavoidably take place." Modern readers will be reminded of the equally mild announcement "Please stand clear of the closing doors" on subways packed like sardine cans during rush hour. Authorities at the Greenock landing on the port of Glasgow, fearing they would be inundated with Irish beggars, threatened to ship them back to Ireland at the shipping companies' expense, and an Act of Parliament set a maximum number of passengers who could be carried on a ship of a given size. But municipal authorities in Glasgow had no means to enforce the act, and as advances in technology led to larger and larger steamboats, more and more Irish passengers in search of work were packed onto their decks.

Once disembarked in Greenock, some laborers remained in the Glasgow area but more headed to the rich agricultural district in southeastern Scotland, to the market towns around Edinburgh. If nature cooperated, they would follow the northwesterly direction of the harvest as the season progressed, from the Lothians to Stirlingshire, along the Forth, and wind up in the Glasgow region by the fall. But because nature was so often uncooperative, many migrants chose a region and returned there year after year, simply waiting until the crops were ripe: "If they are told that they are too soon for the harvest," noted one observer, "they are prompt to answer that they cannot be worse off than in their own country." And like other migrants, they were essential to the economic system of their adopted countries. "The advantage we received from the Irish labourers is very great in harvest," noted a magistrate, "and I am not aware that any inconvenience whatever results from them." And "on a moment's reflection," wrote another, "every one must see that his presence could not, in reality, be dispensed with at the harvest season. But for the presence of these Irish reapers, how much of the finest produce of the land must have this season wasted in the furrows?" Like many migrants, they would do work that local labor would not, at a wage that local labor would not accept, from 8 to 12 pence per day at the start of the season, to 2 1/2 shillings, or even 3 per day for a skilled worker, during the period of greatest demand.

The hiring market for Edinburgh took place in the West Port and the Grassmarket, by the Toll Cross. At 4 A.M. the laborers assembled, and were hired by farmers, or their foremen, in groups or twenty or more. Women received about four-fifths of the men's wages. Workers might be compensated for working at an outlying farm by receiving a traveling allowance; they might receive their food from the farmer, or they might provide their own and earn a few pennies more. All these wages were governed according to the inexorable laws of supply and demand, as it was determined by the employers: where there were so many workers, they could get away with paying the minimum possible wage. Occasionally there was some public outcry, for example during the harvest of 1828, when so many migrants arrived that wages dropped to about a shilling per day. "It is very hard for these poor people," wrote one sympathetic commentator, "that, after traveling several hundreds of miles . . . they should be under the necessity of working for only about one half of an ordinary wage." But laborers who tried to join together to bargain as a group were promptly dispersed, or arrested, by the police. A net gain of only £3 for a season's work was common.

Their employers should have been very well satisfied with the result. "Their output of work, power of endurance and cheerfulness under adverse conditions," noted one writer, "far exceed anything we look for in our young men of this country today." For that reason, he went on, "they are of inestimable and essential value to an ever-growing area of the more intensively cultivated lands in England and Scotland." An apparently inexhaustible supply of cheap, hard-working, cheerful labor—by the 1820s this had become a necessity to the lowland Scottish farmers. It would be pleasant to report that gratitude for the Irish contribution to society was the prevailing attitude in Lowland Scotland, but of course it was not: many would have agreed with the writer who complained of the Irish "spreading like locusts over the whole surface of the kingdom," intent on establishing residency and living off the bounty of Scottish parishes. What farmers, and indeed all employers, wanted was cheap laborers who turned up when they were needed and not a day in advance, for whom they did not have to pay a penny extra for their transportation and subsistence. They railed against the steamship companies, whom they accused of recruiting passengers too early in the season. "Numbers of hand bills were printed up," reported the *Scotsman* in 1827, "stating that the crops were ripe, and shearers in great request in Scotland." As a result, the Irish "abandoned their mud cabins by the thousands, in the vain hope of getting instant employment and good wages in this country." As was common among Scottish commentators, the sympathy of the article was all for the Scots who had to deal with the Irish migrants, rather than the migrants themselves. "The farmers of East Lothian have been for some time grievously oppressed with swarms of these destitute emigrants. They have taken possession of their outhouses and offices, and farmers are obliged to provide them in victuals to prevent their perishing by sheer starvation." Considering how quick the Scots and English were to accuse the Irish of improvidence, they might have been more sympathetic to the forethought shown by Irish laborers who arrived early, as so many of them did, "and are then to be seen walking about the country almost starved, for perhaps a week or ten days, when there is no employment for them." Instead they derided their efforts, viewing the "Irish emigration into Britain" as "an example of a less civilized population spreading themselves as a kind of substratum beneath a more civilized population."

The port of Glasgow even tried to set up a quarantine against Irish immigration, noted a newspaper in Ayr, but without much success. "The means adopted have arrested their entrance by the usual ports, but they still gain a footing as effectually by ports where there is no established police, or by landing on the beach. Two cargoes, we observe, were in this manner discharged lately between Greenock and Glasgow." Of course the Irish migrants made their own accommodations to the system where economic, legal, and social thought all combined to keep them at the bottom of the economic ladder. In some English counties, farmers paid for migrants' travel from Ireland, but refused to pay their way home. Instead of spending their own hard-earned money, some Irish seasonal workers gave their wages to friends or family for safekeeping, and waited to be deported.

By the time Burke came to Scotland, the Irish navvies had acquired, as one commentator put it, "possession of the lower occupations of the people," and were "employed almost exclusively in making ditches and cutting drains, and in carrying loads for masons; and generally in all servile occupations they are employed to the nearly total exclusion of the Scotch labourers." Already by 1817 rumors that a new canal was going to be built, connecting the city of Edinburgh with the existing Forth and Clyde Canal, brought many laborers to the city. In March 1818 work began on the Edinburgh side, digging out the terminus, Port Hopetoun, just down the Fountain Bridge Road from the West Port. Probably this is where Burke joined the other laborers.

Work on the Union Canal was servile indeed. Digging a canal in the era before dynamite required pure, brute force with the pick and the shovel. The Union Canal was a contour canal, meaning that it followed the contours of the hills, wending its way some 240 feet above sea level, requiring aqueducts over the Avon River and Waters of Leith. The eastern portion of the route followed sound engineering principles and was completed within sight of its original budget. Once it reached Falkirk, though, the proprietor of the estate abutting the canal, known as Callendar House, refused to allow the canal to be built within sight of his house and gardens. Workers had to hack out a tunnel 690 feet long and 12 feet high from the solid limestone of neighboring Prospect Hill, using shot holes filled with gunpowder, then picks and shovels to break up the stone. It was arm-numbing, backbreaking labor, where a single miscalculation could lead to crushed limbs and shattered bones. But it paid 2 to 3 shillings per day, enough to support a worker and his family, camped out on vacant land owned by the canal proprietors, building "temporary huts for their own accommodation of turf and wood." These were "pointed out to strangers on the passage boats as great curiosities," since "each, of course, is more wretched than another, and presents a picture of squalid poverty which is new to the people on this side of the Channel. One of them, with the exception, perhaps, of a few sticks, is composed entirely of rotten straw; its dimensions would not suffice for a pig stye." The author did note that "the children appear healthful and frolicsome, and the women contented and happy." But when Burke wrote to his wife to join him, "he got no answer." He probably never saw her, or his children, again.

Soon afterwards he met Helen M'Dougal. She had been born in Sterlingshire, she told the police when taken into custody, so perhaps she had met Burke when the canal went through Falkirk. In 1828, she was thirty-three, described in jail records as tall, with brown hair and blue eyes, round face and a fresh complexion (Figure 8). When arrested she had the marks of a sore on her cheek, but it is not clear what kind. She may never have married, but as a young woman she had lived with a man named M'Dougal as his wife, and her "M'Dougal" connections, like Ann Gray, seem to have regarded her as a blood relative. She "has lived with the prisoner, William

HELEN M'DOUGAL

as she appeared at the Bar
taken in Court

Figure 8. Portrait of Helen M'Dougal during the trial, drawn by George Andrew Lutenor. Reproduced from *West Port Murders*.

Burke, for ten years," she said at the time of her arrest, that is, from about the age of twenty-three. At the time of her trial rumors swirled around regarding her profligate life, but in fact "though not legally married," Henry Cockburn insisted, Burke and M'Dougal considered themselves to be man and wife, faithful to each other and bound by ties of affection. The Union Canal was completed by 1822, and Burke, with M'Dougal, next went to Peebles. Between 1822 and 1827 Burke found work as a weaver and a baker, while still working as a day laborer during the harvest; by 1827, as we have seen, he had learned to mend shoes and gave his trade as "shoemaker" at the time of his arrest.

WILLIAM HARE.

as he appeared in the witness box.
taken in Court.

Figure 9. Portrait of William Hare during the trial, drawn by George Andrew Lutenor. Reproduced from *West Port Murders*.

If the information we have on Burke is limited, it is practically non-existent for Hare. When arrested he gave his age as 21, which would put his date of birth around 1807. He was five feet, four and three-quarters inches, with a "pale complexion," small face, brown hair, and hazel eyes (Figure 9). Neither contemporary nor modern commentators have much good to say about him. Contemporary accounts describe Hare as having "a ferocious and tyrannical disposition, much inclined to quarrel, and very obstreperous when in liquor." Jail records state that he was born in County Armagh, perhaps in Newry Parish. Beyond that, we have no evidence concerning his birth, his life in Ireland, or the circumstances that brought him to Scotland.

Hare seems to have been working in Edinburgh in the mid-1820s, perhaps as one of the "bagmen" at Port Hopetoun, who "provided with a strong coarse sack, . . . follow the coal carts and carry the coals into the houses of the inhabitants." At that time he lodged with James and Margaret Logue at their boarding house in Tanner's Close. Margaret was Irish, and the boardinghouse attracted many immigrants. By that time there were perhaps 10,000 Irish resident in Edinburgh, making up about 5 percent of the population. This was not a very large proportion, compared to their constituting 10 percent of the population of Ayrshire, or 13 percent of the population in Lanarkshire, including Glasgow, where, according to a statistically minded university professor, 1 out of every 9.67 of the inhabitants was Irish. But the Irish in Edinburgh were a conspicuous group, clustered, like the university students, in certain districts. By 1819 there was a Roman Catholic chapel, and by 1823, noted the *Scotsman*, "it may be mentioned as an extraordinary instance of the increased number of Irish people within this city," that the wynds off the High Street "which some years ago did not contain one, is now entirely inhabited by them." The wynds along the Cowgate, Grassmarket, and West Port were referred to as "Little Ireland" or "Little Dublin." By the end of the 1820s, at least three-fourths of the 250 secondhand dealers in the Cowgate, St. Mary's Wynd, and the West Port were Irish; so were most of the porters; and so were many of the hawkers selling all kinds of food, silver watches, prints, handkerchiefs, and cheap linens. Nearly all the 112 scavengers responsible for keeping the streets clean of filth were Irish, including Constantine Burke, William's brother, who had moved to Edinburgh sometime before 1828. The lamplighters were Irish, and so were some of the policemen. The Irish were "small shopkeepers and tradespeople." By and large they got along well with their Scottish neighbors. As one clergyman observed, "The Irish . . . do mix, and are obliged to mix, with the natives in the course of their ordinary employments; and I never observed any disinclination on the part of the Irish to mix with the natives who treat them civilly. . . . There is not much difference between the habits of the northern Irish and the Scotch in the lower classes of life." Indeed, Constantine Burke was married to a Scotswoman, Elizabeth Graham.

After James Logue's death, Margaret continued to look after the lodging house in Tanner's Close. It is not clear when she married William Hare. The lodging house continued to be thought of in the neighborhood

Figure 10. Portrait of Margaret Hare during the trial, drawn by George Andrew Lutenor. Reproduced from *West Port Murders*.

as her establishment, rather than her husband's, who worked principally on the canal, and also "had a horse and cart selling fish." Margaret may have had a child with her first husband, and she also had one with Hare, for she had a baby in her arms when she took the stand at the trial. At that time she gave her age as thirty-one years. She was described in jail records as "middle" sized, with black hair and hazel eyes, an "oblique" face and "fresh" complexion, missing a tooth in her upper jaw (Figure 10). Margaret Hare, like her husband, has aroused little sympathy: if Hare's appearance was taken as "an epitome of all that is mean, subtle, and ferocious," noted one journalist, his wife's aspect "is much upon a par with his own." At the trial she claimed to have been afraid of her husband, and said that she had tried to leave him three times, but there is no outside evidence for this. If she did not plan the murders, she assisted in ensnaring the victims; and she was vehement on receiving her fair share of £1 per murder.

What did the £10 paid for Abigail Simpson's cadaver mean in Tanner's Close? It was three times what a seasonal migrant would make in the harvest; to put it another way, it was three years' worth of hard agricultural labor. If we think of it as 200 shillings and assume Burke made 2 shillings per day on the Union Canal, then the single murder was the equivalent of a hundred days spent hacking the tunnel out of Prospect Hill. The Hares' lodging house had eight beds, which, if let at 3 pence per bed, would bring in 24 pence—2 shillings—per night. But in all the poorer sections of the town, residents eked out a living by "subletting their miserable and dark abodes," according to one commentator, "to as many as can be crammed into them," so that every room, no matter how small, became "a lodging house, and is often tenanted to repletion." During the harvest, lodgings in the "better class of houses"—among which we can probably include Margaret Hare's—ranged from 1 shilling for "Tent-bed, curtains, feather-bed, sheets, blankets, and a piece of carpet in front of the bed," to 2 pence for a "shake-down," consisting of a straw bed and blankets, without sheets. Police officers reported that some lodging houses had as many as "26 beds and about 20 shake-downs in one house and six beds in one room. Three persons are seen frequently in beds . . . and four in shake-downs, the number depending altogether on demand." If we assume three people slept in each of the eight beds in Tanner's Close, at 3 pence per night, we get 72 pence, or 6 shillings per night. If we add some number of shake-downs, we might put the Hares' legitimate income at 7 to 8 shillings per night during the harvest. Thus, £10 was the equivalent of almost a month's income from lodgers, all the more welcome for coming in the off-season.

Perhaps even more important than the pattern of earnings was the pattern of consumption. That £10 was both too little and too much: too little to allow the Hares, Burke, and M'Dougal to move up in the world by purchasing land, setting up a shop, or investing in education, and too much for them to spend on the cheap consumables available in the West Port. They could buy more clothes, more food, the "glittering pieces of jewellery, at prices inconceivably beyond their real value" hawked in the street. They could visit the shops in St. Mary's Wynd, though they would be very much out of place on Princes Street. Perhaps they spent some of the money bribing neighbors and policemen; perhaps they sent some home to relatives, for it seems likely that they kept up with family still in Ireland. But the main form of conspicuous consumption open to them, as to the laboring classes generally, was whiskey. It was cheap—perhaps a penny or two a glass—and widely available at grocery stores. And as contemporaries noted at great length, it was an expenditure that always increased. It was as though Burke, M'Dougal, and the Hares had been walking down the street one day and unexpectedly found diamonds sparkling in front of them; as though they located a resetter—a fence—who paid well, eliminated the evidence, and asked no questions; and as though, having once started to pick up the diamonds, they found they could not stop. As we will see, some men—and women, and children—stole, and stole repeatedly, risking imprisonment and transportation for astonishingly small sums. Burke and Hare did not steal or assault for money; instead, they made shoes, let beds to lodgers, worked during the harvest, and murdered.

The money paid for the cadavers can also illuminate the lives of the murdered. People like Abigail Simpson and Joseph the miller were, of course, poor, much more miserably poor than Burke or Hare: the £10 received for their dead bodies would have taken them a very long time to earn while alive. Scotland in this period was rapidly industrializing. The population in the country as a whole increased about 45 percent between 1801 and 1831, while the population in Edinburghshire increased around 83 percent, from 123,000 to 219,000. Provisions for the poor were completely, woefully inadequate, and literally thousands of families were pushed to destitution during periods of economic depression. Residents of a parish alone were entitled to relief from the parish, and it was the wealthy taxpayers of the parish who decided how much they should pay. Many had been influenced by the Free Church leader Thomas Chalmers, who argued that creating a poor law that taxed the wealthy to support the poor would destroy the wellsprings of human benevolence that led to private charity. He claimed, too, that it would increase, not decrease, the number of paupers, by showing the poor that they could live off the state. "Destroy pauperism, and don't provide for it," proclaimed his adherents.

The result of this "Scotch system of neglect," according to William Pulteney Alison, professor of medicine and champion of poor law reform, was that Scotland had a greater number of destitute, with the concomitant danger to the health and well-being of the wealthy as well as the poor, than any country in Europe "where the relief of destitution is invested with the authority, and administered with the uniformity, of law." As Alison noted in his survey of poor relief, based on questionnaires sent to doctors, ministers, and public authorities, in Scotland overall the system was "extremely irregular, and bears no fixed relation to either the number or the degree of destitution of the poor." The smallest amounts were "awarded, not where destitution is least, but on the contrary . . . in districts where the condition of many of the poor is as wretched as is compatible with human existence." Immigrants to a region had to be resident for three years before being entitled to any relief at all, and when that relief came, it was most often capricious and inadequate. Some country parishes gave no relief at all. A few private charities emerged in the 1810s to alleviate the growing problem, such as the Committee for the Relief of the Labouring Classes and the Committee for the Relief of the Destitute Sick. There were medical charities, too, like the Royal Infirmary and the New Town Dispensary. But again the result was haphazard, and fell far short of the growing need. The treasurer of the Edinburgh Charity Workhouse "attempted to find a system of rules" by which funds would be dispersed "with justice and economy." On reviewing the files, however, he "found there was no written code. It was not intended to give the poor as much as would support them; they were to get a certain allowance and make up the rest as they best could, only they were not to beg nor seek relief from any other charity. Now these being the only honest ways a poor person without health, friends, or employment has of eking out the miserable pittance he gets from the parish, I cannot discover the propriety of this rule."

It took the great cholera epidemic in 1832, and the subsequent Parliamentary Committee to Investigate the Sanitary Commission of the Labouring Classes, to focus attention on urban conditions throughout Great Britain. Knox's assistant Alexander Miller became a district inspector during the cholera epidemic, and his experience led him to agree with Alison that disease was due not to personal failings or ill fortune but to "deficient nourishment, want of employment, and privations of all kinds." He was convinced, he told the Sanitary Commission, "that a fearful amount of destitution prevails . . . very many cases of which private benevolence never reaches, and they are unrelieved by public charity, in as far as the allowances thence derived are totally inadequate." In some respects the existing charitable institutions even made conditions worse, for most parishes would give no money unless the intended recipient had strained every resource, including selling all his or her furniture. For that reason, Miller explained, "the most remarkable feature of such dwellings is the miserable scantiness of furniture, or rather in many cases, the total want of any kind of it. A few of the lowest poor have a bedstead, but by far the larger portion have none; these make up a kind of bed on the floor with straw, on which a whole family are bundled together, some naked and others in the same clothes they have worn during the day." This was particularly noteworthy in midwifery cases. "I have on numerous occasions been compelled to deliver the patient destitute of a bed," Miller testified, "and with nothing to rest upon but a quantity of straw, often upon a damp floor, with an old carpet for a covering; and even where there was an apology for a bedstead, I have often seen a single tattered blanket to constitute the whole stock of bed-clothes. In many instances, I have found it impossible to procure clothes sufficient to cover the infant." It was clear to Miller, who had been on the staff of several of the medical charities, that disease and destitution were closely intertwined. "Isolated cases of continued fever are never totally absent from the dwellings of the poor," he told the commission. "When epidemic, I have observed that it prevails with the greatest intensity, and is diffused most rapidly, where large numbers of human beings are crowded together, inadequately supplied with the necessaries of life."

What do you proposed as a remedy? Miller was asked by the commissioners. He was in no doubt as to "the only effectual, and I should think . . . practicable means," he replied. "Better the state of the poor in respect of the nourishment and clothing . . . , improve the state of their houses by ventilating the localities in which they are situated, and repairing the houses themselves, supplying them with abundance of water, and providing them with water-closets." This was entirely sensible advice that the Town Council was unlikely to follow. The stone buildings of the Old Town were so sturdy and well constructed, one observer noted, "that their destruction alone would be a most expensive undertaking" and their "solidity, and the circumstance of their being entirely built of stone, renders it scarcely possible that a great conflagration should eventually clear them away, as has been the case in so many other cities." Yet though the New Town was as abundantly supplied in worthy philanthropical societies "for the conversion of the Jews and the negroes, and other similar purposes," the writer remarked with exaggerated surprise that "there exists not one for the far more necessary and desirable object of gradually cleansing out the wretched dens of the Old Town, destroying the miserable habitations of the poor, and supplying them with new dwellings, rather more accessible to air and light, and rather more favourable to health and morality."

Disease and misery were exacerbated by Edinburgh's tall tenements and narrow wynds. Though "Nature has furnished [Edinburgh] with a singularly salubrious situation," reported one resident to the Sanitary Committee, he was nonetheless "of opinion that this city is at present one of the most uncleanly and badly ventilated in this or any adjacent country." A physician made the same point: "Edinburgh stands on a site beautifully varied by hill and hollow, and owing to this, unusual facilities are afforded for perfect drainage; but the old part of the town was built long before the importance of drainage was understood in Britain, and in the unchanged parts there is none but by the open channels in the streets, wynds, and closes or courts." The police had the responsibility for supervising "a very active service of scavengers to remove everything which open drains cannot be allowed to carry"—a euphemism for human and animal excrement—"but this does not prevent the air from being much more contaminated by the frequent stirring and sweeping of impurities than if the transport were effected under ground; and there are here and there enclosed spaces between houses too small to be used for any good purpose but not neglected for bad, and to which the scavengers have not access." The height of the tenements contributed to the unsanitary conditions, with their "common stairs, sometimes as filthy as the streets or wynds to which they open." The filth was directly related to the poverty of the occupants, because the height of the buildings increased "the labour of carrying up necessaries, and particularly water for the purposes of purifying." Water was expensive, too, being supplied by private company, "and excepting at two or three wells, all the water introduced into the town has to be specially paid for." It was therefore far less plentiful in the Old than in the New Town; fuel to boil it for tea or broth was also far less plentiful among Old Town residents, especially since few of the tenement rooms had fireplaces.

In fact, almost everything was far less plentiful in the Old Town than in the New, except for disease. "If any malaria or contagion exist in the house," physicians testified, "the probability of its passing from dwelling to dwelling on the same stair is much greater than if there were no communication but through the open air." These tenements were "altogether unfit to be the habitations of men," wrote one social reformer in disgust. The once-respectable tenement buildings "tell their own story, and they almost chuckle when they tell it. They speak in a kind of irony—'Look at us,' say they, 'we are not deficient in architectural beauty, but we are old and incompetent, we cannot stand upright, we are all cracked and creviced, and the frailer we get the fuller we are filled, not with those we were designed to shelter, but with those whom we are in no way fitted to accommodate.'" These were not houses, but rather breeding grounds for the next epidemic: "By curious and clumsy contrivance, rooms have been converted into dens and sepulchres for living men."

Under these circumstances, it might seem that Burke and Hare, and many other economic entrepreneurs, would have had almost unlimited opportunities to dispose of anonymous masses of people. "Our Irish importation have made a great discovery in Oeconomicks," was Sir Walter Scott's caustic comment, "namely that a wretch who is not worth a farthing while alive becomes a valuable article when knockd on the head & carried to an anatomist and acting on this principle have cleard the streets of some of those miserable offcasts of society whom nobody missd because nobody wishd to see them again." But in fact murders of the "Mac the Knife" variety were as rare in the Old Town as in the New. Systematic murder for gain was rare in part because conditions were so crowded, with as many as 48 families, comprising 138 people, resident in a single tenement. Most of these did their best to lead decent lives. The residents of Blackfriars Wynd, one of the most poverty-stricken in the Old Town, included "An old blind woman, whose appearance must be familiar to most of the inhabitants of Edinburgh, and who has been for several years missed from the New Town streets, where she used to exercise a tuneless organ. . . . Old Rosa's chamber is a pattern for cleanness and comfort, and she is contentment itself. She is no longer able to grind her organ, and is now a pauper. . . . When we visited her she had charge of a little girl at the United Industrial School. The little orphan was as clean as Rosa." Other stable families included "a hale and very aged man," a former coach maker, "with his fourth wife, inhabiting a chamber equally remarkable for cleanness and comfort as the one to which we have just referred. . . . In addition to these, we found . . . a journeyman shoemaker, his wife, and four children; two slipper-makers, with their wives and families; a widow, who keeps a small shop and supports her children; and an old shoemaker, with his invalid wife and daughter." None of the members of these households would have been good candidates for "burking": either a sudden death, or a disappearing corpse would have raised the outcry at once.

Even among the truly impoverished, neighbors formed communities. "Neighbours in general are very attentive," Alexander Miller noted in the case of births, and William Pulteney Alison's respondents observed that those most inclined to help the destitute were not the rich, but slightly-less-poverty-stricken neighbors. "Very many of the most destitute are assisted, sometimes altogether supported, by the charity of those who are mostly as destitute as themselves," wrote a surgeon whose practice included poor sections of the Old Town. "This I see constantly, and, while it has led me to admire the kindly Christian feeling which has dictated such conduct, it has struck me that the means of support for the very destitute ought not to be subtracted from the very scanty means possessed by others nearly as poor." This support extended to death as well as birth. Upper-class observers noted with typical condescension that "a death . . . brought a constant succession of visitors to look at the corpse"; they stayed and drank "till they saw it carried off for burial." Opportunities for murder were fewer than one might think.

Irish seasonal migrants, who might be considered prime candidates for murder since they were so far from home, were also safeguarded by their numbers. In some of the lodging houses, noted a surgeon in the Grassmarket, there were "not less than 30 people in one room—men, women, and children." In other cases, there were "asses, swine, and poultry associated with human beings in the same small rooms." Moreover the agricultural laborers were generally sober, anxious to save as much money as possible for the trip back home. There was neither opportunity, nor room, to entice an individual off for a drinking spree followed by murder. For that reason Burke and Hare recorded few murders during the summer months: as Burke said, "They could get nothing done during the harvest-time, and also after harvest, as Hare's house was so full of lodgers."

The main "condition" of the laboring population that made them vulnerable to murder was not unemployment, but partial employment, for it meant that they had to travel from place to place seeking work. We can see that by examining Alison's survey of two closes on the Cowgate, carried out to determine the extent of parish relief for destitution but equally valuable in pointing up how frequently the poor had to leave home to find work. Alison, unlike many other authors, was not interested in documenting depravity: what he wanted was "a fair specimen of the poverty of Edinburgh; in which the people are all of the lowest class, but, in general, of tolerably regular habits, and less migratory than in many of the poorest districts." Still, he found, they were migratory enough, from necessity rather than inclination or dissolute behavior. Of the forty-eight families he studied, only ten had regular employment throughout the year, and of the ten, there were two who made barely 2 shillings per week. The remaining thirty-eight were unemployed from two to ten months a year. Their earnings, during their periods of employment, were generally in the range of 3 shillings per week; only twelve families had earnings between 6 and 12 shillings per week. "When it is considered that hardly any of the families," reported Alison, "whose earnings are thus scanty and precarious, can have their rooms at less than 6 d a-week, and that they are prevented by a strict police from public begging, and even from carrying baskets of goods so small as to appear to be pretexts for begging, some idea may be formed of the privations as to food, clothing, furniture, and fuel, which they have habitually to endure." Only six families in these closes were entitled to parish relief funds, and those families had to share a total disbursement of six shillings a week. "Female field labourers" were particularly vulnerable to seasonable employment, and to having little recourse in the winter but to apply for charity, or become hawkers, but painters were also generally out of work in the winter, and there were so many tailors that "the greater part have only half employment." "I met with cases of every trade in this condition," reported one of Alison's correspondents, "Among the cases I saw were two shawl-weavers, a book-binder, and a slater, all of decent, steady character." Also observed among the floating population of the wynds were "painters, bakers, broommakers, carpenters, tinkers, a confectioner, a paver, scavengers, needlewomen," who came and went in the relentless search for employment. To this floating population we can add Joseph, a miller who had seen better days, and Abigail Simpson in search of her pension, spending part of the year outside the city, and part among the residents of the wynds and closes.

Unlike the completely destitute, the partially employed might even have some money in their pockets; and again unlike the completely destitute, whose earnings, Alison noted, were generally too scanty to be able to afford liquor, they might be persuaded to drink. As we have noted, the "high season" for the harvest was the "low season" for murder, since Tanner's Close was so full of laborers. By the same token, the winter and spring, the "low season" for employment, was the "high season" for the murders, as men and women traveled further for work, and as both Burke's and Hare's opportunities for legitimate income from lodgers and shoemaking declined. The months from November to April also corresponded to the academic year, increasing Knox's demand for bodies for his anatomy class. In this sense we can think of the murders as a particularly gruesome example of the dangers of "scanty and precarious" employment and erratic poor relief.

We can construct, then, a profile of a likely victim of a Burke and Hare killing. The candidate for murder might be male or female, but not especially large or strong, or "burking" would be too difficult. He or she would be poor, but partially employed rather than destitute, residing at least part of the year some distance from the West Port. Victims would have had some form of employment, or they would not have been able to travel to the vicinity of the West Port. Moreover Hare, at least, seems to have preferred whenever possible to get his victims drunk on their own money. But the employment would be intermittent, not steady; nor would the victim be the steady recipient of public or private charity, which would necessitate regular visits from clergymen or inspectors. The ideal victim might be sick, but if so he or she would not be eligible for treatment at the Royal Infirmary or other medical charities. The victim could be either Irish or Scottish, but if the latter, he or she would be comfortable with the Irish and familiar with Irish forms of hospitality. Healthy, not too strong, intermittently employed, tending to travel for work, willing to drink to insensibility: those are the characteristics of a typical Burke and Hare murder victim. He and Hare "made it their business," Burke said, "to look out for persons to decoy into their houses to murder them." But this type of victim did not always turn up, or prove vulnerable enough, for Burke said that they "had a great many pointed out for murder, but were disappointed of them by some means or other." Eventually this led them to increasingly active efforts to obtain their cadavers, as we will see.

We do not know whether Burke and Hare, like modern drug dealers, did a rapid cost/benefit comparison of the wages that could be earned through licit and illicit activity. But like modern drug dealers, they—and

Margaret Hare and Helen M'Dougal—may soon have developed a taste for being "in funds," for in the course of the year they earned around £150 from the sale of the bodies. The whiskey they consumed with their intended victims was both an investment in their operation, and a perquisite of their new occupation. Eventually they could not do without it, for while Hare was not much troubled by the murders, "and could sleep well at night," Burke seems to have required more and more whiskey, in larger and larger doses, to quiet his conscience. After a murder was committed, he "repented often of the crime, and could not sleep without a bottle of whisky by his bedside, and a twopenny candle to burn all night beside him; when he awoke he would take a draught of the bottle—sometimes half a bottle at a draught—and that would make him sleep." Still, he did not stop killing people on that account. Indeed, he said before his execution, "It was God's providence that put a stop to their murdering career, or he does not know how far they might have gone with it, even to attack people on the streets, as they were so successful, and always met with a ready market: that when they delivered a body they were always told to get more."

Chapter 4

Sold to Dr. Knox

"A Native of Cheshire," "Old Woman"

B URKE AND HARE NEVER LEARNED THE NAMES OF THEIR NEXT
two victims, murdered sometime in February or March 1828. The
first was "an Englishman, a native of Cheshire," Burke remembered. He
was a tall man, about forty, with black hair and "brown whiskers, mixed
with gray hair." He sold tinder, "spunks" as it was called in Scotland, and
was probably a kind of regular transient, traveling between the outskirts
of the city and its inner closes. He stayed at the lodging house in Tanner's
Close, and Burke remembered that he had jaundice and lay "in bed very
unwell." Perhaps his murderers thought he was likely to die anyway, or
perhaps he was simply weakened by his illness. He was killed "in the same
manner as the other" and "sold to Dr. Knox for £10."

According to Burke, Margaret Hare had a principal share in the
next murder; he may have wanted to see her accused in place of Helen
M'Dougal, as "guilty of the said crime, actor or actors or art and part."
Hare was out "working on the boats in the canal," and Burke was mending
shoes, on the morning that Margaret Hare "decoyed into the house" an
old woman, name, origin, and occupation unknown. She gave the woman
whiskey, and tried to get her to go to bed, but she apparently kept getting
up, as Margaret Hare had to "put her to bed three times." Finally "she
was so drunk that she fell asleep," and when Hare came home for dinner,
probably early afternoon, "he put part of the bed-tick on her mouth and

nose" to suffocate her. When he came home at night she was dead, and we may wonder if Margaret Hare helped the process along. Burke and Hare removed her clothes, put her in a tea box, and brought her to Surgeon's Square that night. For this corpse, too, Dr. Knox paid £10. Technically the old woman had been smothered, rather than burked, and a modern forensic team would certainly have found telltale evidence of the bed tick around her nose and mouth. But neither Knox nor his assistants were experienced forensic surgeons, and even though this was the fifth fresh, uninterred corpse that "John" and "William" had brought them in three months, they followed their usual practice of asking no questions. What, we may wonder—as contemporaries wondered—was Dr. Knox thinking?

Robert Knox has been an enigma since his purchase of Burke's and Hare's cadavers was first made public. It seemed incredible to contemporaries that a respected medical man could connive at murder, but it seemed equally incredible that he had had no suspicions of the true nature of his purchases. His biographers, starting with Henry Lonsdale, have only compounded the mystery, for they have stressed his brilliance as both scientist and surgeon. Their exertions were as damaging to Knox's later reputation as any of his detractors' accusations. For if Knox had been a great surgeon in the Victorian mode—like Joseph Lister, for example—then he was clearly either a villain or a fool: a villain, if he noticed the evidence for murder and did nothing, or a fool if he did not notice the evidence.

And so we should begin our investigation of Robert Knox by noting that he was not a surgeon in the modern sense: he did not maintain a practice in which he treated patients, performed operations, or carried out postmortem examinations to determine the cause of death. Instead, the goal he pursued throughout his life was research into anatomical science. His models were the French comparative anatomists Georges Cuvier and Etienne Geoffroy St. Hilaire, and his burning ambition was to establish in Edinburgh the equivalent of the natural history research center in Paris, the Jardin des Plantes. The academic year 1827–1828 was only his second year as an independent lecturer on anatomy, but he had already achieved enviable success. Still, in the spring of 1828, as he purchased two more bodies from Burke and Hare, he surely knew he still had far to go.

Knox was born on September 4, 1791, the eighth child of Robert Knox, a mathematician and teacher in Edinburgh, and his wife, Mary Scherer. The Knox family lived at 6 Nicolson Streeet, a few blocks from the main university district to the east and the medical establishments, including the Royal Infirmary and Surgeon's Square, to the west. We have few records of Knox's childhood, but we can probably trust Lonsdale's account of him as a clever, good-looking boy, "of fair complexion, with soft flaxen hair and large blue eyes." An attack of smallpox left him blind in his left eye, but did not affect his studies, and he received medals in Greek and Latin at the High School at Edinburgh, an easy walk from his home, up the South Bridge, then east past the Royal Infirmary. Perhaps he became interested in medicine during his twice-daily walk past the infirmary, or perhaps he had always been interested in science. In November 1810, he entered the College Library to sign the matriculation records and begin his medical classes (Figure 11).

Figure 11. Dr. Robert Knox. Reproduced from a contemporary print, courtesy of the Library of the Royal College of Physicians of Edinburgh.

Knox's medical education followed a typical pattern for a local, well-educated boy of moderate means. He did not have to pay for lodgings, so he only took two or three courses a year, spreading the requirements for graduation out over a four-year period. He attended anatomy lectures at the university given by Alexander Monro *tertius*, and, like many students, also attended private classes in anatomical dissection. His teacher was the well-respected lecturer John Barclay, who became Knox's true mentor in anatomy. The death of his father in 1812 may have limited his funds and therefore his opportunities. He did not join the Royal Medical Society, the most elite of the student societies, perhaps because of the expense, but he was twice elected president of another student organization, the Royal Physical Society. Perhaps he had already determined on a career in science, rather than medical practice. That may explain one noteworthy omission in his education, in light of his later career: he never received any formal training in surgery. He was not apprenticed to a surgeon, the most usual form of surgical education in the early nineteenth century, nor did he attend university lectures on clinical surgery. This too suggests that he had already decided that he would not spend his life setting broken bones, bandaging ulcers, or performing amputations.

Much later Henry Lonsdale published an anecdote, since frequently repeated, that Knox failed his first M.D. exam because he attended anatomical lectures by the incompetent Monro, only to make a brilliant recovery after his assiduous diligence in John Barclay's classes. There is, however, no evidence for this. The Edinburgh Medical Faculty kept detailed records, and in them we find that Knox only took his medical examination once, on November 11, 1814. Professor Monro presided over an examination that required Knox to answer questions, in Latin, on the viscera of the thorax, on pneumonia and phthisis, on ulcers and hepatic ascites. He, like the rest of the students examined on that day, passed with no recorded difficulty.

Knox's first research on human subjects, consisting of himself and one other man about the same age, was carried out for his M.D. thesis, on the impact of stimulants and narcotics on the human body. He continued the research in his first published article on the relations between time of day and action of the pulse. It appeared in the *Edinburgh Medical and Surgical Review* in January 1815, by which time Knox was probably in London. His later writings gave the impression that he was studying with the London anatomist John Abernethy, but he may also have been looking for some kind of military appointment. He obtained the position of hospital assistant on June 16, 1815, one of sixteen such appointments made in anticipation of what became the Battle of Waterloo. His subsequent service after the battle would have given him his first experience of medical practice, but we should not imagine him, saw and scalpel in hand, letting blood and hacking off limbs. Though the allied armies were desperately short of medical attendants they were unlikely to have allowed a set of newly commissioned hospital mates to treat the army "as a huge dissecting room, free to mangle with impunity." Civilian surgeons, far more competent than Knox, flocked to Waterloo to aid the wounded after the battle. It is most likely that Knox carried out the basic, menial tasks of the hospital assistant, the low man on the totem pole: checking dressings, changing bandages, keeping accounts. We may suspect he hated it, for that was the usual reaction of the Edinburgh-bred M.D. trapped at the bottom of the military medical hierarchy. We may further suspect that he was greatly relieved to be allowed to escort wounded soldiers back home to Britain shortly after the battle.

Most of those appointed just before and after Waterloo, as well as the many medical men who had served in the Napoleonic wars, found their positions evaporating after the peace. Knox was fortunate to be spared this fate when, in 1816, he obtained a position as hospital assistant with the 72nd Highlanders stationed in Cape Town in South Africa. His experiences in South Africa had a decisive impact on his life and work. It is not clear now just what his official duties were, though they certainly included attendance during the widespread attack of tapeworm that affected British soldiers at the Cape, which he later wrote up for the *Edinburgh Medical and Surgical Review*. He sounded bored and homesick in a letter to his mother and younger brother Frederick: "How happy am I, and yet how wretched!" he wrote, "Delighted to hear of your health and prosperity, yet miserable at the thoughts of the wide-extended ocean which rolls between us." Africa might offer him prospects for advancement, but they could not compensate "for so long a deprivation of European society," or for having to "resign the pen for the gun; to acquire the art, of managing the reins of my horse whilst traveling on the parched roads of Africa, or pursuing at full speed the swift antelope over pathless flats, whose termination the weariest eye searches for in vain. The amusements of the chase, though interesting at first, soon grow irksome to one whom education and habits of life have led to different pursuits." He hoped to be home by June 1819, but June came and went and found him still at the Cape of Good Hope.

Commendably, and in contrast to many of his brother officers garrisoned far away from home, Knox turned to scientific pursuits, particularly to natural history and comparative anatomy. He seems to have been struck by the availability of freshly killed animals, and he took advantage of every opportunity to dissect them. While on detached duty with a militia regiment under the command of Captain Andries Stockenström, he provided "great service," Stockenström later wrote, "in tracing the nature of [a] horse distemper, by the dissection of the many subjects which unfortunately daily presented themselves." He investigated the habits and the anatomical structure of the spotted hyena, the beaver, and the cassowary, and he began an extensive investigation of the anatomy of the eye and the ciliary muscle, which regulates the shape of the lens. His research on the eye shows him to best advantage as a master of the dissecting knife, able to trace the mechanism that allows the lens to focus without the benefit of modern preservation techniques or high-powered microscopes.

He could do skillful fieldwork, too, as he demonstrated in his research on the spotted hyena. A British naturalist, having found bones of "various animals" in a cave in Yorkshire, had hypothesized that prehistoric hyenas had used the cave "as a place of retreat . . . whither they retired with their prey, in order to feast on it more at leisure than they could well do in the open country." The naturalist had also hypothesized that these hyenas, "by cracking the bones leave nothing they could possibly devour." But this was absolutely opposed to the behavior of present-day hyenas, Knox wrote. In the course of his time in South Africa, he had observed many, many hyenas preying upon carcasses, but he had never observed them to carry off carcasses to their lairs, nor destroy the skeletons. "The carcass they often drag away to a considerable distance from the place where it fell," he wrote, but never back to their caves: indeed, there was no reason for them to do so, for their young accompany them in their hunt. He had never seen any evidence that they devoured the bones of their prey, he wrote, for he had "almost always been able to discover the skeleton, and that often, tolerably entire." And he had "often roused the hyena from his lurking place," but he had never found any animal bones resembling those in the Yorkshire cave. "So that I much question," he concluded, if hyenas "ever carry a portion of their prey, on any occasion whatever, to their dens." It may well have been while at the Cape of Good Hope that he first had the idea of a museum of comparative anatomy, for he seems to have transported some of his animal "subjects" back to Edinburgh, together with other specimens, like the aboriginal skull that became one of his prized possessions.

Knox's South African experience was formative in other ways besides confirming his all-absorbing interest in comparative anatomy. Governed as a British protectorate, Cape Colony exhibited an almost Darwinian struggle of competing groups: the Xhosa and Khoisan—known to most Europeans as the Kaffir and Bosjeman, respectively—who had originally owned the land, the Dutch settlers who had pushed them out or enslaved them but wailed for protection against counterattack or rebellion, and the British colonial bureaucracy which, claiming impartiality, nonetheless adjudicated all claims to its own advantage. From the first Knox seems to have recognized the existence of the struggle, taken for granted by his South African contemporaries but ignored or sugarcoated by observers back in Britain. As a boy he had been given *Travels into the Interior Parts of Africa*, by François Le Vaillant, he later wrote, "five enchanting volumes, full of nature and truth." Ten years later, he continued, "on the afternoon of a bright sunshiny day, such a day as can be seen only in Southern Africa," he ascended the very same spot Le Vaillant had described, over a grassy plain, with the Kaha and Anattola mountain range to the north and east. "What was the living scene before me?" he asked, "Nature in all her wondrous beauty and variety; the dark-eyed antelope, of nearly all varieties, covered the plain; in the distance, stalked slowly the majestic ostrich; over head soared, silent and sad, the vulture; bustards of all sizes; harmless, peaceful, grain and insect-loving animals; the zebra and the quagga; the acacia, the strelitzia, the evergreens, the pasture and the bush, planted by nature; the field which plough or spade had never turned up, on which the cerealia had never been grown." But all this was merely "a panorama, a picture . . . a vast stage, decorated, picturesque, lovely" without man, and Knox, looking through his spyglass, was able to find "on the wooded slopes of the Chumie mountains the curling smoke, telling of the presence of man." Who watched the fire? "It is the savage Bosjeman, or still fiercer Kaffir; the race looked for by Le Vaillant many years before, from the same spot on which I now stood. Nature, then, had stood its ground in the lapse of time; she had remained seemingly unaltered by countless ages up to the moment I then noted her."

But not for long. Into this natural paradise had come "the semi-civilized notions of Europe—the power of combinations, fire-arms, discipline, laws. Before this new element, anatagonistic of nature, her works are doomed to destruction, in as far as man can destroy. The wild acacia he wastes as firewood; the Chumie forests he utterly destroys, converting the timbers thereof into rafters for barracks and other hovels, for men to congregate in like pigs. Over nature's pastures, over the iris, bulbous plants of surpassing beauty, over the strelitzia, and a thousand other wild flowers, he passes the ruthless plough. The antelope is exterminated or disappears; the zebra, the gnoo, the ostrich, the bustard, escape from the land, or are shot down; the mighty onslaught of an antagonistic element, seemingly too strong for nature, defeats even the rhinoceros, the elephant, the lion, so that their skins are become rare, so rare as to be prized for European museums."

Knox was not an environmentalist, and however he might have regretted the destruction of his panorama, he regarded it as inevitable. He also regarded the destruction of the indigenous peoples as foreordained, for they were, in his view, a part of this natural order, and therefore "also must of necessity give way." Their "destiny apparently is sealed," he wrote, and "extinction in presence of a stronger race seems inevitable." Such extinctions were part of zoological history, as the fossils of dinosaurs, saber-toothed tigers, and prehistoric hyenas bore witness. Whether this was just or unjust was immaterial, Knox would later argue: "From the earliest recorded times might has always constituted right, or been held to do so." This view was partially echoed by Knox's superior officer while on campaign in South Africa, Andries Stockenström. But a career spent in civil and military administration led him to vehemently disclaim Knox's poor opinion of the indigenous peoples: "The theory which makes the blacks irreclaimable savages, fit only to be exterminated, like the wolves, was not of Boer origin," he wrote with some heat. Still, he later remembered that Knox's "enlightened political and ethnological views were deeply interesting to me during the many months he remained under my command," and his own experience led him to the same conclusion as Knox regarding practical policy: "We had possessed ourselves of their lands," he wrote, "We wanted more of their land, together with their services." The best that could be done was "to admit what the aboriginal tribes had lost through our progress, and how much it became our duty to mitigate their sufferings."

Knox's and Stockenström's view place them firmly on the dark side of history as far as modern writers are concerned, and in fact Knox is notorious among scholars as "the real founder of British racism." He was, indeed, a literal, thoroughgoing racist, believing that "Race is everything: literature, science, art, in a word, civilization, depend on it," and that all political, social, and environmental conflicts could be understood as the clash of race against race. Knox claimed his view was merely taxonomic, not judgmental: all races have their strengths and weakness, he felt, and "all races have produced men of ability." Nonetheless, he had no doubt that his own race, the Saxon, was dominant, both physically and politically. They had been encumbered by the Norman conquest, eight hundred years earler, but their greatest threat was the Celts, whether across the Channel in France, or at home in the Highlands, Wales, and especially Ireland. The Celtic race "must be forced from the soil," he wrote, "by fair means if possible; still they must leave." Later physiological racists, such as Paul Broca, would search for anatomical features like crania size to justify the supposed superiority of their own kind, but Knox's own starting point was, again, man's "Zoological history," the history of "instinctual, animal man, a part and parcel of nature's great scheme." A careful observer "in the midst of any considerable assemblage of people," he said, could not fail to note significant differences, and if "the assemblage observed be composed of different races, the differences will be still more striking." Indeed, anatomy would provide opposition, not support, for his views, as he noted: "the interior organs of animals, not far removed from each other, vary but little." For that reason he concentrated on the outward form, explaining that "it is to the exterior we must look for the most remarkable characteristics of animals; it is it alone which nature loves to decorate and to vary." This seems an inconsistent position for an anatomist, and indeed modern scholars see "little coherence of thought" or "logical progression" in Knox's arguments. His tactic, found throughout his writings on race, was to state assertions as proven facts, appealing to anatomical structures when it suited his purpose, and ignoring them when it did not. Men simply were of different races, Knox repeated over and over in the face of objections, as though he were pointing out the characteristic distinctions in appearance and temperament between the striped hyena of Egypt and India and the spotted hyena of the Cape. "Call them Species, if you will," he insisted, "call them permanent Varieties; it matters not. The fact, the simple fact, remains just as it was:

men are of different races." And "in human history, race is everything."

Knox's views were not as original as he thought them—they can be found in many of the writers of his day—but that may have contributed to their influence. By the time he publicized them in the 1850s, others had already applied similar theories to contemporary politics and society. Knox complained that his ideas were published without his receiving proper credit, but in fact "Knox on race," particularly on what he called the "dark races," was cited approvingly by name often enough: by proslavery advocates in the United States and anti-Irish in Britain, by the *Journal of Anthropology*, and by the Anthropological Society of London, where he was regarded as "one of England's greatest anthropologists." Many who had never heard of the ciliary muscle were all too familiar with Knox's illustration of the "Kaffir" cranium.

Knox himself was not very interested in African peoples, and he later reported that his British audiences felt the same way. He had first formulated his ideas on race during his journey from Edinburgh to London in 1817, interpreting the Battle of Hastings and subsequent British history as the clash between the Norman and Saxon races. His racial views thereafter became the lens by which he interpreted all current events, from the Irish question in Great Britain to the French colonization of North Africa, from the growth of the United States to the decay of the Austrian Empire. Impossible to pin down, impervious to contrary evidence, and filled with objectionable remarks, Knox's theory of race garnered criticism in his own day and since. Still, it remained unfortunately and undeservedly popular, and Knox noted complacently, "Each race treated of . . . will complain of my not having done them justice; . . . of all others they will admit that I have spoken the truth."

Shortly before he left the Cape, an unpleasant incident may have reinforced Knox's resentment against a Norman government, whose characteristic feature, he wrote with even more vehemence than usual, was "imbecility . . . [and] employment of officials, whose rise in life were impossible, under any other circumstances, but in the atmosphere of a court. Owing everything to patronage, they despise every other human qualification." The governor of Cape Colony, Lord Charles Henry Somerset, could trace his ancestry back to the Norman Conquest, but this did nothing to impress the British and Dutch settlers who chafed under his autocratic rule. His son, Henry Somerset, was a captain in one of the regiments stationed at the Cape, and, according to Andries Stockenström, he made the most of his privileged position. Lord Somerset was "an infatuated parent who could not believe it possible for his son to be in the wrong," Stockenström wrote, with the result that "the young aspirant Captain" became "the focus of a set of hangers-on and flatterers," among whom Stockenström included Knox. Stockenström had more reason than most to complain, as he found his own position as magistrate taken away from him on a technicality, and given to Captain Somerset. He complained more vociferously still when his brother Oloff, an officer in the Cape Regiment, was accused of theft, an accusation supported by Knox's testimony, who gave, according to Stockenström's letters, "whatever colour to his shameful conduct the most refined and plausible cunning could suggest." The accusation was widely believed to have been the product of Captain Somerset's personal spite, and a military court of inquiry exonerated Oloff Stockenström, ruling "That Captain Stockenström's conduct appears to them to be most highly creditable to him as an officer and a gentleman, and that he has conducted himself through a most painful period of calumny and persecution with feelings of the highest sense of honour and propriety." Like many military courts, it took no steps against the high-ranking officer most responsible for the problem, merely remarking that "the Court cannot help observing the backwardness and difficulty with which the officers of the Cape Corps at first answered the questions of the Court, which by coming to the point at once would have tended to have shortened their proceedings." Captain Somerset at length was brought to apologize to Captain Stockenström, and received the thanks of the court. The full opprobrium fell upon Knox, for, the Court of Inquiry said, they "look upon his conduct in such a light that they hope they may be excused from giving an opinion . . . relative to the calumnies issuing from him." That was bad enough, but the affair went further. Knox, all his life, "looked on his opponents as dishonest men and imposters," and his usual response was "sarcasm or invective." That response, directed against one of Stockenström's defenders, led to his being challenged to a duel in turn, and Andries Stockenström, who regarded Knox as the "chief primary tool in the whole affair," reported with satisfaction that he was "publicly horsewhipped and placarded."

Knox was clearly a whipping boy—literally—for Captain Henry Somerset, and we cannot blame his modern biographers for being indignant at such treatment. But for us the affair gives insight into Knox's propensity for being in the wrong place at the wrong time, and his talent for making enemies of former friends. Young officers were notoriously quarrelsome, and duels, though prohibited, were not infrequent, especially on foreign stations. Still, it may be said that it took spectacularly bad luck, or spectacularly poor judgment, for Knox to be involved in a quarrel between a prominent local family and the governor's son. He was a medical officer, after all, with a ready-made excuse for staying out of trouble: directives from the Army Medical Board in London made it clear that medical gentlemen were to hold themselves aloof from the drinking and fighting that was commonplace among other officers. Andries Stockenström had been Knox's commanding officer on campaign, and Knox might have known that he would construe an attack on his brother as a betrayal; Knox might also have known that Captain Somerset was too far above him in rank and consequence to care anything for his friendship or reward his allegiance with patronage. "Of the character of these persons I need not here speak," Knox later hissed, and his experience may have led to his subsequent sharp condemnation of British colonial government. At the time he could do little to justify himself. He had been involved in a very public scandal, and he had ended up on the wrong side of public opinion. He returned to Edinburgh in December 1820, when he, like many other hospital assistants, was placed on half pay.

If Knox was to enter the highly competitive environment of Edinburgh medicine, he needed some special distinction. In the fall of 1821, most likely with financial backing from his family, he left for Paris, "the great school of modern ideas in science." Students and physicians from Britain, America, and elsewhere in Europe flocked to Paris to study pathology and clinical methods, but Knox seems to have eschewed the hospitals and morgue in favor of the natural history and paleontological collections at the Jardin des Plantes. Funded by the government, the Jardin des Plantes became the center for comparative anatomy, presided over by the great Georges Cuvier since 1800. All his life Knox took every opportunity to describe how he had studied under Cuvier, "the discoverer of exact descriptive anatomy" applied to all animals, the "true discoverer of the importance of that branch of knowledge." Cuvier had "laid it down as a principle, that the position of any animal in the animal kingdom could not be well determined, until its descriptive anatomy had been fully laid out." This was a revelation for Knox: it laid out before him a research agenda that allied his talent for precise anatomical observation with a broader theoretical approach to taxonomy. But by 1821, Cuvier's views had been challenged by another great name in French science, Etienne Geoffroy St. Hilaire, "called St. Hilaire by English naturalists," Knox noted contemptuously, "alike incapable of comprehending his name, his genius, his position in science." Knox, who always referred to him as Geoffroy, later wrote of being "intimate with both," but when they later quarreled he followed what he described as Geoffroy's "transcendental anatomy." Unlike Cuvier, who had concentrated on adult males of each species in his study of comparative anatomy, Geoffroy and his followers had studied species through the life cycle from embryos to fully mature adults. The guiding principle they enunciated was that of "Unity of Organization," which was based on repeated observations "that in some animals there existed structures seemingly perfectly developed, whilst in others, the same structures might also, with great care and nicety of observations, be discovered in a rudimentary or undeveloped condition." An example of this was the third eyelid, which was vestigial in man, but "more developed in the ox, horse, dog; still more in the elephant; most of all in the bird." The conclusion Knox and others drew from this was that "one plan existed in all," that is, that all organisms were created according to a kind of blueprint which included all of the anatomical features found in every organism, but that differences among species, and among individuals within species, could be explained by certain features having become vestigial. Take "the cartilaginous skeleton of the nostrils," Knox observed, found in mammals from people to whales; take the pronator muscle, which allows the palm to face backwards or down, and is found in rudimentary form in the horse, even though the "foot of the horse is always prone." Throughout the animal kingdom, we see that "ever the same elements nearly, are found in all; it is merely a question of size and organization, but not of kind or function." The theory of the unity of organization, too, helped define Knox's research agenda: it put emphasis on the vestigial, the rare, the anomalous structures in anatomy. In this enterprise, anatomical dissection was not merely a tool for understanding ordinary physiology and pathology, but rather a method for formulating laws connecting all of zoology.

Knox was back in Edinburgh by December 1822, but it did not take him long to find out that his native city was sadly lacking in opportunities for a man of his talents and interests. He had no wish to abandon science for the mere practice of medicine, which he considered pedestrian and uninspired. Consider the vertebra, he later wrote: "When studied by the surgeon or medical man, it is viewed by him merely as a portion of the skeleton"; while "to the philosophic anatomist"—such as himself—"it becomes the type of all vertebrate animals, of the entire skeleton, limbs and head included; of the organic world, vertebrate and invertebrate. Carried further, it possesses the form of the primitive cell; of the sphere; of the universe." But no one would pay him to pursue his research: Edinburgh had no Jardin des Plantes, and British natural history was moving in other directions, as Thomas Huxley, Charles Darwin, and Alfred Russel Wallace would demonstrate. If Cuvier had been born on the other side of the Channel, Knox later wrote bitterly, he would have found his anatomical views "held in the most sovereign contempt." Forced into "turning his vast intellect to some profitable pursuit," he would have had to abandon science forever, with no choice but to teach "mathematics to boys, chemistry to the apothecary's apprentice, or the anatomy of the parts of the body, concerned in surgical operations, to medical students."

Now thirty-one years old, ambitious and energetic, Knox did not intend that to be his own fate for long. He began presenting scientific papers at a great rate, becoming a fellow of the Royal Society of Edinburgh. He also developed a network of connections among Edinburgh naturalists, including Robert Jameson, professor of natural history, whom Knox assisted with his journal, the *Memoirs of the Wernerian Natural History Society*. In 1824 he married Mary Russell, and the couple relocated, with the rest of the Knox family, to a pleasant suburban house at 4 Newington Street in the southern extension of the city. Henry Lonsdale, much to the delight of later writers, asserted that Knox's marriage "inconsiderately put shackles to his social progress" because of Mary Russell's "inferior rank," and his allegedly imprudent marriage, like his one eye, has figured prominently in Burke and Hare lore. The 1945 movie *The Body Snatcher* depicted the character based on Knox in a clandestine marriage with his housekeeper, while James Bridie's play *The Anatomist* shows Mary Knox being shunned by other professor's wives as "hardly presentable." But Knox's own family was not as high-toned as all that—his sister kept a silk mercer's shop on South Bridge—and it is likely Mary Russell's social background was similar to his own. Moreover his anatomical establishment grew very rapidly in the years after his marriage, and it is reasonable to think that at least some of the money for it came from his wife's family. Eventually Robert and Mary Knox had six children, and he was a very affectionate husband and father.

In April 1824 Knox wrote to the Royal College of Surgeons proposing the founding of a Museum of Comparative Anatomy. "Towards the formation of a Museum of Comparative Anatomy I am willing to bestow my whole labour and time," he wrote, "with that energy which the cultivation of a very favourite pursuit naturally gives." Though the collection would remain the property of the Royal College, Knox stipulated that he be allowed "during my lifetime the use of the Museum for the furtherance" of his "favourite pursuits and studies." The surgeons granted his request, without, at first, allocating him any salary. But they did agree to pay "the attending expenses of presses, glass, spirits, &c." Knox had thus made a start in establishing himself at the heart of a serious museum of anatomy and pathology in Edinburgh, without having to pay for it out of his own pocket. In January 1825, he became conservator of the pathological section of the museum, with a salary of £100 per year. During the next year he supervised the purchase of two major collections, one assembled by Charles Bell, the eminent Edinburgh-born surgeon who had established an anatomy school in London, and the other from John Barclay, Knox's former teacher. By May 1826 Knox was promoted to conservator of the entire Museum of the Royal College of Surgeons, with a salary of £150 per year.

If the museum was Knox's first big break, his second was his association with John Barclay, who, by 1825, began to suffer from ill health. Lecturers had no pension funds to sustain them, and a common practice was to contract with a younger partner, who would become the heir apparent to the lectureship, usually in exchange for the payment of a set fee to the incumbent until the end of his life. On March 2, 1825, Knox and Barclay signed a contract, in which Knox agreed to relieve Barclay "of the whole labour in every branch of the Institution whatsoever during the continuance of the co-partnery." Barclay gave the introductory lecture the following year, but Knox taught the remainder of the classes in 1825–1826. He paid the £250 entrance fee to become a Fellow of the Royal College of Surgeons of Edinburgh in 1825, submitting the required probationary essay on "the causes and treatment of lateral curvature of the human spine." This seems to have been based on Knox's long-standing interest in the beauty of the spinal column, rather than on any clinical experience. In August 1826, John Barclay died, and Knox found himself in the enviable position of inheriting one of the most lucrative lectureships in Edinburgh. He charged students £3 5s the first time they took his course, and £2 4s if they took it a second time, so that he earned £325 for every one hundred new students he attracted. Knox is said to have taught more than three hundred students per year at the height of his popularity; if this is accurate, his income from lecturing, combined with his position as conservator, would have amounted to over £1000 per annum.

Knox's expenses, however, also rose. He spent over £800 in a single year on the operating expenses for his dissecting rooms. He also began hiring staff. His brother Frederick John Knox came to work for him in 1824, to assist with cataloging the Bell and Barclay collections. Frederick Knox was an oddity on the Edinburgh medical scene: thirty years old when he began to work for his brother, he had never attended any medical classes at the university or, apparently, elsewhere. On his marriage on December 12, 1824, he listed his occupation as "Writer." This would usually have meant "writer to the signet," that is, a lawyer, but it seems more likely that he was a lawyer's clerk. Though he later grew adept at anatomical preparations and cataloguing, he "was a great concern, both pecuniarily and otherwise," to his older brother. Knox may have paid him the £150 he earned as conservator; by 1828, Frederick Knox's salary may have been as much as £195 per year. It may have been at the same time that Robert Knox hired David Paterson to assist both himself and his brother as doorkeeper, servant, and anatomical technician. Born in 1805 and baptized, like his employers, in the parish church of St. Cuthberts, Paterson was the eldest son of respectable tradespeople in Wester Portsburgh. He was charged with the disagreeable manual tasks of an anatomical museum and lecture hall, many of which involved getting his hands very dirty indeed, "such as . . . scrubbing the tables, and carrying away and burying the offals of the dissecting-rooms; washing and cleaning subjects preparatory to their being brought into the class-room." By 1828, as we have seen, Knox also had at least three student assistants, soon-to-be or recent graduates who helped keep the account books, teach class, and prepare papers for publications. Knox had need of them: in addition to publishing a dozen scientific articles between 1823 and 1830, he prepared English editions of Continental anatomical works by Friedrich Tiedemann, Antonio Scarpa, Jean Joseph Sue, Pierre Augustin Béclard, and Hippolyte Cloquet. These publications helped establish his reputation, and may have brought in some additional income. It is likely, though, that any money he made was quickly spent, either for his anatomical establishment at Surgeon's Square or for his extended family—including his mother and sister as well as his own wife and children—on Newington Street.

Such rapid advancement in Knox's fortune was bound to make enemies. His success at gaining the conservatorship gained him the enmity of James Syme, later the first professor of surgery at the university, who made it his practice for the rest of his life to attack Knox and his associates. Edinburgh medical quarrels were fierce, frequent, and public, and though Knox had begun his career by behaving with the modesty befitting a newcomer, within a few years he had developed a style as vituperative as any of his colleagues. Even Lonsdale criticized his "want of candour, . . . egotism, and marked disparagement of other people's characters." John and Alexander Lizars were Knox's chief anatomical rivals, and he lost no opportunity of criticizing their teaching. He attacked their use of illustrations, instead of cadavers, to teach students, calling the "Pictorial-Anatomy School," as he termed it, "huge misrepresentations of nature." Rhetoric spilled over into more serious mischief, when a cadaver belonging to the Lizars brothers was stolen and delivered or resold to Knox, requiring Knox to pay for damages.

But Knox picked quarrels, whether in person or in print, with everyone he considered to have a baleful influence on his discipline. His edition of Béclard's *Elements of General Anatomy* begins by criticizing the author's lengthy introduction "which treats," Knox wrote, "of matters with which M. Béclard was not familiar, and of which, indeed, he was almost entirely ignorant." Robert Christison, reviewing Knox's edition of Tiedemann's work, noted that it was not necessary for Knox, in praising Tiedemann, to insult all those who admired the works of other anatomists. Even Charles Bell, whom Knox spoke of as an "esteemed friend" and whose collection had provided so timely an opportunity, was rewarded by having his opinions, where they differed from Knox's, characterized as "orthodox . . . quite safe, and entirely mechanical."

Knox may also have repaid Jameson's early patronage with disdain, according to the letters of John James Audubon, the American naturalist, who visited Edinburgh in 1826. He had letters of introduction to several men of science, but at first could only find Knox in his establishment in

Surgeon's Square. "He came to me with only one eye," Audubon wrote in one of his frequent letters home to his wife "dear Lucy." Knox was "dressed with an over gown, and bloody fingers. He bowed, washed and wiped his hands . . . and wishing me well, promised all in his power, appointed tomorrow to see me and my drawings, and said he would bring some good friends of science to be introduced." Audubon was delighted. "My opinion," he told his wife, "is that Dr. Knox is a physician of great merit." He compared him very favorably to Professor Jameson, whose own publishing project, he feared, put him in competition with Audubon's. But his feelings reversed during his three-day stay. Jameson soon warmed to him, he wrote, "accosted me most friendly, chatted with an uncommon degree of cordiality, and promised me his powerful assistance so forcibly, convincingly, that I am quite sure I can depend upon him." While Knox and his friend, though calling as promised, "talked very scientifically indeed—quite too much so for the poor man of the woods" and spent their time denigrating Jameson's work, so that Audubon remarked ruefully that it was "really amusing and distressing at the same time to see how inimical to each other men of science are."

During the winter of 1828, then, when Burke and Hare delivered the bodies of the Englishman and the old woman, Robert Knox was a very busy man, with both a growing reputation and a growing family to support. Though conspicuously lacking in people skills, he was neither a villain nor a fool. Nor was he a practicing physician or surgeon: indeed, he may never in his life have followed a clinical case from illness to death to autopsy. He was instead a dedicated dissector, with a collector's passion for anatomical oddities and pathological specimens. His contacts with the body trade had probably begun during his partnership with Barclay, and as we have seen, it was standard practice for Edinburgh anatomists to deal with thieves, and to ask no questions. When a "subject" was in the room, whether human or animal, mammalian, fish, or fowl, he had eyes for nothing else, and his many enterprises created a dangerously inexorable need for fresh cadavers.

The closest we can come to Knox in his own dissecting room is in his anatomical notebooks, both his records of "Anatomical and Pathological Appearances met with in the Dissecting rooms during the Winter Session of 1827–8," and his notes for the museum catalogue from the same period. These sources make it clear that during the winter he purchased Burke and Hare cadavers, Knox was busy pursuing the implications of his theory of the unity of organization, concerning anatomical anomalies being evidence of vestigial structures in all organisms. The first of the "Anatomical Appearances" he recorded, most likely from October 1827, noted the presence of an unusual structure, a "Left arm [which] presented a Biceps having three distinct heads," taken from a female subject. Usually a biceps has only two heads, and this interesting anatomical anomaly is found, according to modern authors, in about 10 percent of the population. Similarly, Knox's notes on an unusual "muscular slip" extending from the side across the chest, ending in "a beautifully rounded Tendon," provide a clear account of a structure found in about 7 percent of the population. To Knox, these findings provided evidence that the original "type" or blueprint for all organisms was not simple, but complex. As he wrote in a memoir delivered to the Royal Society of Edinburgh, "An original type seems . . . to have been contemplated for each organ or assemblage of organs; that type generally . . . is extremely complex, and embraces within its range all possible structures." The existence of hermaphrodites suggested that the original type for the organs of generation included both male and female genitalia; the original type for organs of respiration included both lungs and gills. Knox's notebook entries suggest that he considered variants in limb and torso as clues to the original type of vascular structure.

There is no way to link these first "Anatomical Appearances" with Burke and Hare, but some of Knox's later entries may refer to the bodies they delivered. Their first cadaver, Donald, had died "of a dropsy," and some time after November 10, 1827, Knox recorded notes of a dissection of a male subject, described as "generally dropsical." This cadaver, too, presented a triceps instead of a biceps, and the "arteries . . . were likewise remarkably dilated and the nerves large and very distinct." Dropsy was not a rare disease, and it is not inconceivable that Knox could have purchased other dropsical cadavers. They were much prized by anatomical lecturers for their bones, "the marrow," according to one author, "being less abundant and mixed with serum." Still, the entry is worth pondering. No others in the notebook or catalogue can be so persuasively linked to the Burke and Hare victims, though we may wonder whether Knox's kidney specimen "Taken from a healthy looking female subject brought into the dissecting rooms" and donated to the Museum in March 1828 could have come from the anonymous old woman put to bed by Margaret Hare.

We may ponder even more the implication of the notes and museum catalogue entries concerning another anatomical anomaly, an "Altered condition of that portion of the Tendon of the Biceps Flexor cubiti which passes into the shoulder joint." The tendon, which connects the biceps to the joint, was so attenuated as to appear to be hanging by "a few fibrous and cellular looking threads, which could be traced with difficulty." This was a peculiar finding: without the tendon, the biceps would not function properly, and the patient would not have full use of his or her arm; moreover, Knox had, in the course of the previous two years, come across three others "identical to it." "The symptoms are severe," Knox observed, "and the time required for the reparation of the injury much more considerable than in the case of a common bruise," a finding supported by modern sports medicine. The London anatomist Edward Stanley had described a similar condition owing to injury, but Knox did not mention any anatomical indications of prior injury. The condition clearly intrigued Knox, and his catalogue entry concerning it is the longest he wrote. He also contributed an article on it to the *London Medical Gazette* in March 1828. In his notebook, he attempted to link the anomalous appearance to a pathological condition, writing that "Those changes that occurred in the Tendon of the Biceps flexor cubiti seemed to be connected with a rheumatic affection of the other joints as their synovia membranes were in general inflamed." Could this be a finding of significance to medical writers? Had Knox discovered a pathological condition associated with rheumatic fever and previously undetected?

This was Knox's Sherlock Holmes moment. Injury to the biceps tendon was no sort of evidence of murder, especially since Knox had noted the condition in at least one cadaver predating the Burke and Hare deliveries. But by March 1828 he had taken the first steps that could have led toward investigating the origins of his cadavers. He had noted an interesting anatomical finding, and he had speculated about the prior condition that had produced it. Why stop there, when further research was possible? Was it caused by disease? we can imagine him asking. Could it be due to some form of work-related trauma? Were these subjects laborers, or farmers, so that their repeated arm movements injured their tendons? Were comparable anomalies showing up at the Royal Infirmary, or among surgeons who treated the poor? Or could the tendons be injured perimortem or postmortem, that is, at the time of or after death? Could they be artifacts, created by dragging dead bodies by the arm, similar to the postmortem bruises and lividity created by packing them in bags, boxes, and tea chests? And if, at this point in his train of thought, Knox had put down his scalpel, changed his coat and hat, and gone out to investigate the lives of the men and women turning up on his dissecting table, he might have had a far different reputation in the annals of true crime than he subsequently acquired. He had, after all, done just that kind of fieldwork when investigating the habits of hyenas a few years earlier. But Knox did not close his dissecting case and look into the provenance of his cadavers, even when the anatomical evidence seemed to cry out for it. "The appearances I am about to describe have occurred to me only in the dissecting room"; he wrote in his letter to the *London Medical Gazette*, "nor am I acquainted with any of the symptoms preceding or accompanying the pathological condition which the tendon has presented in the dissections to which I allude." He took no further steps to learn about the people he dissected, and his failure to do so would come back to haunt him for the rest of his life. In the end, it was not what he chose to investigate, but what he chose not to, that stymied his ambitions.

Chapter 5

Based on a True Story

Mary Paterson or Mitchell

T HE MOST NOTORIOUS CADAVER, AND THE FIRST TO AROUSE conjecture outside of Knox's notebook, arrived at his dissecting rooms some time during the second or third week in April 1828. In life, she had been Mary Paterson, aged about eighteen, and she lodged with Isabella Worthington in Leith. She had been out the night before with her friend and fellow lodger Janet Brown. According to Worthington, Paterson was "much given to drink," and Brown, in her late twenties, had spent ten days the previous June in prison for being "Drunk disorderly & creating a crowd." William Burke had comparatively little to say about Paterson in his confession. He "fell in with the girl Paterson and her companion," he said, in the house of his brother, Constantine Burke, in Gibb's Close in the Canongate. They had breakfast, and he and Hare "disposed of her in the same manner" as previous victims.

Janet Brown was the chief witness for Mary Paterson's murder, and she came to Burke's trial prepared to testify against him. In fact she was never called, because Burke was tried first, and convicted, for the murder of Madgy Docherty. After spending all day sequestered in the witness room, though, Brown wanted her story to be told, and a version of it, "taken down nearly in her own words," appeared in Thomas Ireland's *West Port Murders* in January 1829. She was the only eyewitness who—as far as anyone knew—lived to tell her tale, and her testimony formed the cornerstone of

all subsequent accounts. Though described by the journalist who interviewed her as "a girl of the town"—which meant she earned at least part of
her living through prostitution—she was a credible witness. Prostitution
was not illegal in Great Britain and she had no reason to hide from the
authorities; furthermore, she was "possessed of considerable intelligence."
Brown had therefore spoken to the police once rumors started circulating
about strange disappearances in Edinburgh. On the night of April 8, she
said, she and Paterson had been taken to the police station on the Canongate. City watchmen made a practice of admitting young women, intoxicated or homeless, to the police office overnight "for protection," though it
is not clear whether it was for protection of the women or passersby. Paterson and Brown were not charged with any offense and were released early
in the morning. They went to a nearby spirit dealer's for breakfast, for Paterson may have had "two pence halfpenny" still clutched in her hand when
her body was delivered to Surgeon's Square later that day. At the shop they
met William Burke. His brother Constantine lived nearby, and though he
might have been paying an innocent visit, his presence in a whiskey shop
early in the morning suggests a shift in behavior: instead of waiting for
victims to come to Margaret Hare's lodgings, he was taking a more active
and predatory role in seeking them out. From this point he and Hare seem
to have made it their business, as Burke later said, to be on the lookout for
persons to murder. He may have noted, like social reformers, that whiskey
for breakfast, poured from pint jars and drunk out of teacups, was a staple
among women in marginal circumstances. "This they called their morning
"budge," according to a mid-century writer, "and they unanimously declared that they would rather pawn their last shift than want it. Indeed
they said that they could not do without it . . . they could not help it; it had
become essential to them."

Burke gave Brown and Paterson a glass of rum, then bought them a
bottle of whiskey each and invited them to breakfast. Brown later claimed
that she had been reluctant to go with him, in contrast to Paterson, who
was "always of a forward fearless disposition," but Burke kept up a continual
banter to allay her fears. He "was very urgent that she should go," Brown
remembered, "saying that he had a pension and could keep her handsomely
and make her comfortable for life." The women may or may not have believed this, but sociable breakfasts were common in Edinburgh's wynds and
closes, and accompanying Burke would save them the price of their own

breakfast. He took his new friends to his brother's house, where they also found Constantine's wife, Elizabeth, with their two sons. They had a good breakfast "of tea, bread, eggs, and Finnan haddocks"; they also consumed the two bottles of whiskey. Constantine left for work during breakfast, later disclaiming all knowledge of subsequent events. "I am often out upon my lawful business," he replied indignantly to Janet Brown a few weeks later when she asked him for news of her friend, "how can I answer for all that takes place in my house in my absence?"

What had taken place, by the end of the breakfast, was that Mary Paterson was unconscious at the table. Brown and Burke may have moved her to a small trundle bed, and then went out for more food and drink. Paterson was still unconscious when they returned, and she did not wake up even when Helen M'Dougal appeared on the scene and quarreled loudly with Burke over his entertaining the two young women. M'Dougal had perhaps been alerted to the possibility of another victim, though that was never proven. Brown became "much alarmed by their proceedings," especially when she learned that M'Dougal was Burke's wife, and insisted that she had to leave. Burke "at her request conducted her past M'Dougal." She promised to return in a quarter of an hour.

Janet Brown told her story "with distinctness and with every mark of apparent truth," and it conforms to Burke's own account of events. Still, the account published in *West Port Murders* included some errors of fact. Brown named the whiskey shop where she had met Burke as Swanston's, but William Swanston, grocer and spirit dealer near the head of the Canongate, took Thomas Ireland to court over that statement, testifying that he lived with his family in Salisbury Street in the south of the city, and that neither he nor his apprentice had been in the shop serving anyone so early in the morning. He had most certainly never had any dealings either with Burke or the two women. Hitherto he had "borne a fair and unimpeachable character for industry, sobriety of demeanor, and propriety of general conduct," argued his attorney, and Ireland, by citing him in connection with the "revolting and inhuman atrocities," had "maliciously slandered, calumniated, defamed, and vilified" him "in his character good name, and reputation and injured him in his feelings and trade." Ireland refused to retract the statement, asserting that it was from "the best authority," Brown herself, but it was common for even careful witnesses to make mistakes when recollecting names and locations after a period of many months. No one seems to have asked Brown to point out the exact shop where she and Paterson met Burke. There was a Swan's whiskey shop in the Canongate as well, so perhaps Brown or the journalist mixed up the two names, or perhaps it was another shop entirely.

There is a similar uncertainty about where Brown went after leaving Constantine Burke's. The journalist who took down her story wrote that she met a "Mrs. Lawrie," and that name has been reprinted ever since. But Crown Office records suggest that Brown went to the wife of John Clark, a baker in Rose Street. Brown told Mrs. Clark about her adventure, at first inclined to make a joke about it. Mrs. Clark, however, thought the whole matter seemed very suspicious. She sent Brown back, with her maid, Margaret M'Gregor, to fetch Paterson away at once. Brown could not find the house again on her own, and had to ask at the shop where she had first met Burke. By the time they had located Constantine Burke's residence, Mary Paterson had disappeared, reportedly out with William Burke. Brown sent the maid back to Mrs. Clark and sat down to wait, but Margaret M'Gregor returned almost at once, that is, within the half hour or so it would have taken to get from the Canongate to Rose Street and back. Mrs. Clark had grown even more alarmed and wanted Janet Brown to come to her house right away. Fortunately for her, she did as she was told. She went back to Gibb's Close again that evening to find her friend, but Elizabeth Burke told her that Paterson was still out with her brother-in-law. Brown never saw Mary Paterson again. Nor did her landlady Isabella Worthington, who also went to look for her at Constantine Burke's house. Brown asked after Paterson whenever she saw Constantine in the street. She had gone off to Glasgow with a packman, he told Brown, only later admitting that he didn't know where she was: "How the hell can I tell about you sort of folk? You are here to-day and away to-morrow."

In fact, Mary Paterson had been disposed of "in the same manner" as the other Burke and Hare victims, and she was "away" at Knox's dissecting rooms within four hours of her murder, by early afternoon. Her clothes had been removed, and Margaret Hare took her skirt and petticoat. They were later found in the possession of Helen M'Dougal and identified by credible witnesses: Jean Sutherland, married to a silversmith in Potterrow, and Jean Coghill, married to a shoemaker in South St. James Street. Constantine Burke knew perfectly well what had become of Mary Paterson, for he had seen her body when it "was put into a tea-box," which he helped transport to Dr. Knox's. He told his wife about it, but not their sons, who remembered seeing the two women at breakfast but did not know what became of them. By this time, Burke remembered, he had grown "more bold," and the two brothers carried the tea chest through High School Yards in broad daylight. There were a great many boys about, who followed them, crying, "They are carrying a corpse," but they "got her safe delivered."

At Surgeon's Square, Paterson's cadaver brought £8. "It was cold, but not very stiff," Burke said, and for the first time the staff at Number 10 grew uneasy. "Mr. Fergusson and a tall lad," said Burke, "who seemed to have known the woman by sight," asked "where they had got the body." One of the students said, "she was like a girl he had seen in the Canongate as one pea is like to another," and Alexander Miller later told the police that

MARY PATTERSON OR MITCHELL.

Figure 12. Artist's conception of Mary Paterson. Reproduced from a contemporary print, courtesy of the Library of the Royal College of Physicians of Edinburgh.

Fergusson had recognized the woman, giving her name as "Mary Mitchell" (Figure 12). According to Hare's later statement, Fergusson went further than this: he said "he thought he knew the lass, that she lived in the Canongate and that in his opinion she had died in her usual health," so recently that it seemed "if he had a lancet he could bleed and recover her." David Paterson too, had noted "the beautiful symmetry and freshness of the body," and he later claimed that he, too, asked Burke where he had got the body. But when Burke responded that he had purchased it from an old woman at the back of the Canongate—the equivalent of the modern "it fell off the back of a truck" as an explanation for stolen property—no further questions were asked. One of the students gave Burke a pair of scissors to cut off her hair.

When the case became known, public outcry was loud that this was the moment to have sent for the police. Knox's assistants had been presented with a young girl, recently dead, never buried, with no obvious signs of disease, brought in to the dissecting rooms with no better explanation than that her body had been bought "from an old woman in the Canongate." But Knox, when he arrived, was delighted with the cadaver, treating it like a prized possession rather than a piece of contraband and preserving it in whiskey for three months before dissection. "He brought in a painter," Burke said, "to look at her, she was so handsome a figure, and well shaped in body and limbs." The painter may have been Edward Mitchell, the engraver working with Knox and his assistant Thomas Wharton Jones on the anatomical plates in Knox's *Plates on the Arteries of the Human Body*. According to David Paterson, many of the students made their own sketches of the woman's body, one of which he kept. There is no sign that Knox attempted to conceal his possession of Paterson's corpse, and his supporters have argued that had he suspected murder, he would not have displayed it so publicly. David Paterson later said that he "had not the slightest suspicion as to the deceased having met with a premature death." Instead he "did think that it really was sold by the relatives, or by some one who kept a brothel or lodging house for paupers, from whom the resurrectionists purchase subjects."

This became the one Burke and Hare murder that everyone remembers, its elements repackaged and incorporated into both fiction and annals of true crime. The story was told and retold, of a young girl, strikingly beautiful and strikingly promiscuous, betrayed by her own immoral life into the hands of callous murderers, only to be recognized by her medical student lover as she lay upon the dissecting table. Her image was formed from the picture of Edinburgh low life common among Victorian social reformers and writers, of dark yet alluring wynds filled with thieves and prostitutes, drinking themselves into early graves, their clothes stolen and cadavers sold by old women even more disreputable than themselves. That there were lodgings where this sort of thing went on might be gleaned from the reports of the Police and High Courts published in the *Scotsman*. Just a few days before Mary Paterson was murdered, for example, there was an account of several "infamous" lodging houses, described as "nuisances of vice and crime." In July—about the time she would have been dissected—the *Scotsman* reported a "state of confusion" in Halkerston's wynd "by a fray among a few of the abandoned women who roost in the low houses. Six of them had a regular set to, and they not only tore each other's hair and clothes, but they bruised and battered each other. . . . Though some people witnessed the onslaught with mingled feelings of pity and indignation, there were creatures present, who walked upright and wore the human form, who appeared highly elated with this degrading and demoniac display of female ferocity." When the policeman arrived—John Fisher, who would later arrest Burke and M'Dougal—three of the women "ran into their lodging, a noted brothel." Surely bodies would be plentiful in such places, if anywhere.

We can watch the story of the lovely and licentious Mary Paterson build through the many supposedly trustworthy accounts of the Burke and Hare murders, starting with the published *Trial of William Burke and Helen M'Dougal*, widely advertised as the most accurate record of the trial. To enhance the value of the work, the publisher, Robert Buchanan, and his bookseller associate, John Stevenson, had the idea of inviting the noted antiquarian and literary gossip Charles Kirkpatrick Sharpe to write the preface. "The first victim named in the indictment, Mary Paterson or Mitchell," Sharpe wrote, "was a person of disorderly life, and is said to have been well known to Burke before he murdered her. She was of low stature, and not calculated to make much resistance, even had the opiates been withheld. She was cut short in her sinful career, and hurried (O, dreadful thought—how much unprepared!) before the judgment-seat of her offended Maker, at the early age of twenty-one." Published on December 31, 1828, this preface assured Paterson's posthumous notoriety, and all subsequent writers have portrayed her encountering Burke while seeking refreshment after a night plying her trade. The publishers, possibly aided by Sharpe once again, elaborated on the story in the preface to their *Appendix* to the trial, published several months later. By that time, rumors had spread that "numbers of the unfortunate females around the town" had disappeared, no one knew how. Indeed, it was reported, "Natural deaths have become rare" among girls of the town, "and for some time past the interment of one of them has scarcely been heard of." One story concerned a young, well-dressed woman, "with her shoes and stockings on," whose body was delivered in a sack to "a most respectable teacher of anatomy." On examining the corpse the surgeon found "an enormous fracture in the back part of the head, and a large portion of the skull driven in, as if by a blow from the blunt part of a hatchet." "You damned villains," he exclaimed to the men who brought it, "where, and how did you get this body?" It belonged to a whore, he was told, who "had been popped in a row (murdered in a brawl) in Halkerston's wynd."

Later nineteenth-century writers recognized the entertainment value of Mary Paterson in imparting erotic interest to the Burke and Hare tale. Alexander Leighton's *Court of Cacus* combined Janet Brown's story with Sharpe's preface in describing Paterson as "a young girl of eighteen or nineteen years of age, of remarkably handsome form . . . who turned her attractions to no other use than that of *the old abuse*." Henry Lonsdale's biography of Knox plagiarized from Leighton while assuming an air of spurious authority: Lonsdale described "Bonny Mary Paterson" and her "voluptuous form and beauty," as if he had seen her, adding a homily on "the whisky tendency of all such women . . . their reckless life and exposure, and their frequent abandonment when at death's door." Lonsdale added the titillating detail that Knox, "wishing for the best illustration of female form and muscular development for his lectures," made use of Paterson's body, "so that when he came to treat of the myological division of his course"—that is, the muscles—"a further and daily publicity was given to Paterson's remains." By the time we get to William Roughead's account of Burke and Hare for the Notable Trials series, both Mary Paterson and her companion Janet Brown had become "girls of about eighteen," who, "though young in years, were old in everything else, having early enrolled themselves among that sorry company whom the French incongruously term daughters of joy."

Roughead added two other elements to spice up the story. The first was publication of an engraving of a naked young woman, labeled in his book "Mary Paterson" and attributed to "J. Oliphant." Of its provenance, Roughead said only that "The picture of that pale piece of mortality accompanying the present volume, and curiously reminiscent in its graceful pose of the famous Rokeby Venus of Velasquez, is reproduced from one of the contemporary drawings referred to in the text." This rather circuitous sentence could be taken as implying that the sketch was drawn from life, as Roughead perhaps intended. Certainly later authors took it that way, concluding that "art students who frequented the rooms also made drawings of Mary Paterson, after the manner of the Rokeby Venus."

We can see here how a number of disparate sources were condensed into a narrative whole greater than the sum of their evidentiary parts, and the same process is at work in Roughead's second contribution to the sex angle, his casual assumption that William Fergusson was one of Paterson's customers. This was first implied by Lonsdale, who wrote of "a pupil of Knox's, who had been in her company only a few nights previously," standing "aghast on observing the beautiful Laïs stretched in death, and ready for the scalpel of the anatomist." Roughead assumed as a matter of course that sexual activity had taken place; he also assumed that it had to be kept hidden, that "such mere males as might have had some casual knowledge of the dead girl when in life, would, naturally enough in the circumstances, hesitate to claim acquaintance with her." All this intimate connection of sex and murder undeniably enthralls the audience, and that heartrending, soul-destroying moment, in which the bereaved sees his loved one, once warm and vibrant, now laid out on a slab, has become a staple of murder dramas. But did it really happen in 1828? What reason do we have for believing any of these accounts of Mary Paterson? How much did these writers really know about her life, or her death?

If we begin with Sharpe, the answer is, not much. It is not clear why Stevenson and Buchanan approached Sharpe to write the preface, except perhaps that as the acknowledged authority on local history and artifacts he was one of their best customers. "Intensely aristocratic, he cared nothing for the interests of the great multitude," wrote his friend, the Edinburgh historian Robert Chambers. On his daily walks he appeared the very model of an Edinburgh eccentric, with his "thin, effeminate figure," his high-pitched voice, his "long blue frock-coat," old-fashioned even then, his "black trousers (rather wide below and sweeping over white stockings and neat shoes), something like a web of white cambric round his neck, and a brown wig coming down to his eyebrows."He struck another close friend, Sir Walter Scott, as a throwback to an earlier era. His knowledge of Scottish history was considered second to none, and Scott drew upon Sharpe's research for many of his novels. Stevenson, who had known Sharpe for many years, must have approached him about writing the preface soon after the indictment was made public in early December 1828. The trial was scheduled for December 24, and Stevenson and Buchanan planned on having a reporter in court, ready to take down all the proceedings in shorthand. Unlike the other Edinburgh publishers, Buchanan was not aiming to be the first in print. That honor ultimately belonged to the *Caledonian Mercury*, which printed a rough transcript the day after the trial. Buchanan's intention was to be the most literary of the Burke and Hare publications and thus corner the high end of the market. To that end, he had all the principal lawyers and witnesses review and, if necessary, revise the raw transcript. An "illustrative preface" by Sharpe, a noted scholar, with connections to families of rank and fortune, could only enhance sales of what his publishers called "a full and correct report" of the trial.

Sharpe was fond of murder stories, especially if they had a historical bent, and his friend Chambers described him as delighting in "any case of a Lady Jane stabbing a perjured lover." He also delighted in indecent ballads and scurrilous letters from centuries past. Like other men of his age and class, he had a horrified fascination with transgressive female sexuality, and he contributed a frontispiece montage of "portraits of celebrated London courtezans"—an artist's conception if ever there was one—to a limited edition printing of the seventeenth-century *Whore's Rhetorick*. This work, its editor was careful to point out, should not be considered as contributing to the immorality of the age, for "its tendency is not of a description to inflame the passions, but on the contrary, to check them, by laying bare the system of deceit practised by those miserable creatures, whose hypocritical endearments lead the unwary to destruction." After Sharpe's death he was remembered for "scandalous anecdote and reminiscence . . ., a habit of cynical sarcasm on all sorts of persons, living or dead," and "speculations of the sexual order."

Let us not, therefore, look to Sharpe for historical accuracy or investigative journalism. His research for the preface to Burke's and M'Dougal's

trial consisted primarily of gathering apposite quotes from Milton and Ju-
venal, and transcribing a broadsheet illustrating "An Account of the most
horrid and unchristian actions of the Gravemakers in Edinburgh" from
1711. He persuaded Hugh Alston, who had the key to Burke's house in
the West Port, to let him in to sketch the premises, and his "Interior of
Burke's Room" was published in Buchanan's *Trial*. Though frequently reprinted, it is rather less precise than it appears. Alston, showing commend-
able integrity, refused to charge admission for entry to Burke's house, even
though a more self-interested steward was purportedly making a fortune
doing just that with Hare's residence in Tanner's Close. Alston had even
inventoried the household goods before locking them in a cellar, in order
to foil the souvenir seekers who would otherwise have stripped the room
of anything they could carry. Burke's and M'Dougal's bed, "consisting of
2 sides 2 ends, and seven spars," their "3 chairs & one stool," and their
"29 old shoes," two awls, and nine lasts were all put away for safekeeping.
For that reason the household furnishings so carefully depicted in Sharpe's
drawing, including "The Bed, or wooden Frame, full of Rags and Filth,"
and "The Straw, under which the body of the old Woman was hid," were
probably not Burke's at all, but instead were imported for the occasion, like
props for a play.

Sharpe, of course, knew nothing of Alston's inventory, which only
turned up in a scrapbook years later; indeed, he had very little hard information at all. For once the indictment was served to the defendants and
their legal counsel, the Scottish judiciary imposed a blackout on the press
until after the trial, to ensure that potential jurors would not be preju-
diced by their reporting. Journalists were forbidden to interview witnesses,
though they could interview other people not specifically named in the
indictment. But they could not publish anything until the verdict had been
handed down. That meant that Sharpe did not have Brown's testimony, or
Burke's confession. The only information he had was the indictment, and
the few scraps of information that had been published in the newspapers
before the indictment was issued. One of these, published on December
6, 1828, reported that "the two men and two females who were apprehended on suspicion of murdering an Irishwoman, and selling her as an
anatomical subject, have undergone repeated examinations at the Sheriff
office; and various rumours are afloat regarding them." The reporter had
heard that "one of the gang" had agreed to testify against the others, "and

has divulged their whole plan of procedure, which, if true, must strike the most unconcerned with horror for its atrocity and cruelty. He mentions that twenty people have been murdered by them, and sold to the lecturers on anatomy, and that the major part of these were unfortunate girls of the town." The term "burking" had not yet been coined: the murderers were reported, at this early stage, to have carried out their crimes by luring their victims "into the house of one of the gang, and there, plying them with spirits until intoxicated," at which point "they were strangled with a hand-kerchief." Such were the rumors that were "circulating generally regarding this mysterious affair for the truth of which, however, we cannot vouch." These rumors were all Sharpe had to work with when he penned his account of Mary Paterson.

Sharpe was not very interested in the other victims, and his original draft left them out completely; he added only a few paragraphs about them later, at the request of his publisher. John Stevenson helped ground Sharpe's historical overview in the here and now by locating "an old man, James Maclean, a hawker," who claimed to have known Burke, M'Dougal, and the Hares, and transcribing his account for inclusion in the preface. Stevenson had hoped to get Sharpe a ticket to the actual trial, so that he could round out his account, but that proved impossible. Instead Stevenson appended two articles from the *Caledonian Mercury* on recent events. Within twenty-four hours of the trial, Buchanan had reviewed the preface and returned it to Sharpe with several small corrections. By December 26, the preface was in press, with the trial transcript added over the course of the week. Five days later it was published, well before Janet Brown's story, or Burke's confession, had been made public.

Sharpe's avowed intent in his preface was to put the murders—"dreadful proof of the deep depravity of human nature"—into historical perspective, to lecture "the poorer classes in Edinburgh" on the evils of whiskey, and the wealthy on their irrational prejudice against bequeathing "their bodies to the public for dissection." But his masculine fantasy of a prostitute's life and death, together with its elaboration in the preface to Buchanan's *Appendix to the Trial of William Burke and Helen M'Dougal*, was echoed in all subsequent accounts. The first novel based on Burke and Hare, entitled *Murderers of the Close*, was issued on February 28, 1829, by the London publishers George Cowie and William Strange. The anonymous author had very little time to cobble together a coherent narrative, and large chunks of this work were plagiarized from both Thomas Ireland's *West Port Murders* and extant broadsides. He had the grace to admit that he had interspersed fictional episodes of his own invention among the facts gleaned from Edinburgh sources. "Some sort of explanation appears necessary for presenting the following narrative to the public in its present shape," he wrote, "inasmuch as it may be objected to, as neither an actual or bona fide statement of the events it undertakes to record. This is, perhaps, to a certain degree, the case." As he admitted, "the conversations put into the mouths of the different persons, as well as a few of the events, trifling in themselves, are indeed fictitious." Still, he felt justified in calling the book "a record of transactions hitherto unparalleled in the history of crime," for "the main features of this diabolical affair are carefully preserved, and the above unimportant interpolations have been introduced merely to lighten and relieve the heavier portions of the narrative."

The novel's depiction of Mary Paterson on that April morning in Gibb's Close is straight out of the penny dreadful imagination. Later nineteenth-century authors may well have read it, for the novel depicts Mary Paterson as a "destitute and houseless prostitute," and Janet Brown, "an equally hapless fellow-sufferer and fellow-sinner." Their presence in the tale added the enticing combination of sex and women in peril to the built-in violence, for such women, said the author, "offered a secure game" to Burke: "for who would care for the fate of those whom all had abandoned? who would institute inquiries after beings so lorn?" Hearing that they had spent the night in the watch house, Burke invited them to breakfast, "with an air of pleasantry." "'Come along, girls,' he said, 'a basin of strong tea, with a dash of the whiskey in it, will be no bad thing after your cold night's lodging. I warrant they gave ye but a scanty supper at the lock up yonder.' 'Devil a sup or a crust either,' exclaimed Paterson, 'did they give us; so we all night through cursed them for their hospitality; did'nt we, Janet?' . . . 'In troth and we did,' answered Brown, 'and I'm thinking they were'nt sorry to get rid of us at daylight.'" Hearing, this, Burke "laughed heartily. 'Ha, ha, ha! Ye are spirited girls, any how.'" He purchased two bottles of whiskey. 'There now, we're ready to jog after the proper fashion,' said he 'bad luck to me but a man or woman either is no good without whiskey.'"

During that fateful breakfast, as the level of whiskey in the bottle fell, "Burke, dragging a seat close to Paterson, began to exhibit towards her marks of extraordinary fondness. He pressed one arm round her waist, while the other was thrust into her bosom, and kissed her repeatedly, and with much seeming warmth." This set up the graphic murder scene, when Mary lay, alone and unconscious, on the bed. Burke "cast a horrid and searching glance around the room, and then rapidly clutching the mouth of the sleeping girl with one hand, grasped her nostrils tightly with the other." Her gasps and twinges were accompanied by dialogue illustrative of the heartlessness of the murderers—"'Thou hast not finished thy work now,' said Hare, 'she still moves.' 'Tis but nature's last kick,' replied Burke, coolly, 'she'll give no more trouble, I'll warrant.'"

In *Murderers of the Close*, Paterson's death became a cautionary tale on the dangers inherent in an immoral life. It illustrated "the cold blooded indifference usually manifested by the world" toward "those wretched outcasts known as abandoned females (and true and sad is the appellation)." No one, exclaimed the author, "scarcely its own members, sympathizes one with another in this unhappy class; and when an unfortunate female has disappeared, there may have been an expression of wonder, perhaps a meaningless laugh or ribald joke among her companions, and the subject hath then dropped." This concern for dissolute, "unfortunate females"— and with exploiting their potential in sensationalist fiction—is typical of the nineteenth-century preoccupation with prostitution. Social reformers, political economists, and authors of penny dreadfuls all painted sad portraits of destitute, fallen women, their faded rags all that was left of the wages of sin.

Running parallel to the narrative of the abandoned woman was the narrative of the medical student discovering someone he loved on the dissection table. The basic idea was caught in doggerel in one of the earliest broadsheets printed after the trial of Burke and M'Dougal. "In Edina town," it begins,

> *Where your friend you may meet.*
> *At morning, in health, walking forth in the street,*
> *And, at evening, decoy'd and depriv'd of his life,*
> *His corpse fresh and warm is laid out for the knife.*

It was only a short step from this to the medical student recognizing his "friend," fresh and warm, under the knife, though it seems to have taken a few years to turn up in print. By the 1840s it was as familiar a plot device as the hard-boiled detective and the dame in the pulp fiction of the 1930s. The cadaver thus displayed—the student standing "aghast"—was commonly a female, family member if not a sweetheart of the student in question. The essential element was the recognition of the female cadaver, which allowed the author, either directly or through euphemism, to invite his readers to dwell on the beauties of the naked female form. In Edinburgh at least, the belief lingered that the dead woman beloved by the student was somehow morally suspect; perhaps an artist's model if not a girl of the town. In Robert Wise's 1945 movie *The Body Snatcher*, concern for propriety turned her into a street singer, but Dylan Thomas's 1953 screenplay restored the transgressive love affair between the prostitute Jennie Bailey and Dr. Murray. Jennie and her gentleman lover have to meet in a tavern, for she refuses to consider either "loving in the lanes, with all the trees dripping down your back and the thorns tearing your petticoats" or "sitting holding hands in your lodgings all the evening, and your brother studying books in the other corner." She tells Dr. Murray, "You know you could come home with me," but upright young gentleman that he is, he cannot bear to think of her in "that house, ever. I don't want to think of the others, and your smiling at them and letting them . . ." For her part, Jennie will not consider giving up her way of life to marry him: "Oh, a fine young doctor's wife I'd make. Wouldn't the ladies love me? 'And from what part do you come, Mrs. Murray?' 'Number 23 Pigs' Yard. Your husband used to call on Wednesdays.'"

This aspect of the story was no doubt enhanced by the portraits of supposedly dead naked women which circulated, probably by the 1830s but certainly by the 1860s, given new impetus after the publication of Leighton's *Court of Cacus* in 1861. One of these was the original of the illustration published in Roughead's *Burke and Hare*, which can still be found in a book of Burke and Hare ephemera in Edinburgh Central Library. One look and it is clear that Roughead did not tell all he knew. The illustration, and the rest of the Burke and Hare material, was probably in the possession of the Edinburgh antiquarian William Cowan, and perhaps even in 1921 gentlemen did not publicize their ownership of drawings from the nude. The illustration is not dated, but it bears the inscription "Jessie Patterson—model for the Life Academy—murdered by Burke and Hare—drawn by J Oliphant." The inscription suggests strongly that the illustration is not contemporary to the murders. Every document from 1828–1829 speaks of "Mary" Paterson, so an allusion to "Jessie" indicates less than perfect knowledge of the events. So does the attribution to "J Oliphant," for John Oliphant, artist, appears in the Edinburgh City Directories only from 1831, and his extant works all date from the 1830s and 1840s. He was never a member of the Life Academy, later to become the Royal Scottish Academy. And the academy itself, though founded in 1826, did not offer classes for students until a much later period. Roughead's comment can be taken to imply that Oliphant was the artist Knox brought in to sketch the dead Paterson, but there is no evidence whatever that Oliphant ever knew Knox or attended his anatomical classes. Nor is there evidence that the surviving illustration depicts anything other than a reclining, but warm and still-breathing, nude.

Roughead did not mention that the collection contains a second drawing, in pastels, of a different, though again, obviously still living, female nude. He presumably did not know that another version of the second illustration appears in a collection of Burke and Hare ephemera now in the National Library of Scotland. Whereas the model for the illustration in the Central Library is clearly lying on her side with her back to the viewer, the identical scene in the National Library has been cropped to look as though the woman were face down on a table. This would have placed her arms at a most awkward angle, though whoever wrote the inscription "The unfortunate girl Paterson as she lay exposed on the table of Dr. Knox for dissection the day after her murder" was probably not interested in her arms. "One of the students had been with her the night preceding," the inscription continues, "and his feelings may be well conceived when he saw the body which but a few hours had been clasped in his embraces thus exposed." Indeed they might, and no doubt artists and booksellers were happy to exploit their customers' desire to re-create those feelings as they gazed upon the naked form of the alleged "Mary Paterson." By the 1850s, reported the *Scotsman*, "lithographed studies from the life" were "continually . . . exhibited in the windows of our printsellers." And it seems likely that Henry Lonsdale's authority for his image of the "beautiful Lais" outstretched in death came from just such an illustration, rather than any eyewitness account.

But if the stories, the illustrations, the allegedly authoritative works are all suspect, then what are we left with? Can we say anything about Mary Paterson? What was the origin of the rumors circulating about her? Was any part of the narrative actually "based on a true story"? The one person in the best position to know, Janet Brown, was indignant at the description of her friend widespread in the Edinburgh newspapers. She was "irregular in her habits," Brown admitted, "but not so low as she has been represented." Then who, or what, was she?

To answer that question, we have to go back to sources which have some purpose besides narrative fireworks, which exist for reasons other than telling a good story. The first of these is the warrant issued for the arrest of William Burke and Helen M'Dougal on December 4, 1828, on suspicion of murdering "Mary Paterson alias Mitchell." In it, Paterson was described as "a Girl of the Town . . . who had no fixed place of residence." Rumors concerning this warrant, and the investigation which followed, were the most likely sources for the December 6 article in Sharpe's collection, which mentioned "unfortunate girls of the town" as the main victims of Burke and Hare. By December 19 Sir Walter Scott had heard from official circles that "one of the creatures who perishd was a prostitute of uncommon personal beauty." The formal indictment against Burke and M'Dougal, however, did not designate any occupation for Paterson, describing her only as "residing with Isabella Burnet or Worthington." There is no Mary Paterson to be found in surviving police records from the 1820s, though both Janet Brown and other Burke and Hare victims appear in them. What reason could there be, then, for assuming she was a prostitute?

There are other surviving records carefully preserved in Edinburgh's outstanding archival collections, including those of the Magdalene Asylum, a cross between a refuge and reform school for penitent "girls of the town." According to the asylum minute books, on September 18, 1826, "Mary Paterson aged 16—daughter of Peter Paterson, Mason" applied for admission. She had been "in the service of Mr. Deuchar, Engraver," probably Alexander Deuchar, "seal-engraver and lapidary to his Majesty," who had a shop at 57 North Bridge, not far at all from Surgeon's Square. Possibly she had been seduced and then dismissed from service. In any case, the minutes recorded, she had subsequently spent "4 months on the Town." The forty or so inmates to the asylum earned their keep by working either as seamstresses or in the laundry. Most of the income thus generated went to support the asylum, but the women were also allowed a share. It was therefore a mark in her favor that young Mary Paterson could "both sew and wash." She was precisely the kind of young penitent the Magdalene

Asylum preferred, of respectable family, caught early in what would otherwise be a downward spiral of infamy. She was admitted, conditional upon her being examined by the surgeon and found free from venereal disease.

Did the four months "on the town" make her a prostitute? Not necessarily, according to the surgeon William Tait, whose 1842 book *Magdalenism: An Inquiry into the Extent, Causes, and Consequences, of Prostitution in Edinburgh* was carefully researched and widely cited. Tait, like many other reformers, made a distinction "between the terms prostitution and prostitute." Prostitution, he said, "is merely an act, which may be an isolated one in the history of the individual who is guilty of it. . . . Prostitution may arise from various causes," including seduction and desperate economic need, "and may involve a greater or less degree of guilt." In contrast, a prostitute, according to Tait, was a woman "who openly delivers herself up to a life of impurity and licentiousness, who is indiscriminate in the selection of her lovers, and who depends for her livelihood upon the proceeds arising from a life of prostitution." The distinction was important, because Tait, like other reformers, assumed that women, even those as young as fifteen or sixteen, had complete control over their own sexuality. They could be misled and seduced—"led astray" in the phrase used by the asylum—but then it was their duty to return to the straight and narrow path of true religion. A young girl, like Mary Paterson, might fall into prostitution, but she could be rescued from it under the salutary influence of the asylum. A hardened prostitute—like the fictional Jennie Bailey in *Doctor and the Devils*—could not, and would be refused admission.

Once admitted, women were expected to conform to a strict code of behavior. They had to agree to remain in the asylum for at least two years, and to adhere to all the regulations set by the directors and the staff, which included a matron, who had overall authority for running the institution, as well as staff members to supervise the laundry and sewing details. Inmates were expected to work every day except Sunday at their assigned tasks, to attend all religious services, and to learn to read the Bible. They were also expected to remain within the asylum at all times and to refrain from all contact with former friends and family, unless given express permission. The purpose of this regimen was steeped in medical metaphors: the women were to be "cured" of the wayward tendencies that had led them astray, and inculcated with the moral precepts that would inoculate them against temptation in the future. They had to be isolated from their former associates to prevent contagion, or they would fall back into their immoral way of life.

Some of the inmates found the "cure" far worse than the disease, and within a week of being admitted clamored to get out. Others absconded at night, or while the other women were at work, sometimes taking other inmates' clothing or household items with them. When confronted with their wrongdoing, they refused to confess. "No reliance can be placed on any thing they say," complained Tait of women he had dealt with, "Dissimulation has become so natural to them, that they fail to speak the truth even when it is for their advantage. . . . If . . . they are asked where they reside, they will mention any street but the right one. . . . If they are tipsy, and be told so, they will swear that they have not tasted spirits for a month." But we might be more inclined to see the formal appeals for admission, the highly informal exits through the laundry windows, and even the lying as strategies utilized by young women living on the social margins. The Magdalene Asylum records reinforce what has long been known to social historians, that though commonly referred to as "the oldest profession," prostitution in the 1820s was emphatically not a profession at all. Instead, it was a form of economic makeshift for girls, generally in their late teens and early twenties, and generally only for a few years. As the social historian Judith Walkowitz explained, "Most were single, and more often than not their previous occupation had been casual maids of all work. They were local girls, indigenous to the region. They overwhelmingly lived outside the family—indeed, they would most likely have been half or full orphan." Their sexual partners were much more likely to be men of their own social status rather than gentlemen; they had sisters, friends, and neighbors who were respectably married, and with some luck they might end up respectably married themselves. Like conscientious teachers, the directors and staff of the asylum took pride in their successes, in the young women who were received once again by their families, who found good positions in respectable households, who married and continued to read their Bibles. They sighed and scolded the others.

We can make a strong, if not airtight, case that the Mary Paterson admitted to the asylum was "our" Mary Paterson, that is, the murder victim. Certainly it would explain the origin of the rumors of her irregular life. Her age at the date she entered tallies with what we know of her. So does the information, provided by Janet Brown, that Paterson was a native of

Edinburgh, "well educated for one in her situation," her mother dead. It is possible that the two women could have met at the asylum, for the minutes record both a "Jess" and a "Janet" Brown. Mary Paterson who entered the asylum must have been reasonably contented there, for her name did not turn up in the records again until almost a year and a half after her admission, when she would have been about eighteen years old. On April 7, 1828, she appeared before the directors "desirous to be permitted to leave the Asylum." She was "admonished" but, persisting in her determination, she was "permitted to go" with the money she had earned. The date should give us pause. According to Janet Brown's interview, it was the day before Burke encountered Brown and Paterson in a whiskey shop. And the asylum was located on the Canongate.

In the spirit of good legal counsel we should note the holes in our case. Mary Paterson figured prominently in the most sensational murder case in Edinburgh, her name and description published and republished, often accompanied by a hand-colored print purporting to be her likeness. We would expect some response from the Magdalene Asylum directors on hearing that one of their recent inmates had been killed the day after leaving the institution. In fact, the asylum minutes make no more mention of Mary Paterson after her departure than before, and they likewise make no mention of the murders. The only entry that could possibly be construed as a response to the public agitation over Burke and Hare referred to a "Circular urging the Claims of the Institution" and requesting funding for the asylum from the religious institutions in the city. It was dated January 5, 1829, less than a week after the publication of Sharpe's Preface.

Another hole has to do with the timetable of events. If Mary Paterson left the asylum on April 7, only to be murdered the next day, she had a single afternoon to pack up her few belongings, meet up with Janet Brown, and make Isobel Worthington acquainted with her fondness for drink, before she wound up dead on a table in Surgeon's Square. Even if we assume that she had arranged to join Brown at Worthington's lodgings before her release from the asylum, surely she would need less than an afternoon to show her clothes to witnesses Jean Sutherland and Jean Coghill, located in Potterrow and South St. James Street respectively. Had she spent the afternoon paying calls? Again, surely someone would have mentioned that? It is, however, possible that the date usually given for Paterson's death, April 9, was only an approximation. The Crown Office indictment merely places the alleged murder "on one or other of the days between the 7th and the 16th days of April 1828." Our best witness, Burke, placed the murder in April but not on any specific date, and we know from other parts of his confession that, like many people, he tended to keep track of events by holidays rather than by month, day, and year. Janet Brown was quoted as specifying April 8 for the night she and Paterson spent in the Canongate watch house, but we have already found reasons to question the details of her interview. Knox never allowed access to his record books, if indeed he even kept track of the dates on which he received the cadavers. Given the precision of the Magdalene Asylum records, we may assume that the former inmate Mary Paterson did indeed leave on April 7, 1828. But Burke's victim could have been killed any time from one day to one week later. And if Paterson were wearing the same clothes in which she left the asylum, that would have been another reason for her friends to remember them. For women generally left with a new set of clothes, and Janet Brown especially objected to the print of Paterson "represented in the garb of a servant, a dress in which she never appeared."

The strongest argument that the asylum Mary Paterson and the murdered Mary Paterson are one and the same is that it explains one aspect of the murder so puzzling that most accounts have either altered or ignored it: the oddly passive behavior of Paterson herself as she breakfasted in Gibb's Close. As we have seen, Janet Brown described Paterson as of a "forward fearless disposition," the starting point for all her fictional avatars. Yet Brown's story tallies with Burke's that Paterson got very drunk very quickly, and lay insensible on the bed by the end of their alcoholic breakfast. Neither witness recorded her bantering, flirting, or indeed saying anything at all. It was Brown, the older of the two, who spent the better part of the morning talking, laughing, and, inevitably, drinking with Burke. Why should a "forward fearless girl" show so little personality, as little personality, in fact, as Paterson from the Magdalene Asylum? Why should she have eaten, drunk, and fallen asleep so quickly on the bed? What if she were not forward and fearless in a sexual sense at all, but instead a young woman recently released from the strict discipline of the asylum, not so much "given" to drink as susceptible to it? What if she was, for the first time in eighteen months, encountering the freedom of the street? What if she felt comfortable in the Canongate, having lived so long there, and suspected no danger in breakfasting with a police employee and his hospitable family? Why would she have expected any danger if, feeling woozy, she lay down on the bed?

One important question remains to be answered: where could a young woman from the Magdalene Asylum have met one or more medical students? The assumption that Mary Paterson was sleeping with William Fergusson, or any of Knox's assistants, has never rested on any contemporary evidence. At the time of the trial, the three men lived far removed from each other and from Surgeon's Square, William Fergusson with his brother John, a writer to the signet, in George Square, Thomas Wharton Jones with his mother in West Circus Place in the New Town, and Alexander Miller in lodgings in Clerk Street, on the edge of the southern suburbs. We have no reason to think that they went to the same taverns for drink or debauch, or even spoke to each other outside of Knox's dissecting rooms. There is no evidence linking any of them to the brothels on Halkerson's Wynd, or the ones closer by on Eldin or West Richmond Streets. Edinburgh students did form liaisons with women of the "poorer classes," but they were typically attracted to household servants, who were conveniently located and presumably less expensive. This is clear not only from student diaries, but from the personal histories of Magdalene Asylum applicants, like Margaret Hill, aged seventeen, seduced "while a servant with Dr. Campbell by one of the young men there." It was highly unusual for medical students to go into the back wynds and closes, looking for "houses of bad fame," for the women in them were believed to be disease-ridden, in league with cutpurses and pickpockets. As for the real "destitute and houseless prostitutes," women who, Tait said, strolled the streets "from night to morning for the purpose of earning as much as will suffice to meet the necessary wants of life for the ensuing day," their "particularly dirty and wretched appearance" cannot be reconciled with the "beautiful symmetry and freshness of body" David Paterson noted in the murder victim. Where, then, could medical students have met an inmate of the Magdalene Asylum, and seen enough of her to be able to recognize her cadaver, naked, on the dissecting table? Was there any place in town, outside of their own households, where three young men would come into regular contact with any young women of the "poorer classes"?

The obvious answer is the Royal Infirmary, which functioned as both a public hospital and a teaching ward, treating the poor of the city at no charge in exchange for using them as clinical material for medical students.

And on March 15, 1828, a woman named Mary Paterson was admitted into the Royal Infirmary for "Rheumatism," probably rheumatic fever. She was admitted to the Clinical Ward, that is, the ward used in teaching. She remained until March 29, when she was dismissed, cured.

Again, we must ask: can this be "our" Mary Paterson? Again, we can make a strong if not airtight case. This is the only record of a Mary Paterson in the infirmary during the period 1826–1828, and other inmates of the Magdalene Asylum are found in infirmary records for those years. Once again the dates fit what we know of both inmate and murder victim, and it is certainly plausible that a stint in the infirmary, Paterson's first time away from the asylum since her arrival, might have increased her desire to leave the institution. We cannot be certain that Fergusson or the other assistants would have seen her there, but Fergusson attended the infirmary on a regular basis. There is another point in support of the identification as well. On December 28, 1827, a woman named Mary Mitchell was admitted to the Royal Infirmary, and was placed in the Clinical Ward. She died there on January 3, 1828.

It has never been explained why the murder victim was identified by Knox's assistants as "Mary Mitchell." Judicial procedure required that all persons named in legal documents had to be identified as fully as possible: married women were listed with both maiden and married names, and criminals were identified by all known aliases. But no witness ever suggested that Paterson was married, or had a criminal alias. Why, then, should she have been Mary Paterson to William Burke and Janet Brown, and Mary Mitchell to at least some of the students? The simplest answer, given by the Royal Infirmary records, is that there were two "Marys" admitted to the Clinical Ward at about the same time, one named Mary Mitchell and the other Mary Paterson. Seeing the cadaver several months later, Fergusson or another student might have mixed up the names. We have found enough mistakes in names among both witnesses and journalists that this kind of slip seems plausible.

If Fergusson had seen Paterson in the infirmary, it gives a slightly different cast to the questions he put to Burke about her cadaver, one more in keeping with his professional pursuits and therefore more likely to have been on his mind that April afternoon. At that point he had no reason to suspect murder, but he might have had reason to suspect theft. If he had last seen the woman alive in the Royal Infirmary, then it was reasonable to suppose she had died there, in which case her body "belonged" to that institution unless claimed by relatives. That meant she should have been dissected for the benefit for students at the infirmary, and the only way "John" and "William" could have gotten hold of the cadaver was by stealing it. Indeed a cadaver was "fraudulently obtained" from the infirmary by Edinburgh body snatchers on at least one other occasion. And the question he asked, as Burke phrased it, was "where we got the young woman Paterson." Perhaps what concerned him was not *how* she had died—not that he had last seen her alive, and now she was dead—but *where* Burke had gotten the body—in other words, had he stolen it from the Royal Infirmary. We would like to know whether Fergusson investigated further, whether he went to the infirmary and asked questions or checked the books. The indications are, though, that once Burke had explained the cadaver's supposed provenance, Fergusson did not pursue the matter.

There is another, rather gruesome reason for supposing that neither Fergusson nor Knox's other assistants had been involved with Paterson on a personal or sexual basis. As the many fictional accounts of the murder prefer to overlook, Burke said that Paterson's body was preserved in spirits for three months. That means that her former lover or lovers—if present—would have had to view her naked body in a vat of spirits, day after day, as the fluids and color leached out of it, as her features altered beyond recognition, and as decomposition progressed, slowed by the preservative fluid but not stopped altogether. The most macabre of nineteenth-century tales of terror did not choose to dwell on that part of the story, or conceive of the feelings of the medical student, standing aghast at the body of his dead lover as he added fresh alcohol to her vat.

Surely it is easier to assume that medical students met Paterson in the course of their professional education. An experienced anatomical student would have to get used to dissecting the cadaver of a former patient; indeed, that was all in a day's work for a practicing surgeon. If Fergusson or his fellow assistants were distressed or titillated by her youth and well-developed figure, they would have to learn to deal with those feelings. If we agree with Roughead that men would hesitate to identify the cadaver of a woman they had slept with, then that is really an argument against the supposed liaison of Paterson and Knox's assistants. Fergusson, and "the tall lad" mentioned by Burke, identified her body quite openly, and in the presence of servants and supposed resurrectionists. They later testified as much to the police. If their inquiries were professional, not personal—if they were merely doing their duty by the Royal Infirmary and ensuring their cadavers were not stolen—it would explain their readiness to ask questions, and the lack of shamefaced silence.

And once the story of the prostitute started circulating, there was a practical, if ugly, reason why Fergusson and his colleagues might have hesitated to speak out against it: it provided a perfect justification for why they had not gone to the police. It was clearly a common assumption that girls like Mary Paterson ended up dead in brothels. "Everyone knew" that resurrectionists made the rounds of disorderly houses, whose inhabitants might wish to dispose of inconvenient bodies, no questions asked. Who could blame mere assistants for believing Burke had purchased the cadaver under just such circumstances? Who could have expected them to know any better? Even the tales circulating by the 1860s—which the former assistants must have heard—of the doomed love between the medical student and his mistress may have seemed easier to live with than the truth: that they could have called the police—right then, in April 1828—and stopped the killers before they went any farther. Perhaps it was that reflection, rather than any delicacy of feeling, that kept them silent.

If Mary Paterson's murder marked a shift in Burke's behavior, it may also have marked a shift in Knox's. He kept the cadaver for three months, something he did for no other victim, female or male, young or old. Perhaps it occurred to him that someone might make enquiries for so young and striking a cadaver; perhaps he was waiting to see if anyone reported her missing. When no enquiries were forthcoming, he may have felt justified in accepting "John's" and "William's" story concerning her death. In that way his experience with Paterson's body might have allayed, rather than increased, his suspicions.

Mary Paterson's story served as a cautionary tale: for young women, that promiscuity led to a nasty death, and for medical students, that the body they dissected might be one they loved. But the evidence we have uncovered beyond it suggests that murder was more random though no less poignant: that a woman whose brief life is preserved through entries in the archives died simply because, one April morning, she encountered a murderer in a whiskey shop. We have no reason to accept the "conviction" on the part of contemporary journalists that Burke targeted "girls of the town." It is simply not true "that the greater number" of his victims "were selected from this unfortunate and degraded class," despite their propensity to drink. Burke was no Jack the Ripper: there is no sign that he enjoyed killing women, and he must have been very drunk when he killed Mary Paterson. Even more important, whatever Constantine Burke might say, that "sort of people" were not "here today and away tomorrow." Girls of the town were, like Janet Brown and Mary Paterson, likely to be local. They were not literally "abandoned" women, deserted, as middle-class moralists liked to think, "by the relatives and friends whom they dishonoured, and excluded from all notice or regard by the virtuous part of society." It was manifestly untrue that "there was none to care for, and none to inquire what had become of them": they had families, friends, connections in town. Janet Brown never stopped looking for Paterson, and she had allies in Isabella Worthington, Mrs. Clark, and, eventually, the police. Burke and Hare, more observant or with more self-interested motives than middle-class moralists, may have come to realize that even "girls of the street" could not just disappear. Janet Brown's persistent searching for her friend may have helped the cause of justice in more ways than one.

Chapter 6

The Dangerous Classes

Elizabeth Haldane, Margaret Haldane

SOME TIME DURING THE SPRING OF 1828, "A STOUT OLD woman," Elizabeth Haldane, turned up at Margaret Hare's lodging house in Tanner's Close. According to Burke, she "had but one tooth in her mouth, and that was a very large one in front." Thomas Ireland's *West Port Murders*—where she is referred to as "Mary" Haldane—described her as "a dissipated character, who used to infest the Grassmarket and neighbourhood," but Burke claimed he knew "nothing farther of her" than her name when he found her "asleep among some straw" in Hare's stable. "She had got some drink at the time," Burke said, "and got more to intoxicate her," and he and Hare suffocated her. They kept her in the stable overnight, "and took her to Dr. Knox's next day."

Margaret (or Peggy) Haldane, one of Elizabeth's daughters, was murdered several months later, during the summer of 1828. She, too, had lodged with Margaret Hare, and like her mother, Burke said, was "of idle habits, and much given to drinking." Burke murdered her on his own, without the help of Hare. He and M'Dougal had moved away from Tanner's Close, and he may have encountered Haldane on the street or, as with other victims, at a whiskey shop. In fictional re-creations of the scene, she has been depicted looking for her mother, but though this has proved an ever-attractive plot twist Burke said nothing about it. Strictly speaking Peggy Haldane was not burked. Instead, she drank a great deal, Burke explained, and then lay on the bed "with her face downwards." He "pressed her down, and she was soon suffocated." Indeed, she "was so drunk at the time that he thinks she was not sensible of her death, as she made no resistance whatever." She, like Mary Paterson, was taken to "Dr. Knox's in the afternoon in a tea-box"—that is, again within a few hours—"and £8 got for her." Her cadaver apparently aroused no comment, though it was the second young woman to turn up dead with no obvious signs of disease.

It was probably rumors about Peggy Haldane which fed the stories later associated with Mary Paterson. Haldane may well have known Burke previously, from lodging with Margaret Hare. In addition, the description of Peggy in *West Port Murders* as "a woman of the town" who "led a very dissolute life" is supported by police records, which show that Margaret Haldane, unlike Mary Paterson, had a criminal record. Haldane had been arrested twice in eight months for "vagrancy" and "infesting the New Town to the great annoyance of Passengers." Thirteen other women, aged nineteen to twenty-seven, some with prior convictions, were arrested at the same time on similar charges. And so with the Haldanes' murders we enter the world of "the dangerous classes," as the lawyer and social theorist Jeliger Symons was to call them in mid-century, consisting of "criminals, paupers and persons whose conduct is obnoxious to the interests of society," as well as "that proximate body of people who are within reach of its contagion, and continually swell its number." We enter, in other words, the criminal underworld, so intriguing to readers of the *Newgate Calendar*, of Charles Dickens and William Thackeray, so intractable a problem to social reformers.

Symons and like-minded writers believed that criminality was on the rise, threatening all civil society. He was not concerned with what he termed "crimes of passion and poverty"—crimes committed by amateurs, as we may think of them—which he viewed as comprising a small proportion of the total criminal element. His main targets were the professional criminals, "offshoots of an extent of moral disease which they by no means accurately measure, but of which they attest the magnitude." He was particularly concerned with theft, "a craft," he wrote, carried on by "an organised corruption of young persons and servants." It was "out of all proportion the most extensive crime," and it was "gregarious"—that is, involving numbers of perpetrators, from gangs of thieves to their "resetters" or fences. It was, he pointed out with great concern, "especially adapted to children." Symons was also concerned with vagrancy, as the chief means by which crime spread from place to place. Men and women "experienced in the crimes and vices of the criminal associations of the larger towns from whence they sally forth," he wrote, form "large proportions of the population of the gaols in the rural districts." They stayed in lodging houses, meeting up with colleagues from other towns, and "tell one another all they know." By mid-century some 30 percent of all arrests were for vagrancy.

Views similar to Symons's had led the Edinburgh Town Council to authorize the creation of the Police Establishment in 1805, with the charge "to establish more effectual regulations for apprehending and punishing vagrants and disorderly persons, suppression of common begging, removing nuisances, lighting and cleaning the streets and passages, and in general, for the preservation of peace and good order." The police functioned as a branch of city government, and the superintendent in 1828, Captain James Steuart, was under considerable pressure to keep the police force "efficient," that is, low cost. That was not easy, considering its many duties, which required as many as fourteen committees to carry out. The Police Establishment was responsible for collecting human excrement from the city, which, when sold for fertilizer, accounted for a substantial proportion of Captain Steuart's total operating budget. The directive for "lighting and cleaning the streets and passages" meant that the supervision of both the fire department and gas line installation devolved on the police. So did cleaning and maintaining public lavatories—"necessaries" as they were called—and responding to any complaints about their condition. The police superintendent acted as public prosecutor for cases in the Police Court, held twice a week for minor offenses, in addition to his other administrative duties. He was also expected to work closely with other entities involved in criminal procedure, including the Burgh Courts within Edinburgh, the sheriff's office, which had jurisdiction over lesser offenses, and with the Crown Office, which had jurisdiction over serious crimes throughout Scotland. And Captain Steuart took an active role in criminal investigation in especially important or well-publicized cases: it was Steuart, we may recall, who came to the West Port to arrest William and Margaret Hare.

The "great object" of the police, a later superintendent was to write, was "Prevention of Crime," and to achieve this object, Captain Steuart's force consisted of 26 watchmen—so called because they were assigned to be on duty at the city watch houses—and another 24 patrolmen, who walked a specific beat throughout their districts. There were a much greater number of night watchmen, 149 of whom were dispersed throughout the city. All these men were empowered to act as constables, that is, "to apprehend persons who have committed crime—or who are strongly suspected of doing so." Persons so apprehended could be searched immediately, even without a warrant, and though a warrant was recommended before searching a suspect's residence, much was left up to the watchman's judgment. The watchmen "were to be civil and attentive to every person; bearing bad language, and even reproach, from such passengers as are in liquor, when they appear to have no bad intention; and exercising, under all circumstances, all the humanity compatible with the due and firm discharge of their duty." Their task was, for the most part, made easier in that watchmen were seldom threatened or challenged by the felons they arrested. Injuries in the line of duty were more likely to come from unruly crowds or rioting students than those who ended up on trial for serious crimes.

Since the watchmen were generally first on the scene of a crime, they had broad responsibilities for gathering the evidence that would later be used by the prosecution if the perpetrator were brought to trial. As a city institution the Police Establishment was under separate administration from the Crown Office, which handled prosecutions, just as a city police department in the United States is under separate administration from the district attorney's office. Still, the Edinburgh police were expected to work closely with the sheriff-substitute and the procurator fiscal—as an American police force would work with a sheriff or district attorney—to provide evidence and give clear testimony when a case came to court. Policemen giving evidence were enjoined to properly identify all parties and witnesses, with occupations and places of residence, maiden names of married women, and all designations for children. They had to "exert the utmost care in ascertaining the true spelling of names of parties, witnesses, and places." If they wrote down the testimony of witnesses, they had to write it down "from the mouths of those examined, from beginning to end of the transaction, and in the parties' own words." Under no circumstances were they to hint "that it might be for the prisoner's advantage to be candid," in order to "induce delinquents to confess the crime upon which they have been apprehended." Nor were they, in giving their own testimony, to "make the evidence appear stronger than can be fully supported at the time of trial," or the Crown Office prosecutor, whether the lord advocate himself or his delegates, the advocates depute, would be justifiably furious. Finally—and by this time we can hear the rising exasperation in the hardworking superintendent's voice—when a constable gave evidence in court, he was enjoined to "promptly answer the questions put to him, either by the Public Prosecutor, Sheriff, Judge, Prisoner's Agent, or Jury, in a direct manner, and not, as is frequently the case, enter into a rambling statement."

From 1822, the police force included six "criminal officers," hired specifically to be a visible presence among the criminal element in the city. They were to keep track of "loose and disorderly persons, whose behaviour is such as to excite just suspicion" and make it "evident to the parties that they are known, and under the surveillance of the Police, and that detection will follow any commission of, or attempt to commit, a crime." Like all policemen, they were empowered to go "in hot pursuit" after criminals and make arrests, but their specialty was investigation, their duties closer to the Victorian police detective than the constable on his beat. Criminal officers were expected to attend the Police Court on a regular basis and make a note of repeat offenders. In this they cooperated closely with the hardworking clerks of the police establishment, who were on the job from 9 A.M. to 5 P.M. every day, and from 6 to 9 P.M. every evening. The clerks were expected to "make searches every day" through both city and county records "of all persons accused of theft, fraud, &c before the Court to ascertain whether they have been formerly punished & whether they have been three times convicted." They had to keep a record of all persons committed to the three city jails, with offense and dates of commitment, "referring from one to another" to keep track of individual offenders as they moved around the city. They had to keep records of persons removed to other jurisdictions. They had to keep track of all persons indicted and brought to trial for felonies at the High Court of Justiciary. And they were expected to stand ready to provide up-to-date crime statistics on a regular basis to the police superintendent as well as the lord provost of Edinburgh, the Sheriff's Office, and the Crown Office. According to one such tabulation, 731 persons were arrested for felonies from January 1827 to December 1828. One quarter of these were women. About half of all the defendants, and two-thirds of the women, were charged with simple theft, that is, theft of items of small value, which did not include breaking and entering. About two-thirds of these came to trial. The most common sentence was thirty days in jail for a first offense, and sixty days for a second offense. It was very easy to cross the line from simple theft to housebreaking, but it was a line well worth avoiding, because the punishment was much greater even if the value of the goods stolen remained the same. Theft aggravated by housebreaking, or by repeated offenses, earned the harsher penalty of transportation to the colonies for seven or fourteen years. Robbery with assault was the least common form of theft, averaging about twelve cases per year. It carried the harshest penalties: defendants were sentenced to transportation for fourteen years or life if the victim recovered from the assault, execution if he did not. "Ordinary" murder, unaccompanied by theft, had, oddly enough, the highest rate of acquittal. Fully half of the two or three cases logged in each year resulted in a verdict of "not guilty" or "not proven." The police clerk's tabulation reinforces the point that the lord advocate knew well: Edinburgh juries were slow to convict in capital cases.

Yet where the police recorded crimes, we may see an economy of makeshifts, just on the wrong side of the line public authorities drew between the "unfortunate" and the "criminal." The murder victim Elizabeth Haldane might have been regarded as "unfortunate," but she had another daughter, Mary Ann Haldane, with a full-fledged criminal record. Mary Ann's first arrest had been at the age of sixteen. She gave her occupation as "hawker," but she was clearly living on the margins, like the young people from the London slums, who when asked by reformers, "What do you do to get your living?" responded, "What we can." Her first trial at the High Court of Justiciary was for theft committed on Saturday, February 24, 1827, at 18 Northumberland Street. This was a very elegant address, but she had not stolen anything from the householder, John Corson, and his family, residing on the upper floors. Instead, she had gone downstairs to the servants' rooms and stolen a gown, muslin hats, and a half-pound box of tea from the laundry. Several of the servants saw her as she came out of their quarters, "carrying something white in her hand," and five of them gave chase. They "apprehended her at the foot of Dundas Street, and brought her back to Mr. Corson's house, and sent for the police." Officer George Foulis came from his house in Canonmills and recognized Haldane at once as "an old offender, she having been repeatedly in the Police Court, accused of theft." Theft was, as Symons had noted, a "gregarious" occupation, for at least two people were needed, one to take the goods and the other to act as lookout and hide the stolen property if anyone gave chase. For that reason Haldane's "great companion," Margaret Finlayson, was arrested at the same time. Aged twenty-four, daughter of a weaver in the West Port, Finlayson was also well known to the police as "an idle character." At the jail Haldane was described as fair haired with blue-gray eyes, fresh complexion, and a round face. She "had been out of service"— that is, unemployed—"for three years past," a sobering reminder that the police treated young people as adults, and expected them to be at full-time work, not school. Mary Ann had probably spent little time in school, as she could not write, though she may have been able to read. She claimed that she and Finlayson "were in Great King Street together selling sticks about three o'clock, and they were again the new Town that evening, about seven o'clock" but she could not say where Finlayson was in between. She further claimed that she had never been in the house in Northumberland Street, and that she certainly had not taken any trunk or any other items, and that she knew nothing of the matter "until laid hold of by two men and three women in Dundas street."

In a case like this, much depended on whether the defendants were first-time thieves or repeat offenders. One of the criminal officers, Sergeant John Stuart, testified that he had known Haldane for about five years and considered her by "habit and repute a thief," and Finlayson an "idle character." Officer Foulis gave similar testimony: the two women were seen "constantly walking about together," he said, "and both of them are very bad characters." They had been in Police Court about a year earlier for stealing three coats from 24 Dublin Street, another New Town address. In that case, it had been Margaret Finlayson who had gone inside, while her partner had waited in the street. That earlier complaint was proved against Finlayson, for the coats were found in her possession, and she was sentenced to sixty days in prison. The charge against Haldane was dismissed: since no witness had seen her with the stolen property, the Crown could not make its case against her. With the Northumberland Street robbery, the situation was reversed, and it was Finlayson who was cleared of all charges, while Haldane had to stand trial. Once again she was lucky, or skillful: even though the servants had seen her "dart past them" from their rooms, and had "caught her at the foot of Dundas Street," the stolen property was not recovered in her possession. For that reason the judge directed the jury to return a verdict of not proven, and Mary Ann Haldane was set free on May 28, 1827.

In the meantime, her friend Margaret Finlayson had been arrested again, for breaking the laundry-room window to a house on Melville Street and pulling out "a white silk or cotton shawl" belonging to a servant. Since Haldane had been incarcerated, Finlayson had been working with sixteen-year-old Elizabeth Paterson, daughter of a gentleman's servant, who did not come up for trial. The broken window ratcheted up the charge from theft to housebreaking. Finlayson was found guilty and sentenced to fourteen years' transportation. By the end of the month Mary Ann Haldane had met the same fate, and since she must have known the difference between housebreaking and theft we may wonder if she did it deliberately. On June 29 she was arrested for stealing a "blue and white checked printed cotton wrapper" from a servant at the house of Dr. Thatcher in Elder Street. She had to wait for trial until the High Court was again in session, and the jury heard her case on November 9, 1827. They found her "unanimously guilty," and she, too, was sentenced to fourteen years' transportation. After almost a year in prison, Mary Ann Haldane left Edinburgh on April 18, 1828. We have no way of knowing if her mother or sisters were allowed, or wished, to see her before she left (Figure 13).

Figure 13. Parliament House in Edinburgh, where the High Court of Justiciary met. From Thomas Shepherd, *Modern Athens*, reproduced by West Port Books, Edinburgh.

Forced removal to the other side of the world for stealing three coats, a gown, and half a pound of tea seems intolerably cruel, particularly since contemporary records make clear that once young people found their way into the criminal justice system, they were unlikely to find their way out. Most expected to be "lagged," or transported, sooner or later, and when enjoined to repent "their evil ways," wrote one observer, "they laughed and shook their heads; and one of them told us not to suppose that their present life was a matter of choice with them, but that it was either steal or rob, or—starve." There were no social welfare programs adequate to deal with the rising crime rate, and the best the Edinburgh judiciary could do was shake its collective head and lament "the immorality of the age." The Edinburgh public appeared to have scant sympathy with those "obnoxious to society," holding them accountable for their actions whatever their ages or circumstances. On April 5, 1828, the *Scotsman* reported what it called "one of the most appalling scenes of juvenile depravity that has come before this court for a number of years." Six girls aged between thirteen and fifteen were brought before the Police Court, together with their landlord, arrested for keeping a disorderly lodging house, probably not so much a brothel as a resort of thieves, "rogues and vagabonds." The girls, "though young," according to the report, "were by no means incipient in crime, for, from the familiar, wholesale sort of way in which they were named and addressed by the Clerk of Court, it appeared that they had been very troublesome, and that they were no strangers" to the inside of the city jail. Three, who came from outside of Edinburgh, were banished from the city; the other three were "admonished and released." The landlord was fined £2, and had to leave £20 with the court, which he would forfeit if arrested again.

But where were the girls to go? "In no other city in Europe, perhaps, is there less employment for the female part of the population than in Edinburgh," wrote William Tait in his analysis of *Magdalenism*. In his view it was a prime cause of crime as well as prostitution. There was little factory work, so that women could find work only as house servants—often in lodging houses—or in the trades relying on hand sewing: "sewers, dressmakers, milliners, bonnet-makers, stay-makers, colourers, book-stitchers, shoe-binders, hat-binders." The average amount women could earn through sewing was 6 shillings per week, assuming constant employment. But there was no reason to make that assumption. There were so many women looking for work that, Tait noted, "the supply of labourers exceeds the demand," and by the "well known" facts of political economy, "the rate of wages inevitably falls." One shop owner in the Lawnmarket paid only 3 pence for a man's shirt, and "How can a woman maintain herself," Tait asked indignantly, "if she is paid so little for her work? A very good sewer can with difficulty make three shirts in two days, and an ordinary hand cannot finish more than one in a day." Even assuming a constant supply of work, the fastest sewers could earn—at best—2s 3d per week, while the less talented would only earn 1s 6d, a sum which puts Mary Ann Haldane's theft of muslin caps and a half pound of tea in perspective. In the absence of any other public institutions, some of the women came to the police to "beg for honest employment," according to the Glasgow chief of police. "A dozen sometimes in a day of these poor things . . . but what can I do?—the factories are all overstocked, the benevolent institutions would not contain one-hundredth of them; besides, they have no characters, and if they had, there is no employment."

Women with no employment wound up on the street, hawking or begging, leading to their arrest, like Peggy Haldane, for "vagrancy" or "infesting the New Town." The laws against vagrancy were at least as harsh as those against theft, and "Suppression of Vagrancy" as significant in police regulations as "Prevention of Crime." Indeed, the two were related, for the Edinburgh Police Establishment followed closely Symons's view that vagrants were criminals waiting to happen. A watchman "may, and should, arrest any one whom he has just to suspect of being about to commit felony," according to police regulations, "any night-walkers who cannot give a good account of themselves—any sturdy beggars and gypsies found encamping on the road side, or upon any other place—any idle persons whom he knows to have no means to live upon, and who will not betake themselves to any labour, trade, or occupation." Watchmen had broad discretion to arrest all such persons and bring them before the Police Court. The *Scotsman*'s crime reporter praised the police in 1828 for "clearing the town," as he put it, "of the inveterate thieves and dissolute characters who followed no lawful calling, and had no means of subsistence."

Did all these arrests really reduce crime, or did they simply shift its location? That was the question raised when the police, in response to complaints by merchants and shop owners, arrested thirty itinerant hawkers who had set up their stalls in the High Street, in February 1829. The hawkers were brought before the Police Court. "Anxious to encourage every person willing to earn a subsistence in an honest way," the magistrate told them, "you have been allowed to remain as long as could possibly be done; but the cumbering of the streets with your stalls is completely against the Police Act, and, in fact, the magistrates have no choice." Though the court "had no intention to enforce the law in a harsh or imperious manner," the stall owners were given one week only to sell off their remaining stock; after that point they would not be allowed to "cumber the streets." A similar policy enacted in 1850 drew protests. "We cannot, for the life of us, conceive what has tempted the head of our police to proceed as he has done in his late system of, what we will venture to call, *ejectments*," argued one writer. Families who had "previously earned a scanty and precarious subsistence by keeping a barrow—as a sort of stall—on the street, in which they hawked whatever might be in season at the time—food, fish, or confectionary" now were subject to fines and imprisonment "if they venture with their barrow on the public streets." True, the streets might look "better and cleaner" but was "the appearance of the streets . . . all we have to show" for the increased crime and destitution caused by "depriving some 200 families of the means of making a miserably poor, but still an honest living?" Even the police could hardly consider "an increase of prisoners of a morning" an improvement. Very probably they did not, but as the Police Court magistrate had said, they "had no choice." That meant enforcing policy in which human "annoyances"—whether criminals, hawkers, vagrants, or drunks— were considered just another urban nuisance, to be picked up and cleared away like garbage or human excrement. The problem was the people were much harder to manage than manure or street lighting. Landlords fined for disorderly houses would just shift to a new location, moving as did the fiddlers on Saturday night, from one disreputable part of town to another. Hawkers would move to more isolated, and thus more dangerous, parts of town. And young people picked up in one part of the city for "infesting the streets" would simply turn up in another part, earning longer and longer sentences, until they were branded "habit and repute" and transported. "Day by day, they had the melancholy spectacle of boys entering on life, placed at their bar," said one High Court judge, after sentencing John MacLeod, age twelve, chair maker, and Alexander Shaw, age fourteen, cabinet maker, to transportation for fourteen years for the theft of a silver hunting watch and gold chain. And he sincerely wished, he went on, "that the large sums expended on missionary and other foreign societies, were applied at home in procuring moral and religious instruction for unfortunate children, neglected, or otherwise deserted, by their natural guardians."

One reason for the large number of children before the bar was that they often stole for adults involved in fencing—no surprise to anyone familiar with *Oliver Twist*—and were more likely to be caught than their older and more experienced mentors in crime. In 1827, nine-year-old William Campbell was arrested for reset of theft, that is, for fencing stolen goods, in a tenement off the Grassmarket. He was described in court records as a beggar from Dundee, and he confessed as soon as he was arrested. On trial for the same offense were the mother and son team Elizabeth M'Donald or Kelly, aged forty-five, and William Kelly, aged twelve. They pleaded not guilty, but it was evident that Elizabeth was the chief instigator, making use of Campbell to protect herself and her son. Though regarded by the prosecution as the "worst offenders," the Kellys were acquitted when the chief witness against them did not appear in court. Campbell was duly found guilty and because of a prior conviction for theft could be transported. One of the judges proposed, however, that Campbell "should suffer the punishment of imprisonment rather than of transportation, because he was a very young boy." The hope was that eighteen months spent incarcerated, "subject to the rules of the house would afford him an opportunity of receiving instruction and being reformed." The governor of the jail was directed "to take pain to procure him some instruction, and to teach him some useful trade." The formal sentence read to nine-year-old William Campbell was that he be imprisoned for the eighteen-month period "and kept at hard labor." Twelve-year-old William Kelly was arrested again the following year for theft, this time without his mother. After that he dropped out of judicial records.

Were there no refuges or resources for young people? we may ask at this point, like Scrooge on the verge of his reformation, and we may expect to hear the echo of the Ghost of Christmas Present: "Are there no prisons? Are there no workhouses?" There were certainly no schools and few jobs. The commissioners of police did put together a committee in 1824 to look into "the Practicability of establishing a House of Refuge in Edinburgh for Male Juvenile Delinquents, and of teaching them a Trade, whereby they may be enabled to gain an honest Livelihood." Their suggestion was a kind of Magdalene Asylum for thirty boys aged twelve to eighteen, intended to keep them hard at work and off the streets, for "confinement of young delinquents" in prison, the committee found, "does not seem to have any effect" as a deterrent. The plan called for a schoolmaster to teach the boys for one hour per day, and also for thirty weaving looms. Weaving seemed an appropriate choice for vocational training, the report explained, because it required no special skill to learn. What the report does not mention is that Scottish weavers were often involved in labor activism, and we may suspect that committee members had in mind the provision of a more docile labor force. The House of Refuge seems to have been met with little enthusiasm and no funding at the time, either as an educational institution or a breeding ground for incipient strikebreakers.

Reformers then, as now, feared that the prisons served only to introduce children to more hardened criminals a year or two older, and lead them further into a life of crime. One habitual offender later recalled his first jail sentence, twenty days for stealing two dozen empty bottles from his employer, a spirit dealer. He was "sad enough the first night in jail," when he found himself in a large room, called the "school," with some thirty or forty other prisoners. But it was like being in a barracks, or on board ship, and "his fellow prisoners were very attentive to him—far more than one could possibly have expected from such a set of *roughs*—and showed him how to sling his hammock." The result was that he formed firm friendships, which lasted in and out of prison. Another man found his life companion in jail, and the two of them formed a partnership in theft. And have you married her? he was asked. "Married!" he replied, "what need o'that? We've robbed thegether, we've been in jail thegether, ay, and we've starved thegether; and that wi' us is far stronger than a' the marriages since the world began." To prevent those associations, the Edinburgh police generally placed children in a separate section of the jail, away from the adult offenders.

Yet there seems little point in romanticizing the criminals either. The dangerous classes appear to have been most dangerous to their near neighbors, those slightly above them in the social and economic scale. Poor-on-poor crime was much more prevalent than the master criminals stealing jewels from gentleman's houses so beloved of later Victorian detective fiction. Convicted pickpockets interviewed by London police commissioners estimated that "they must steal about six pocket-handkerchiefs or things of the same value" in order "to live," that is, to gain money for food and lodging, so that "a career of depredation" became "more eligible to them than a livelihood of honest industry." Most of the money went into the hands of the fences, who were, as we have seen, hard to convict. It was much easier to steal those six pocket-handkerchiefs from people of their own social background, from servants, or wives of small tradesmen, or from women involved in the sewing trades, than it was from the gentry. The thousands of pounds lost due to property theft each year fell disproportionately on those least able to afford it.

Certainly Margaret Sudhope Leslie was justly indignant when a trunk containing her own clothes and those of her four-year-old son was stolen from her one-room flat in Greenside. Her husband was a painter serving in the carpenter's crew on board ship in the West Indies, and she earned her bread by doing washing in gentlemen's houses. On the evening of Monday, April 6, 1829, she locked her door, and, leaving her son with her mother-in-law, went to work at the home of Adam Black, the bookseller and publisher, in London Street in the New Town. She did not mention to anyone that she was leaving, but most of her neighbors knew she went to Black's on Monday evenings, in order to be there early Tuesday morning for washing day. In this instance, she stayed through Wednesday morning, when a neighbor came to tell her that "her house had been entered and the trunk carried away." She reported her loss to the police, giving an itemized list of all the articles stolen, but heard nothing more for about two weeks. During that time she left her lodgings in Greenside and moved in with her in-laws, who lived on the north back of the Canongate, the safer and more respectable side of the district.

On April 22 she heard from one of her brothers-in-law that a woman named Agnes Brown (no relation to Janet) had been seen wearing one of her missing dresses. Brown had also been seen with Thomas Nesbit, whose parents lived next door to the flat in Greenside. Leslie and her two brothers-in-law patrolled the streets from 6 P.M. looking for Brown and Nesbit, and finally encountered them on the High Street about midnight. The brothers-in-law ran to get the police—presumably leaving Margaret Leslie on the High Street—and returned with Sergeant John Stuart, who arrested Nesbit and Brown and brought them to the Police Office. Brown was, indeed, wearing Margaret Leslie's dress, already carefully described in the police report, and the rest of the stolen articles were found in Brown's and Nesbit's lodgings in Castle Hill, where they had "cohabitated together" as "husband and wife."

The theft was a particularly thoughtless one. Margaret Leslie had always believed her neighbors the elder Nesbits to be "decent people," and their son Thomas, aged twenty, "a quiet sober lad." He gave "blacksmith" as his occupation, but had been most recently employed at the Caledonian Theater "in lighting and extinguishing the gas Lamps and shifting the Scenes." His father, a saddler, testified that his son had been "behaving very ill for some time past," and had not slept at home "for about six weeks preceding his apprehension." His mother was "more indulgent to him during that time," and so Thomas would visit her when his father was at work, telling her only "that he slept on the High Street with a companion." On his recent visit, his mother testified, "in the course of conversation she mentioned to him about Mrs. Leslies house having been entered; and he was sorry he said, to hear it"; at that time she "had not the most distant suspicion that her son was guilty." For his part, Thomas was clearly terrified to find himself on the wrong side of the law. On his getting to the police office, Stuart testified, "he began to cry," and asked the officer "whether he would advise him to plead guilty," but Stuart "told him that he could not give him any advice." In the end Thomas chose to protest his innocence. Yes, he had "known the prisoner Brown about three or four months and became acquainted with her upon the Streets she being a girl of the Town, and he used sometimes to visit her in her Lodgings." No, he had not lived with her as husband and wife in the lodgings where the stolen property was found, but had slept at home every night with his parents in Greenside. No, he knew nothing about any stolen property and had not been concerned with stealing anything.

Unfortunately, we do not know the end of the story: whether Thomas got off, whether his parents took him back, whether he kept or was dismissed from his job at the Caledonian Theater. But it is likely he came to a happier ending than Agnes Brown, age seventeen. She had once been employed as servant to a linen draper but had been out of service for the past fifteen months, and could give no satisfactory account of how she earned a living. Nor would she "give any satisfactory account of her residence," according to Stuart, but only indicated that she lived in lodging houses, "saying that she was a night here and a night there." She, too, protested her innocence. She testified that she "had no concern in breaking into any house in Edinburgh or the neighbourhood and taking the articles." When asked how she came to be wearing a dress reported as stolen, she declared "that she met a man late in the street one night . . . who was carrying all the articles, and other articles of the same kind. That she does not know his name and never saw him before to her knowledge, and does not know where he is to be found." He told her "he was going out of town and had occasion for money, and they went together into a public house, which she thinks was in a close off the High Street, but which she could not point out, and she there purchased all the articles now shewn her" for about 25 shillings. She and this mysterious man parted on the street, and no, she did "not know of any person who saw them together." Where had she obtained so much money? she was asked, for witnesses testified that they had never seen her with more than a shilling or two. How on earth had she come by 25 shillings to buy the clothes? "From an acquaintance named McGregor," she replied, "who was a clerk in a wareroom somewhere about the Cowgate and who has now gone to the Highlands." No, she did not know "where he is now to be found," and no, "no other person knew of her having the money." And "when she received the articles she had no suspicion that they had been stolen otherwise she would not have purchased them." It seems likely that Brown, at least, spent some time in prison, and we can only hope she stayed out of the criminal justice system thereafter. For if Sergeant John Stuart could have given her advice, it would have been what everyone knew: that repeated apprehensions for theft would lead to a character as "habit and repute" a thief. As many as two-thirds of the prisoners in jail in 1827–1828 had prior arrests. For many of them, transportation was only a matter of time, for three convictions—three strikes, we might say—and the felon was out.

The system therefore provided a strong incentive for offenders to avoid a conviction at all costs, in much the same way that modern insurance policies provide incentives for drivers to contest that first speeding ticket. Even one ticket, particularly for a new driver, can push up the cost of car insurance by thousands of dollars, and even one appearance before the Police Court marked the difference between a "good" and "bad" character. Catherine Douglas, an orphan, aged sixteen, had always had a good character, according to her employer, Ann Calder, a respectable married woman who kept a lodging house for students. But Douglas was arrested on March 27, 1830, and charged with theft of small articles of clothing and linen from Calder's house. The arresting officer was again Sergeant John Stuart, and he and his colleague had no trouble apprehending her as she headed south toward the Edinburgh city limits with her younger sister. After dropping off the sister, the two men took Douglas to the Police Office on the High Street. She readily confessed her theft to the police lieutenant on duty, who directed that Douglas be put in a cell in the women's jail, upstairs. These were detention cells, where women were kept while awaiting a hearing at the Police Court. Since Douglas was arrested on Saturday, she would have to wait until the following week for her hearing. Conveying her to her cell was really the turnkey's job, but he was unavailable, and so Officer Stuart took her upstairs and brought her to cell number 45. It was the first room on the right off the main passage, separated from cell 46 by a wooden partition from floor to ceiling.

At this point the accounts diverge. Stuart testified that he stood at all times by the door of cell 45, and did not approach Douglas or the bed. Douglas asked him to "go for her mistress to see whether she would take her home," and Stuart agreed to speak to Ann Calder. She asked for water, and he "took her to the water cistern" just on the other side of her cell, "where there were some jugs, and she filled one of them for herself, and took it into the room." He then "locked the door." The whole interchange had lasted "between five and ten minutes." Douglas, however, testified that after leading her to the cell, Stuart had closed the door behind him. He had taken off her bonnet, thrown her down on the bed three times, and without her consent had "had connection with her." She had never had intercourse with a man before, and blood on her shift had come from the rape. After that, Stuart had left, locking her in. When the turnkey came, Douglas was in tears. She told the turnkey that Stuart had raped her, later making a formal complaint to the lieutenant on duty.

Rape was a serious offense, but one that was notoriously difficult to prove. There were seldom eyewitnesses, and Edinburgh juries disliked convicting for rape almost as much as for murder. The initial impression of the procurator fiscal, Archibald Scott, was "that it was doubtful whether the charge was well founded." Indeed, he noted, "it was rather thought that Stuart was not guilty." First, Douglas had a motive for lying: she had been accused of theft, and might have as "her object to incite compassion, in order to escape with a mild punishment, for her own offence." Her main witness was Mary Lockhart, who had been in the next cell and claimed to have heard her crying after the assault; she further claimed that Douglas had told her about the rape on the night it occurred, that is, the night of March 27. But Lockhart had an "indifferent character," Scott noted, and "all such characters" had a desire "to injure Stuart, on account of his activity and usefulness." In contrast to the women was the "good character of Stuart," a police officer of twelve years' standing, "who had for many years been well known for his uniform propriety & decency, and respectability of conduct to all persons connected with the criminal department in this county, and also his attention and kindness" to his wife and eight children. To the modern reader, the most convincing argument was the one Scott put last: "it seemed hardly credible," he wrote, "that any experienced & intelligent Police Officer should be so imprudent as to attempt to commit a rape in an apartment in the Police Office," when the next cell, 46, was already occupied and "separated only by a slight partition of wood."

But we should not be as quick as the procurator fiscal to take Stuart's side, for there is no more reason to romanticize the police than the offenders. Policemen were dismissed from their jobs for a range of offenses, including drunkenness, dereliction of duty, and outright theft, and at least one police officer was involved in both reset of theft and murder, as we will see. Though it was plausible that Douglas, perhaps on the advice of more experienced women prisoners, viewed a rape accusation as a way of escaping conviction, it was also plausible that she was telling the truth. That was the view of the lawyer for the Crown Office, and believing the case "was likely to attract public attention," he did not want to show Stuart "more than usual indulgence." The case was duly placed before the lord advocate, who decided that the investigation should go forward. Stuart was formally indicted and imprisoned, awaiting trial.

What had begun as a minor skirmish in the border wars fought to define criminality in Edinburgh became a very public conflict. The usual relationship between miscreant and police officer was set on its head, as Catherine Douglas was redefined from accused to victim, and Stuart from witness to accused. As word spread through newspapers, broadsides, and word of mouth, new witnesses came forward with testimony to blacken the character of both accused and accuser. Two women claimed Stuart had raped them, too, when they were in the Police Office overnight; two other witnesses, one of whom was a night watchman, claimed that they had seen Douglas having "connection" with men in disorderly houses and back alleys. Each claim had to be patiently investigated and, eventually, discounted. The night watchman was later dismissed from the Police Establishment, and though no reason was given, it may well be for lying during an investigation. What the stories show is how easily rumors swirled around police investigations, how readily supposed witnesses came forward claiming to know something pertinent, and how much time and energy went into substantiating or discrediting their stories. The testimony for this case ran to over 250 pages, "longer than was necessary upon the merits," Archibald Scott noted, "but it was thought proper to make other inquiries to ascertain the character of Catherine Douglas and test the truth of her statements, so that a judgment may be formed of her credibility."

The chief witnesses for the prosecution were Mary Lockhart and Margaret Fraser, the women who had spent the most time with Douglas. Had they seen or heard anything? Had she confided in them? Or—as the defense believed—had they encouraged her or helped her to fabricate her story? Lockhart, as we have seen, initially backed up Douglas's complaint. Margaret Fraser had heard Douglas tell the turnkey "of the usage she [Douglas] had got from Stuart." Both women had subsequently been released, and it took several weeks for the police to locate them again. During that interval, that first complaint to the turnkey, dealt with in-house, had become a full-scale investigation into a capital crime. It is likely that the gravity of the situation was impressed on both witnesses, as they made their formal declarations before the procurator fiscal, and neither chose to confirm Douglas's story. Margaret Fraser testified that she, personally, had heard nothing of any assault. She had slept in the same cell as Douglas the following night—that is the night after both the alleged rape and Douglas's formal complaint—and "she particularly asked her whether Stuart had had connection with her and she said that he had not and she repeated the same statements" on succeeding nights. Fraser believed that accusing Stuart may have been Mary Lockhart's idea, for Douglas told her "she would not have told any thing about it if it was not the woman who was in the next cell who had wished her to tell it." But Lockhart, when questioned, vehemently denied that: she had never advised "Douglas to tell that Stuart had had connection with her or recommend her to say anything about anything that had passed in the cells with them." She had, in fact, known nothing about it until the rumors had spread through the prison the next day. She was "positively certain that Douglas during the whole night between Saturday the 27 and Sunday the 28 of March" never told her that Stuart "had had connection with her." On the contrary," Fraser said, Douglas had told her "that nothing of that kind had been going on."

Douglas was thus left high and dry by her former prison companions, the same ones who, by her own account, had been so supportive when she lay crying in her cell on Saturday night. In her own formal declaration, she persisted in testifying that over the course of the few nights she had shared a cell with Margaret Fraser, she had had "different conversations with her about what had happened and that she always told Fraser distinctly that Stuart had had connection with her." She never told Fraser, she declared, "that it was the woman in the next cell who had advised her to accuse Stuart," and "in point of fact that woman (that is Lockhart) never did give . . . her any such advice." All of which she solemnly swore to be the truth. But the case for the prosecution increasingly came to look more like the case for the defense. This was certainly true of the testimony by the police surgeon, Alexander Black. He had examined Douglas on Sunday, the day after the alleged rape, and though he had concluded that "some person had had connection with Douglas," he "certainly did not think that if for the first time"—as she had claimed—"it could have been so recently as the preceding Saturday." He had "found not the slightest appearance of injury of any kind" to indicate that she had been forcibly restrained, thrown down on the bed three times, or raped. The blood on her shift, he believed, was her menstrual blood, as she admitted she had been wearing it since her last menstrual flow.

The High Court of Justiciary heard the case on June 21, 1830, by which time Stuart had spent nearly three months in prison. He was therefore relieved and gratified when the presiding judge directed the jury "that as they had heard the female (a convicted thief) with whom the charge originated, repeatedly perjure herself before them, it was their duty to find a verdict, not of 'not proven,' but of 'not guilty.'" The Police Establishment passed new regulations ensuring that female prisoners were accompanied at all times by a female turnkey when in the presence of a male officer. Catherine Douglas went home to her mistress, Ann Calder, who seems to have been completely bewildered first by the theft and then by the subsequent judicial proceedings. Douglas had always been a very good girl, Calder said, and the missing items were "of trifling value." If only Douglas had come to her first, this whole affair could have been avoided.

In a fitting end to this very Dickensian chapter, Catherine Douglas was rescued from the fate of the convicted thief by private kindness rather than by governmental policy. Mary Ann, Peggy, and Elizabeth Haldane were not so fortunate. No reformer bemoaned the sad fate of "inveterate thieves" who were cleared from the streets, but loss of illegal income could prove just as disastrous to their families as a loss of a barrow on the High Street. Whatever the impact Mary Ann Haldane's transportation in April 1828 had on her own future, it is likely that it acted as a kind of economic domino effect on her mother and sister. At the time of her last arrest, Mary Ann and Elizabeth had been living together in Castle Bank, and it may well have been the loss of her daughter's earnings that pushed Elizabeth out of her lodgings, into Hare's stable and to her death. Likewise, her mother's death may have pushed Peggy Haldane into Burke's apparent hospitality. She had been sentenced to thirty days for her first vagrancy offense, in June 1827. On her second offense in January 1828, she was sentenced to sixty days. Her arrests corresponded to increased efforts on the part of the police to sweep the streets of anyone found loitering, or vagrant, or idle. Given those efforts, her sister's and mother's disappearance, and her own history, it was likely that she would end up "infesting the streets" again. If arrested, she would spend anywhere from three to six months in prison. By the summer of 1828, then, her options when it came to makeshifts had dwindled, making her all the more vulnerable to predators of all kinds. Any offer of food or drink might have seemed a welcome alternative to another arrest for vagrancy or begging, and Burke's room a far safer place to lie insensible in than the street. This time there really was no one left to "institute inquiries for one so lorn," as *Murderers of the Close* had put it, and so the Edinburgh streets were cleared—permanently—of two of their "nuisances" through murder.

Chapter 7

Anonymous Subjects

"Effy the Cinder Gatherer," "Old Woman and Grandson," "Woman Murdered by Hare"

B Y LATE SPRING, THE AGRICULTURAL SEASON HAD STARTED and the West Port was crowded with immigrants. That meant fewer, rather than more, opportunities for murder, as the house in Tanner's Close filled with lodgers. Yet Burke and Hare took their opportunities where they could find them, like the cinder gatherer whose name, Burke thought, was Effy. "She was in the habit of selling small pieces of leather to him, as he was a cobbler," which "she gathered about the coach-works." That did not keep him from taking her "into Hare's stable," and giving her "whisky to drink until she was drunk." She lay down in the straw and fell asleep, and they "then laid a cloth over her." They suffocated her "as they did the others," and brought her to Robert Knox's dissecting rooms in Surgeon's Square. Her cadaver sold for £10, slightly higher than usual; perhaps it was in especially good shape, or perhaps Knox had particular need of it.

In late June—around midsummer, as Burke remembered—an old woman came from Glasgow with her grandson, "a dumb boy," about twelve years old, "who seemed to be weak in his mind." Once lodged at Margaret Hare's house, the woman "got a dram" of whiskey, and fell asleep, and "he and Hare suffocated her," removed her clothes, and covered her with the bedding. The boy, in the meantime, "was sitting at the fire in the kitchen," and Burke carried him inside to the bed under which his grandmother lay. The room may have been the one shared by Burke and M'Dougal, for Burke speaks of carrying the boy "ben to the room," meaning from an outer chamber to an inner one; that description would apply much better to the small box bedroom than to the large open area used by regular lodgers. If so, both M'Dougal and Margaret Hare must have known what was going on. The men may have given the boy some whiskey, too, and waited for him to fall asleep; they then "murdered him in the same manner, and *laid* him alongside of his grandmother."

During the trial, the rumor circulated that Burke had murdered the boy himself, "almost charitably," by setting him on his knee, and breaking his back. "He describes his murder as the one that lies most heavily upon his heart," according to *West Port Murders*, "and says that he is constantly haunted by the recollection of the piteous manner in which the boy looked in his face." But this is a most unlikely story. Burke was not a large man, and the bones of even a small, undernourished twelve-year-old would have been very hard to break. The vertebrae, as Robert Knox could have told the *West Port* author, are very strong and flexible, designed and cushioned by muscle to withstand all but the most traumatic injuries. And why should Burke have done any such thing? Why choose an ugly, bloody, painful, protracted, and almost certainly noisy murder, likely to arouse comment when the body was examined, over a quick, quiet, easy one, tried and true in its results? It seems that once again we have a story "of a peculiarly touching description" shaped by the desire to wring the greatest possible pathos out of the murders. Burke maintained in his confession that the boy, like his grandmother, was murdered in the same manner as the others, and his is the most plausible account.

The bodies were left undisturbed for an hour, perhaps to be sure that no one raised the alarm. They were then packed into a herring-barrel. Burke was very specific that the barrel was dry, with no brine in it. He and Hare put the barrel in the stable, and the next morning transferred it to Hare's cart. To their alarm, the horse refused to draw the cart more than a little way through the Grassmarket, so that they had to get a porter with a barrow to transport it the rest of the way. Hare and the porter took the barrel up to Surgeon's Square, with Burke going on ahead, "as he was afraid something would happen." They made it to Knox's dissecting rooms, but rigor had set in, and "the students and them had hard work" to get the cadavers out, they "being so stiff and cold." They received £16 for the two bodies. Hare must have been spooked by the horse refusing to draw the cart, for he took it to the tanyard behind his house, and shot it. Hare stuffed the two large holes in the horse's shoulder with cotton, Burke said, "and covered over with a piece of another horse's skin to prevent them being discovered." Why this was important Burke never explained. Perhaps Hare was afraid that their secret would somehow be betrayed through the balky horse. Perhaps he was superstitious and feared that the horse's refusal to carry the cadaver was some kind of sign. Or perhaps, more prosaically, he simply thought the horse had outlived its usefulness, and it was time to purchase another. Burke's detail about covering up the bullet holes is an interesting touch, for there was surely nothing illegal about shooting one's own horse. Perhaps the murderers did not wish to call attention to the fact that they had a gun.

Later that month, Burke and M'Dougal went to visit M'Dougal's father in Falkirk. Burke remembered that it was around the time of the anniversary of the Battle of Bannockburn, June 24. When Burke left, he said, "he knew Hare was in want of money; his things were all in pawn." Since this would have been soon after the double murders, it suggests that Hare was going through money very fast, either spending it himself or sending it away. On his return, Burke found that Hare had plenty of money and asked him "if he had been doing any business?" Hare responded that he "had been doing nothing," but Burke did not believe him. He checked with Knox, who told him "that Hare had brought a subject." Hare, confronted with this testimony, confessed that he "fell in with a woman drunk in the street at the West Port. He took her into his house and murdered her himself, and sold her to Dr. Knox's assistants for £8."

This doleful catalog of people, who trusted Burke and Hare and paid with it for their lives, highlights once again the inexorable demands of the body trade. What did Knox and his associates do with these anonymous subjects? What was it that drove the price of these most human of raw materials so high? What made cadavers so important?

The answer lies in the structure of anatomical teaching, the messy, smelly business of turning the gory slashing stab wounds of the beginning student into the precise, delicate incisions of the advanced dissector. Anatomy was—and is—a labor-intensive, and cadaver-intensive, subject to learn. "A knowledge of the anatomy of the human frame," Robert Knox wrote in his textbook, *The Edinburgh Dissector*, could "be best acquired" by what amounted to the functional equivalent of a modern laboratory course: attending "the lectures of an experienced anatomist," and participating in "actual dissections in practical rooms." Knox offered the first of these, a "full and complete course" of lectures "on human anatomy, in all its details," on Tuesdays and Thursdays, November through April. It was his most popular course, attracting about four hundred students per year. This was too many to fit into his lecture room at one time, so he offered two sets of lectures, at 11 A.M. and 1 P.M. A smaller number of students carried out dissections in the practical anatomy. Either Knox or William Fergusson demonstrated the anatomy of the soft parts of the body—that is, the muscles, blood vessels, and viscera—at 9 A.M. daily. The dissecting rooms were open for student use thereafter until 4 P.M., and were under the supervision of an assistant while Knox lectured. The practical class required an additional 3 guinea fee to pay for the cadaver, over and above the class fee of 3 guineas. It fulfilled the requirement that the student had been "actually engaged in the dissection of the human body," necessary to obtain any formal certification as surgeon. Knox also offered advanced students a three-month course on surgical anatomy, which he taught himself, followed by a three-month course on operative surgery, taught by William Fergusson. These additional courses were widely regarded as imperative for any practicing surgeon.

Knox thus followed the example of many successful Edinburgh lecturers in offering courses for students of a range of abilities and interests, with many more students attending his lectures than his practical dissection class. This is an important point, for both contemporary observers and later writers have assumed that any cadavers delivered by Burke and Hare would have ended up in front of a class of four hundred students. As Knox's biographers have pointed out, he was hardly likely to knowingly exhibit a murder victim in front of so many witnesses. In fact, though, he was not likely to exhibit any fresh, whole cadaver in front of so large a crowd, where the detail would be visible only to those in the front row. Lecturers typically used skeletons and anatomical preparations to illustrate their presentations, reserving whole cadavers for practical dissecting class and their own research. If Knox followed the common practice, only a comparatively select group of students would have seen any of Knox's cadavers during the fateful period of the Burke and Hare murders. And the cadavers themselves—stretched out on a table, shoulders or hips raised on blocks, head hanging down and limbs positioned with hooks—would have revealed little or nothing of their origins.

Why did medical students need all this anatomical instruction? Could they not study books, or illustrations, or wax models? These questions were asked and answered by the London physician Thomas Southwood Smith, in his 1824 essay "Use of the Dead to the Living." "The basis of all medical and surgical knowledge is anatomy," he wrote. "There can be no rational medicine, and no safe surgery" without it. Since "the organs on which all the important functions of the human body depend are concealed from view," he went on, "there is no possibility of ascertaining their situation and connections, much less their nature and operation, without inspecting the interior of this curious and complicated machine." For that reason the most knowledgeable and humane medical practitioners were those with the most dissecting experience. An "enlightened physician and skillful surgeon," according to Smith, "are in the daily habit of administering to their fellow men more real and unquestionable good, than is communicated . . . by any other class of human beings to another." What made it possible for them to do so—what separated them from their ignorant brethren, more deadly to the community than plague, in Smith's view—was their knowledge of anatomy based on dissection. "Naming parts first, then describing, then dissecting them," as a prominent surgeon explained, "dissecting them again and again in different directions, and in a variety of subjects; dissecting, till names and parts are rightly associated in his mind, till he recollects, and can represent with ease . . . all their relations to each other . . . till, by placing his finger on any point of the body, he can name the parts which lie within": that was the foundation of medical progress.

Smith pointed to the preceding fifty years of medical and surgical advances to support his case. Diagnosis of diseases of the epigastric region—stomach, liver, small and large intestines—had improved dramatically, due to a better understanding of the anatomical connections among the parts. Arterial aneurism—a bulge in the artery, prone to rupture—had previously been fatal, but had been transformed by modern surgeons into a treatable condition. Amputation, once the scourge of the battlefield, had also been tamed: "not more than one person in twenty loses his life in consequence of the operation" when performed in hospitals, and "in private practice, where many circumstances favor its success, it is computed that 95 persons out of 100 recover from it, when it is performed at a proper time, and in a proper manner." These statistics may still sound horrific to a modern reader, especially when "favorable circumstances" referred to operations performed without anesthesia or antisepsis, with patients strapped down to the operating table and not quite insensible from wine or opium. But for many conditions from cancer to compound fracture, surgery offered the only possibility for the patient's survival, and precisely in those circumstances, skill with a knife could make all the difference. "All incisions, more especially through the skin, the most sensible part of the animal machine," wrote the Edinburgh surgeon Robert Liston, "should be effected with rapidity, and in such a way as to give as little pain and shock to the nervous system as possible." To be able to do that, students had to spend many hours in the dissecting room, for "it is only when we have acquired dexterity on the dead subject," said Liston forcefully, "that we can be justified in interfering with the living." The London surgeon Charles Averill agreed, deploring the fact that so few British students learned to operate by practicing on dead bodies. "The ultimate benefit of any surgical operation must, of necessity, depend greatly on the dexterity of the operator. . . . The importance therefore to the student, of actual practice on the dead body, can not be too highly estimated." This was true whether he expected to treat private patients, or charity patients in public hospitals. "The infliction of unnecessary pain," as Liston put it, "through want of adroitness in the use of instruments, and consequent protraction of the operative procedure—the hazarding in the slightest degree the safety of any one who puts confidence in us, and entrusts to us his life, or of one who, as in public practice, is, by chance, and without the means of appeal, thrown upon our care—cannot by any means be palliated or defended—and is, in point of fact, highly criminal."

Often the skill of the surgeon consisted in knowing when not to operate, and here, again, was a use of the dead to the living. The difficulties involved in the operation for inguinal hernia, wrote Averill breezily, "have been much exaggerated. . . . Two or three dissections of hernia, and having been a witness to an operation for this disorder, will do more to instruct the student, than the longest lessons and most minute explanations." But that did not mean that the condition itself was easy to diagnose and treat, for hernia could appear in a variety of forms, from "inconvenient complaint, attended with no evil consequences whatever," to one "which may prove fatal in a few hours," when the protruded membrane became blocked and infected. "The disease itself occurs in numerous situations," Smith pointed out; "it may be confounded with various diseases," like most abdominal complaints; "it may require, without the loss of a single moment, a most important and delicate operation; and it may appear to demand this operation, while the performance of it may really be not only useless, but highly pernicious." The surgeon examining the abdomen required skill and experience with "the parts which lie within," in order to make the correct diagnosis, and make it quickly enough to save the patient. Only a thorough understanding of anatomy, based on repeated dissections, could convey that skill.

Indeed, we can see the benefit of the dead to the living in one of Robert Knox's own contributions to medical practice. In October 1827, he took from the neck of an anonymous female subject "A remarkable Tumour . . . coinciding with one in the Edinburgh Infirmary of which a drawing has been taken." As he explained in more detail, "The situation and external appearance of the tumor resembled in a very remarkable manner that of a patient in the Royal Infirmary of Edinburgh. The case was attended with great difficulty, and was generally supposed to be an aneurism" of the carotid artery. Only within the previous twenty years had surgeons discovered how to cut and ligature this vessel, and though the operation had, according to Charles Averill, "been performed many times with success," it still required the utmost skill to avoid hemorrhage or wounds to the jugular vein. Slightly over half of the patients who underwent the operation were pronounced cured, a favorable rate by surgical standards of the day, but just under a third of them died. For a tumor, such an operation was worse than useless. Indeed, it might well prove a fatal mistake. "The dissection therefore of the dead subject was peculiarly interesting," Knox continued; so was the anatomical specimen he preserved from it, as it demonstrated that the "state of the arteries . . . would have rendered an operation . . . a very hazardous undertaking." The "patient in the Infirmary was dismissed a good deal relieved but without any operation having been attempted." Knox's "female subject" had probably saved the patient's life. No clearer example could be found of the benefit of anatomical dissection for the living patient.

Even laypeople seem to have accepted the value of anatomical dissection that was clearly connected to medical treatment. Autopsies in both private practice and in public hospitals were fairly routine in both London and Edinburgh practice, and occasioned little comment. Smith argued that such autopsies served a valuable educational purpose for the whole community, not just medical students. When he began practicing in a public dispensary, he found at first that friends and family objected to autopsies, but "by reasoning with the poor," he said, "and explaining to them the importance of such inspection, I could generally succeed in gaining their consent; ultimately I found very little difficulty, and it was always greatly lessened by allowing the friends to be present." They could see exactly what was going on, which they attended to "with great calmness and interest"; and Smith "recollected no instance of a relative or friend having been present at such an examination, who did not become convinced by it of its usefulness and importance." Indeed, "in very many instances I went away, receiving the warmest thanks of the people, for what I had done." Smith, as an advocate for dissection, may have been inclined to exaggerate its acceptance among families of the deceased, but it may also have been true that their presence at autopsies added to the "decorum," and reduced "indelicacy and levity," in the examination of the body. In any case Smith was convinced "that in the state of mind at present prevailing in the British public, the poorer classes are as much open to conviction as those above them, and perhaps more so; that they are quite able to perceive the reasonableness of the measure if it were properly represented; and that their feeling is so good, that they would ultimately acquiesce in it." The same good effects were observed by an Irish surgeon who decided, when he first opened his dissecting rooms, "as the thing was known to all the persons employed in the neighbourhood," that "the best way to carry on his anatomical pursuits was to leave the door open, that the public might come in and look at his dissections and attend his lectures; and the consequence was, that a great number of porters and ostlers, and the poorer people came in to his lectures; and after they were finished, he took the opportunity of pointing out to them the structure of the body, and the importance of this being known, &c; the effect produced was, that the whole lower orders around became so interested and so favourably disposed to dissection, that they brought him bodies themselves." By being brought into the process, the patient population could also claim oversight of how the cadavers were used; this benefited the anatomical establishment, too, by deflecting rumors of improper traffic in dead bodies.

But these men were unusual in their advocacy of what we might call community-based dissection, the recognition that anatomists had obligations to the dead of whom they made use, and to the neighborhoods from which cadavers were drawn. Most anatomists, Knox among them, preferred to make "these matters as little public as possible." Certainly they did not open their establishments to families of the deceased, unless those families had a warrant, as we have seen. For anatomy to be dignified with the name of science, they believed, the dissecting room had to be treated as a laboratory, cadavers as scientific commodities like saws and scalpels, solvents and substrates. Who asked the chemist to account for his reagents? Or required the physicist to seek permission for his magnets and copper wire? Why then should Edinburgh anatomists concern themselves with public opinion, what they considered the prejudices of the multitude? Surely it was safer to shroud their practices in "secrecy and mystery," to bar the door to laymen and concentrate on the work at hand.

For the work at hand required students to leave behind their religious beliefs in the sanctity of burial, and their superstitious fear of dead bodies, as they crossed the threshold of the dissecting rooms. Every October, a few weeks before the semester started, Knox began to get ready for classes. He had the green felt repaired for his dissecting tables and purchased instruments, spirits, and salt. He also purchased from four to six cadavers from his reliable suppliers. His subjects were nearly all anonymous, acquired without concern for their provenance and subsequently discarded without burial. The very term "subject," like Burke's and Hare's "shot," distanced the cadaver from its human origins. Medical student pranks reinforced this distance. Anatomy students stole fingers from skeletons, or poked holes in jars with preparations, so that the alcohol evaporated. They collected body parts and played macabre jokes. These were all psychological mechanisms necessary, perhaps, to remove the traditional reverence, and traditional distaste, students might feel on encountering a cadaver. They also marked clearly the line separating those who had been initiated into the rituals of anatomical training, and those who had not. We may wonder if students crossed that line more readily because the subjects were anonymous, that is, had been deprived of the most basic individual identity; or because they were clearly from a different social and economic class, as the calluses on their hands and feet bore witness. And we may also wonder whether, in adapting to cadavers, students realized they were moving from presumably more-or-less law-abiding lives to frequent, persistent, illegal activity.

The first set of body parts introduced to students was the skeleton, the foundation of any anatomy course. Frederick John Knox explained, in his manual *The Anatomist's Instructor*, the difficulties in preparing "the *perfect* adult skeleton" for use in lectures. The subject's age had to be "above twenty, and not exceeding forty," he wrote, and the bones had to be "free from any pathological condition." It was best if the subject had died of "some lingering disease," that would cause no trauma to the bones. The most usual procedure for removing all skin and muscle was maceration, soaking in a closed tub, for between six weeks and two months. Since, "in Great Britain, in the open air, without the assistance of any artificial heat," this could only be carried out in the summer, lecturers had to acquire the cadaver by late spring if they wished to have it ready by the start of the semester. Once the macerating process was completed, Frederick Knox continued, "the bones must now be collected, with great care and patience, from amongst the putrid remains; and, indeed, this will require to be done by a person perfectly acquainted with all the bones of the body, so that he may name each as it turns up to him, and place them immediately in dishes of pure water, each section in a separate vessel; by this means he will be quite certain when he has got the entire skeleton." Each piece then had to be carefully cleaned and dried, so that they all could be assembled into an articulated skeleton, "by which is meant," as Robert Knox explained to his students, "the bones connected together by means of iron or brass wire, and suspended in a frame." It seems likely that Robert and Frederick Knox together prepared their first skeleton in 1824, but by 1829 they employed a skeleton maker, George Stewart Campbell, who conveniently resided in nearby High School Yards. They supplied the bones, as well as the cork and the wire to string them together; Campbell supplied the labor and skill.

Students really needed several skeletons to learn the anatomy of the bones properly, Knox wrote in *The Edinburgh Dissector*. The first skeleton should be articulated, made "from a set of bones which have been simply macerated," and which showed no signs of disease. "The articular surfaces must be entire, untouched," Knox went on, "and no artificial means used to whiten or polish the texture." Ideally students should be also able to study a skeleton with its own ligaments—called the "natural skeleton"—but because the ligaments changed appearance when dried, the natural skeleton was less useful for teaching purposes. There were other ways in which the prepared skeleton inevitably differed from natural, living bone, most notably in one of Robert Knox's favorite parts of the body, the spinal column, "which combines lightness with solidity and flexibility," and "serves to support the head and chest. It is the seat of all the motions of the trunk, of which it transmits the weight to the pelvis. It lodges and protects the spinal marrow and the membranes which invest it. It gives passage to the spinal nerves and to many vessels. It affords insertion to numerous muscles and ligaments, both anteriorly and posteriorly." Unfortunately the remarkable "elasticity and flexibility" of the spine was lost in the articulated skeleton, because the "pieces of cork, putty &c" could not be made to behave like the natural cartilage that connected the vertebrae. Still, Knox said reassuringly, students would be well able to see the beauty of the spinal column for themselves on examining "the fresh bones in the dissecting room." Perhaps Effy, or the old woman, or her grandson, provided those fresh bones.

Using the spine as his base, Knox took his students through the thorax, "composed of an assemblage of bones and cartilages." He did not linger over the bones of the thorax, however, because "It has always appeared to us," he told his students, "that it is here where the teacher is least aided by his museum in conveying to the student a proper idea of the thorax as a whole," because the ribs gave little indication of the size, extent, or arrangement of the thoracic cavity. For that reason "The articulated skeleton conveys an erroneous idea of the physiology of the region," he wrote, "and the *form* alone is correctly represented."

From the thorax Knox moved back up the spinal column to the head, or cranium, "a spheroid, . . . placed at the upper extremity of the trunk. Like the pelvis, it is really an appendage of the trunk." Perhaps he used a dissected skull to show his class that "The *head*, without the lower jaw, when placed on a horizontal plane, rests upon the incisor teeth and occipital condyles, which are so disposed as to be opposite the middle of a line drawn from the incisor teeth to the most prominent point of the occiput. The centre of gravity of the head is in the middle of this line, and thus we see why the head, notwithstanding its great weight is so easily supported on the spine." From the head, Knox moved to the other extremity of the spine, the pelvis, which "forms at once a powerful bony girdle for the articulation of the inferior or pelvic extremities, and a deep nearly circular cavity, in which is lodged a portion of the intestines and many of the urinary and genital organs." Its anatomy was less interesting in its own right than some other regions of the body, "but its importance and surgical relations are so great and numerous," and so many of the procedures in common use in childbirth or diseases of the urinary tract required a deep understanding of the anatomy of the region, "that," Knox told his class, "we shall run the risk of shortening the description of some other part rather than omit any thing regarding the pelvis." Perhaps he preserved extra pelvises for the use of his class, for "no student of a month's standing," he wrote, "should be without one."

From here Knox went on to the limbs: first the "upper extremities," from the collar bone to the clavicle to the bones of the arms and hands, and then the "lower extremities, from the femur, through the thigh, knee, and foot," which Knox admired as much as the vertebrae. The "arrangement in the human foot when well formed," he told his class, "yields in beauty and perfection to no part in the human body. This part of the skeleton seems indeed perfected in man." Quite apart from their intrinsic beauty, their arrangement, and indeed the articulations of all the bones of the limbs, was of the utmost importance to any surgeon wishing to perform amputations successfully.

Knox's lectures on anatomy were enhanced by his style. He was the quintessential showman, dressing "in the highest style of fashion, with spotless linen, frill, and lace," according to Henry Lonsdale, indicating this or that anatomical structure with "raised arm and pointed forefinger, upon which he wore an exquisite diamond ring." His lectures attracted numerous auditors outside his own students. If "the class appeared a little wearied with the description of a bone, say the sphenoid"—the bone at the base of the skull—"the minute portions of which were invisible to all but the front benches, Knox would show his skill by refreshing his audience by a pause; then saying in a distinct voice, 'Gentlemen, the sphenoid bone is the most important bone in the body.'" This pronouncement, like his opinions on the beauty of the spinal column and the human foot, "startled the class by its novelty and abruptness." Indeed, Lonsdale reported, "nobody could ever say that [Knox] gave a dry lecture, or one that was not specially instructive."

Those students who chose to attend his practical dissection class finally began their own hands-on dissection in December, as the weather got colder. The standard practice was for them to work several students to a cadaver, rotating around the body as new topics were introduced. They began with "a subject for the muscles," explained a Glasgow anatomy professor, with each taking a part of the cadaver. "The second subject is for the blood-vessels; and as the students shift places, he who had a lower extremity before, gets a superior one now. The third subject is for the nerves and absorbents" and the students shifted again; "the fourth, for the viscera, and a more minute examination of connection and relative position." In that way every student had the opportunity to dissect during every topic, and to examine four cadavers, "all of which are not long in hand, and of course the less offensive; at the same time, leisure is afforded to examine every thing minutely, and to fix the whole in the memory." The bodies were probably preserved in spirits on arrival, to be brought out as the course progressed. By that time any idiosyncratic resemblance they had to their living owner would have disappeared, so that they could serve as exemplars of the ideal human form. At no point in Knox's *Edinburgh Dissector* did he refer to a subject as young or old, male or female: what mattered was the structure of their body parts, not their human identity.

The cadavers would arrive about the time Knox finished up his discussion of the skeleton. "Thus the student perceives," he wrote, "how the skeleton has been described as a frame work, affording at once support and protection to the soft parts, giving to the body its general form, and lastly, when acted on by the muscles, serving the purpose of a series of levers, and hence denominated the passive organs of locomotion." When students stood up and sat down in his class, they were to consider the mutual inter-relations between the feet, the knees, the pelvis, the spine, and the head; when they picked up a pen, they were to consider the delicate balancing act performed by the shoulder, the arm, the elbow, and the twenty-nine bones of the hand.

Dissecting manuals advised students to wear flannel jackets and carpet shoes, to counteract the "bad effects of sitting several hours in a cold dissecting-room." If a student wore a coat, it should not be the same one he wore on the street, but one purchased specifically for use in the dissecting room, for reasons of hygiene. A cap, again specifically for dissecting-room use, should be used instead of a hat, which "very quickly acquires a bad smell." An apron, "so loose as to give him perfect freedom in all his motions," was also recommended, preferably coated with a preparation of India rubber. Students' equipment, kept in a dissecting case, included saws, knives of various sizes, chisels, and pincers, and all the blades were to be kept very sharp. In making incisions, the knife "should be held like a writing pen in the right hand," while the part to be cut "should be held perfectly tense with the other hand, or with the forceps." The knife should be passed "with a steady and light stroke" in the direction of the fibers to be cut, "and in such a way as to just graze them," so as not to injure the parts underneath. Each student should keep his own sponge handy to clean away any oozing blood or pieces of tissue, "for where a sponge is used by several it becomes nobody's business to clean it; the consequence is that it is seldom fit for use." Damp cloths, soaked in chloride of lime, a bleaching agent, should be kept on hand to place over a dissection, in order to retard putrefaction. Even better, students should take care to remove only as much skin as was absolutely necessary to view the parts beneath, for the skin, even of a cadaver, was the best protection against decay.

Cadavers were known to cause infection, especially where the cause of death was hernia, erysipelas, or puerperal fever. To guard against illness when emanations from a dead body were "very putrid and offensive," one author suggested a "fumigating mixture" composed of black oxide of manganese, salt, sulphuric acid, and water. This mixture, left in the dissecting rooms overnight, would clear away the smell, so that dissection could safely resume. Wounds and abrasions, whether preexisting or contracted during dissection, could also be very dangerous for the student. To prevent infection, students were earnestly advised to protect their hands with oil or lard, and to take "the utmost care" to shield cuts and sores from contact with the cadaver by coating them with silver nitrate, or covering them with "proper dressing, and a slip of bladder bound over it." Pricks or punctures from dissecting tools had to be cleaned immediately and treated by application of some strong mineral acid, for if left alone, they might well lead to serious illness.

Knox probably separated his class into two groups, those who had no experience dissecting, and those who had. The first group needed to learn basic techniques of saw and scalpel, and concentrate on the major structural components of the body, muscles, bones, and larger organs. The second, whom Knox assumed to be planning a career in operative surgery, needed to hone their manual skills, trace the blood vessels and nerves, and pay particular attention to the articulations of the joints. Knox would clearly have preferred that students undertake "a second, and even a third examination of the same parts upon different subjects" and he provided incentives for students to take his courses more than once by lowering the price to 2 guineas for students who attended a second time. Students who attended three or more courses were admitted free of charge, and may have served as teaching assistants. William Fergusson remained Knox's chief assistant, supervising the dissecting rooms while Knox was lecturing.

Among the beginning students, dissection "should almost uniformly be commenced on the back," Knox wrote, with "the subject being placed on its face, a block of moderate height under the centre of the thorax, and a second under the abdomen." This was the posterior view of the subject. The first, shallow cut was to go from the base of the skull to the bottom of the spinal chord; three more cuts were to be made across the breadth of the back. Careful removal of the skin and fat exposed the muscles extending up and down the back, so that all six students in each group "have a share in this dissection, and they ought mutually to assist and examine each other's dissections." The students with the least experience were usually given the lower portion, involving the muscles of the buttocks, since an inexpert incision in the gluteus maximus would do the least harm. The more experienced or skillful of the six were given the head and neck, where a cut in the wrong place would ruin the subsequent dissections. With Knox as mentor, any willing student could learn the graceful sweep of the scalpel, the interconnections between anatomy, physiology, and surgery. And if a student did need correction, Knox administered it, as when, observing a pupil "slashing away at the muscles of a part," he "touched the young man's shoulder, and said: 'Ah, sir! I see you are dissecting for the sake of the bones; would it not be well to pick up a few facts as to the attachments and uses of these muscles before you reach the skeleton?'"

From the muscles in the back, Knox proceeded to the arm, or, as the student had to learn to think of it, the "thoracic pectoral superior extremity." Beginners in anatomy, again, had "principally to do with the muscles," and he started them off with dissecting those muscles which connect the arm to the trunk. Advanced students, taking a "surgical view," would turn the subject over on its back, "the shoulders raised by means of a narrow block of six or eight inches in depth, so that the arm may hang freely over the sides of the table, and the head at the same time be depressed." This would give the anterior, or front, view. The arm was to be positioned "nearly at right angles with the body," so that, once the skin and fat were cut into flaps and drawn back, the muscles, tendons, ligaments, and joints would be clearly exposed.

This process was probably much more interesting for the advanced than for the beginning students, who were by this time getting tired of one muscle after another. But the body could not be moved until a particularly tricky, but important, piece of dissection was completed: the examination of the muscles on the thigh leading to the popliteal space of the knee, with the veins and superficial nerves. The operation for aneurysm in the popliteal artery had become an essential part of the surgeon's toolkit, and any medical practitioner had to be prepared to diagnose it accurately, even if he did not operate himself. "All this will require more than usual industry" on the part of the two students assigned to that region, Knox admitted, because the back of the head and trunk "present few objects of interest, and are soon gone over by the students engaged in examining those parts, and who, of course, demand the subject to be turned." If those industrious students held out for the popliteal space, we may hope that any ill feeling was not permanent, for once the body was turned to reveal the anterior side, the six students would have to cooperate to somehow divide up the four extremities, beginners, as usual, concentrating on muscles and tendons, and advanced students carefully exploring the structure of the joints (Figure 14).

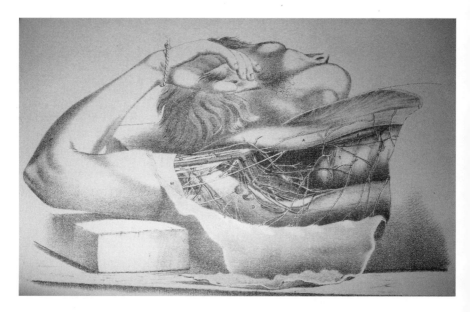

Figure 14. Dissection of the right arm demonstrating the use of block and rope to hold the limb in the correct position. Reproduced from Ellis, *Illustrations of Dissections*.

The remains from the preceding dissections being cleared away—by David Paterson or other servants—students were left with the head and trunk, face up. We can only assume that decomposition had begun, though it may have been retarded if the body was previously immersed in alcohol. We have no information on how long students took with each subject, but the rate at which Knox recorded anatomical structures in his own notebook suggests that corpses could be used up within a week. Knox noted that "the dissection of the Thorax should be undertaken immediately after one of the extremities," for at this point, "the student, for the first time, perhaps, gets a view of its actual form when the shoulders and limbs have been removed, and he will find it quite unlike what he anticipated, unless indeed he has previously given the skeleton a more than ordinary share of his attention." Indeed, Knox went on, evincing some heat, "if the student has really ne-glected this part of the articulated skeleton, he will find it an unprofitable waste of time to dissect the recent subject." The thorax could be likened to a cone, "somewhat truncated above, flattened behind, expanded below, with an extremely sloping basis . . . towards the abdomen." That base was the diaphragm, and, Knox said, "if the cavity of the abdomen happens to have been previously laid open by another dissector," the student should explore its position "and how far it ascends into the chest, contracting, as it were, that cavity most where least expected." Once again Knox emphasized that the beginning student was required to learn the muscles, bidding him to "carefully go over with the demonstrator, or with a more advanced stu-dent, the attachments of all the muscles" to the walls of the thorax.

The muscles having been committed to memory, the students would next create what was in effect a window into the chest cavity. First, Knox instructed, "cut through the cartilages of the second, third, fourth, fifth, and sixth ribs on each side," likewise the soft tissues "in the same line of incision." Next, "introduce the fingers cautiously into the opening so made, in order to protect the diaphragm . . . , and carefully tear through any adhesions which may exist between the contained organs and the walls of the thorax." Finally, "saw the ribs . . . so as to allow of the removal of a large portion of the walls of the chest." In this way, "the student exposes the interior of the chest most favourably for taking up a correct idea of the mechanism of the interior," including the important organs of the chest—the lungs, heart, trachea—in their natural positions.

Look first at the organ in situ, before making any incisions, Knox told his students; make sure you understand how it is connected to the rest of the frame, or you will mangle the very structures you are trying to examine. The same instructions, look well before you cut, applied to the abdomen and pelvis, which, Knox said, "form but one great cavity internally, as may be observed by an inspection of the skeleton, and they must always be dissected together." They "contained most of the principal viscera of the body," and a thorough knowledge of their pathological anatomy was essential to any medical man. Surgical students who expected to perform the well-established operations of lithotomy (removal of urinary stones) or paracentesis (draining of fluid from dropsical tissues) had to pay special attention. Knox, like other anatomists, took the male viscera as his prototype, "noticing afterwards, in a separate section, the peculiarities of the female and of the foetus." Perhaps the three women murdered in late spring provided examples of female "peculiarities."

Dissection of the pelvis began on the subject's back, with the muscles that acted as one wall of the cavity; if they had not been examined earlier, "the student had better turn to these at once and dissect them accordingly." Once completed, the subject could be turned, face upwards, "with a block under the loins, so as to put the anterior and lateral parts of the walls of the abdomen on the stretch." The dissection itself was, literally, multilayered, requiring the students to peel away, first, the skin, and then the muscles to "display the organs of digestion, which occupy the greater part of the cavity thus laid open." A cut into the abdominal cavity would penetrate the peritoneum—the membrane that covers the abdominal organs—as well, and "it is in this space, which the student now sees fully laid open, that fluids collect in dropsies." Having examined the peritoneum, students could—one at a time—insert their hands into the abdominal cavity, noting the abdominal muscles, the diaphragm, the spine, portions of the liver, the stomach, intestines, and the bladder if extended.

The abdomen contained more organs, such as those of generation, and some anatomists prefer to examine those next, Knox noted, but "this would require the student to have command of another abdomen, which might not be convenient at the time." Knox took his students slowly, point by point, through the intestines and colon; gave them precise instructions on removing and cleaning the "stomach, duodenum, liver, spleen, and pancreas in a mass" so as to examine them more thoroughly; and finished up with "the great trunks of the arteries and muscles and their branches." The kidneys and ureters were left for the dissection of the pelvic region, which immediately followed, the subject having been "put as in the situation for the operation of lithotomy," face up, "and a thin block placed under the pelvis; a grooved staff introduced by the urethra into the bladder, and secured there, and the scrotum well raised up with hooks." With the cadaver—or what remained of it—in this condition, students could examine the organs of generation in males and females.

The final dissection was of the head and neck, "with which the student generally, and very properly, completes his anatomical studies." The hair should be closely cropped, if that had not already been done, so that the student could make incisions from the tip of the nose across the top of the skull, and around the forehead above the eyebrows, drawing back the flaps of skin to examine the muscles. The next step was to saw, carefully, all around the skullcap, and lift it off the base of the skull. "Having removed the brain," Knox went on, the student ought to preserve it "in alcohol of sufficient strength, until such time as he can return to its examination with advantage." Before he came to that, the student was to complete the dissection of the face, and this was very difficult, requiring careful, neat incisions to expose glands, hooks to draw out and pin muscles, small saws and bone nippers to remove sections of the jaw. Knox supposed that the student made himself "well acquainted with . . . the muscles, by devoting one side of the head and neck to their almost exclusive consideration, and that having redissected and carefully cleaned all the muscles, preserving the arteries and nerves, in a second dissection, he is now prepared to consider the anatomy" of the blood vessels and nerves. So complicated were some of these anatomical structures, like the larynx, that Knox, uncharacteristically, told students they would have to examine already prepared specimens: "with these," he wrote, "and a careful dissection of the larynx belonging to the head and neck he has just dissected, he will readily make himself master of this organ, which no existing manual of practical anatomy, aided by the dissection of a single larynx, could ever enable him to accomplish." Perhaps at this point students returned to the human brain, so carefully preserved in alcohol months previously. In this way the six students would cycle through their allotted cadavers, generally by mid-March.

In the spring, William Fergusson offered a course on surgical operations, and Knox purchased an additional set of about fifteen cadavers. "There cannot be a greater mistake in a young surgeon's education," Fergusson later wrote in his textbook, *A System of Practical Surgery*, "than to commence the performance of operations before he has acquired a thorough knowledge of anatomy." Without it, "he can neither operate with safety to his patient nor satisfaction to himself; all must be hap-hazard; whilst on the other hand, in prosecuting his dissections, he takes the surest way of acquiring that dexterity in the use of his hands and instruments, which will be of infinite service to him." This was as true in what was called minor surgery—"bloodletting, bandaging, dressing sores, opening abscesses, and the numerous little manual proceedings which constitute the routine of surgical practice"—as it was "in the dexterous removal of a limb, or the rapid and successful extraction of a stone from the bladder."

Dissections carried out as part of surgical education required additional skills. "The cutting instruments," Fergusson noted, "are now in general to be used in a more free and bold style than in ordinary dissection, and more extensive movements are required in the hand and arm." Students should practice holding the parts to be cut with their left hand, slightly stretched between fingers and thumb, while making the incision with the right hand, without pressure or bruising. In addition to scalpels and forceps, they needed to master the use of the saw. "As it is difficult to use in a workmanlike manner," Fergusson wrote, "it will be well to practise with it on wood or bones, the latter being preferable when they can be procured in sufficient abundance; for it is not by sawing through the bones or one or two extremities merely that a dexterous use of this instrument can be acquired." Indeed, students must become acquainted with all the "requisite apparatus for an operation," usually placed on a small tray near the surgeon: "the knife, to cut the soft parts; saw to divide the bones; cutting forceps to remove spiculae of bone; forceps and tenaculum to lay hold of the arteries requiring to be tied; ligatures to apply to these vessels; needles with thread to stitch the wound; straps of adhesive plaster, lint, and bandages, to dress it; sponges with water, cold and hot, to wipe away the blood." Ideally, a good operative surgeon would have several assistants to hand him instruments, compress the arteries, sponge off the blood, and "assist in securing the patient during his struggles." In some cases, though, the surgeon would have to rely on his own resources, "which he will have little difficulty in doing, if he be possessed of that natural coolness, aptitude in emergencies, and knowledge of what he is about, which are almost equally essential to the welfare of his patient and his own comfort." The moral was clear:

knowledge, aptitude, and even coolness when confronted with living patients could best be acquired by extensive experience with dead bodies.

Perhaps the most successful operation Knox's anatomy classes performed was a kind not mentioned in the manuals: the transformation of once living people into anonymous dissecting material, and the concomitant transformation of novice students, imbued with the religious principles of their day, into proficient dissectors who could contemplate a dead body without a qualm or pang of conscience. Conservative writers denounced anatomical dissection precisely for that reason, arguing that it hardened the anatomist's conscience, weakening the natural reverence men ought to feel for mortal remains. "It is not to be expected, or wished," wrote one, "that a surgeon should possess strongly sensitive feelings upon matters where his firmness and philosophy are essential to his own success and the safety of his patient." That was no excuse, though, for violating basic decency. "A surgeon," the writer continued, "to be fully qualified for his profession, should have . . . an eagle's eye, a lion's heart, and a lady's hand," but "a hard heart, and a brave one are as different as light from dark."

The criticism is deserved: for all that early nineteenth-century medicine owed to cadavers, there were no mechanisms to ensure the dead were treated with respect. Indeed, because of the "mystery and secrecy" with which anatomists shrouded their dissections, the cadavers may have ended up discarded in the forgotten corners of Edinburgh's medical district. In 1983 a small "assemblage of 63 items of bone" was found by workmen cleaning out the town wall, at the site of what would have been the northeast section of Surgeon's Square. The Edinburgh city archaeologists who examined the bones were able to identify the remains of animal skeletons, including a bear and a seal. Fifty-five of the bones could be identified as human, belonging to a minimum of five individuals, one of whom was a child of six to eight years of age. The most likely provenance of these cadavers was the Edinburgh anatomical schools, though we have no way of knowing which one. And it may well be that the remains of all the Burke and Hare victims, including Effy, the old woman and her grandson, and the woman murdered by Hare alone, met a similar fate.

Chapter 8

The Criminal Mind

"Drunk Old Woman," Mrs. Hostler, Ann M'Dougal

T HE SUMMER OF 1828 APPEARED TO MARK ANOTHER SHIFT IN Burke's and Hare's behavior, toward even more reckless targeting of potential cadavers. They saw one opportunity in a drunk woman being dragged to the West Port watch house by two policemen. Burke, seeing them, said, "Let the woman go to her lodgings." The officers said "they did not know where she lodged," to which Burke responded that "he would take her to lodgings." They "gave her to his charge," and he took her to Hare's house. Burke said that they "murdered her the same way as they did the others," and got £10 for her from Dr. Knox at Surgeon's Square. "Did the policemen know him when they gave him this drunk woman into his charge?" he was later asked. Yes, replied Burke, "he had a good character with police," for "if they had known that there were four murderers living in one house they would have visited them sooner."

About the time of the murder, Burke moved, with Helen M'Dougal, to the snug little house between Weaver's and Grindlay's Closes, where Madgy Docherty was to meet her death later that year. At the time a day laborer, John Brogan, and his family occupied the room. Brogan's wife was some sort of relation to Burke, and both Burke and Hare had stood security for Brogan's rent of £3. It was in Brogan's house that Burke, acting alone, murdered Margaret Haldane during the summer, as we have seen. It is possible that Burke moved because he wanted to get Helen M'Dougal away from his partners. He later said that Margaret Hare had urged that M'Dougal be killed, for, she told him, "they could not trust to her, as she was a Scotch woman." It is also possible opportunities for obtaining murder victims in Tanner's Close continued to decline during the summer. The next two cadavers did not come along until late September or early October.

In life, the first had belonged to Mrs. Hostler, who was the washerwoman in John Brogan's house. She had been washing one day, Burke explained, "and she came back next day to finish up the clothes, and when done, Hare and Burke gave her some whiskey to drink, which made her drunk." It was still daytime, but the two men were able to persuade her to go to bed, and then "murdered her the same way they did the others." They "put her in a box, and set her in the coalhouse in the passage, and carried her off to Dr. Knox's in the afternoon of the same day." Knox gave them £8 for her. The reason for the haste was that Brogan's wife was away from home, as Burke was careful to state; but she still must have wondered what had become of her washerwoman when she returned. Burke did not mention her husband or their seventeen-year-old son, also named John, a boatman at the canal basin.

Perhaps Mrs. Brogan noticed something and spoke to her husband, for by the next murder, which probably took place within a week or two of Mrs. Hostler, John Brogan had become suspicious. Ann M'Dougal was a cousin of Helen M'Dougal's first husband. According to Burke, she was married, and had come to Edinburgh on a visit. Perhaps they had met her during their trip to Falkirk earlier in the summer and invited her to stay. She, like the others, was "given whisky until she was drunk," and put to bed. Burke had some misgivings about killing her, and told Hare he would have to "have most to do to her, as she being a distant friend, he did not like to begin first on her." Hare therefore "murdered her by stopping her breath," with Burke acting as his assistant.

Once again Brogan, his wife, and their son were out, but when Brogan returned from work he noticed a "fine trunk"—obtained from David Paterson—"and made inquiries about it as he knew they had not trunks there." Burke offered him some whiskey, and the three men discussed the situation. The upshot was that Brogan received £1 10s from each man then and there, and an additional £3 after they delivered the body. In return, he agreed to leave Edinburgh for an unspecified period. His wife and son seem to have remained at home. It is likely that John Brogan the younger—later to be pressed into service to keep Ann Gray away from Madgy Docherty's cadaver—knew about the bodies. But he had already been arrested twice for "assaulting and maltreating a woman," and so had good reason to avoid the police if another one turned up dead. Knox paid £10 for Ann M'Dougal's cadaver, so with the payments to Brogan, and Mrs. Hare's usual £1 fee, Burke and Hare netted less than £2 each from Ann M'Dougal.

This set of murders has not garnered much attention, "First ae drunk auld wife, and then anither drunk auld wife—and then a third," as Christopher North put it. Yet they are remarkable for deviating from what has long been assumed to have been the profile of the victims: long-distance migrants, those "whom nobody missd because nobody wishd to see them again," in Sir Walter Scott's phrase. All three of the victims had a direct personal connection to Burke, and there were plenty of witnesses who saw them together. The policemen who gave the drunk woman into Burke's charge could be expected to remember it. Not just the Brogans but also their neighbors would remember Mrs. Hostler. And Ann M'Dougal's husband and other relations would certainly know that she had gone to Edinburgh and never came home. The murderers were becoming reckless indeed to have chosen such well-connected victims, and they must have realized that John Brogan, once he returned from his travels, would require an additional share of the profits. Perhaps they simply did not know how to stop killing, for they had become used to the money, and had no idea how to get it other than by the methods they had perfected. Or perhaps Burke, at least, was subconsciously hoping to be caught, so that the murder spree would end.

The fact that the Burke and Hare murders were serial killings fascinated contemporaries. For a person to commit even one murder was dreadful enough but the burgeoning taste for true and fictional crime stories had accustomed the public to the idea that such things might happen. Men, and in some cases even women, might be caught up in strong passions like rage or jealousy. They might lose control of themselves in an unguarded moment. But why would anyone, in full possession of his reason, resort to murder? And above all why would he resort to murder over and over again? Were such murderers simply morally deformed from birth, brought into the world without conscience or proper moral sense? Were they, in other words, born with a criminal mind, so imbued with villainy that no matter the good intentions of their parents or friends, no matter how many chances they had to reform, they always ended up returning to their wicked ways?

The rise of crime journalism added fuel to debates over the nature of criminality, as reporters eagerly sought interviews with murderers awaiting trial or already condemned to execution. The well-known London journalist Pierce Egan set the standard for this in his interview of John Thurtell, imprisoned for the 1823 murder of his longtime gambling associate, William Weare. Before the murder Thurtell had been an on-again off-again member of the London sporting world, often in financial difficulties but without any reputation for violence. In fact, he swore he was not guilty, but had been framed by his associates, one of whom turned witness against him. Few, even among his friends, believed him innocent, but that made the whole affair all the more fascinating, for what could have led him, charming and well spoken as he was, to such depths of depravity? What kind of a person was this Thurtell? Pierce Egan set out to satisfy public curiosity. He had known Thurtell in London, and was able to interview him twice before his trial. "You know my forte," he said to Thurtell: he had come, he told him, "to cast my eyes around; to report what is going on." For his part, Thurtell welcomed the interview, greeting Egan "with a cheerful step and a smiling countenance."

Egan began with the question on everyone's mind: was Thurtell guilty? He denied it strenuously: "I never committed any serious crime in my life," he told Egan. "My friends know it full well." Egan must have expected that reply—for the governor of the prison was present, and the trial had not yet taken place—but he must have known, too, that his readers expected him to do more than simply take Thurtell's word for it. He brought up Weare's name, watching Thurtell carefully as he did so. But "the name of Weare did not make any impression," though Thurtell's eyes met his, he reported. That is, Thurtell did not blanch or look ashamed. Indeed, Egan felt he had never seen him "look better," and Thurtell was angry at the newspapers reporting him to be "sullen and dejected." That would have been a sign of guilt, as he knew full well: "Those who know me well," he assured Egan, "know that I have done nothing to be dejected about." As far as motives attributed to him for the murder, they were all false. "My enemies assert I committed this murder for the sake of money," he said, but "I could have plenty of money to set up in business to-morrow, if I wanted it."

The most prevalent theory concerning criminal behavior in general was that it was promoted by bad company, because repeated exposure to miscreants weakened the moral sense. Small crimes led to bigger ones, and the first, small self-indulgence could lead to murder. For that reason, many writers claimed it was Thurtell's connection with gambling and the sporting life that led him to the deed: though once a talented man, he had become hardened by a life spent among horse racing, prizefighting, public houses, and evil companions. Thurtell would have none of that. If "the judge attacks me for my attachment to sporting," he told Egan "with great warmth," he would explain "that if I have erred in these things, half of the nobility in the land have been my examples, and some of the most enlightened statesmen in the land have been my companions in them." But in fact "no person behaved more honourably than I did," he said, "or spent his blunt [money] more freely."

In fact Thurtell was convicted and subsequently executed to great fanfare. Thousands—including Egan—attended his execution, and thousands more purchased the books and broadsides detailing every aspect of the crime. One group, though, ignored the public sensation surrounding the murder, and went straight to an investigation of what they saw as its cause. These were British phrenologists, who made a practice of obtaining casts of the skulls of famous criminals as well as other noteworthy individuals. Their goal was to study the features of the brain that distinguished murderers from nonmurderers; their higher purpose, to discover the mental mechanism that had allowed some people to become criminals, in order to counteract that mechanism before it appeared in others.

The theory of phrenology originated around 1800 with the German physician Franz Josef Gall, and was disseminated in Great Britain by his associate, Johann Spurzheim. By the 1820s it had adherents throughout Europe and the United States. It has not been treated kindly by modern neuroscience, and even in its own day it had many detractors, but its hold on the popular imagination continued well into the early twentieth century. Phrenologists divided up the human brain into thirty-five parts, called "organs," each of which was held to be the site of a specific aspect of personality, such as Benevolence, Destructiveness, Veneration, and Individuality (Figure 15). The size of each organ was believed to result in more or less of that aspect of personality. Since it was impossible to examine the brain directly while a subject was still alive—and brains decayed so quickly after death—phrenologists studied the size and proportion of corresponding sections of the skull as a guide to the brain beneath. They preferred to work directly on the cranium, using calipers and measuring tape to map the bumps and expanse of bone. Where skulls were not available, though—or would be available for only a short period of time—they took plaster casts, as accurate as they could make them. The use of casts meant that numerous copies could be made of the same skull, and phrenologists throughout Europe and America exchanged or sold casts regularly. Thus the cast of Thurtell's skull could be added to collections of murderers' skulls, to be examined for what it would reveal about criminal tendencies.

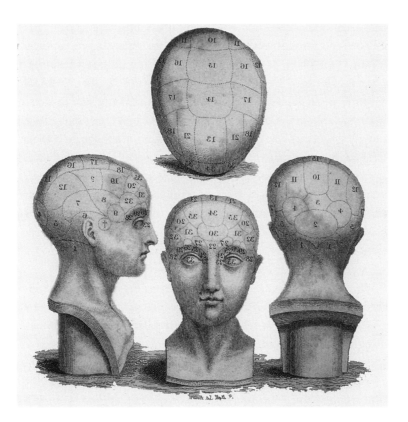

Figure 15. Heads indicating the position of the phrenological organs. Phrenologists located organs of perception like Form (23), Size (24), and Weight (25), at the front of the brain; they placed the organ of Destructiveness (6) on the side, and those of the higher sentiments, like Benevolence (13), Veneration (14), and Conscientiousness (16) at the top.

What phrenology revealed, according to its adherents, was that the brain was not a unitary organ, like the the stomach or kidneys, which performed only one function. For that reason there was no such thing as a unitary "criminal mind," entirely different in its construction from the minds of law-abiding people. Instead, there was a "correspondence between the formation of the brain, and the constitution of the mind," wrote the physician and belletrist Robert Macnish, who was fascinated by the mind during altered states of consciousness, like sleep or drunkenness. The brain was "in reality a congeries of organs, so intimately blended, however, as to appear one. Each of these is the seat of a particular mental faculty, so that, as the whole mind acts through the medium of the whole brain, so does each faculty of the mind act through the medium of a certain portion of the brain." But what reasons were there for supposing there were such divisions in the brain, or indeed in the mind? The reasons were numerous, explained Macnish. "Were the brain a single organ . . ., there could be no such thing as partial madness: if a portion of the brain were diseased, the whole mind should suffer; whereas, we often find that one faculty is insane, while all the others are perfectly sound." The same principle explained the phenomena of dreaming. If the brain were a single, unified organ, "we should be either completely awake or completely asleep; whereas, in dreams, one or more faculties are in operation while the rest continue in perfect repose. The perversion in madness, and the wakefulness in dreaming, of certain faculties, can be explained only by supposing that each of these faculties has a separate locality in the brain."

Similar reasoning, according to phrenologists, might finally lay bare the mind of the murderer. For murderers, even the most violent, were not murderous all the time. Thurtell, as we have seen, had no previous history of crime, and accounts of his last days were filled with anecdotes demonstrating his kindness and human sympathy. Surely phrenology could explain the mental mechanism by which they murdered. Surely the theory of the brain as "congeries of organs" could clarify how they could be ordinary, decent human beings one minute, and vicious killers the next.

This was the view of George Combe, Edinburgh's leading phrenologist, whose public lectures and numerous publications made enormous numbers of converts to what he called "the true philosophy of the mind." A socially progressive advocate for educational and prison reform, Combe felt that phrenology provided a better way of explaining criminal behavior than the supposition that a murderer had been born bad, his "heart ever peculiarly wicked." Phrenologists argued that the brains of criminals did not differ in kind from those of virtuous people, but only in the particular structure of their organs. Murderers, like everyone else, were born with organs leading them to both constructive and destructive behavior, but they committed their crimes when the destructive organs got the upper hand. Benevolent organs grew stronger with use, and so early intervention, as we might call it, could keep them active and healthy. Unfortunately, malevolent organs also grew stronger with use, so that a criminal, once having overcome his natural inhibitions against crime, might well become habituated to it and even glory in it. Combe's ideas remained enormously influential throughout the nineteenth century, finding their most famous literary echo in Robert Louis Stevenson's *Dr. Jekyll and Mr. Hyde*. In Stevenson's story, Dr. Jekyll was born with a "congeries" of personalities, comprising inclinations both to good and to evil. He could transform himself from one to the other with a potion, a change that, according to Combe's ideas, came about by changed circumstances in a man's life. This was how phrenology related to criminal psychology, Combe wrote, by explaining "the effect of external circumstances in bringing into predominance different elements of the mind." The key was to make use of this knowledge: Combe believed that "evil tendencies" inherent in criminals could be restrained "by placing them in circumstances calculated to cultivate the good."

Phrenology was a science based on research, supporters asserted, and Combe carried out pertinent research by interviewing an accused murderer, David Haggart, while the latter was awaiting trial. Haggart was a well-known thief and swindler, who had killed a jailer when escaping from prison in Dumfries. He had not meant to do it, he later explained in his autobiography, composed while awaiting execution. "I gave only one blow with the stone and immediately threw it down." He managed to get away and hid in a haystack, when he "heard a woman ask a boy if 'that lad was taken that had broken out of Dumfries jail'; the boy answered 'No, but the jailor died last night at ten o'clock.'" That was the first he knew that he was a murderer, and, he wrote, "His words struck me to the soul; my heart died within me, and I was insensible for a good while; on coming to myself, I could scarcely believe I had heard them," for the possibility of the jailor's death "had never entered my mind." Like Thurtell, he had not previously committed any violent crime, though he had enough counts of theft, swindling, and criminal aliases to find himself at home among the "dangerous classes." His undoubted skill at provoking sympathy for his cause, combined with his "genteel and prepossessing appearance," led to a gentle, one might almost say supportive, tone in the broadsheets reporting his trial and execution. It was a foregone conclusion that he would be hanged, for, the judge told him, "the law would most decidedly avenge the violence done to keepers of his Majesty's prisons." Nonetheless the "unfortunate prisoner preserved a steady composure throughout the whole trial, and appeared at one time to be much moved during the passing of this judgment. . . . The meeting with his father" just before his execution "was truly affecting." Even the publication of his account of his life, which might be criticized as providing a model for criminal behavior, could be excused as originating first "in a wish to atone in some degree for his crimes, by disclosing them" and second "to benefit his father's family, upon whom it was his express desire, that a portion of the profits . . . be bestowed." The rest, according to his editor, was to be given away to charity.

Haggart therefore seemed a perfect example of a man with conflicting personalities, with both good and bad personality traits, and the interplay of those traits was the focus of Combe's questions. Since Haggart was still awaiting trial at the time of the interview, Combe did not question him upon his case. Instead, he carefully examined his skull, and then wrote up his character study, "drawn from the development of his head." This was then sent to Haggart for his own commentary, with the assurance that it was "entirely confidential, and will not be abused." Combe's higher purpose in conducting the study, he said, was "not to indulge an idle curiosity, but to throw light upon the natural dispositions which particularly lead a young man into a sporting line of life." Once illuminated, it would be possible to devise "effectual means to reclaim young offenders at the outset of their career."

Combe adopted the usual view that Haggart, like Thurtell, had developed bad habits by his acquaintance with young sporting gentlemen, whose demeanor and lifestyle he wished to emulate. This led him to leave home at an early age, and to fall in with dissolute companions. He explained this in phrenological terms: the organs of Conscientiousness and Benevolence, which would have been fostered had he remained in his parents' house, had not had time to develop properly. Instead, the evil ways of Haggart's companions had led to the overdevelopment of his organs of Combativeness and Destructiveness. Your greatest errors, Combe suggested to Haggart, "have arisen from a great self-esteem, a large combativeness, a prodigious firmness, a great secretivness, and a defective love of approbation." In other words, "In your earlier years of boyhood, you would often fight because you were insulted, or supposed yourself to be so. You would maintain the battle with desperate obstinacy." Haggart responded that he "never was much given to quarreling, excepting when I was insulted." He agreed, though, that "if it did come to a fight, I seldom left the field till covered with wounds." And at home, Combe continued, "you would be excessively self-willed and obstinate, very little regardful of what your parents or others thought of you, and rarely submissive to command, except when it pleased yourself to obey." "Neither have you mistaken me in this," responded Haggart, "for, at home or abroad, I never, or at least seldom, would do any thing that was required of me. . . . When I was ordered, I took but little notice of it, as I thought my own way the best." Haggart agreed, therefore, with Combe's analysis of his combativeness and firmness, and he also agreed about his secretiveness. "You would all your life feel a peculiar facility in concealing your real motives, in completely commanding your feelings when inclined to do so, and appearing impenetrable to the eyes of others?" asked Combe. "There were few that ever knew any of my secrets," responded Haggart, "for I knew that if I could not keep my own mind, another would not do it."

Haggart did not feel that Combe got everything right. "You would not be the slave of the sexual passion, nor greatly given to drink?" Combe asked. "You have mistaken me in this point of sexual passion," replied Haggart. "For it was my greatest failing, that I had a great inclination to the fair sex." "You would never be cruel or brutal?" asked Combe. "Cruel to my inferiors I never was," said Haggart "but rejoiced to pull the lofty down, to make them on a fair level with their brethren in the world." What we seem to have here is dueling images of what cruelty might mean, for Haggart elsewhere admitted that he had behaved cruelly in being "the means of leading away and betraying the innocence of young women, and then leaving them to the freedom of their own will." Indeed he seemed proud of it: "I believe," he said, "that I was the master of that art more than any other that I followed." But on the subject of his conscience, Haggart believed that Combe had gotten it right again. "You would often be perfectly conscious," Combe wrote, "that your own mind upbraided or accused you for your conduct: Did you ever try to appease your conscience, by believing that the rest of mankind were doing exactly the same thing as you?" "There is no doubt," responded Haggart, "that my conscience upbraided me in this point, but I thought that I was no worse than others who had been before and would come after me."

In the end, Haggart provided Combe with support for his beliefs in the dual nature of the criminal mind. "Your nature is, in many respects, so different from your actions and situation, that you are a hypocrite in the opposite sense to those who are usually styled such," Combe wrote in his concluding notes. "You affect to speak lightly of your sporting adventures, and to feel less; but you positively feel a great deal more internally than you pretend to do. You feel that there is a war within yourself—two principles in your own mind—one telling you, that this course of life was not for you, and that you might have made a figure in another path; another trying to stifle these reflections, and to persuade you that you have done nothing amiss." Scholars have noted the influence of Combe's Calvinist upbringing on his own ideas, and it certainly seems to be present here, with "two principles in your own mind" substituted for the traditional angel and demon perched on Haggart's shoulders. If only he had listened to his guardian angel—or, as Combe would have said, exercised his organ of Benevolence—then he would have avoided his short, lonely walk to the gallows.

Phrenological analyses of murderers became a kind of professional specialty with Combe, and he made a point of examining the crania, or casts, of as many as he could procure. He naturally was attracted to the Burke and Hare case, for he had to investigate whether phrenology could explain not one but sixteen murders. It was easy enough to see how Haggart's Combativeness and Firmness could lead to his attempted escape, and then to his accidentally killing the jailer who came after him. But could any set of mental faculties explain repeated murders, each one, apparently, undertaken more readily than the last?

Combe visited Burke in his condemned cell to take the measurements of his skull, which he then supplemented by measurements from a plaster cast after his execution. He took Hare's measurements, with his permission, while the latter was in prison. He explained that Hare's had been as accurate as possible: his hair had been "so closely cropped as completely to present the appearance of a cast moulded on the shaven scalp, except along a marginal line in front, where Hare would not allow the hair to be cut away." Combe then compared their measurements with those of other well-known murderers, including Thurtell, and with one gentleman, a certain Rev. M, a man whose "dispositions" were "naturally virtuous."

Combe used these findings to argue that there was a distinction between "two classes of criminals,—those who are habitually violent, and those who are tolerably virtuous till excited by temptation." John Bellingham, who shot Prime Minister Spencer Perceval in 1812, was, according to Combe, one of the former, "habitually fierce, passionate and unreasonable," and his phrenological examination showed that "in his head Destructiveness is very large, and Benevolence and Intellect small." Murderers who, like Burke, "possessed a calm exterior" and had behaved "with some degree of propriety" at periods of their lives made up the latter group. They would manifest not only a "combination of large Combativeness and Destructiveness," but also "some portion of Benevolence." Something never comes out of nothing, Combe asserted: if murderers like Burke behaved in particular ways, then the wellspring of that behavior could be found in phrenological analysis of his skull. If, then, Burke "was intensely selfish, a correct exposition of his character must exhibit the selfish principles strong in his nature; if he was atrociously murderous, the element of Destructiveness must appear; but if Burk actually manifested also some portion of attachment, of kindness, and of honesty, the elements of these better feelings must likewise have existed in his mind."

What Combe was suggesting was that criminals, even murderers, were not creatures set apart from everyone else, devoid of all moral sense. Neither were they, precisely, good men gone wrong. Instead, they were people with the potential for being good men, for leading upright lives, until circumstances led to the strengthening of their antisocial mental organs. Combe went over what was known of Burke's early life, focusing on the evidence of Burke's good behavior, such as his early religious upbringing, his service to men of known moral character, and his "fidelity and propriety" while in the army. "Here, then," he noted, was evidence of Burke "having in his youth possessed some intellectual acuteness, and having been active, cleanly, and well-behaved for a considerable numbers [*sic*] of years; or, in other words, at this period of his life he manifested intellect and moral sentiment." Indeed, these manifestations continued during his early period in Edinburgh, when he was remarkable for being attentive and reverential at church, "industrious and serviceable" at his trade, and "inoffensive and playful in his manner."

What, then, went wrong? What drove him to the "intense selfishness, cold-blooded cruelty, and calculating villainy" of the sixteen murders he committed? "Phrenology," asserted Combe, "is the only science of mind which contains elements and principles capable of accounting for such a character as that before us, and it does so in a striking manner." In examining Burke's head, phrenologists found, as they expected, that "the middle lobe, in which are situate the organs of Destructiveness, Secretiveness, and Acquisitiveness, is very large; at Destructiveness in particular the skull presented a distinct swell." The anterior lobe, that of Intellect, "though small in proportion to the hind and middle lobes, is still fairly developed," especially in the section denoting perception. One of the most striking features was the organ of Self-esteem, which was "prominent, and has indented its form distinctly on the skull." As Combe interpreted it, "the general result of this development is, that the animal feelings are very strong; the moral feelings are proportionately feebler, but not wanting; while observing intellect is present in a considerable degree, but reflecting intellect much less."

The conclusion was that all those inhibitions—like "reflecting intellect"—that should have prevented Burke from becoming a multiple murderer had initially been comparatively weak, while those faculties that would lead him to violence, like "animal feelings," were disproportionately strong. As long as Burke remained prosperous, and was surrounded by examples of good behavior, for example in the army, his good qualities, Benevolence and Intellect, kept those strong faculties in check. Even in adversity, many of his good qualities continued: his organ of "Philoprogenitiveness"— love of children—was "strongly developed," and Combe repeated the story, often reprinted, that "the children who lived in the neighbourhood of his house were ready at all times to run errands for him, or serve him." Of course, Combe noted with apparently no sense of irony, Burke must have overcome this feeling when murdering the old woman's grandson, "as he did his Benevolence in murdering adults." Combe also noted that Burke's organ of "Adhesiveness" was full, and used it to explain Burke's fidelity both to M'Dougal and to Hare. But all these organs were eventually overcome by negative ones: by Burke's "Amativeness," or sexual attraction, which "led him into habits"—presumably living in adultery with M'Dougal, though Combe did not say so explicitly—"which terminated in his greatest crimes."

It was the habits that mattered to Combe, rather than the organs, for he believed not that environment produced character but that it operated selectively on specific attributes. Difference of circumstances, he wrote, bring forth "a discovery of *the real* character," rather than altering it. "There *is* a change, in so far as one set of feelings gain the ascendency in the new situation which were subordinate in the old." In Burke's case, while he was comfortably at home, or under the beneficent influence of religion and honest work, his benevolent organs came to the fore. But the change in his circumstances produced the change in his behavior: "poverty, habits of vicious pleasure, intoxication . . . gave an ascendency to Destructiveness which in happier circumstances it did not possess."

Once Destructiveness had the upper hand, each new murder only served to strengthen it, at the same time as Burke's natural allotment of Benevolence and Philoprogenitiveness inevitably lost ground against his baser instincts. Combe classed Hare—referred to as Burke's "infamous accomplice and companion"—as one of the negative influences that allowed Burke's Destructiveness to emerge. Like most commentators, he saw Hare as "the more brutal and disgusting" of the two men. The organ of Benevolence was much smaller in Hare than in Burke, he wrote, while "the organ of Acquisitiveness, which lies in the temples, and which gives the love of gain, is very large, and stands broadly out." The next most prominent organs were "Destructiveness, Combativeness, and Self-esteem, forming altogether a combination of the lowest of the propensities." Since Hare was "unguided . . . by any considerable endowment of moral sentiment," the result "was abundantly strong to fit him for the scenes in which he acted so brutal a part." In short, concluded Combe, "the development of Hare turns out to be as complete a key to his mental character as that of Burke has been shown to be to his, and harmonizes in every respect with what is known of his manifestations."

Yes, it harmonizes in every respect, and no wonder, said Combe's opponents, when phrenologists did no more than make up their cranial analyses to match the known accounts of the criminals. "Merely telling us that such and such protuberances on the skull denote such and such faculties," wrote one antiphrenologist, "does not at all account for the character." Combe's critics pointed out that he had been credulous indeed in believing everything Burke said about the murders after the fact. The remorse that Burke claimed he felt for the murders—and that Combe cited as a sign of his Benevolence—was not corroborated by any other witness. Even if it was believed, "the mere fact of a murderer's slumbers being haunted with the image of his victim for a brief space, cannot prove the existence of benevolence." But, as one author pointed out, there was no reason to believe it, even according to the tenets of phrenology. Combe himself had pointed out that Burke's organs of Imitation and Secretiveness had led him to play the part of the decoy during the murders, and to adapt his responses while in prison to the expectations of his many visitors. "We shrewdly surmise" that the whole talk of guilt "is a fiction of Burke's," the writer went on, "and that he narrated it at a time when the well-developed organ of Imitation, combined with his large Secretiveness, was excited to such a degree as to produce *acting* or simulation."

Most offensive to many readers was the implication of phrenologists that criminals were not a separate and inferior subspecies of human but instead had the same mental equipment as everyone else, differing from moral people only by degree, not by kind. The idea shocked polite society, just as it would be shocked sixty years later by Sigmund Freud's comparable assertions regarding sexuality. "An ordinary person cannot think of bloody crimes with too great agitation of abhorrence," growled Christopher North, "but a philosopher, like Mr. Combe, is superior to these delusions of the imagination, and therefore thinks and writes rationally of murders and murderers." Most commentators rejected utterly Combe's attempt to show that Burke had had the capacity to take another path. "It is altogether too much," wrote one, "to elevate this unnatural and anomalous monster into a being possessing some of the best and noblest attributes of humanity, merely that the dogmas of a favourite pursuit should be supported."

Antiphrenologists also refused to be persuaded by the causality described by Combe, that Burke committed the murders because his baser instincts, kept in check by his organs of Benevolence and Intellect for so long, had been brought to the fore. How could it be, wondered one writer, that these beneficent organs, "which modified and gave respectability to his character for as many as thirty years, all of a sudden cease to exercise any influence, and acquisitiveness and destructiveness, arising like two arch fiends on both sides, leave the state of inactivity in which they had reposed for so long a period, and gain a most unaccountable control over the physical powers under which they had for so many years succumbed." It is not as though phrenological analysis had imparted any new insight into the criminal mind with its protuberances and organs: "many ignorant people" who had never measured a cranium "might inform us, that frequently a man does not get desperately wicked all at once, that there is nothing very uncommon in a person behaving tolerably well for a length of time, and afterwards abandoning himself to the most profligate courses."

The most comprehensive attack on Combe's findings was launched by a medical student, Thomas Stone, perhaps with the assistance of some of Combe's longtime opponents. His pamphlet *On the Phrenological Development of Burke, Hare, and Other Atrocious Murderers* was "one of the most efficient knock-down blows which Phrenology has yet received," according to the *Edinburgh Literary Journal*. Stone asked three questions relating to Burke and Hare. First, did the structure of Burke's skull, as understood by phrenologists, "correspond with his acknowledged character?" Second, did the structure of Hare's skull correspond to his acknowledged character? And third, was it possible "to distinguish the crania of murderers from other crania, by the Phrenological indications attributed to them?"

From the point of view of strict logic, Stone won his case hands down. He examined Burke's skull himself when the opportunity arose, and carefully compared its measurements to one hundred crania collected by both phrenologists and their opponents. Though Combe had called Burke's organ of Destructiveness "large," Stone found that seventy-two of the hundred crania had organs of Destructiveness larger than Burke. A similar anomaly occurred with the organ of Benevolence: Burke's was "above the average size" of the majority of the comparison crania. Stone also had measured Hare's head "the evening before this miscreant was liberated from prison . . . with the assistance of an able Phrenologist" as well as some other witnesses. He compared the measurements to other crania, separated into Englishmen, Scotsmen, and Irishmen, and found that there was nothing distinctive, and certainly nothing conclusive, about the size of Hare's protuberances. His organ of Destructiveness was by no means greater than those of ordinary individuals, and his organs of Benevolence and Conscientiousness were larger that those of "many individuals of exemplary character." Consequently, Stone noted, neither Burke's nor Hare's crania were "indicative of that moral degradation" which they exhibited. The most remarkable organ in Hare's skull was that of "Ideality," having to do with invention and artistry. "At the time we took the measurement," Stone declared, "one of the most highly-gifted and popular of our living poets was present, whose genius is peculiarly characterised by the vividness and power of its *idealism*." According to phrenological measurements, though, "Hare possessed a larger organ of ideality than the poet." Indeed, it was larger than the published phrenological studies of Laurence Sterne, Edmund Burke, and Voltaire.

That was only to be expected, Stone asserted, for the crania of the worst murderers of modern time simply did not have the distinctive characteristics attributed to them by phrenologists. Murderers were supposed to have "a large endowment of the organ of Destructiveness," and "a deficiency in the development of the alleged organs of the Moral Sentiments." In comparing the published measurements for skulls of fifteen executed murderers to his one hundred comparison crania, though, Stone found that they were generally below the average in Destructiveness, and above the average in Benevolence. How, then, could phrenologists possibly argue that there was anything distinctive about the crania of murderers? And by extension, how could they argue that there was any science, or indeed any value whatsoever, to phrenological study?

Stone did not speak to Burke, but he provides us with one of the few known interviews with Hare. It is not especially illuminating, succeeding primarily in the unlikely task of provoking some sympathy for Hare's having to put up with such a battery of impertinent questions. Hare— the "stupid and miserable wretch," as Stone referred to him—refused to answer anything "until repeatedly assured by the Governor that we were not sent by the Sheriff to make any investigation into the particulars of his case." Are you a Roman Catholic? Stone asked, but Hare would only respond—with what Stone considered a "contemptuous sneer"—that he "did not rightly mind what he was." When asked whether his conscience ever troubled him, "he answered, with a laugh, 'No, with the help of God.'" By this point Stone had concluded that Hare's "whole demeanor was that of a man evidently devoid of every moral reflection." Though his head was "adorned, as if in mockery of Phrenology, with large organs of Ideality, Causality, and Wit," Stone said, Hare was "only a few degrees removed from the very lowest of the brute creation."

As tough-minded and pugnacious as his critics, Combe was up to countering Stone and other detractors, whom he portrayed as capitalizing on sensationalism to gratify their own low tastes. "The wild cry of indignation, and the amazement of horror manifested by the public," he wrote, "are mere ebullitions of feeling, which lead to nothing. It is a cheap and easy way of being virtuous to express strong detestation of vice; but the true lesson to be learned from this dreadful and disgusting tragedy is to inquire into and remove the causes which gave it rise." The point of phrenology was to show "the effect of external circumstances in bringing into predominance different elements of the mind. We have never taught, that a man cannot commit murder who has an organ of Benevolence, for every individual has all the organs; but that a man cannot commit a cool murder without possessing Destructiveness largely developed, and here Destructiveness is very large." Burke's "moral powers" had been sufficient to hold it in check for years, but could not restrain it when external circumstances changed for the worse. "We perceive that a considerable degree of moral feeling has been as dust in the balance when weighted against the excitement of the animal powers of Burke, stimulated by the external temptations offered to them."

The importance of these findings went well beyond the individual case, argued Combe, for phrenology showed that criminals were not freaks of nature, but were indeed part and parcel of the human community. "A Phrenologist would say, that there are still Burkes and Hares in society,—that is, individuals who, while preserved from temptation, may pass through the world without great crimes, but in whom the capability exists of similar atrocities, if similar facilities are afforded them." The solution was a call to social action: "Society ought to take the lesson to itself, that it is its duty, by means of education and rational institutions, to remove excitement to crime from such wretches to the greatest possible extent." Though Combe and other phrenologists were never as effective as they thought themselves in translating their tenets into practice, they took much more seriously than their critics the goals of educational and prison reform. "This is active practical goodness," Combe wrote fiercely, while all the public outcry against inhuman monsters was "mere indulgence of excited feelings, fleeting as the day on which they arise, and leaving no trace behind after time has caused them to subside."

Phrenology gave, perhaps, as good an explanation for serial killing as was available in the 1820s. For the first murder, a phrenologist might say, Burke's and Hare's organs of Destructiveness and Acquisitiveness had to work hard to overcome their Benevolence and Cautiousness, and they experienced aching and soreness, just like someone who tries to make strenuous use of any muscle for the first time. Through exercise in the form of murder, their organs of Destructiveness and Acquisitiveness grew in strength and facility. At the same time their organs of Benevolence and, especially, Caution, atrophied through lack of use, so that by the summer of 1828 neither moral principles nor fear of discovery acted as a brake to their crimes. It was an explanation that made sense to contemporaries, whether or not they used the language of the "philosophy of mind." As Pierce Egan put it, "at the *first* murder" Burke committed, "he felt agitated, unwell, and sick at his stomach; at the *second*, a little sort of compunction operated on his mind; the *third* murder scarcely ruffled his feelings; but on the *fourth*, he grew quite firm; and the murders he committed afterwards were to him mere matters of *routine!*"

Chapter 9

Crime Scene: Edinburgh

James Wilson, alias Daft Jamie

T HE MURDER OF JAMES WILSON, BETTER KNOWN AS DAFT
Jamie, marks another departure from the pattern. Jamie was an established and popular figure on the streets of Edinburgh, where he wandered,
barefoot and bareheaded, in all sorts of weather (Figure 16). Rumors later
circulated that he "had been for some time watched by the gang of murderers, and marked out as one that might be easily taken off without exciting suspicion." But he did not fit the usual profile of the Burke and Hare
murder victims at all, being young—probably in his twenties—vigorous,
and not much given to drink. He was not so much "daft," or crazy, as what
would now be called mentally challenged: "imbecile and incapable of any
continuous mental exertion," as Ireland's *West Port Murders* put it. Perhaps
he was an idiot savant, for he could be prevailed upon to perform odd,
but useful, forms of calculation, such as telling the day of the week on
which a given date would fall. Indeed, for "the boys of Edinburgh," it was
said, he served as a walking calendar. Jamie sang as well, and told jokes in
broad Scots. He did not actually beg, but he was often given gifts of food,
drink, snuff, and small coins, and benevolent households made it a point to
provide him dinner and see he was "kindly entertained." He came from a
local family; his mother was still alive, and he lodged with his sister Janet,
married to a porter and living in Stevenlaw's Close off the High Street.
She and her daughter Mary looked after him well, for "he was scrupulously

clean in his person and linen, changing it frequently," and his "hands and feet, though uncovered, were also observed to be always clean." Surely it was asking for trouble to target him, rather than a more anonymous subject, for Knox's dissecting room. Well-known murder victims would have identifiable physical features, which could be used by the Edinburgh police and medical inspectors to investigate the crime. For, though modern forensic techniques like fingerprinting and blood type analysis were years in the future, the scientific investigation of crime scene, cause of death, and murder weapon was a well-established part of the Edinburgh legal process. A victim whose appearance, clothes, and habits had attracted public attention in life was sure to attract that same attention in death.

Figure 16. James Wilson, known as Daft Jamie. A portrait drawn after his death, reproduced from a contemporary print, courtesy of the Library of the Royal College of Physicians of Edinburgh.

The decision to murder Jamie seems to have been made by Margaret Hare, who had none of Burke's practical sense of a successful murder plan: how to choose a susceptible victim, how to charm neighbors out of their suspicions, how to ward off awkward questions. According to Burke, she found Jamie in the Grassmarket one day in early October, thinly clad and looking for his mother. She persuaded him to come home with her, leading him, Burke said, "as a lamb to the slaughter, and as a sheep to the shearers; and he was always very anxious making inquiries for his mother, and was told she would be there immediately." Leaving Jamie with her husband, she went in search of Burke. She found him at the counter at Rymer's shop, where she went under the pretext of buying some butter. Asking him for a dram, she "stamped him on the foot" while she drank it. Burke knew very well what that meant: there was a new victim in the offing, and after a discreet interval he followed her home. Once Burke arrived at Tanner's Close, Margaret Hare left, locking the door behind her, while Jamie, Hare, and Burke had a companionable drink, and then perhaps another. At some point Jamie lay down on the bed, and Hare lay down next to him. "When they had laid there for some time," according to Burke, "Hare threw his body on the top of Jamie, pressed his hand to his mouth, and held his nose with his other. Hare and him fell off the bed and struggled. Burke then held his hands and feet. They never quitted their grip till he was dead. He never got up nor cried any." It was about 12 noon by the time they were finished.

Jamie had more personal effects than most of their victims. Hare took his brass snuffbox, and Burke, his copper snuff spoon. Usually Burke and Hare destroyed the clothes of their victims, "to prevent detection," but this time Burke gave Jamie's clothes to his brother Constantine for his sons, Richard and William; "they were almost naked, and when he untied the bundle they were like to quarrel about them." Young Richard soon traded Jamie's green waistcoat, with telltale snuff stains, to one of his friends in exchange for a dog. The clothes were noticed. A baker in the Cowgate saw Constantine Burke wearing a pair of trousers that he had originally given to Jamie. One of his sons was likewise observed wearing one of Jamie's kerchiefs. But that came later: on the day of the murder, Burke and Hare, with the porter M'Culloch, delivered the cadaver to Knox's rooms between seven and eight that evening.

David Paterson received the body as usual, directing Burke to lay it on the table so he could check it over before agreeing to payment. It was hard to see, he later testified. The "only light in the room was from a closed lantern having one bundle, and by it the Declarant saw that it was a full grown male subject, but he did not then look at it particularly and did not recognise it as the body of a person he had seen before." It never occurred to him—he testified—that it could be Daft Jamie's, whom he had seen just a few days before, hale and hearty. He gave Burke and his associates three or four pounds, with instructions to call back the next day after Dr. Knox had had a chance to examine the cadaver.

As was customary, Paterson was the first to arrive at the dissecting rooms the next morning, and Dr. Knox and his assistants came in shortly thereafter. "This is the body of Daft Jamie!" exclaimed William Fergusson as soon as he arrived, and the other assistants, too, agreed that it was Jamie's body or a striking likeness. Paterson claimed to be of two minds: he "looked at the body, and actually thought it was that of Daft Jamie, but he could hardly credit the circumstance as he saw that person in the street a few days before in perfect health." Knox, for his part, took one look at the cadaver and ordered it to be made ready for dissection. He assured his students that this ever-so-fresh male subject—the first he had received during the term—could not possibly be anyone they knew.

Once the scandal broke, all of Edinburgh was ready to believe that Knox must have recognized Jamie. There could not be any of the "scientific individuals" who did not know him by sight, according to one pamphlet, "for he was two or three times daily, for hours at a time, in the Necessary (head of College Wynd), the moment he sat down to do his need, he gabbled away at some nonsense or another, which attracted the attention of all who saw or heard him; sometimes, from those who were humane, he got a halfpenny or a penny." Paterson presumably believed it, for his testimony emphasized the speed with which the body was consigned to the dissecting class, out of its turn and ahead of the subjects already obtained for dissection. The cadaver was placed on its stomach, so that the beginners could get to work on the muscles of the back and buttocks—but perhaps also so that the face could not be seen. The arm muscles were cut and feet removed, to facilitate the study of the extremities—but perhaps also so that no deformities or other identifying features remained. After four or five days, when rumors circulated of Jamie's mysterious disappearance, there was no longer any physical evidence to connect him to the severed body parts in Surgeon's Square. Paterson testified that Knox had kept "the Cranium of the head . . . entire for preservation," in his collection, a macabre trophy like his aboriginal "Kaffir" skull.

The police were not interested in Jamie's cranium, but instead, in distinctive anatomical features that could unambiguously identify the male subject delivered to Surgeon's Square as James Wilson of Stevenlaw's Close. Yet though Paterson appeared certain in his published statements, he nonetheless kept equivocating in his official testimony. Yes, the body looked like it could be Jamie's, but he hadn't thought to examine it closely since Dr. Knox had stated so definitely that it was not. Yes, Jamie could be assumed to have some physical deformities: he had been "distorted upon one side, . . . had a halt in his gait" and was "in the practice of walking with one of his arms contracted upon his breast," but of course he never saw the male subject's gait. Jamie's feet were known to be "peculiarly formed," with one foot "twisted or diseased by contraction," but he had never observed "whether the feet of the body on the table were diseased or not." The most he could say was "that the feet were those of a person who appeared to have gone without shoes, That they appeared to be thick and bruised, and often walked without protection, and he does not remember to have observed the same appearance on any other subject." Moreover, he declared, "the face of the body appeared to be sun burnt and equally dark, and the hair to be hard and dry as in the case of a person being exposed in the open air without the head being covered." Yet that could have been true of any number of people on the streets of Edinburgh in October, and the subject "looked more stout and fleshy than he would have expected the body of Daft Jamie to be, but he could hardly form any opinion with regard to the body of Daft Jamie from seeing him slouching along the streets in loose dress." In the end, all the police could get from Paterson was "that if he were upon oath he could not swear that it was [the body of Jamie], and he could not swear that it was not, but he could do all but swear that it was."

William Fergusson never wavered in his conviction that the body was Daft Jamie's. Careful, observant, and dexterous, Fergusson later became one of the most eminent London surgeons of his generation, with a reputation for never forgetting the face of a pupil. Though the cadaver was smaller than he expected, he told the police, the toes were distinctively wide, and he believed it was Jamie. Why, then, did he not go to the police at that time? we may ask. Or when rumors of Jamie's disappearance began to circulate? Paterson strongly implied that both Fergusson and Alexander Miller were involved in some kind of cover-up. Fergusson "seemed doubly anxious to have the feet of this subject, which he received from the students that dissected the body," said Paterson. "It is a common practice amongst the students that when they wish to preserve the bones of any limb entire, to immerse it in a jar of water until decomposition takes place, when the soft [tissue] is cleaned from the bone." But in this case, Fergusson deviated from this practice, "for he immediately was at the no small trouble of detaching bone from bone PREVIOUS to their being immersed in water. I do not present to offer any opinion upon his so doing, I merely state facts."

The police were interested enough in the facts to follow up, but when called upon for an official statement, Paterson gave his story a somewhat different emphasis. He told the police, indeed, that he heard Fergusson "make anxious enquiries for the feet of the above body," and he at last obtained either one or both of them from a medical student, James Evans. Ferguson then "detached the several bones, put them in water and preserved them all" in Paterson's presence. But, as the police found out, Evans had no suspicion that the leg he dissected had come from Daft Jamie until questioned by the police. Surely, if Fergusson were trying to conceal a crime, it would have made more sense to let the feet go to other students and be dissected away, rather than make "anxious enquiries" about them.

Still, we cannot discount the possibility that Fergusson, like his mentor Knox, was so absorbed in his own anatomical research that he deliberately chose not to inquire into the provenance of his cadavers. In 1828, Fergusson was in the process of preparing his probationary essay on the arch of the aorta, required for becoming a Fellow of the Royal College of Surgeons of Edinburgh. "Having been connected for nearly four years with a great Anatomical Establishment, and for a considerable period of that time taken an active share in its management," he wrote in his preface, "I have consequently had many opportunities of examining the anatomy of that part of the body to which this paper applies." Within the next year Fergusson presented a marvelously lifelike preparation of the blood vessels of the feet to the Royal College of Surgeons, and it remains one of their prized possessions. It is likely to have required meticulous examination of the soft tissues of many pairs of feet, and it is possible that Daft Jamie's were included.

Whatever the explanation for the missing feet, it is clear that this was the second cadaver that Fergusson had recognized as having been in health just a few days before turning up on the dissecting table. If he thought this was anything other than an odd coincidence he did not say so, but it seems likely he was growing increasingly uneasy. He certainly appears to have cooperated fully with the police during the subsequent investigation. He remained convinced of Knox's innocence throughout his life, seeing him as much a victim of Burke and Hare as Jamie himself. Many years later, when he was attacked by James Syme in the pages of the *Lancet* for his connection with Knox "of whose dissecting room he had the principal charge during a very eventful period," Fergusson was quick to respond in the same public forum. "I have ever been proud to acknowledge my early association with that distinguished anatomist and teacher," he wrote; "my success in life I gratefully attribute to the advantages I enjoyed as one of his assistants . . . for an 'eventful period' of about seven years, during which time I was favoured with much of Dr. Knox's professional confidence." He had nothing to be ashamed of, for that position "gave me an influence and a start in life which few men between the age of 19 and 26 ever possessed." The period of their professional collaboration also corresponded to the peak of Knox's success, which may have been more due to Fergusson's influence than Knox's biographers recognized. Certainly we might interpret Fergusson's careful record keeping for Knox's dissecting rooms, instituted in the fall of 1829, as his way of ensuring that his mentor would never be imposed upon by miscreants again.

And yet it surely seems to us, as it did to contemporaries, as though Knox and Fergusson must have missed some telltale evidence—or refused to look at it. Jamie was the only one of the victims known to have struggled with his murderers. Surely, surely, some decisive evidence must have remained. "Tyro as I am on matters of anatomy," wrote Paterson in an anonymous pamphlet, "I have always been led to consider that suffocation or strangulation causes the blood to flow to the head, consequently makes the face of a strong livid colour, with a small discharge of blood from the mouth, nose, and ears." Since Jamie, like the other Burke and Hare subjects, "had suffered death by suffocation. . . . I think it is but natural to infer, that if the Doctor saw these bodies, he is either horribly ignorant of his profession, or he wilfully withheld that information he ought to have given." The *Caledonian Mercury* went further. Burke and Hare, so expert in other murders, from "impatience and impetuosity" missed the opportunity to pin down Jamie's chest, "and only grappled him by the throat." In consequence, "the poor creature was able to exert his whole strength—and a desperate, a mortal struggle ensued, in the course of which several external wounds were inflicted on him. . . . That such traces and marks were left on the body of Jamie is sufficiently proved by the fact that his body was kept four or five days in spirits before it was laid on the dissecting table. The effect of immersion in spirits, we need scarcely say, is to remove the lividity consequent on external bruises or contusions, to corrugate the skin, and to give it all one uniform colour." The *Caledonian Mercury* was quite incorrect: neither Paterson nor any other witness had seen Jamie's body kept in spirits, let alone any "external bruises or contusions." But that phrase, "we need scarcely say," is a tribute to the high level of sophistication the *Caledonian Mercury* expected of its readers when it came to forensic pathology. James Wilson, aka Daft Jamie, had been murdered. There had to be physical evidence.

Edinburgh was an unusually favorable environment for the emerging field of forensic science. The first chair in medical jurisprudence and police was established at the University of Edinburgh in 1807. It was the brainchild of an enterprising medical professor, Andrew Duncan senior, and it combined his long-standing interest in public health and hygiene with his overwhelming desire to have his son appointed to the medical faculty. Andrew Duncan junior was a conscientious lecturer, but like his father he framed the subject matter of the course around legal issues of public health. The chair had marginal status within the medical faculty, and Duncan was pleased to be able to move to the chair of physiology within a few years. He was succeeded by William Pulteney Alison, equally conscientious, but equally pleased to move on to other pursuits, like social and medical reform. Neither Duncan nor Alison had any practical experience with criminal trials. Nor did Robert Christison when he was appointed to the chair in 1822, largely on the basis of his family's political connections. He had, however, studied chemistry in Paris, where the newly appointed professor of medical jurisprudence, Mathieu Orfila, was in the process of creating the field of forensic toxicology. Christison transformed the chair of medical jurisprudence: forensic pathology, especially the detection of poisons, took center stage, and public health was relegated to a few summary lectures. He attracted a devoted student following and played academic politics effectively enough to earn his discipline a more secure position in the medical curriculum. His testimony in a series of high-profile homicides involving arsenic led to his reputation as "the highest authority that this country (or Europe) could produce."

Christison's appointment came at a time when the police establishment, too, was shifting its focus toward a more modern concept of policing. The position of police surgeon had been carried over from the old Edinburgh watch, and had originally entailed provision of any kind of medical services, including caring for injured patrolmen, aiding victims of assault, and testifying as to cause of death. By the 1820s, though, the police surgeon, Alexander Black, had taken on the role of frontline medic, the first to be called in cases of violent crime and therefore the first to be in a position to detect and preserve the medical evidence. Two more medical inspectors were appointed by the Crown on a case-by-case basis. Their job was to establish the cause of death and uncover any existing physical evidence. Christison was frequently appointed medical inspector, especially in cases of suspected poisoning, while members of the College of Surgeons were more frequently appointed in cases of assault or asphyxiation. Under John Hope as solicitor general, the procurator fiscal's office took medical jurisprudence very seriously indeed. Even outside the university and courtroom, the long-standing association of legal and medical professionals in Edinburgh society, often from the same families, fostered a familiarity with legal and medical concepts. Perhaps the combination of literacy and litigiousness prevalent in Lowland Scots culture did the same. Sir Walter Scott surely knew his audience when he built *The Heart of Midlothian* on a set of criminal trials, holding closely to existing documents and his own familiarity with legal procedure.

There were two aspects of Scots law that encouraged the use of medical evidence. The first was that it could be used to corroborate the testimony of the *socii criminis*, "partners in crime." These were suspects who were offered the chance to turn king's evidence, that is, to testify against their erstwhile associates in exchange for immunity from prosecution. Their testimony was particularly vulnerable to attack from the defense counsel, for they could be accused of lying to save themselves. Judicial practice was very rigorous: it was, in the words of one judge, "clear and settled law" that the testimony of a "*socius*" could go to a jury, but only "if corroborated in some points," and if " it appeared to be consistent with itself, and with the other proof." Medical evidence could provide essential corroboration for their testimony. The second aspect of Scots law that supported medical witnesses was a set of restrictions on interrogation of suspects. Once a defendant had been indicted, he or she could no longer be interrogated. That made it much harder for prosecutors in Scotland to get a confession, for once the indictment was served, the defendant had only to remain silent and await trial. Under those circumstances, medical witnesses could provide key testimony.

Though called by both prosecution and defense, medical experts retained their character as independent witnesses, who were bound to give accurate testimony no matter what it might do to a carefully prepared case. As in modern crime scene laboratories—in real life rather than on television—forensic science was considered to be most valuable in confirming or rebutting the testimony of witnesses or suspects, what would now be called exclusionary evidence, rather than in detection. Indeed, Christison wrote in a handbook for medical inspectors, *Suggestions for the medico-legal examination of dead bodies,* medical testimony was most important where it "furnishes good tests of the value of otherwise doubtful evidence." He would have liked to see them given even more information, and at an earlier stage of the case. "The Procurators-fiscal should supply the Inspectors with such parts of the precognition as may have been previously taken," he wrote, adding that "one or more of the persons best acquainted with the circumstances of the case should accompany the Inspectors, and be on hand during the examination to answer their questions." In more complicated cases, where the medical evidence might be crucial to a verdict, "advantage would often be derived from requesting one of the Medical Inspectors to aid the law-authorities in conducting the precognition, wherever it touches the medical evidence."

According to Christison, the medical examination began with the crime scene. He directed medical inspectors to take careful notes on the position of the body, and of the surrounding area, "with a view to discover the objects on which it rested, marks of a struggle, signs of the presence of a second party about the time of death, or after it, weapons or other objects . . . the remains of poisons, marks of vomiting," and marks of blood. Where "marks of blood are of importance, and doubts may arise as to their really being blood, the articles presenting them must be preserved for farther examination." Clothing was important, as were any stains, "of mud, sand, or the like, of blood, of vomiting, of acids, or other corrosive substances . . .

marks of injuries, such as rents or incisions." Rips and tears on the clothes should be compared to the position of injuries on the body, and "where stains apparently from poison are seen, the stained parts were to be preserved for analysis."

Once the crime scene had been investigated and all such matters noted, the body should be transferred to the police station, or other convenient location, for examination. Medical investigators had to think about their role in building a prosecutor's case, wary of defense attorneys who could cast doubt on the medical testimony. Christison's *Suggestions* counseled that the "examination and dissection of the body should not be undertaken, if possible, except with sufficient daylight in prospect to allow the whole inspection to be made without artificial light." There should be two inspectors present, one to conduct "the practical details of the examination," and the other to "take notes of its successive steps." The notes should indicate "all the points inquired into, with the observations made, and appearances presented, negative as well as positive,—and stating simple facts only, without either generalizations or opinions." Necessary equipment, besides what would ordinarily be found at a dissection, included "a foot-rule, and an ounce-measure graduated to drachms, for measuring distances and the quantities of fluids,—a few clean bladders for carrying away any parts of the body which it may be necessary to preserve for future examination,— and, in cases of possible poisoning, three or four bottles, of 8, 12, and 16 ounces, with glass stoppers or clean corks, for preserving fluids to be analyzed." All distances, lengths, and surfaces which might bear on the case should be precisely measured, the authors asserted, as should all weights and volumes. "Conjectural estimates and comparisons, however common even in medico-legal inspections, are quite inadmissible."

All this describes idealized circumstances, when an uncontaminated crime scene could be examined at leisure and an undecomposed body carried clear sign of the cause of death. We can, however, see similar procedures followed by police surgeon Alexander Black, late on a summer's evening, when he was called to what proved to be a fatal stabbing just off the High Street. He found a woman, Mrs. Gow, in the stairwell, "lying on the floor all covered with blood," and when he examined her he found "a large incised wound betwixt the third and fourth rib which perforated the thorax; likewise an incised wound on her right and left arm." One of the bystanders showed him a shoemaker's knife on which there was some blood, and "having measured the wounds," Black was "of opinion that they had been inflicted with the said knife and he marked it." "Blood was issuing profusely from the wounds," Black testified, and he "considered her in the greatest danger." He asked her "how she got herself so severely hurt and she said she had been stabbed by Gow her husband & thought she was dying." Another stabbing victim, Alexander Polson, was "sitting on a chair in the same apartment supported by two people & vomiting much." Black found he had "a large wound on the leg all bleeding most profusely," and considered him to be in the greatest danger as well. He compared the same knife to Polson's wounds, and was "of opinion that they had also been inflicted by it." Polson, too, told him that "Gow stabbed him & that he conceived he was dying." Black dressed their wounds and sent them to the Royal Infirmary; when both died, James Gow was charged with the murders. Both the knife and Mrs. Gow's heart were preserved as evidence and are now held by the Royal College of Surgeons of Edinburgh.

We may note that there is not much detection necessary here. Both Mrs. Gow and Alexander Polson accused Gow of stabbing them; there were other witnesses; and Black did not even have to search for the murder weapon, for one of the bystanders handed it to him. Murders that came to trial in Edinburgh were not typically whodunits. Most occurred during fights in front of plenty of witnesses, the murderer quickly apprehended as he stared down, dazed, at the body of his wife or neighbor. No one would have had the least doubt of Gow's guilt even if Black had not measured the knife wound and knife. But of course it was not Black's job to detect guilt or innocence. Nor did he have the luxury of a fictional detective, to point the accusing finger and let someone else build the legal case. His task as part of the Police Establishment was twofold: to care for the crime victims, and to follow the evidence from assault, to injury, to cause of death. His testimony was essential to the prosecution in Gow's case, because a clever defense attorney might have admitted Gow's guilt in the assault, but argued that his two victims died in the infirmary from other causes. The jury might therefore find him not guilty of murder, or find the charge not proven. So Black's testimony was a model of careful and precise medical observation. Witnesses, including the two victims, testified that Gow had perpetrated the stabbing. Black identified the knife at the crime scene, and ascertained that it could have inflicted the wounds. The victims believed that they had received mortal wounds, and he believed them in the greatest danger, that is, unlikely to recover. The medical staff at the infirmary testified that the wounds had been severe, and there was no medical evidence to assign any other cause of death. Finally, both knife, and incised wound to the heart, had been preserved. One look at the specimens and no jury would doubt the cause of death.

What if Gow had been innocent? What if someone else had stabbed his wife and Polson, what if the victims had been dead when Black arrived, and what if that "someone" had then handed the knife to Black and disappeared? Could the medical evidence have helped bring the perpetrator to justice, or saved Gow from being arrested and tried for murder? Probably not. There would be no way to use fingerprints to track down a killer or exonerate the accused for another seventy years. Alibis were seldom useful, for the Police Establishment did not have the manpower to check every story. Had Gow been innocent, his recourse would have been his defense attorney and the Scottish legal system, not the medical evidence. Still, the evidence appears to have been generally adequate to the task. Since knives and blunt-force trauma were the usual causes of death, victims often survived long enough to name their killers; since most crimes occurred in the heat of the moment, there were often neighbors and other witnesses available to testify. And since there were surgeons available in every part of the city, medical experts were seldom more than a few streets away.

When James Brown, a laborer, was assaulted by John Gray near the seaside suburb of Musselburgh, the local surgeon and sometime poet David Moir was called as the medical inspector. Brown had been taken to the infirmary but died the next day, so that Gray was accused of having "wickedly culpably and recklessly inflicted several severe blows upon the head or body of James Brown . . . by which the said James Brown was repeatedly knocked to the ground and his head having by one or more of the said blows been driven against a stone or other hard substance of the pavement of said Street his skull was thereby fractured and he was severely and mortally wounded." Again, there was no doubt about the assault, which took place in front of witnesses who provided over one hundred pages of testimony. The question was whether the assault was the cause of death, and that was the question Moir set out to answer.

Christison's *Suggestions* set out the standard procedure for a postmortem dissection. The body itself should be examined on all sides, "not neglecting the back, as is often done." This should be done before cleaning, so as not to wash away "marks of mud, blood, ligatures, injuries, stains from acids." The medical inspectors should also look for "foreign bodies, or injuries within the natural openings of the body, namely the mouth, nostrils, ears, anus, vagina, and urethra." If they are in any doubt about whether stains are blood, the skin must be preserved for later analysis. "If there are impressions of finger-marks" left on the skin, the medical inspectors "will consider which hand produced them." They must also look for ligatures, commonly found on "the neck, the wrists, the ankles, and the waist." Time of death could be investigated through the extent of decomposition: "the degree of looseness or rigidity of the joints . . . , the degree of warmth of the trunk and extremities . . . , the odour of the body, the looseness of the cuticle, the colour of the skin, and formation of dark vesicles on it, the evolution of air in the cellular tissue, the alteration of the features, the softness of the muscles, the shriveling of the eyes, the looseness of the hair and nails."

All this duly noted, the body was to be washed and the head "shaved, or at least closely cut." Once again, the medical inspectors should minutely investigate the body on all sides. What they were looking for specifically was "the appearance of lividity," where the blood seemed to deposit itself once it was no longer kept circulating by the beating heart. By "noting its chief seat and its relation to the posture in which the body was found," the medical inspectors could determine whether or not it had been moved. They might also be able to discover "impressions on the skin of objects on which it had rested." Careful inspection at this stage might show them "marks of injuries, more especially contusions . . . , marks of disease, such as eruptions, ulcers, and the like . . . , marks of burning . . . , marks of concealed punctures in the nostrils, mouth, external openings of the ears, the eyes, the nape of the neck," and other less visible parts of the body.

Whether Moir really did all this is open to question. This murder, like the previous one, was not a mystery. All witnesses agreed that Brown had been knocked to the ground and repeatedly hit his head, so there was no point in looking for marks of suffocation, or burning, or concealed punctures. Instead, the medical inspectors concentrated on Brown's very obvious head injuries. "We could discover nothing externally," Moir wrote, "except a puffy swelling, immediately above and behind the left ear; and on proceeding to dissection found a considerable quantity of blood extravasated between the scalp and temporal muscle." They removed the muscle, and found that "liquid blood continued to ooze copiously through the skull."

Its source was soon apparent: "a fracture was discovered about four inches in length, with depressions about the centre to the extent of a full inch in diameter, the lower portion of the depressed piece being completely detached." Once the skull cap was removed, a large clot of blood "of considerable size and probably more than three ounces in weight" was found between the skull and brain just under the fracture, the position of which was precisely identified. It produced "a very extensive and deep indentation on the Lateral and Posterior Lobes of the Brain." From that, Moir concluded, "We have no hesitation in stating that the Fracture of the Skull and its consequences were the cause of death." Moreover he was "decidedly of opinion that the fracture could not have been occasioned by the blow of a man's fist, but might have happened by a fall on the edge of a stone, or other hard substance," such as the cobbled pavement of the street on which James Brown was assaulted. Once again, the medical testimony supported the prosecution's case that the assault was the direct cause of death.

Daft Jamie, though, had not been stabbed, with the murder weapon considerately left around for bystanders to present to the police; nor had he been repeatedly battered against cobblestones. His cause of death, suffocation, was much harder to prove beyond a shadow of a doubt, unless the murderer was caught in the act. Christison's *Suggestions* gave detailed instructions on how to examine bodies "in cases of suspected death by hanging, strangling, or smothering." The first thing to attend to was "the state of the face as to lividity," for it should appear flushed, as blood was forced into the face. The eyes should appear bloodshot, the tongue, lolling out of the mouth. The medical inspectors should look for "nail-scratches, abrasions, or small contusions in the throat, chin, and lips," and for congestion of the lungs and organs of the abdomen. "The mark of a cord or other ligature round the neck must be attentively examined," according to the handbook, "and here it requires to be mentioned, that the mark is often not distinct till seven or eight hours after death, and that it is seldom a dark livid mark, as is very commonly supposed, but a pale greenish-brown streak, if made with a rope." Other "effusions of blood and lacerations" should be looked for, as well as "accessory injuries on other parts of the body, most especially on the chest, back, and arms."

The cases on record involving suffocation required little effort to uncover the cause of death, or near death. Early on the evening of February 6, 1827, Margaret Petrie went to visit Thomas and Catherine Graham, who lived a few doors down from her flat in the southern suburbs of Edinburgh. She knocked and knocked, and was very alarmed when "Grannie," as Mrs. Graham was known, told her to come in and see her husband, who had hanged himself. She looked in and saw Thomas Graham "lying on the floor with his head about a foot from the ground." She ran off to get a knife, but by the time she had returned another neighbor, John Anderson, had cut him down and sent for the surgeon. Graham was lying insensible a few feet from the bed, and his face was swollen and black. The neighbors were sure "he would not have lived two minutes, if he had not got assistance." The surgeon, Patrick Campbell, agreed. The police were called, and after Alexander Black examined Graham, he was sent to the Royal Infirmary, where he soon recovered.

The main suspect was Catherine Graham, aged sixty-nine, who behaved throughout "like a person deranged with passion, or in drink," cursing and swearing, and shouting "roast him alive, roast him in Hell!" Thomas insisted that he had not tried to hang himself. He had felt ill and had gone to bed, but had no memory of what had happened that day until he woke up and "found his neck very sore." He bore no particular animosity toward his wife, to whom he had been married for forty-six years. They had had ten children, he said, and his wife had "brought up her family in as decent a way as any poor man's wife could do." She had been addicted to "take a glass 'for a gae time back,'" but he "would have no particular dislike to take her home, if she were now at liberty." One of the judges tried to get Graham to say that he would henceforth keep her from drinking anything stronger than water. This seemed too cruel to Graham: "He would be sorry to confine her to that," he responded.

Despite Graham's inclination to forgive and forget, his wife's trial had to go forward. Margaret Petrie had testified that "there was no other persons" in the room but Thomas and Catherine Graham when she "opened the window-shutter," and looked into the apartment. There was napkin and rope around Thomas's neck, according to John Anderson, and "the rope was below the neckcloth, twisted tight round his neck, and fastened to a nail in the beam above." Mrs. Petrie did not see the neckcloth, for she came in after Anderson had removed it, but she saw the rope, which "had been wound three times round his neck. . . . There were three black marks, as large as her finger, round the neck" as well. Alexander Black also reported "a *broad red mark round his neck*, which was swollen as thick as the declarant's forefinger" as well as "a very considerable swelling up the left side of Graham's head" with a high fever. Mrs. Petrie identified the cord as "such as is used for an eight-day clock," and it was produced at the trial. Yet if the weapon was clear, the manner of the assault remained murky. The nail on which the rope was hung was very high up: "A person standing on the chest of drawers could not have put a rope round the nail in the beam," testified Mrs. Petrie, "nor could a person, by standing on the end of the bed, have done so." There was a table in the room, though, and she thought that by "standing upon a high table" it would be possible to reach the nail. The jury was left with two unlikely scenarios. One was that Thomas had stood on the table, hung a rope on the nail, wound it three times around his own neck, then jumped off without overturning the table, to end up with his body on the floor and his head, suspended by the rope, hanging about a foot off the floor. The other was that Thomas had been sleeping in bed, perhaps with a fever, while his wife climbed onto the table and attached the rope to the nail. She had then tied the rope three times around his neck, somehow dragging him out of bed and suspending him without any effective struggle on his part. "It was one of the most melancholy cases he had ever known," noted Solicitor General John Hope, "and in some respects inexplicable. It appeared to have been in a fit of temporary derangement, produced by intoxication," that the act had been committed. Neither excuse could be used by the defense, and the jury found Catherine Graham guilty as charged, though they "recommended her to the lenity of the Court, on account of her years." She was sentenced to eighteen months in prison, "to be allowed no drink stronger than water." It is possible that the judge considered this preventative treatment, rather than punishment.

Both the quick-thinking neighbors, Margaret Petrie and John Anderson, showed a striking awareness of the importance of physical evidence, and this lay understanding was demonstrated time and time again in murder trials. It was as though Edinburgh was populated with Sherlock Holmes's aunts and uncles, directing the attention of police to clues they may have missed and vying with expert witnesses to see who could give the more precise testimony. James Robertson, for example, a goldsmith on the High Street, was awakened on the night of October 27, 1827, at about midnight, by cries of "Murder, Murder, I am burnt!" He knew they came from his upstairs neighbor, Archibald Campbell, who had been threatened repeatedly by Hugh and Euphemia McMillan, living just down the hall.

The trouble seems to have started with a trivial disagreement: Mrs. Campbell had left a chair in the common passageway to prevent her child from leaving her flat, and Mrs. McMillan objected to it. She picked up the chair, and threw it back into the Campbells' room, damning Alexander Campbell "for a bugar," and crying "that if he came out she would lick his skin for him." Mrs. Campbell ran to call the police as Mrs. McMillan pushed her way into the room and shook her fists at Campbell, cursing him repeatedly. When the patrolman arrived, Mrs. McMillan "appeared to be in liquor and was in a dreadful rage," he testified, shouting "that she would have the bugar's life as soon as she got out, altho' she should hang at the head of Liberton's Wynd for it." Mrs. McMillan spent the night in jail and was brought before the Police Court the next day, when Campbell gave evidence against her. The judge ordered her to find caution—that is, lodge payment with the court—for her good behavior for the next twelve months, and to pay all the expenses of the court. She was released when her husband paid the bail, but both continued to be incensed: once back in their building McMillan pushed open the Campbells' door and called out "Damn you Campbell, I shall be revenged on you yet." He continued to harass Campbell for the next two days, declaring he would wash his hands in Campbell's heart's blood.

When he heard the cries upstairs on October 17, therefore, Robertson feared that Campbell had been assaulted while returning to his own flat. He had his son call out the window for the night watchman "to guard the stair in order that no one might escape," and headed upstairs. Mrs. Campbell also heard her husband's cries. She "opened her room door and she saw McMillan's door closing as she went out." It was dark in the passage as she went downstairs, calling out, "Is that you Archie." Yes, he called back, "I am burnt and I am certain it is with vitriol." She, her father-in-law, and Robertson helped Campbell up the stairs to their flat, where "they saw that his eyes and face was dreadfully scorched." He said "that as he was coming up stairs he heard McMillan's door open, and something was instantly thrown in his face but he did not see the person who had done it." By that time the watchman had arrived. He forced open the McMillans' door and positioned himself in the flat; he was still there when Lieutenant John Home arrived to take charge of the investigation, having been notified in the Police Office that a serious case was under way. Home found the McMillans in bed, and when he asked them if they had been out and committed the assault they "affected to be ignorant of what had happened." Home arrested them, and proceeded to examine the premises. He began by examining the stair, where he "saw drops of some liquid extended from the place where he was told the acid had been flung upon Campbell, along the passage to McMillans door." He then "searched the house minutely in the hope of finding the vessel in which the acid had been contained, but without success." It occurred to him that it might probably "have been flung out of the window and the window having been opened he examined particularly if there was any drops on the frame but he saw none. That he then went down stairs with the Watchman and saw him pick up in the Close right under McMillan's window the broken pieces of what appeared to have been a small jug or cup." He touched "a piece of it to the tip of his tongue and found that it had contained something of a sour burning nature."

Mrs. Campbell and James Robertson had already noted the significance of the liquid in the passageway. They had traced it, Mrs. Campbell testified, "from the place where her husband was standing on the Stair when the Vitriol was thrown into his face, to McMillan's Door." The lower part of the door, she noted, was "an inch or two above the level of the floor, & some of the liquid was lying on the floor immediately below the Door." She tasted it, and noted that it had a sour taste, but she could not say for certain that it was vitriol. Robertson could, though. He "examined these drops which he saw extended from a window in the stair case to McMillan's very door, and upon testing them he knew it to be muriatic acid or oil of vitriol, and his reason for knowing it so well is that he uses the same acid, after he dilutes it, in the course of his business." He went back upstairs to test Campbell's clothes, which appeared burnt, "and upon applying the tip of his tongue to the neck of his cloak," he knew "that it had been done by the same acid as that spilt on the floor."

In contrast to the neighbors, the expert witnesses did little to move the case along. Alexander Black was not in attendance that night; instead, the acting police surgeon was his son, Alexander Black junior, a second-year medical student. He looked after Campbell, noting the presence of acid on his face and applying water before taking him to the infirmary. "Someone" called upon him "to examine some liquid upon the post of the outer door on the passage," but he did not "examine the stair or passage leading to McMillans house to see whether there were any drops of the acid upon it." He assumed the liquid was sulfuric acid, without, apparently, investigating it further. Robert Christison, who tested the broken cup and Campbell's clothing for the presence of acid, made the same assumption. But the lord advocate was aware of the discrepancy: "All the witnesses, except the medical call this substance 'vitriol,'" he wrote in his notes on the case's loose ends, "the Medical, 'sulphuric acid'—They are not the same." It is likely that the goldsmith Robertson had correctly identified it as muriatic (hydrochloric) acid, not quite as dangerous as sulfuric when spilled on the skin. Campbell might have recovered, but he developed an infection at the infirmary and died two weeks after his assault. Though the medical testimony gave the cause of death as inflammation "originating from the wound made during the operation of blood-letting," Euphemia McMillan was nonetheless convicted under an 1825 statute making it a capital offense to assault with acid "with intent to murder or maim, or disfigure or disable." She was sentenced to death, later commuted to transportation. Her husband, Hugh McMillan, was found not guilty.

Despite the acumen displayed by laymen and professionals alike, forensic science was still limited. Deliberate destruction of evidence was less of an obstacle to criminal detection than forces of nature: once decomposed, a cadaver would no longer reveal the cause of death. Christison's *Suggestions* present the optimistic opinion that even lapse of a "considerable period" between death and inspection was no reason to forgo the examination. It "must in all cases be proceeded with," and if the body was putrid, it "will be rendered greatly less annoying to those present, by frequently washing the parts successively exposed with a solution of chloride of lime." Indeed, according to the *Suggestions*, "It is of moment to remember, that the internal organs are often in a great measure entire, though the external parts are much decayed." But this was wishful thinking in the real world of an urban homicide investigation. If the "external parts" of a cadaver showed any marks of violence, they would be entirely removed by decomposition. Careful murderers could therefore escape conviction if they could hide their victim's body long enough for telltale bruises or punctures to decay.

Perhaps policeman Charles MacMahon had learned how to stymie the medical experts through his work, for the murder he and his wife, Margaret, allegedly perpetrated was one of the rare instances of a cold-blooded killing for gain. Alexander Phillips, a Jewish fur dealer, left his lodgings on

North Richmond Street on July 3, 1827, and was never heard from again. He had just quarreled with his father over a watch he had purchased from a man in Leith, and had gone out to return it and get his money back. At that time he was carrying perhaps £200 in bank notes, and another £50 in gold, as well as several watches and a silver snuffbox. His father grew anxious about him when he did not return, but as a recent immigrant from Poland, he did not contact the police, believing that he could not make himself understood well enough in English. On July 7, a porter, James Heymer, took a shortcut following a narrow footpath through a field of oats, and "found the body of a man lying across the path, his left arm below the body, and his right stretched out." He did not see any signs of a struggle, but he did find a hat lying a few feet away, with a very little blood upon the inside.

By the time he returned with patrolman Alexander Moir, "two dozen of people were standing round," and the grain "was now considerably trampled." Apparently they knew not to touch the cadaver, though, for it was left the way Heymer had found it, "lying on the face," Moir testified, "with the right arm stretched out, and the hand turned up." The body was already decomposing, and there was no sign of blood. This meant, as everyone was aware, that the man had probably died elsewhere and then his body concealed by dumping it amid the oats. Moir testified that "there was thick moisture below his face, and his beard sticking to the ground, and partially separated from the face." No money was found on the corpse, but his pocketbook contained letters and certificates giving his name and address. Phillips's father was duly notified, and identified the cadaver as his son. His clothes were still intact, and his silver watch was found in an inside pocket. The rest of his valuables were gone.

The police had little to go on in what the procurator fiscal called a "mysterious and unsatisfactory Case," and so Phillips's father called in a friend, Moses Leisenheim, to investigate his son's death. Leisenheim located the MacMahons and worked with the police to set up a sting. On August 20 he went to their house to purchase two gold watches, taking a servant girl who, at a prearranged signal, fetched the police. They searched the premises, finding the watches and the snuffbox identified as belonging to Phillips. Margaret MacMahon tried to hide Phillips's purse by dropping it into a tub of washing. But Leisenheim saw her and directed the policemen to search the tub. When he saw the purse, Leisenheim exclaimed,

"You are the murderer of the Jew, for this is the Jew's purse." Margaret sat down, Leisenheim testified, "and grew as white as death."

Many of the valuables last seen on Phillips were found at the MacMahons' flat, and they were charged with murder and theft. The police also found enough other articles of clothing and jewelry for the couple to be charged with receiving stolen goods. This was just as well, for the prosecution had the unwelcome experience of watching the murder charge unravel in court. The problem was that the medical testimony was not conclusive, and the defense attorney attacked it vigorously. Alexander Black was the first to examine the body when it was brought into the Police Office. He "ordered the clothes to be stripped off preparatory to the body being inspected by the Surgeons," and noted carefully that they "were not in any way cut or torn . . . the pockets & waistband of the trousers were whole." The only damage that he could find was "the pocket in the left breast of the coat which he was told had been done by the Policemen to take out the pocket book." The medical inspectors called into this case were experienced surgeons, William Brown and Alexander Watson. They testified that they believed Phillips met a sudden death, for his "limbs were plump and firm," with no sign that he "had been bed-rid." Internal organs—what was left of them—showed no pathological signs. The *"brain was in such a state of decay being almost fluid,"* so that it was *"impossible to ascertain the existence of any disease."* The "lungs and heart" were also "considerably decayed, but seemed in a healthy state," and "the stomach and intestines so far as examined had no appearance of disease." Thus all evidence pointed to Phillips's having been perfectly healthy when he left home on July 3. But did the evidence necessarily indicate death by violence? That was trickier to determine. There was no sign of a blow to the head, for "Upon cleansing the Skull," Watson noted, "no fracture or mark of injury could be observed, and the brain was quite in a fluid state from decomposition & its exterior membrane entire." Nor could he detect signs of assault, for "the skin upon the parts of the body which were covered with clothing was nearly of its natural colour so that any marks of violence could clearly have been discovered but none could be seen."

That left strangulation or suffocation as the most likely form of homicide, if homicide it was. Watson gave as his opinion "that if the man died by violence it most *probably was by strangulation.*" However, "from the state of decomposition of the head and neck no evidence of that could be observed." It was not for want of trying. Brown carefully examined the head, neck, and chest, but as he testified, the *"face and neck were so much disfigured that they could not ascertatain whether there were marks of strangulation or other violence,* nor whether his face had the appearance of a person who had been strangled." Blood had collected beneath the skin under the neck, "which might have been caused by a tight ligature round the neck, but that the state of decay from innumerable maggots made it impossible to ascertain whether there were any marks of such ligature." The maggots were a problem for Watson, too. He testified that "if there had been any blood upon the face it must have been eaten off by the maggots along with the exterior surface of the skin and from the state of the flesh and skin it could not be discovered whether there had been any injury of the flesh or skin so as to allow blood to escape or not." But Watson did not think there had been very much blood, or at least not sufficient to cause death, because "the skull appeared quite uninjured."

The two inspectors could not say for certain how long Phillips had been dead. Brown thought three or four days, but had to admit that "he has had very little experience with regard to the time which dead bodies take to putrefy when exposed to the air." It was Watson's opinion, based on the recent weather—it had been hot, with thunderstorms—as well as "the appearances on the body" that "the man must have *been dead four or five days* at least." The lack of precision weakened the case, as did the lack of any shred of evidence linking the accused to the dead body. The victim "might have been strangled for aught you can say?" asked the presiding judge. "He might. He was a stout man," Brown replied. But that was easily countered by the defense during cross-examination. "When you say that for aught you know he *might* have been strangled, we are to understand, of course, that for aught you can tell, he *might not* have been strangled." "Certainly," Brown replied. "You cannot say whether he may not have died of apoplexy?" the defense attorney continued. "No," replied Brown, "I cannot."

That settled the matter. The lord advocate, in his address to the court, had to admit that he had no case for murder. Certainly "there were the strongest grounds of suspicion that the deceased had lost his life by unfair means," he told the jury. "There was pregnant suspicion of a murder having been committed," and committed by the accused at the bar. But "from the medical evidence . . . it was too narrow a case against them, as what formed the first inquiry in every case of this kind, the cause of death, was left in uncertainty." The judge directed the jury to find the murder charge against the MacMahons "not proven." Members of the jury were not happy about this, and appeared to be about to deliberate further, but they were informed in no uncertain terms that they legally "could not touch a hair of the prisoner's head." So the case of murder was dropped, but the MacMahons did not get to leave the court. They were immediately tried on the charge of theft and reset of theft, found guilty through their own confession, and sentenced to fourteen years' transportation.

Alexander Phillips's case shows that even Edinburgh forensic science was still limited in the 1820s by the ages-old problem of proving murder without an intact corpse. Hence the widespread outrage at Burke and Hare, who had hit upon a way to destroy the single most incriminating piece of evidence—the cadaver—and be handsomely paid for it as well. For supposing that Jamie, like Phillips, had been suffocated but not dissected? Supposing his body had turned up more or less intact? The police would have been called, and his body turned over to Alexander Black and two medical inspectors. They could have examined the body, noting any of "the external bruises or contusions" caused by the struggle leading up to his death. Jamie's face might have been congested with blood, and his eyes bloodshot; though there would have been no marks of a cord on his neck, postmortem examination might have revealed the "nail-scratches, abrasions, or small contusions in the throat, chin, and lips" indicating the use of force to stop the flow of air into his lungs. Even if there were no forensic signs clear enough to convince a jury, there would, at least, have been enough to warrant a thorough police investigation. Medical witnesses would have testified to the fact that the victim was strong and appeared to be in good health, with no physical evidence of fatal disease. Other witnesses for the prosecution would have testified that they saw Constantine Burke and his children wearing Jamie's clothes, and Constantine would have had to explain where the clothes had come from. That line of questioning would have led directly to Burke, and eventually to the Hares, who had kept Jamie's snuffbox and other possessions, and would have had no satisfactory explanation of how they had obtained them. Even if the evidence was not sufficient for the lord advocate to indict them for murder, it would have been enough to keep them in prison while the investigation moved forward. It would have been enough to save Madgy Docherty's life, when she arrived in Edinburgh some six weeks later.

We do not, in fact, know whether there was forensic evidence of Daft Jamie's murder that would have been apparent to Knox and his assistants. The difficulty, as Christison noted in the *Suggestions*, was that careful forensic analysis really required examining the body "before it is undressed or moved from the spot where it was first found," that is, where the death could be presumed to have occurred. "If the body has been previously removed or meddled with," the text continued, medical men "ought to inform themselves accurately as to its original position. In many cases it is material that they personally visit the place where it was first seen; and they should inquire minutely into all the particulars connected with the removal of it." Knox and Fergusson had not seen the cadaver in situ, but only on the table on the dissecting room, by which time any "traces and marks" could have faded, or been plausibly attributed to packing and handling.

More important, though, was the anatomist's customary environment of "secrecy and mystery," which so deliberately separated the cadaver from its previous existence as a person. Confronted with a young male "subject," no one in Knox's dissecting establishment undertook the active inquiry of the kind assumed by Christison and his forensic colleagues. "If this is not Daft Jamie, then who is—was—this male subject?" Fergusson might have asked. "If he is not Daft Jamie, then why has Jamie been reported missing?" He might have left Surgeon's Square to undertake further investigation, might have asked "John" or "William" to point out the boardinghouse or street in which their cadaver had been found. But like Knox six months earlier, he made no awkward enquiries. With eyes fixed determinedly on their cadavers, with scalpels held firmly in hand, the anatomists at Number 10 Surgeon's Square moved steadily, disastrously, toward the approaching scandal. Some writers blame the Edinburgh magistrates for the murder, wrote Christopher North during the trial, and some the London Parliament, "but I canna help blamin', especially, Burke and Hare—and neist to them Dr. Knox and his assistants." Let Knox go to sleep at night in a lonely wood, "and by skreich o'day he will be seen flyin' wi' his hair on end, and his een jumpin' out o' their sockets . . . pursued, as he thinks, by saxteen ghaists a' in a row wi' Daft Jamie at their head, caperin' like a paralytic as he was, and laughing like to split . . . at the doctor or the doctor's man, distracted at the sicht o' sae mony spirits demandin' back their ain atomies."

Chapter 10

Day in Court

William Burke

T HE CADAVER WAS A MALE SUBJECT, THIRTY-SIX YEARS OLD, not very tall, but muscular and well built. In life, it had belonged to William Burke, laborer and shoemaker, "whose hands," according to *West Port Murders*, "were more deeply dyed in innocent blood than those of any other homicide recorded in the calendar of crimes." Arrested, with Helen M'Dougal, William Hare, and Margaret Laird or Hare, he was tried, with M'Dougal, for the murder of Margaret Docherty or Campbell on December 24, 1828. The case was covered in exhaustive detail in newspapers and broadsides, in *West Port Murders,* and in *Trial of William Burke and Helen M'Dougal.* For the Scots loved their trials, and they were justly proud of their legal system, among the most equitable and humane at that time. Burke and M'Dougal were represented, free of charge, by the best legal counsel. They were tried under judges who protected the rights of the accused and before juries who demanded the strongest possible evidence before convicting on a capital case. During their day in court—literally a day, for the trial ran continuously for twenty-four hours—they therefore derived more direct benefit from eminent men than they had met with in their entire lives. The Scottish legal system saved M'Dougal's life, though it did nothing to guarantee her future. It convicted Burke and executed him on Wednesday, January 28, 1829.

In the end, it was neither the police nor the medical men who were responsible for putting a stop to the series of murders, but the lodger, Ann Gray, filled with that investigative spirit apparently so prevalent in Edinburgh neighborhoods. She had come from Maddistone, near Falkirk, where she had known Helen M'Dougal, who had lived with her father as if his wife. That made her a kind of stepdaughter, and so she and her husband, James, were very pleased to renew the acquaintance in October 1828, shortly after their arrival in Edinburgh from Aberdeen. James Gray had been born in the Grassmarket, where his father had kept a public house. Though listed as a laborer in court records, he had been trained as a jeweler and had worked in both Glasgow and Edinburgh. When business failed, he had joined the army and served for a number of years, probably in Ireland. He had returned to Edinburgh to look for work, and ran into Burke on the High Street. Burke sought out the Grays' company, inviting them "to remain at his house." Helen M'Dougal even accompanied Ann Gray to pay the ninepence owed their former landlord. At the time, Gray imputed this friendliness "to his wife being a town's-woman of Burke's wife, and Helen Dougal"—as he insisted was her correct name, rather than "M'Dougal"—"having had two children by Gray's wife's father." Later, he told interviewers, he had "every reason to think that Burke had an intention of making Gray and his wife victims also." That seems plausible, from the pains Burke and M'Dougal took to ensure that the Grays lodged with them; by this point we have no reason to trust their unsolicited friendliness. Perhaps, as an outraged journalist later assumed, their success at purveying their former victims had emboldened them still further. Perhaps "a year's impunity had produced the effect of making them consider themselves as engaged in a species of profession which had indeed, like illicit distillation, or any contraband traffic, to be concealed from the authorities, but which, except for this annoying accompaniment, was pursued with nearly as little compunction as any other profession would have been." Perhaps Burke thought his good character with the police—bolstered, according to James Gray, by treating the local watchman to a bottle of whiskey every night when he came off duty—would keep him safe from all suspicion. Or perhaps by this time Burke and M'Dougal, William and Margaret Hare were beyond asking themselves any questions, and simply, horrifyingly, thought of anyone who came within their grasp as a potential cadaver.

If the Grays had been their original targets, Burke and Hare had no difficulty in turning their attention to Margaret Docherty when she appeared in Rymer's shop on October 31, 1828. And as it turned out, their apparent hospitality to the Grays proved their undoing. What excited Ann Gray's suspicions the morning after Docherty's murder, she told her husband, was Burke's and M'Dougal's "not allowing her to clean the house." She thought "they had stolen goods concealed among the straw," and she told her husband she intended to look into it. "This put them on the search for the body," James Gray told journalists, and "Now," said his wife, once the room was clear, "I will see the mystery." As we have seen, after finding the body Gray went for the police, despite M'Dougal's plea and offer of £10 per week. *Murderers of the Close* reflected the common view that Ann Gray, who gave her testimony in court in "a very distinct manner," was the real heroine of the story, while her more pusillanimous husband had hung back to avoid trouble. "'But Nanny, dear,'" said the "irresolute husband" in the story, "fearful perhaps of embroiling himself and his wife, 'were it not best just to let the matter rest.'" "'Shame on ye!'" the fictional Ann Gray retorted, "'would ye see murder done and remain silent? At the least I will not.' And without waiting to hear anything further from her cautious husband, Nanny Gray hastened on her way to the police office." Sherlock Holmes fans might remark on the historical coincidence that she, like their hero, smoked a pipe. But both James and Ann provided evidence crucial to the prosecution, for they alone could swear to seeing the dead body actually in Burke's house, lying naked under the bed, face to the wall and blood on the nose and mouth. The Grays were much praised in the newspapers for not allowing themselves to be bribed into silence, and the publisher Robert Buchanan, at that point hard at work on his forthcoming *Trial of William Burke and Helen M'Dougal,* asked the public for donations to reward for their honesty. "Books," wrote John Stevenson to Charles Kirkpatrick Sharpe, "lie at the three Shops for the Signatures of those who feel well disposed to the cause," a useful piece of advertising conveniently located next to order forms for the soon-to-be-published *Trial.* James Gray was ultimately offered a position on the Edinburgh Police Establishment, "from the great services he rendered the Public in this matter." If this were historical fiction it would be pleasant to imagine them a husband and wife detective team, lodged in the Grassmarket above Gray's father's old pub, solving crimes in the Old Town and New. In historical fact Gray was dead within a few months, and his wife applied to Charles Kirkpatrick Sharpe for assistance. "You are the only friend that I have, in this place," she wrote to him shortly after her husband's death. "I have not any other person to apply to." She had been left "a very poor widow indeed" and "owing to your former goodness I would take it very kind of you if you could have the goodness to assist me as I have nothing to depend upon on to get him interred and pay any lodgings." She wrote Sharpe again about a year later, when she and her child had been ill, but after than she disappears from the archives.

Not even the Grays were enough for the lord advocate, Sir William Rae, to build an airtight case. "Sensible, cool-headed, and firm," according to his good friend Sir Walter Scott, "always thinking of his duty, and never of himself," Rae enjoyed a good reputation in the highly politicized world of the Edinburgh legal profession. He had previously served as sheriff of Edinburgh, and his appointment as lord advocate in 1818 signaled the government's desire for a cooling of partisan fury. Adopting an understated, conciliatory demeanor in court, he supported Whigs as well as Tories for promotion to High Court judgeships. His correspondence with the procurator fiscal, Archibald Scott, shows an insistence on high standards and rules of evidence in criminal cases, and he was instrumental in the 1830 revision of the Scottish legal system which largely defined its modern form. Still, for all Rae's sympathy for reform, he was determined that it should come from the government, not in response to public clamor. During the Burke and Hare sensation, the public press complained repeatedly that the lord advocate was not providing enough information. Rae took no action against them, but neither did he respond to their complaints. He clearly felt that access to information, like criminal justice administration, should remain firmly in his own hands.

Once the seriousness of the crime became clear, Rae took an active role in the investigation. Burke and M'Dougal had been arrested on Saturday, November 1, and had been placed in separate cells. William and Margaret Hare were arrested a day later. They did not see each other again until the trial, though they may have been able to pass some information back and forth through other prisoners or the guards. On Monday, November 3, a formal warrant for their incarceration was sworn out for the murder of "Mysie or Madgy McGonnegal or Campbell or Duffey." Burke's and M'Dougal's first statements were taken on November 3, and presumably the Hares' were as well, though they have not been preserved. Burke's declaration invoked that mysterious man we have met in other depositions, who always seemed to appear just before the crime and disappear to some untraceable location immediately thereafter. In this case, Burke alleged, the man, whose name he did not know and whom he had never seen before, had paid him sixpence to leave a box in his rooms for a day or so. When he left, he had placed something under the straw of the bed, and Burke, investigating, had found a dead body, but he could not tell whether it was a man or a woman. Take it away, he told the man when he returned, it was wrong for you to have brought that here, and the man promised to return later that evening. When he did not, Burke and Hare arranged to sell the body to Knox, through Paterson. The woman Docherty was entirely separate: he admitted that she had stayed with him but knew nothing of what had become of her. The cadaver he had delivered to Knox was certainly not hers. He had never seen the mysterious man again.

In the meantime, the medical investigation had begun. Police surgeon Alexander Black had first examined Docherty's body when it was brought into the Police Office on Sunday morning, November 2. Black did not find any bruises or wounds "of any consequence." Her face was swollen, and "of a blackish hue." Her eyes were swollen, too. There was "blood about her nose, and there was saliva," but Black could not find any cuts on the face that would explain it. He had gone to Burke's house the night before, where he had found "a quantity of blood, mixed with about 15 or 16 ounces of saliva." Black had been told at that time that "the woman had lain in that place," and therefore concluded that the "saliva must have come from her mouth and nose."

Once Black had examined the body, it was time for the two medical inspectors, Robert Christison and William Newbigging, appointed by the lord advocate. At Rae's request, Professor of Medicine William Pulteney Alison assisted them. He probably kept in close contact with his brother, Archibald Alison, who was one of Rae's advocates depute, that is, part of the prosecution team. Christison, Newbigging, and Alison examined Docherty at 3 P.M. on Sunday, November 2, and again at 11 A.M. on Monday, November 3. The choice of Christison for medical inspector is an interesting one, since his specialty was toxicology. It suggests that poison was being considered as a cause of death. Christison did examine the stomach, but found little there except "about a pint of this grayish pulp, like half digested porridge, entirely free of any spirituous or narcotic odour." The skull, brain, and other internal organs were all "perfectly natural," only the liver showing early signs of "the incipient stage" of the "disease of drunkards." The most important sign of trauma they uncovered was during the examination of the spine, consisting of the rupture of "nearly the whole posterior ligamentous connexions" between the third and fourth vertebrae. As Christison later wrote, they "were at first disposed to look upon the laceration of the spine as an injury produced during life, and adequate to account for death." It did not seem to fit, however, with the pattern of other contusions found on the body; moreover, a blow that would lacerate the ligaments of the spine would be expected to produce other effects on the body. Christison could not find any answers in the medical literature, so he decided to carry out experiments of his own while consulting with other experts in the field. He and his colleagues took three fresh cadavers—where they obtained them was never explained—and subjected them to a variety of blows to the back and other parts of the body. After studying them carefully over a period of twenty-four hours, they came to the conclusion "that the marks of contusions were almost certainly inflicted during life," but that the "injury of the spine might have been caused seventeen hours after death, as well as during life," that is, by being packed into a tea chest prior to being transported to Knox's dissecting rooms.

By Burke's second statement, made on November 10 after witnesses had identified the cadaver as Docherty's, he was prepared to admit that she had, in fact, died in his house. It was from natural causes, he claimed. They had been drinking, the Hares, M'Dougal, and himself, and when Docherty came in she had joined them. They were all in front of the fire, "but he cannot mention the hour." At some point he and Hare "had differed," while the three women continued to drink. The men began to fight, and M'Dougal and Margaret Hare tried to separate them. When they had cooled down, and sat drinking again, they noticed Docherty was nowhere to be found. On searching, they found her, dead, under the straw of the bed, "lying against the wall, partly on her back and partly on her side." There was vomit from her mouth, but no blood; she was still warm, but not breathing. The women left the house, and the men stripped the body. "It was then proposed by both of them," Burke said, "but he cannot say by which one of them first, to sell the body to the surgeons." This story made a valiant effort to establish that all four of the suspects were together, and otherwise occupied, at what could be construed as the moment of Docherty's death. It also protected the women from the charges of theft or trafficking in dead bodies, by establishing that they had left the room before he and Hare had mentioned the surgeons. It may not have occurred to Burke that either M'Dougal or Margaret Hare could be tried for murder. Burke himself, he said, had "no concern in killing the woman," and "no knowledge or suspicion of Hare, or any other person, having done so." It was "his opinion that the woman was suffocated by laying herself down among the straw in a state of intoxication."

But the medical evidence, as Christison was later to point out, together with testimony of when Docherty was last seen alive, told against Burke's story. "At eleven the woman, though intoxicated," Christison said, "was sensible enough to be able to dance and sing"; a few hours later she was dead. "Now death from simple intoxication in so short a time was impossible, because then we should certainly have discovered spirits in the stomach." The same would be true of death by suffocation, caused by the falling into "an awkward position by which the access of air to the lungs was mechanically obstructed." Moreover the victim would have had to be completely insensible and unable to move even her head, let alone crawl under the straw. Taking all the information together, Christison and Newbigging gave it as their formal opinion "that the fluidity of the blood, the ruffling of the cuticle over the throat, the lividity of the face without lividity elsewhere, and the great redness of the eyes, with the blood found where the body had lain, were signs," together with those already mentioned, that made it "probable" that Docherty "had died by violence." The hyoid bone, a rather fragile bone in the neck, was "further apart than usual" from the thyroid cartilage, but it was still intact. A modern medical examiner would therefore have ruled out strangulation as a cause of death, but this was still largely uncharted territory in 1828, and "throttling," Christison wrote, "was the form of strangulation we suspected."

The guarded words of the medical inspectors—"probable" death by violence, "suspicion of death by strangling," and the clear statement that the appearances of the body would justify "nothing more" than a probability—would not by themselves guarantee a conviction, especially since the medical evidence did not directly link the cadaver to the prisoners. Under no circumstances could Rae risk releasing the prisoners for lack of evidence. Once rumors of the murders began circulating, sending the four prisoners home would lead to exactly the kind of public tumult he was determined to avoid. It was necessary, he later wrote, "that a conviction should be *ensured*." Moreover, he felt it "his imperative duty, not to rest satisfied without having the matter probed to the bottom, and that he should, for the sake of the public interest, have it ascertained what crimes of this revolting description had really been committed,—who were concerned in them,—whether all the persons engaged in such transactions had been taken into custody—or if other gangs remained, whose practices might continue to endanger human life." The usual strategy employed against any group of suspects was to find one willing to turn king's evidence, that is, to testify against the others in exchange for immunity from prosecution. Perhaps Rae thought that Hare, as the younger of the two suspects, was the less culpable, or perhaps he thought the case would be easier to prove against Burke, because of "the particular murder which led to the whole discoveries," as the *Edinburgh Observer* noted, "having been perpetrated under Burke's roof." In addition, Burke's actions in inviting Docherty to his home, and his conversation with Paterson concerning a subject, "naturally point out him and his guilty partner [M'Dougal] as the more immediate objects of legal vengeance."

Had Hare seen this coming? The author of *Murderers of the Close* depicted him dancing about the room when told of the lord advocate's offer, "glad that I got my neck out of the halter . . . and as for poor Bill (Burke), why he must go hang, I suppose." In real life it is not so clear that Hare was the villain in chief, or that he had planned so far ahead. But the real Burke may have been as dumbfounded as the fictional one to learn that Hare was to be a witness against him and M'Dougal. The first indication may have come with the arrest warrants sworn on the murder charges. The initial warrant for Docherty's murder had, as we have seen, allowed for the incarceration of all four prisoners. The second, for the murder of "James Wilson a young man of weak mind," was initially dated November 19, and was likewise sworn against all four. On November 29, though, it was amended to authorize incarceration of Burke and M'Dougal only. If the warrants were read to them, as seems likely, then Burke, at least, must have pondered the meaning of the change. By December 4, when the final warrant for incarceration in the murder of Mary Paterson was drawn up naming only Burke and M'Dougal, Burke may well have realized they had been betrayed. We can only imagine his response to this blow, as did the author of *Murderers of the Close*: "The infernal—the deliberate villain," the fictional Burke muttered when he heard. "He is worse than me! this man

. . . this false and turncoat villain—false to his God and to myself; 'twas he first tempted me to this, and now . . . he purchases his own security by denouncing him he hath ruined." The real Burke would have had another source of anguish: it was not only he, but also M'Dougal, with whom the Hares had purchased their security.

But was M'Dougal truly a "guilty partner," as the *Edinburgh Observer* put it? Surely it was Hare who deserved to stand trial with Burke—was it altogether fair of Rae to retain M'Dougal in the indictment, when he knew full well that the much more culpable party would go free? But Rae had made his position clear in other criminal cases: if there was evidence justifying an indictment, then it was his duty to indict, and to build the strongest case possible for the prosecution. It had been his "painful duty" to the public, he told the jury, to put Burke and M'Dougal on trial, in order "to remove that alarm which prevails out of doors, and to afford all the protection which the law can give to the community against the perpetration of such crimes." He had been fortified in his decision by the knowledge that the defendants were entitled to legal counsel: "the Bar of Scotland," as he put it, "does itself honour by undertaking the defence of the unhappy persons who are brought before this Court accused of offences." He knew, therefore, that "the most distinguished of my brethren" were "engaged in the defense." If the prisoners at the bar were acquitted, he hoped that it would be acknowledged that he nonetheless had had sufficient reasons for trying them. If they were convicted "the country must be satisfied that the conviction will be just, when the defense is in the hands of counsel so eminent, and so universally and deservedly respected." In other words, Rae had no intention of sparing M'Dougal the ordeal of a trial if that would imply weakness on the part of the government, or leave questions in the public mind. His was the sword of justice to wield. It was up to his "honourable and learned friends on the other side of the bar" to convince the jury to temper it with mercy.

In fact Burke and M'Dougal got the best legal team assembled anywhere, for the Whig opposition, so well represented among Edinburgh advocates, saw the trial as the perfect opportunity to take on Rae and the rest of the Tory establishment. James Moncreiff, a longtime and passionate advocate for reform causes, was the chief legal counsel for Burke; Henry Cockburn, eloquent and outspoken critic of the Tory administration, was chief legal counsel for M'Dougal. It is not clear when, or how often, they met with their clients, nor what Burke or M'Dougal told them. This was not a case for Perry Mason: counsel for the defense did not need, or perhaps even want, to hear the whole truth. What they needed was a strategy to weaken the case for the prosecution sufficiently so that the jury would return a verdict of "not proven."

By the 1820s, after so many years of appearing for the defense, Cockburn and his colleagues knew that strategy by heart. Cockburn and the young advocate Duncan M'Neill had in fact scored a spectacular victory against the Crown almost exactly a year earlier, when they had defended James Dewar, an iron founder in the district of Silverfield in Leith, against the charge of reset of theft, in this case receiving pig iron bars that he had known to be stolen from the Shotts Ironworks. The prosecution must have felt they had an open-and-shut case. The two chief witnesses were two carters who worked for the Shotts company, Potter and Mitchell. They swore that they had consorted with Dewar to steal the pig iron from their loads and deliver it for £3 per ton, well under the usual Shotts foundry price of £6 10s. It was under his direction, they said, that they first broke the bars into pieces, and then covered them with salt and water, "that they might acquire a coat of rust, and appear like old iron." This disguise did not work very well, for Dewar's foreman could not help wondering about why he was asked to receive new pig iron, broken into pieces. He had also wondered why the carters brought their load so early in the morning, and received payment from Dewar's daughter. He "suspected something wrong," but when he mentioned this to his boss, Dewar replied "If I do not take it, another will, and it is as well that I should get a bargain as another." The clerks at Shotts testified that slightly over nine tons of iron had gone missing, and there were "occasional irregularities" in paperwork for deliveries made by Potter and Mitchell. By the time the prosecution finished its case, James Dewar appeared very guilty indeed.

But Cockburn and M'Neill did not have to prove him innocent; they only had to demonstrate that the prosecution had not proven its case, that the indictment had not been sufficiently proven. Any hole they could punch in the evidence brought forward would support their case, that the Crown had not been sufficiently careful in its investigation. Any inaccurate statement, weak inference, or sloppy reasoning was fair game. For that reason, the only witnesses brought forward by the defense had nothing to do with the theft. Instead, they had legal authority over the land on which Dewar's foundry was placed, and they swore it was not, as named in the indictment, part of the district of Silverfield, which lay perhaps fifty feet away. That was all, and when the lord advocate addressed the jury, he pointed out that this was a trivial distinction, "and there could be no ambiguity" in the indictment, or suggestion that Dewar owned some other foundry, for there was no other iron foundry in the parish. When Cockburn, in his turn, addressed the jury, he argued that such distinctions were anything but trivial. It was the prosecution's job to ensure that the indictment was founded on facts: the correct address of Dewar's iron foundry "was a fact on which the Prosecutor was bound to obtain correct information, and having failed in so essential a part of his case, he was not entitled to ask a verdict on evidence which had now no foundation on which to rest." The whole indictment was shot through with ambiguities, he implied, for the prosecution had not even verified the existence of Shotts Ironworks as a company, or proved that those persons claiming to be its representatives and managers were really so. This was an important point, for it addressed the question "To whom did the iron belong?" Before Dewar could be found guilty of reset of theft, it had to be proven that a theft had taken place, that is, that an entity really existed that had been robbed of its lawful possessions.

If this was all a little nit-picking for the jury, the strongest part of Cockburn's defense came when he attacked the prosecution's chief witnesses, Potter and Mitchell. "No jury was ever asked to believe the evidence of a thief," he told them, unless "it was amply confirmed by that of good witnesses." The only evidence of what was said at the meeting between "those miscreants," as Cockburn described them, and the defendant, Mr. Dewar, came from the thieves themselves. And Potter and Mitchell had a perfect motive for lying, for it was "the interest of all thieves to give up a resetter, as the only means of saving themselves." The consequences would be "extremely dangerous" for the general good if the jury "by their verdict . . . should sanction the doctrine that respectable persons in business were to be at the mercy of every infamous wretch, who might have an interest to swear any thing against them."

Once both the prosecution and the defense had presented their closing arguments, it was the task of the lord justice clerk, David Boyle, to charge the jury. In a modern trial this would involve his explaining aspects of the law that applied to the case, while maintaining strict impartiality as to the verdict. Boyle, however, generally used the charge to direct the jury's atten-

tion to the most important points presented by the Crown, in effect plead-
ing on behalf of the prosecution. But in Dewar's case neither he nor the
Crown attorneys convinced the jury, which returned a verdict of not guilty,
to the expressed "disapprobation" of the Justiciary Court judges, but presumably to the entire satisfaction of Cockburn and M'Neill. We can think
of this case as a dress rehearsal for the trial of Burke and M'Dougal, for the
defense deployed similar strategies in both trials. The first was to weaken
the indictment by any means possible. The second was to attack the credibility of the *socii criminis* who were the chief Crown witnesses, arguing
that they were the true criminals, whose lies threatened to deceive the jury
as they had once deceived the prisoners at the bar. And the third was to
leave the jury with the impression that the defendants were not miscreants,
but rather respectable people caught up in a web of circumstances beyond
their understanding.

Cockburn and Moncreiff came to court on Wednesday, December 24,
prepared to put these principles into practice. "No trial in the memory of
any man living has excited so deep, universal, and, we may almost add,
appalling an interest," reported *West Port Murders*, and on Monday and
Tuesday people could talk of nothing else. "The coming trial," people expected, "was to disclose something which they had often dreamed of, or
imagined, or heard recounted around an evening's fire, like a tale of horror,
or a raw-head-and-bloody-bones story, but which they never, in their sober
judgment, either feared or believed to be possible." By 7 A.M. on Wednesday a large crowd had gathered outside the High Court of Justiciary, filling
Parliament Close. The first group the sheriff's officers admitted were the
jurymen, shepherding them into the court buildings through a separate
door off the Signet Library. Just before 8 A.M., the officers admitted the
gentlemen of the public press. The witnesses had been previously sequestered in a separate room. Precisely at 9 A.M., the full complement of the
Faculty of Advocates and Society of Writers to His Majesty's Signet, all
of whom had the privilege of attending the High Court proceedings, were
seated in the courtroom, taking up half the available space. And "in fact,"
noted *West Port Murders*, "the narrow dimensions" of the courtroom, "which
have been often complained of . . . were never more seriously felt."

The prisoners, Burke and M'Dougal, were brought in about twenty
minutes before 10 A.M. They had probably not seen each other since their
arrest, but now they were seated together. Observers commented that they

appeared "without any visible signs of perturbation," and "to attend very visibly to the proceedings." Burke was especially attentive to M'Dougal, speaking to her calmly and occasionally smiling. The likeness we have of him, drawn during the trial, shows a round-faced man, with sandy hair and "a determined, though not particularly sinister expression," noted *West Port Murders*. He was dressed in his best clothes, which look entirely respectable to modern eyes, with buttoned coat, which we are informed was shabby and blue, a striped waistcoat, high collar, and cravat. Helen M'Dougal also appears neat and respectable in her portrait, though contemporaries inform us she was "miserably dressed in a small stone coloured silk bonnet, very much the worse for wear, a printed cotton shawl, and a cotton gown." She looks sad and anxious, her "large, full, black eyes"—though they were blue according to the jail records—open wide, and there is no record of any smiles from her during the trial.

At 10:15 the court was in session, and all those expecting a grand legal show were gratified within the first few minutes. The first order of business was reading the indictment, but Patrick Robertson, counsel for the defense, promptly objected to it. We might call this step one of the defense strategy, the weakening of the indictment. Robertson intended, he said, to show that the indictment was inadmissible, and argued that reading it in its present form would create prejudice in the minds of the jurors. The judges could see where this was going. "I am against novelties; I am against interfering with the discretion of the court," said Lord Meadowbank, the most outspoken though probably least competent among the six justices, and so the indictment was read, formally charging Burke with the murders of Mary Paterson, James Wilson, and Margaret Docherty, and M'Dougal with being "art and part of"—aiding and abetting—the murder of Docherty.

Once the indictment had been read, the defense moved to their formal challenge. James Moncreiff, defense counsel for Burke, submitted that he was not bound to answer to an indictment that charged him "with three unconnected murders, committed each at a different time, and at a different place," and was combined with the trial of another defendant "who is not even alleged to have had any concern with two of the offenses of which he is accused." Similarly, M'Dougal, through Moncreiff, submitted that she was not bound to answer to an indictment that placed her together with "a different person, who is accused of two other murders . . . it not being alleged that she had any connection with either of those crimes." This accumulation of defendants "and of offences is not necessary for public justice, and exposes the accused to intolerable prejudice."

The next few hours were spent negotiating these points in front of the judges, with both the defense and the prosecution quoting arguments and precedents against or for the indictment as written. The judges ultimately decided that the court could best protect the right of the defendants to a fair and unprejudiced trial by splitting the indictment into three separate murder charges, which would come to trial separately. The lord advocate could decide which murder charge he wished to try first, and Rae chose the murder of Docherty. This decision has generally been considered a victory for the defense, and certainly it provided essential protection for M'Dougal. But Rae might not have been entirely displeased at the outcome, for murder charges without bodies were always hard to prove. The prosecution's strongest evidence lay in the Docherty murder, and Rae may have felt he lost little by jettisoning the other two charges.

By early afternoon, the prosecution was allowed to present their case. All those who had seen or heard Margaret Docherty on or before the night of October 31 came forward to give their testimony. They were clear and direct, the kind of witnesses the prosecution looked for when presenting a case. Early on during the trial "a large window was thrown open as far as it could be done, and a current of cold damp air beat, for twenty-four hours, upon the heads of the whole audience." Since most of the audience consisted of "Advocates and Writers to the Signet in their gowns, these were wrapped round their heads, and, intermingled with various coloured handkerchiefs in every shade and form of drapery," gave the audience "such a grim and grisly aspect as assimilated them to a college of monks of inquisitors . . . grouped and contrasted most fantastically with the costume of the bench and crowded bar engaged in the trial." M'Dougal, at least, had her silk bonnet, but Burke had to sit through the proceedings bareheaded. They were both allowed water to drink, and around 4 P.M., Burke asked when they would be given dinner. When told it would not be until 6 P.M., Burke asked for a "biscuit or two." At dinner, both Burke and M'Dougal "ate bread and soup heartily." It is not clear whether the trial continued as they ate, or whether the court as a whole took a short break. There was no formal recess, however. To formally postpone the proceedings, even for dinner, would raise procedural questions about the validity of the trial.

The cornerstone of the prosecution's case, of course, was the testimony of William and Margaret Hare, who were also depicted by artists during their court appearance. Hare was described by a journalist as "one of the most squalid looking wretches we have ever seen," but in his engraving he appears a self-possessed young man, with head held high and steady gaze. Margaret Hare, described as "a short, stout, round-faced and fresh-complexioned personage," was cast in the popular mind as Lady Macbeth. In her engraving, her angry, brooding expression is mirrored by the child she carries; the engraving is more a caricature than a portrait. The child cried, off and on, during the trial.

Hare testified that Burke, together with M'Dougal, had plotted to kill Margaret Docherty. He and Burke had been drinking in a public house, and Burke said "he had an old wife in the house, and that it was a *shot* for the doctors." That night, after all the drinking, he and Burke had quarreled. Docherty had run out twice, and, Hare said, "It was Nelly M'Dougal that brought her back both times." Finally, when she lay drunk and unconscious, Burke "got on the old woman with his breast on her head, and kept in her breath." All Hare had done was help deliver the body to Dr. Knox. Margaret Hare had not been an eyewitness to the murder, but the conversations she had with M'Dougal were damning. M'Dougal, she told the court, had come to her house earlier in the afternoon or evening, "and said there was a shot in the house," a woman, and that "Burke fetched her in out of a shop." Did M'Dougal say they intended to murder the woman? Margaret Hare was asked. "No," she replied, but she "understood from the word *shot* they were to do it" for she "had seem some of the same *tricks* before."

The Hares' testimony led directly to step two of the defense strategy, the discrediting of the chief witnesses for the prosecution. Hare was certainly vulnerable to attack, as Cockburn made clear in his cross-examination. "Have you been connected in supplying the Doctors with subjects upon other occasions than those you have not spoken to yet?" Rae objected, and Cockburn asked that the witness leave the courtroom while he explained his strategy. He intended, he said, to ask Hare "this specific question— Have you ever been concerned in murders beside this one? I am ready to admit he is not bound to answer; but I am entitled to put that question, let him answer it or not as he pleases. It will be for the Jury to judge of the credit due to him, after seeing how he treats it." The justices engaged in a learned discussion over whether Hare could be asked about other crimes he had committed, or whether the defense had to restrict themselves to this case alone. The outcome was that and other potentially incriminating questions might be put, but the witness would be warned in advance that he was not bound to answer the question. When Hare was recalled, Cockburn himself issued the genial warning. "I am going to put a very few questions to you, and you need not answer them unless you please." Since Hare did not please, the effect was a rapid-fire assault that the prosecution could not prevent. How often have you seen your associates carrying subjects to the doctors? began Cockburn. "Was there murder committed in your house in the last October?"—a clear reference to Daft Jamie's murder. When Burke told him he had "got a *shot* for the doctors," did he understand "that Burke meant to murder that woman or somebody?" At no point did Hare deny the implications of these questions, so that the jury could infer that such an answer would be perjury. It was clear that he knew what Burke meant by the word "shot." It was clear he knew to equate it with murder. It was clear he had received money from Dr. Knox, though he claimed it was Burke who gave it to him, in exchange for helping to "transport" the body. And the climax to the series of questions left Hare's credibility in shreds: "And did you sit in the chair," Cockburn asked, all the time Burke was murdering Madgy Docherty? "And did you sit ten minutes on that chair without stirring one hand to help her?" "You did not cover your head?" "You stood and saw it with your own eyes?" "You did not call murder or police?" "You took the body to Surgeon's Square. . . . And you took money for it?" "And the next day, in the police office, you denied that you knew anything about it?" To all of these, Hare answered, simply, "Yes." Small wonder that one of the illustrations for *Murderers of the Close* made Hare, looking on from a chair, as prominent in the picture as Burke committing the actual murder.

Cockburn attacked both William and Margaret Hare mercilessly in his closing remarks. Hare was clearly "a monster, whose will, as well as his poverty, will consent to the perpetration of the direst crimes." His wife was no better: "I never saw a face," said Cockburn, "on which the lines of profligacy were more distinctly marked." She did not even look at her child "with one ray of maternal softness," but instead used the infant "merely as an instrument for delaying or evading whatever question it was inconvenient for her to answer." It was "in vain" to say their stories were corroborated, for "though you may corroborate a *doubtful* testimony," the "idea of confirming the lies of these miscreants, is absurd."

Step three of the defense strategy was the recasting of the defendants into respectable people, caught in a web not of their own devising. Ann Gray's testimony, so strong for the prosecution, could also be worked into the defense. When she was in the witness box, the court requested her "particular attention" to the interchange she had had with M'Dougal before going to the police. "When my husband went up the stair," she said, he "mentioned to her that he had found a corpse in the house; and she said hold your tongue, and she would give him five or six shillings"—or perhaps, on further reflection, it had only been two or three—but she had also said "that he might be worth £10 a-week if he would be quiet; and he said, 'God forbid that he would be worth that, for he could not keep it on his conscience.'" Ann Gray asked her "what she had been about, I had found such a thing in the house"; and she echoed her husband's rejection of money in exchange for silence. What did M'Dougal mean, she asked "by bringing her family into disgrace" by such a thing? "My God," replied M'Dougal, "I cannot help it."

Did this attempt at bribery mean that M'Dougal was an accessory to the murder? Absolutely, argued the lord advocate in his closing argument to the jury, and "recollect, I pray you" he said to the jury, "the nature of the bribe,—£10 per week—a truly enormous sum, recollecting the price immediately paid for the bodies destined for dissection." The implication, which the jury could no doubt figure out for themselves, was that M'Dougal was prepared to kill a subject a week to keep the Grays quiet. But the counsel for the defense also highlighted Ann Gray's testimony, and both Moncreiff and Cockburn fastened on her last reported phrase from M'Dougal, "my God, I cannot help it." Cockburn argued that, "in a moral sense," M'Dougal was as completely under Burke's influence "as any wife could be to any husband. Great allowance, therefore, must be made in judging of her conduct, from the control which he may have exercised over her; and for the interest which she may naturally, and most properly, have had in concealing her husband's crimes."

What "proper" reason could M'Dougal possibly have for lying about her husband's activities? Cockburn explained that Burke "was a professional resurrectionist. His trade consisted in supplying anatomical teachers with subjects; a trade which, when conducted properly, is not only lawful, but absolutely necessary. The remains of mortality form the materials of that science, by which the sufferings of mortality are to be alleviated, or its date prolonged." This was a stroke of brilliance on Cockburn's part, for it tied into the public debates on anatomy in a most satisfying way. We may wonder if Burke was surprised to hear his supposed resurrectionist activities asserted as a fact to which it was, in Cockburn's words, "impossible to shut one's eyes." After the trial Burke was to state, positively, that he had never supplied subjects for dissection "by raising dead bodies from the grave." But by that time M'Dougal had already been acquitted, and indeed Cockburn guarded against the possibility of being contradicted by his own client under cross-examination by carefully reserving his argument for his closing statement. He did not, of course, speak out in favor of grave robbing. There is no doubt, he told the jury, that it was an occupation "which necessarily corrupts those who are engaged in it. It is shocking in itself;—it is generally conducted in violation of law—and it must always be conducted by a disregard of the most sacred and reverential feelings of our nature." In phrenological terms, as we have seen, that meant that the trade would lead Burke's moral sentiments to atrophy from lack of use. And prolonged contact with a man engaged in such a morality-numbing activity could only blunt M'Dougal's own moral sense, all the more since her interest—her husband's livelihood, and her own—depended on it. So "in judging of her delinquency," Cockburn went on, the jury should take into consideration that she "was the wife of a person who had a professional connection to dead bodies, and with whom no woman could live, without seeing many things, which are better imagined than told. A thousand circumstances may concur in the life of such a woman, even where she is perfectly innocent, any one of which would be fatal to the idea of innocence in an ordinary sense." M'Dougal's proffered bribe indicated a none-too-clear conscience, certainly. But it did not prove she was accessory to the murder.

Cockburn used similar reasoning to explain why M'Dougal had lied to the police. Her statements were clearly false, he admitted, "fallen upon to conceal the crime." But they were exactly what could have been expected, given "the suspected, or the guilty, trade which her husband was engaged in; and I have not a doubt that she was obliged to resort to similar deceptions every week. It was her misfortune to live in a situation in which, even when there was no idea of anything like murder, she was habitually obliged to make false statements to account for the possession of dead bodies, or to avoid the suspicion of having them." In this way Cockburn redefined the defendants into respectability: William Burke a professional purveyor of medical supplies, and Helen M'Dougal a dedicated housewife, making excuses to the neighbors for the weekly nuisance of dead bodies turning up in her parlor.

The orations of the opposing counsel went on for six hours, and it was early in the morning by the time they had concluded. In his summing up, the lord justice clerk once again took the prosecution's side, and Burke assumed, after the directions Boyle gave the jury, that M'Dougal would be found guilty as well as himself. "In view of which," according to *West Port Murders*, "he gave her directions how she should conduct herself, desiring her to look at and observe him when the Lord Justice-Clerk was pronouncing sentence." But when the verdict against M'Dougal was pronounced "not proven," he at once exclaimed, "Nelly, you are out of the scrape." He requested permission from the authorities for her to stay in prison for a few more days, "for her personal protection." He seems to have remained calm when confronted with his conviction of murder "of a blacker description," the lord justice clerk told him, "more atrocious in point of cool-headed deliberation, and systematic arrangement, and where the motives were so comparatively base," than they, or any other court of law, had ever seen. The sentence was execution, and there could be no hope of pardon, due to the "necessity of repressing offences of this most extraordinary and alarming description." The only question was "whether your body should not be exhibited in chains, in order to deter others from the like crimes in time coming," an archaic, but still legal, form of punishment for truly heinous crimes. But times and manners had changed, and "taking into consideration that the public eye would be offended with so dismal an exhibition," the lord justice clerk pronounced the usual sentence for murder: that William Burke be taken to "the common place of execution, in the Lawnmarket of Edinburgh, and there . . . be hanged by the neck, upon a gibbet, until he be dead, and his body thereafter to be delivered to Dr. Alexander Monro, Professor of Anatomy in the University of Edinburgh, to be by him publicly dissected and anatomized . . . which is pronounced for doom."

Burke was transported back to the jail early in the morning of Friday, December 26, so as to avoid any publicity that might spark a riot. Helen M'Dougal was released later that night. The lord justice clerk had stated to the jury, when thanking them, "that your verdict appears to be perfectly well founded. Entertaining, as you did, doubts of the guilt of the female prisoner, you gave her the benefit of those doubts." The *Blackwood's* writers, on the whole, agreed: "The jury might," said Christopher North, "with safe conscience, have found Macdougal guilty; but with a safe conscience, they found the libel in her case, *Not Proven.* They did what, on the whole, was perhaps best." "I doot that," responded both the Ettrick Shepherd and Tickler, and "So perhaps did they," replied North, "but let her live. Death is one punishment, Life another." And so it proved. After formally pronouncing the verdict to M'Dougal, the lord justice clerk added, "The jury have found the libel against you *not proven;*—they have not pronounced you *not guilty* of the crime of murder charged against you in this indictment. You know whether you have been in the commission of this atrocious crime. I leave it to your own conscience to draw the proper conclusion. I hope and trust that you will betake yourself to a new line of life, diametrically opposite from that which you have led for a number of years." But that implied that she had deliberately made the conscious, immoral choice to live in adultery and collaborate with a convicted murderer, instead of drifting into it through circumstances that, as Cockburn had argued, must have seemed beyond her control. It is not clear how much she understood of her situation, and so, like most people released from jail, she went back home, to the West Port. Did she look forward to sleeping in her own bed, sitting in her own chair? Had she counted on seeing friends, neighbors, who might comfort her after her trial? Did she hope to meet with sympathy for Burke's unhappy fate? To quietly pack her few belongings and leave town by the Glasgow Road?

But there was no sympathy for "the burkers" to be had. "The citizens of Edinburgh are by no means blood-thirsty," reported *West Port Murders*, "and, on ordinary occasions, would rejoice to learn that a fellow-being had escaped the fearful death that the law adjudges to great criminals." But in this case the death penalty for Burke was considered entirely justified, and there was public dissatisfaction that M'Dougal, "who was considered equally guilty, should not have been equally punished." It was as though "the enormity of their offenses had stopped the channels of pity, and an unanimous requisition for vengeance was made by a whole population." For that reason the author characterized M'Dougal's return to "her old haunts" as "audacity or folly," though it was more likely that she simply had nowhere else to go. She was quickly recognized—indeed, there was no sign that she attempted any disguise—"and a mob collecting, was in danger of being roughly handled." Someone called a policeman, "and with some difficulty she was conveyed to the watch-house" in Fountainbridge. The officer on duty was in a quandary, for he had only a few men, and the numbers of people in the street grew larger. To prevent a full-scale riot, he resorted to a trick: "a ladder was placed at a back window, by which it was pretended that she had descended." The crowd dispersed, and M'Dougal was taken to the main Police Office on the High Street. Some accounts later added the picturesque though unlikely detail that she was disguised in men's clothing. She was attacked and forced to seek police protection several times over the next month, and she appears to have been lost without Burke: "her attachment to him," noted a journalist, "is undoubtedly strong." Eventually she made her way to Constantine Burke, who accompanied her in an attempt to see his brother. William Burke had continued to speak "in terms of great affection towards her," and hoped to be allowed to see her, but the governor of the prison refused to allow him to receive any visitors. M'Dougal "sent a message, saying that she wanted money," and Burke sent her all he had left, together with his watch. "Poor thing," he said, "it is all I have to give her, it will be of some use to her, and I will not need it." She left town the next day. She was said to have returned to her father's house in Stirlingshire, but we will never know for sure.

Burke, now a condemned criminal, was placed upon the "gad," described in Walter Scott's *Guy Mannering* as a "round bar of iron, about the thickness of a man's arm above the elbow," which "crossed the apartment horizontally at the height of about six inches from the floor;" and was firmly attached to the wall at each end. The prisoner's "ankles were secured within shackles, which were connected by a chain at the distance of about four feet, with a large iron ring, which traveled upon the bar. . . . Thus a prisoner might shuffle along the length of the bar from one side of the room to another, but could not retreat further from it in any direction than the brief length of the chain admitted. . . . A pallet-bed was placed close to the bar of iron, so that the shackled prisoner might lie down at pleasure, still fastened to the iron bar in the manner described." All other restraints were removed, so that Burke could make himself comparatively comfortable. But his "condemned cell, as he observed, is but a comfortless place, cold and cheerless and dreary, where hope, at least in such a case as his, never enters to enliven it." His only way of keeping warm was by staying in bed, for no fire was allowed. He was reported to be in pain from a cancerous sore, and to be fed only on "coarse bread and cold water," to which some broth was added on the recommendation of the surgeon who examined him. It is not clear why the execution was delayed. "The law in this part of the island," noted *West Port Murders*, "humanely allows a period for the purpose of giving an opportunity of repentance to the criminal, and time to make his peace with God," but Burke was imprisoned for five long weeks after the trial. Both Protestant and Catholic clergymen came forward to offer him spiritual counsel, and he finally settled on two Catholic priests, Reverend William Reid and Mr. Stuart, paying "due attention to their exhortations" and reading "the Bible or some religious book constantly in their absence." He was said to have fully understood the need for preparing "for the great and awful change which he must soon undergo," and despite the skepticism of some contemporary accounts we have no reason to doubt his contrition.

Burke had been asked to give a full account of all the crimes, and after consulting with his spiritual advisers, he notified the sheriff on January 3, 1829, that he was ready to do so. The confession was given in the presence of the sheriff-substitute, George Tait, and the procurator fiscal, Archibald Scott, with the priest Mr. Reid present on his behalf. The Crown Office had been very anxious to get a full statement of all the murders, in order to establish whether there were any other people involved in the gang, or any other, as yet unreported, murders. After investigating Burke's sworn statement, the prosecutor's office concluded that "after a very full and anxious inquiry . . . no circumstances have transpired, calculated to show that any other persons have lent themselves to such practices in this city, or its vicinity." Moreover, Burke's confession matched that given the preceding December by Hare "in point of number, of time, and of the description of persons murdered." There was therefore no reason to believe "that any other crimes have been committed by Burke and Hare, excepting those contained in the frightful catalogue to which they have confessed."

The official confession was not made public until a month later, and in the meantime Edinburgh newspapers looked for copy: "Whatever is interesting," wrote one journalist, "our readers may rely upon receiving." Interviews with condemned criminals were highly publishable, and Burke's conviction led many to hope for a first-hand account. According to the prison officials, Burke had asked that he be shielded from visits of the merely curious "to the end that he might . . . be allowed to remain undisturbed, and apply his mind to things fitted to his situation." But he was a naturally gregarious man, used to spending time with people, and conversations even about his crimes must have seemed better than solitude. The *Caledonian Mercury* provided the first published Burke confession "received from a most respectable quarter." The name of the interviewer was not stated, but his questions were those that all Edinburgh was asking: "How comes it . . . that you who, by your own account, were once under the influence of religious impressions, ever formed the idea of such dreadful atrocities?" Were there thirty murders in all? Had Burke any accomplices besides Hare? How far were the anatomists involved? Was Burke "tutored and instructed, or . . . [did he] receive hints from any one as to the mode of committing murder?" Had he been a resurrectionist? What did he think of Hare's escaping prosecution? To these questions Burke appeared "to have opened his mind without reserve, and to have given a distinct and explicit answer to every question which was put to him." Though first printed in the *Caledonian Mercury*, it was quickly reprinted and distributed in Thomas Ireland's *West Port Murders* series, and in broadsheets.

Burke's next confession was apparently bespoken by a lawyer, J. Smith, though it ended up at the offices of the *Edinburgh Evening Courant*. Smith seems to have induced Burke to write a letter to the lord provost of the Town Council of Edinburgh, asking to be allowed to give Smith a detailed account "regarding the crimes with which he had been connected." The provost did not believe for a moment that the idea had originated with Burke, though "*signed* by him," and turned the matter over to the lord advocate, who promptly refused permission with some asperity. "It appears to me of importance," he wrote, "both to the individual himself, and to the public, that no second statement, which might be contradictory of, or inconsistent with, the first (so solemnly and deliberately given) ought now to be impetrated from this man by irresponsible parties, with the avowed object of publication." Rae had in fact gone in person to Burke and explained the reasons for his refusal, assuring him that if he had anything else to communicate, he could add to his original statement. Burke asked that the sheriff come to him for that purpose, and the coda, added to his official confession on January 22, shows the points of most concern to him less than a week before he was to be hanged. Yes, he agreed with all his previous statements regarding the murders. No, there were no other murders besides those he had already mentioned, and none of the rumors of other murders or attempted murders were true. No, he did not know of other murders committed by Hare, or by anyone else, in order to sell cadavers to the anatomists. He had never been a resurrectionist. He and Hare had operated independently of the anatomists: he had no surgical instruments in his house, and neither Knox nor any of his assistants knew where he lived. "And all this he declares to be truth."

There remained one last confession, for J. Smith seems to have ignored the lord advocate's refusal to grant permission for his interview, or else he carried it out before formally asking for permission. However improper that may have been—and, one might think, rather foolhardy for anyone planning a legal career in Edinburgh—historians have reason to be grateful for it, for Burke's *Courant* confession, as it is often called, contained the fullest detail about many of the victims, the dealings with Knox's anatomical establishment, and the relationships among the murderers. Burke wrote out in his own handwriting "that docter Knox never incoureged him, nither taught or incoregd him to murder any person, neither any of his assistents [*sic*]." He also insisted that Helen M'Dougal did not commit any of the murders, "nor saw them done." This was his story and he stuck to it, so that the four confessions—or three and a coda—which make up an ongoing conversation between Burke and his interlocutors are remarkably consistent on those points. They are also, for the most part, consistent in enumerating the victims, though by the *Courant* confession Burke may have begun to ramble and repeat details. Virtually all who have studied the documents with care have concluded, like Sheriff-Substitute Tait, that Burke's account was as trustworthy as he could make it. Burke knew what he was saying, and he, like Ann Gray, spoke "in a very distinct manner."

The *Edinburgh Evening Courant* intended to publish "their" confession the day after the execution, but they were forced to delay owing to the ongoing legal actions regarding Hare.

Burke's official January 3 confession had been a disappointment to the authorities in one respect: they had hoped he would provide them with evidence of crimes of which the Hares, or at least William Hare, could be charged. Public opinion in Edinburgh was loud in its condemnation of Hare's immunity from prosecution, and the Crown Office hoped for information from Burke that would allow them to put Hare on trial. Burke, too, was "particularly anxious that his associate Hare should be brought to trial." His spiritual advisers had told him that he should not go to death with any hatred for Hare in his heart, so he explained that his desire came not from vengeance, but from concern for the common weal. "If Hare should be again let loose upon society," he was reported to have said, "he would recommence his murderous career when he wanted money," and Burke was afraid that "the spirits of [Hare's] future victims would reproach him in the regions of bliss, for not having taken means to get Hare executed, and thereby preventing their violent and untimely deaths." The language sounds most unlike Burke, but he may have said something similar; certainly we can believe he wanted Hare to hang. In this he was at one with the rest of Edinburgh. "The sacrifice of Burke alone will not appease the present righteous cry for vengeance against a horde of systematic and scientific murderers," wrote the *Caledonian Mercury*. That "subtle fiend," Hare, "was Burke's master in the art of murder, and he has been longer engaged in the trade than his apt scholar, who is now given over to justice."

Unfortunately Burke and the rest of Edinburgh were to be disappointed. The lord advocate's position was clear: after "the most anxious inquiry," Rae wrote, it was found "that no crime could be brought to light in which Hare had been concerned," excepting those for which he had been granted immunity. That included all three of the murders named in the original indictment, the only ones, in truth, for which the prosecution could make a convincing case. The writer for the *Caledonian Mercury* argued that, since Burke was only tried for the murder of Margery Docherty, Hare only had immunity from that charge, and so could easily be tried for either Mary Paterson or Daft Jamie. But that simply was incorrect, Rae explained in court. Margaret and William Hare were ready to be called as prosecution witnesses, no matter which of the three murders was on the indictment, on the assurance—the unqualified assurance—that "the *possibility* of future trial or punishment was thereby entirely excluded." If Burke had been acquitted on the first charge, the Crown would have tried him on the second and third, and the Hares would have been called as witnesses in each case. That meant that they had immunity from prosecution for all charges, and indeed for the entire series of murders for which they had given evidence to the Crown.

Since the Hares could not be brought to trial, the Crown did not have just cause to detain them in prison. Margaret Hare was set free on January 19, and seems to have made it out of Edinburgh without incident. Newspapers reported her in Glasgow a few days later, where she was living under an assumed name while waiting for passage to Ireland: a drunk woman in the street called out "Hare's wife; burke her!" and a loud, angry crowd soon gathered. Like M'Dougal, she had to be rescued by the police, who managed to shepherd her onto a steam packet for Belfast with only a few more incidents in the street. She was reported to have "burst into tears while deploring her unhappy situation, which she ascribed to Hare's utter profligacy, and said all she wished was to get across the channel, and end her days in some remote spot in her own country, in retirement and penitence." Whether she did or not, we will never know. Her husband did not accompany her, for on January 16, George Monro, agent for Janet Wilson and Janet Downie, the mother and sister of Daft Jamie, had instituted a private criminal prosecution for the murder of James Wilson. The sheriff issued a new warrant for Hare's arrest, retained him in jail upon the new charge, and began a new series of depositions related to the murder.

Private prosecutions in criminal cases were—and are—legal in Scotland, but this was not really a private matter. The Wilsons, as Jamie's closest living relatives, were the obvious choices to begin the prosecution, but there was some sort of committee in the background to raise the necessary funds for both George Monro and their eminent legal counsel, the noted Whig lawyer Francis Jeffrey. Jeffrey's decision to act as counsel was a shrewd political maneuver. Moncreiff's and Cockburn's defense of Burke and M'Dougal, however true to the equitable principles of Scottish law, had not put the Whigs on the side of the angels. If they could, now, succeed in nailing Hare where the Tory Rae had failed, it would be a distinct triumph. Burke's former counsel, Duncan M'Neill, took on the task of defending Hare. He filed a "Bill of Advocation, Suspension, and Liberation," demanding that the prosecution be stopped. Hare did his part in his own defense by remaining belligerently uncommunicative when questioned by Monro and sheriff's officers. When "interrogated whether he was acquainted with or ever saw a person of the name of James Wilson commonly known by the name of Daft Jamie," he declared, "that he saw him but he was not acquainted with him, so as to call it acquainted." When asked "whether he was ever in company with him," he declared "he never was." When asked when last he had seen Jamie, he said that it was in his own house, with no other person present except William Burke, but when asked the follow-up question, "how Wilson came to be in his house," he declared "that is all which he has to say about that." Asked how long

Wilson was there, he declared "a few minutes." A few more questions, and he had had enough: "it is not fair to ask him those questions now," he said, "because no person except himself or Burke could have said any thing about it." What did he mean by saying "any thing about it," George Monro wanted to know, but Hare just repeated "that it is not fair at any rate and he will answer no more." With that the agents for Daft Jamie's family had to rest content.

This case presented a number of important legal points and engaged the best minds of the Scottish bar. The most important point for Hare, though, was that the High Court of Justiciary decided the case in his favor by a vote of four to two: his immunity extended to private as well as public prosecution, so that he could not be put on trial for the murder of Daft Jamie. The decision amounted to a vote of confidence for the lord advocate's handling of the case, and even the two dissenting justices made a point of commending Rae's "wisdom and prudence," by which "the law and justice of the country have been rescued" from the "indelible disgrace" which would have occurred if Burke and Hare had been brought to trial, and acquitted through lack of evidence. Monro, acting for Daft Jamie's family, immediately notified the sheriff of their intention to raise a civil suit against Hare for £500 as indemnification of the damages done them through the murder, and entered a petition for Hare to be detained in prison until he could provide security for that sum. But it would have been this side of never that Hare would be able to pay £50, let alone £500, and the family was persuaded to drop the case. On February 5, 1829, Hare was finally released from prison, having got away with murder.

The now-familiar set of reports and angry crowds followed Hare in his unsuccessful attempt to leave the country without attracting attention. He was given an old cloak as a disguise, and escorted by policeman John Fisher to the mail coach at Newington, in the south of the city. Hare seated himself on the outside, still wrapped in his cloak, but as it was a cold night, that would attract no attention. "Good bye, Mr. Black, and I wish you well home," Fisher called out, and the coach left, heading south for Dumfries. When it stopped at an inn en route, Hare, like the other passengers, went inside. At first he tried to keep in the background, but the others, seeing him so far from the fire on such a cold night, urged him to join them. Unfortunately for Hare, Erskine Douglas Sandford, one of the lawyers employed by Daft Jamie's family, was also traveling on that coach. Perhaps this was a coincidence, but it is not impossible that either the family or their legal advisers had been keeping a watchful eye on Hare's release. When the coach was ready to set out, Hare tried to take a vacant seat inside, but Sandford refused to allow it. By the time the coach arrived in Dumfries, all the passengers knew who was traveling with them, and "the news flew like wild-fire in every direction." According to the *Dumfries Courier*, thousands of people came to see Hare, who had to sit, penned in the King's Arms Inn, for four hours while waiting for the mail coach to Portpatrick, where he could get passage to Ireland. "By these successive visitors, he was forced to sit or stand in all positions"; noted the journalist, "and cool, and insensate, and apathetic as he seems, he was occasionally almost frightened out of his wits." At one point he tried to walk out and face the crowd, "determined, as he said, to let the mob 'tak' their will o' him.'" An unnamed "medical man" refused to let him. There was no question of letting him take the mail coach to Portpatrick, for he and it would have been attacked at once. But of course the landlord of the King's Arms was anxious to get rid of him without any damage to his inn, and so, with an elaborate feint—sending one carriage to the front of the inn and ostentatiously loading it with Hare's trunk, while he surreptitiously crept into another carriage at the back—Hare was transferred to the Dumfries jail for safe-keeping.

He stayed there for the rest of the day, protected by the police, the militia, and eventually a hundred constables specially sworn in for the purpose of keeping the peace. Outside "nothing but clamour and rioting were heard," as the populace "laid regular siege" to the jail, smashing the front windows and gas lamps, and attempting to prevent anyone from going in or out. By 1 A.M., the crowd had been dispersed, and Hare was told to gather up his things and be ready to move. He "enquired eagerly for his cloak and bundle," but they could not be brought quickly enough, so he "was told that he must just go without them, and thank his stars into the bargain that he had a prospect of escaping with whole bones." The whole, well-traveled route from Dumfries to Portpatrick was in an uproar, and it was clear Hare could not be transported that way. According to the *Dumfries Courier*, the police put him on the Annan road heading towards England, and washed their hands of him. "He was last seen on Sunday morning last, about two miles beyond Carlisle. He seemed to be moving onwards, trusting to circumstances, and without any fixed purpose, if we except the wretched one of prolonging, as long as possible, his miserable life." But these final reports are not very convincing, and suggest only that the *Dumfries Courier* had lost track of Hare once he left town. No reliable information has ever been recorded of what happened to him. It is possible that he went home to his family in Ireland, for according to the *Dumfries Courier*, a Dumfries city official received a visit from Hare's sister a few weeks later. "Hare's sister! and what the deuce are you seeking here," he said to her, "we have had enough of trouble with your family already, and if you don't get out of the way as fast as possible, the town will rise, Irish and all, and tear you to pieces." She was on her way home from the shearing in England, she told him, and had been asked to come via Dumfries in order to retrieve his bundle. It was found in "a corner of the tap room," at the King's Arms; "the woman got it, and some cold meat to boot, and departed as quietly and privately as she arrived."

By the time Hare left Edinburgh, Burke was already dead and dissected, his skeleton in the possession of Professor of Anatomy Alexander Monro. He had been moved to a cell near Liberton's Wynd, the traditional venue for executions, at 4 A.M. on Tuesday, January 27. "The time was purposely fixed," noted *West Port Murders* "at this unusual hour to prevent any annoyance from the crowd, which would undoubtedly have assembled had it been delayed to a later time of the day." He appeared exhausted, and it was reported that he slept soundly until the next morning. He had expressed the desire for a suit of clothes to be executed in, for "since I am to appear before the public," he told his other spiritual advisers, "I should like to be respectable." When it was brought to him later in the day, he "exhibited deep emotion, and by his own confession he felt it." Reverends Reid and Stuart, and the Protestant ministers Reverends Marshall and Porteous, remained with him throughout the day, and through the night.

Burke slept soundly for about five hours that night, the last night of his life. There was no custom of the condemned man's last meal in this period, but his jailers agreed to remove his shackles when he woke up at about 5:30 A.M. on Wednesday, January 28. The crowd had been gathering outside the jail since before daybreak, in order to obtain a place to view the execution. Every room with a window in the surrounding buildings had been rented out for the occasion. Charles Kirkpatrick Sharpe was there, as was Sir Walter Scott. Presumably Sir William Rae, Henry Cockburn, James Moncreiff, and the rest of the legal establishment were present as well. "Many well-dressed ladies" were also seen "at the windows of the lofty and sombre looking lands in the Lawnmarket, as well as those of the county buildings." The cold rain, falling through the night, discouraged some from arriving until it stopped about 7 A.M. At that point "though it was a cold raw disagreeable morning," the entire public area between the West Bow and Tron Kirk "presented an aspect of such an immense and closely wedged mass of human beings" as had never before been seen, at least by the author of the account. The same author carefully calculated the total number of spectators as "nearer to forty thousand souls than to thirty-five thousand," but other estimates put the number closer to twenty thousand. In any case it took its place in the annals of public spectacle. The police had taken the precaution of swearing in an additional seventy constables to keep order. Several enterprising printers had taken the precaution of having broadsides describing Burke's "last moments," "dying declaration," and "execution" made up the day before, so they could be "cried in the street" as soon as the crowd assembled. For obvious reasons these sheets were filled with accounts of the murders, the trial, and Burke's conduct in jail, with only a line or two purporting to describe the actual execution (Figure 17).

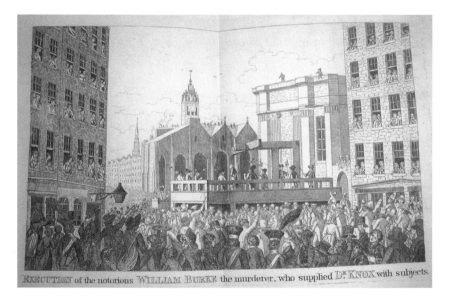

EXECUTION of the notorious WILLIAM BURKE the murderer, who supplied Dᴿ KNOX with subjects.

Figure 17. Contemporary print of the execution of William Burke on January 28, 1829. Many engravings purporting to show the execution were really printed the day before, so they could be hawked on the street to the thousands of spectators crowding the High Street.

The crowd was too large, and Burke too much hated, for the usual "respectful and solemn deportment," to be maintained. The crowd cried, "The murderer! *Burke* him! Choke him, hangie!" as soon as 8 A.M. struck and Burke appeared climbing the stairs to the scaffold. He looked thin and pale in his black suit, hair "of a light sandy colour approaching nearly to white," with boots "which seemed to have lain uncleaned for a length of time in some damp place until they had become mouldy." It was 8:05 when he appeared on the platform, and he knelt and prayed with the clergymen, his back to the crowd. "Stand out of the way," and "turn him around," the spectators called, but the public officials adhered to the letter of the statute and continued with their task. Burke's prayers "seemed to be very fervent," and he was reported saying to one of the priests "that he died in the full assurance that he would be saved through the mediation of our Saviour."

The priest stood with him as he went to stand directly under the gallows, above the drop. He had a white neckcloth, which got in the way of the executioner when he tried to adjust the noose. "The knot's behind," Burke told him, and the executioner removed it and made sure the noose was properly fastened. He put on a white death-cap, too, as the crowd grew more impatient, calling out "Where is Hare?" "Give him no rope," "You will see Daft Jamie in a minute," and, again, "Burke him!" Mr. Reid prayed with him one last time, and the executioner fitted the cap over his face. Burke stood "unflinching and motionless"; then, after "beseeching mercy" from God one last time, he signaled that he was ready. The trapdoor opened, and the next moment he was hanging, lifeless. The whole process took barely ten minutes and was over by 8:15 A.M. There were cheers from the crowd, and many remained, watching the body's "very gradual swinging around . . . produced by the wind," and the head, which "leaned a little to one side." Perhaps half an hour passed before it was cut down and taken inside the lockup house, and at that point the crowd dispersed.

The spectacle now shifted to the anatomical theater at the University of Edinburgh, where early on Thursday morning Burke's cadaver was turned over to Professor Alexander Monro for dissection. Again, the authorities had decided to wait until after dark, for a crowd had assembled in front of university buildings after the execution and remained there all day Wednesday, in spite of the continued rain. The first people admitted on Thursday morning were those interested in scientific inquiry, including the phrenologist George Combe. A sculptor made a cast of Burke's skull. Several students were there as well, and made sketches. At 1 P.M., Monro began the dissection in front of a crowded lecture hall. "It was commenced," according to *West Port Murders*, "by first taking off the scalpel to show the muscles of the upper part of the head; these being removed, the skull was sawn through, and the brain with its covering exposed." The smell must have been very noticeable, as "the quantity of blood that gushed out was enormous, and by the time the lecture was finished," two hours later, "the area of the class-room had the appearance of a butcher's slaughter-house, from its flowing down and being trodden upon," as spectators came forward for a closer look at the anatomical structures. The only disturbance came from groups of students who tried to push themselves in and were prevented by the police. Feeling that this in some way violated the privileges of the university, the students hooted and pushed harder, refusing to disperse. According to *West Port Murders*, they threw stones at the building, breaking "a good deal of glass," but this seems unlikely as it is not mentioned in any other source. Eventually Professor Robert Christison was able to calm them down by promising them that they could enter the classroom in groups of fifty, if they would behave themselves.

In contrast there was no trouble at all when the doors were open to the general public on Friday morning at 10 A.M. The room had been arranged to control the flow of traffic, so that spectators "were admitted by one stair to the Anatomical Theatre, passed the table on which lay the body of the murderer, and made their exit by another stair." The crowd on the way in sometimes pressed forward, so that even those people who, on approaching the two-day-old cadaver, were suddenly overcome by the urge to step backwards, had to continue on. Some women attended—seven, out of the thousands who filed through the doors that day, according to *West Port Murders*—but they were hissed at as "void of decency," for the body was naked, entirely exposed. It was pale, from the blood having drained away, and the "features had entirely lost that decidedness and sharpness they yesterday possessed. The nose was thickened, as the lips likewise were, producing that bloated appearance usually seen in the faces of those who have died from strangulation." The cap of the skull had been replaced and the skin drawn back over it, reported one journalist, but the face no longer looked like Burke. If there were those in the crowd who mourned the change, we may be sure they kept as still as death.

On Sunday, February 1, Alexander Monro arranged for the final dismemberment of Burke's body. He kept some hair from Burke's leg, tinged with blood, and he may have retained some skin, for the Royal College of Surgeons of Edinburgh still has a pocketbook allegedly made from it. Burke's cadaver was presumably immersed in water, to remove the remaining flesh, and the skeleton was given to the University of Edinburgh. It remains today the property of the Department of Anatomy, thus fulfilling the hope of Lord Justice Clerk Boyle that Burke's skeleton would be preserved, "in order that posterity might keep in remembrance" his "atrocious crimes." But before disposing of the cadaver, Monro, in an anatomist's ritual as macabre as any we have seen, dipped his quill into Burke's blood, recording that "This is written with the blood of Wm Burke, who was hanged at Edinburgh on 28th Jan. 1829 for the Murder of Mrs Campbell or Docherty. The blood was taken from his head on the 1st of Feb. 1829." And so it happened that Burke's career ended with anatomists' hands, too, deeply dyed in blood.

Chapter 11

All That Remains

Robert Knox

THE FINAL CADAVER WAS NOT DISSECTED, BUT INSTEAD WAS buried on December 29, 1862, intact, in Brookwood Cemetery, in Surrey, England. In life it had belonged to Robert Knox, anatomist and public lecturer, most recently pathological anatomist to the Cancer Hospital at Brompton, London. It is an irony of nineteenth-century medical history that few anatomical lecturers chose to donate their own bodies to science, and though Knox had cited lack of cadavers as one of the "obstacles which impede the progress of anatomy in Great Britain" he chose a churchyard over the dissecting table for his own remains. He had been complaining, Henry Lonsdale said, "of the enfeebled action of the heart, and his inability to ascend a staircase," and he came home from the hospital on the evening of December 9 "tired and exhausted." Shortly after he went to bed "the noise of laboured breathing was heard proceeding from his room," and he was found "apoplectic," that is, suffering from some form of stroke. He never again regained consciousness, and he died on December 20, 1862. His wife, five of his six children, and his sister Mary had all predeceased him, leaving his son Edward, who lived with him, the only family member to attend his funeral. He had often spoken "of the heather and wild flowers blooming in great beauty" in Brookwood, and he was interred, as he had wished, "in some spot where the sun might shine longest on the green sod above his grave."

There is no question that the Burke and Hare murders ruined the career Knox had envisioned, branding him with a notoriety he could never escape. "Through the close and up the stair," ran a popular song,

> *But and ben wi' Burke and Hare.*
> *Burke's the butcher, Hare's the thief,*
> *And Knox the boy who buys the beef.*

David Paterson was a key witness in the trial, and his evidence focused much unwelcome attention on Knox's dissecting room practices. It was made abundantly clear that Burke had had an established relationship with Paterson and with Knox, for he called at Paterson's house after midnight on October 31 to say "he had procured something for the doctor." Paterson had seen Burke the next day, speaking to Dr. Knox, and Paterson "got orders from Dr. Knox if they brought any package, I was to take it from them." When they brought the "package"—now known to be the murdered Madgy Docherty—Paterson had "previous orders to divide the money and give each a share." Burke and Hare had been told to call back on Monday, after Knox had had a chance to examine the cadaver and decide what it was worth. "Did they frequently bring subjects that had not been interred?" defense counsel asked Paterson. "Frequently, my Lord," responded Paterson. "I suppose they had not been interred." The image of Knox, coolly examining the body of a murdered woman to judge its price, was captured in a widely reprinted set of caricatures by the lithographer R. H. Nimmo. One shows Knox in front of his lecture hall, examining a pig's carcass, with the caption "The Lecturer, not quite pleased with *his* subject" and a quote from a cook book, "If you can get them when just killed, this is of great advantage."

The result of these disclosures, as the *Caledonian Mercury* put it, was that "the present impression on the minds of the People is that one gentleman stands in the same relation to Burke, that the murderers of Banquo did to Macbeth." This slightly confused analogy equating Knox with Macbeth was printed as the caption for another of Nimmo's caricatures. Still another made an even more graphic analogy between Knox and Richard III, indicating that Knox had commissioned the murders. Knox is depicted in his anatomical museum, holding a mask to his face and speaking to a ragged, barefoot Hare. There is a cranium on a table behind them and a set of tea chests off to the right. The dialogue is taken from Richard's query to his page, concerning a man to carry out the murder of the princes:

> *"Know'st thou not any, whom corrupting Gold*
> *Would tempt unto a close exploit of death?"*
>> *"I know a discontented Irishman,*
> *Whose humble means match not his haughty mind.*
> *Gold were as good as twenty Orators,*
> *And will, no doubt, tempt him to any thing."*
>> *"What is his name?"*
> *"His name! My Lord, is* BURKE.*"*
> *"I partly know the man; go, call him hither."*

The author of the *Caledonian Mercury* article went on to say that he believed the public impression to be "ill-founded," but to satisfy all those who required reassurance, to convince them that their trust in anatomical teachers overall, and in "one gentleman whose name has unfortunately been too much mixed up with the late proceedings," had not been misplaced, that same gentleman, and all other anatomical lecturers, ought to demand a full inquiry. "For the honour of a most respectable profession, for the public safety, for the character of the country, for the credit of its laws, and for the sake of humanity itself, the Public Prosecutor ought to interpose, and have this matter probed and sifted to the very bottom."

But Knox refused to make any public statement. The Edinburgh botanist Robert Greville, like Knox a Fellow of the Royal Society of Edinburgh, had heard that Knox "kept silence in compliance with the advice of his Counsel," which he thought "had an ugly sound about it." It was, in fact, excellent legal advice, for even if Knox had known nothing of the murders he could be implicated for reset of theft of other cadavers, or "art and part" of violation of sepulchres. Certainly until Hare's case was decided Knox had to tread very carefully. If Hare was charged with Daft Jamie's murder then Knox could expect to be a key witness, for he had dissected the body and might still have the cranium. And there were other matters he would no doubt have preferred to keep quiet. As he put it, "the disclosures of the most innocent proceedings of even the best-conducted dissecting room must always shock the public and be hurtful to science," and we may question whether Knox ran his rooms any better than his rivals

John Lizars or Thomas Aitken, who within a few weeks would be implicated in purchasing cadavers stolen from the Lasswade churchyard. Knox had his assistants to think of, who had accepted most of the cadavers and urged Burke and Hare to bring more. He also had his brother's family to protect, for it seems likely that Frederick had known about the deliveries from "John" and "William." The younger brother kept a very low profile indeed during the entire period, and his name was never mentioned in the press despite all the public scrutiny accorded the elder Knox. It is possible that Frederick, whose wife was pregnant with their third child, had thought it prudent to spend the winter with his family outside the city. He seems to have been back in town when his daughter was born on March 9, 1829, though, for he gave his address in the baptismal record as number 6, Surgeon's Square.

Knox continued to lecture while the scandal mounted. His friend and fellow physician Alexander Lesassier sat in on Knox's class the day that Fergusson, Jones, and Miller were called to give evidence before the lord advocate. Lesassier noted that Knox "evidently laboured under great agitation" during the whole of his "luminous demonstration." But like many among Knox's friends and associates, Lesassier was "thoroughly convinced" that Knox was "absolutely guiltless of the faintest suspicion of the late murders." He made a point of shaking Knox's hand warmly, giving his opinion that "the popular ferment" was "mere hypocritical cant & twaddle." He knew first hand how bitter internecine warfare among the Edinburgh medical community could be, and he told Knox his belief that the outcry stemmed from "jealousy . . . that is to say on the part of the other teachers of anatomy." "All a conspiracy—eh?" responded Knox. To which Lesassier replied, "Nothing more, nor less." The poor fellow, he noted in his diary, was due to appear before the College of Surgeons later that day, and "they will crush him if they can." Knox also seems to have believed that the attacks on him were personal, and deliberate, attempts by his rivals to destroy his reputation. If they had been mere "popular prejudice," he said, they would have "passed away, by its being seen that I had been exposed to a mere misfortune." The fact that, as he put it, "every effort" had been "employed to convert my misfortune into positive and intended personal guilt of the most dreadful character" argued for a deliberate smear campaign, for "scarcely any individual has ever been the object of more systematic or atrocious attacks than I have been."

Whether or not the Fellows of the College of Surgeons were conspiring against Knox, they certainly did not rise in his support. The surgeon James Syme made it clear to anyone who asked, and many who did not, that he considered Knox to be seriously implicated in the murders. Knox had always had a knack for making enemies, and if the rest of his Surgeon's Square rivals did not go to the length of rejoicing in his misfortune, they were in no hurry to defend him. Professor Alexander Monro carefully collected broadsides and newspaper clippings connected with the trial, out of historical interest or of *schadenfreude*. The Royal College of Physicians "expressed their deep and sincere regret that the anatomical instruction, which they conscientiously believe to be an essential part of the education of physician and surgeons, should ever have furnished a temptation to such unexampled atrocities," while helpfully pointing out "that no one of their number has ever been in the smallest degree connected with the perpetrators of those crimes."

When involved in a controversy, Knox remained his own worst enemy. On January 14 he was scheduled to read a paper at the Royal Society of Edinburgh "on some dissections," as Sir Walter Scott put it. "A bold proposal truly from one who has had so lately the boldness of trading so deep in human flesh," wrote Scott. "I will oppose his reading in the present circumstances, if I should stand alone. . . . It is very bad taste to push himself forward just now." Some members of the Society hesitated in making an issue of Knox's presentation, believing that "declining to receive the paper would be a declaration unfavourable to Dr. Knox." But Scott stated forcefully that "hearing it before Mr. Knox has made any defence (as he is stated to have in view) would be an intimation of our preference of the cause of Science to those of Morality and Common Humanity." Knox reluctantly agreed to postpone his essay. "I believe," sighed Robert Greville, "the very name of Doctor stinks in the nostrils of the whole place."

Knox had, in fact, been perilously close to being indicted. In questioning his assistants, Rae was following the suggestions of the home secretary, Sir Robert Peel, to whom he had sent a copy of Hare's deposition. Peel, later famous as the founder of London's Metropolitan Police, was horrified at the disclosures of so many murders, "these proceedings for which language has no epithets," as he called them. In his view, Hare's testimony "implicated, in a most obvious degree—morally certainly if not legally— other persons besides those who have been placed upon their trial." In the case of the woman and her grandson, he noted, "Burke went to Dr. Knox and told him he had got two bodies from the country. Dr. Knox received the bodies on the evening of the day on which the boy was murdered. When did he unpack them? When did he examine them?" In that case and in others, "did it not occur to Dr. Knox—on actual anatomy of the bodies—that the bodies were recently dead—that Burke's account to him of their being received from the country—or as to the period of their death—were untrue?" Had he not been "struck by the singular similarity there must have been to this mode by which life became extinct in those bodies which Burke brought him?" Peel concluded that "there is ground for the most painful suspicions and it certainly appears that there might have to be—if there has not already been—the most sifting investigation into everything deponed by Hare."

The questions put to Burke at the time of his official confession on January 3 echo those suggested by Peel, and it was Burke's answers which, ironically enough, proved Knox's salvation. It is clear from the structure of the confession that Burke first gave an account of the murders, and was then asked a series of direct questions, easy enough to reconstruct from his responses. Had suffocation been suggested to them by any persons? No, he deponed, but it "occurred to Hare on the first occasion before mentioned, and was continued afterwards because it was effectual, and showed no marks." Did they take their victims by the throat, or leave any marks on them? No, he deponed, "That with the exception of the body of Docherty, they never took the person by the throat . . . and [he] declares that there were no marks of violence on any of the subjects, and they were sufficiently cold to prevent any suspicion on the part of the Doctors; and at all events they might be cold and stiff enough before the box was opened up . . . and no suspicions were expressed by Dr. Knox or any of his assistants, and no questions asked tending to show that they had suspicions." And in his later deposition, he testified "they never allowed Dr. Knox, or any of his assistants, to know exactly where their houses were, but Paterson, Dr. Knox's porter or door-keeper, knew." He reaffirmed this in his later confessions, even putting down in his own handwriting, as we have seen, that "docter Knox . . . nither taught nor incoreged him to murder any person."

Without Burke to incriminate Knox, Rae could not possibly make a case against the anatomist, and to indict him with no likelihood of conviction would merely prolong public agitation. He would have preferred all along to "conceal from the public the extent to which such crimes have been carried," and it was probably, again, at Peel's suggestion that he finally agreed to publish Burke's confession. "Now that the trial has taken place," Peel wrote, "I doubt whether uncertainty as to the extent & history of these murders—is as great an evil as any exposure of facts can be."

However valuable Burke's two confessions had been for Knox in a legal sense, though, their publication in early February only blackened his reputation further. Burke's statements made it clear that Knox and his assistants "asked no questions" as to how the bodies had been obtained. The newspapers italicized the phrase "asked no questions" whenever it appeared, as well as other choice phrases: "they would be glad to see them again when they had any other body to dispose of," and "Dr. Knox approved of its being so fresh, but did not ask any questions." In the *Courant* confession, Burke's phrases "Sold to Dr. Knox" and "taken to Dr Knox" appear as regularly as the tolling of a bell or the gavel on an auction block, resonating with readers already indignant that anatomists stole decently buried folk from local graveyards. Both confessions were reprinted with running commentary on the significance of Burke's phrases, probably added by Robert Buchanan and John Stevenson. "When the reader notices what is printed above in *italics*," went the first note, "he will see that the *facility* with which Burke and Hare got a *purchaser* for the *body* of Donald, and the *desire* to 'see them again when they had *any other body to dispose of*,' must have been great *inducements* to such miscreants to *commence* their career of *murder*." "They were always told to get more," points out a later note, "alas! It is now too apparent what effect these words carried in the minds of Burke and Hare." Not even Burke's own exculpatory remarks about Knox were enough to counteract the effect on the popular imagination of so many murdered bodies—"sixteen in whole," as Burke said, purchased and dissected with so few questions. "Men, women, children, old and young," went yet another verse,

> *The sickly and the hale,*
> *Were murder'd, pack'd up, and sent off,*
> *To K—'s human sale.*
> *That man of skill, with subjects warm,*
> *Was frequently supplied.*
> *Nor did he question when or how*
> *The persons brought had died!*

During Burke's execution there had been calls from the crowd for "Knox and Hare" and Knox had to take precautions entering and leaving his dissecting rooms. Lonsdale portrayed him as a "man of thorough pluck," who refused to give in to the "rabble" threatening him, but Knox did his best to stay off the streets. To a friend in the country, Robert Greville could tell very little. "You ask me for something correct about Knox," he wrote, "but we know as little here as you do." He had not seen Knox "since the business" but heard "he sleeps every night in Portobello," the seaside town a few miles away. "They have got him caricatured in all manner of ways in the shops—& he hangs along side of Burke, Hare, Mrs. McDougal &c." Presumably his family had moved out of the house in Newington as well. The caricatures must have caused the relatives remaining in Edinburgh

CROPPING A NOX-I-OUS PLANT
OR AN OLD VIRTUOSO APPROPRIATING A NEW CURIOSITY.

Figure 18. Caricature of Robert Knox published shortly after Burke's and M'Dougal's trial. Reproduced courtesy of the Library of the Royal College of Physicians of Edinburgh.

great distress, for they made use of every unpleasant pun on "Knox" available. "In one the devil is cropping a Nox-ious plant," Greville reported (Figure 18). In another, Knox was portrayed cutting open the body of a woman, with the heading "Dedicated without permission, To a most distinguished finishing Lecturer: close of an obnoxious Session." The puns on "ob*nox*ious" were, of course, a way of referring to Knox without running afoul of the libel laws. When, one morning, boys hawked a broadsheet with Knox's head on it, crying "Here you have a likeness of Dr. Knox and a poem on the murders, for a ha'penny," they were brought to the Police Office. By evening the same broadsheet was back on the street, advertised with the cry, "Here you have a new poem on the Surgeon's Square doctors, for a ha'penny." The next day, though, the boys were back to naming names: "Here you have a new poem on Dr. Knox and his resurrectioners, for a ha'penny."

The *Scotsman*, which had a reputation to maintain, used the same circumlocution as the caricatures in describing the "popular tumult" on Tuesday, February 10, when "a number of young men assembled on the Calton-hill," around 3 P.M. They "proceeded to equip a large effigy of an Anatomist"—"bald head and all," Greville heard—"who has been rendered very obnoxious to the public by recent events." At first the young men were "few in number," but as they filed over the bridges to Newington, the figure "high in air," they attracted more adherents, "till the whole southern suburbs seemed in motion." The police were notified, but it took them some time to arrive, and in the meantime, the shop owners on nearby Clerk Street took the precaution of closing early. On arriving at No. 4, "a number of lads deliberately proceeded to 'Burke' the effigy, amid loud huzzas. Having squeezed and throttled the figure for some time, they tied a rope about its neck, and suspended it from a small tree in the shrubbery before the house, but the branches giving way, the effigy was pulled, battered, and tossed about." The intention was to burn it, but, Greville heard, "he would not consume." At that point the police arrived, led by the superintendent, Captain Steuart. The crowd threw rocks at the police and the house, and when Greville went to Knox's house the next day he "found they had broken every pane of glass in the house, & not only his, but the windows of several houses on either side—which certainly was not like the discrimination of an *Edinburgh* mob." The demonstration was dispersed from Newington, but moved to Surgeon's Square, and was rumored to be heading for the lord advocate's house as well. The police prevented them from getting close to either place, and "huzzaing and cheering through several streets," the crowd "began to abate their noisy demonstration." By 8 P.M. all was quiet, and "the city had recovered its wonted 'propriety.'" A few weeks later, another effigy was burnt in Portobello, on the former site of public executions.

We do not know Knox's feelings, or his wife's or sister's, when they saw their home with the smashed windows, or spoke to their neighbors whose houses had also been damaged in the attack. By the time of the incident, Knox's resolve had been shaken, and he had decided to seek public vindication. Characteristically, he did not for a moment suggest that he had done anything wrong, asserting instead that his friends, without his permission, had gone ahead and appointed an agent to look into the matter. The agent, after conferring with legal counsel including James Moncreiff, dean of faculty and former defense counsel for Helen M'Dougal, recommended that a private committee made up "of a few persons of undoubted weight and character" be asked to conduct an investigation. Sir Walter Scott was approached to be part of that body, but he reflected the general view that its members were not impartial, but rather were "to sit as Mr. Knox's friends" with regard to "his late traffick with the West port. In other words to lend a hand to whitewash this much to be suspected individual." That was not fair to committee members, who were not all "doctors and surgeons" as Scott supposed but included lawyers and businessmen known for their probity. But Scott felt no call to lend his own, highly respected countenance to the proceedings. Knox "shall ride off on no back of mine," he wrote, "and I feel no call to mix myself in the business at all. . . . I will travell in no such boat."

The report of the "Committee of Investigation as to the Dealings of Dr. Knox with the West Port Murders," to give the full and unwieldy title, contained material to satisfy both Knox's supporters and his detractors. His friends could be satisfied with the first point made by the committee, that they had seen "no evidence that Dr. Knox or his assistants knew that murder was committed in procuring any of the subjects brought to his rooms, and the Committee firmly believe that they did not." They could also be pleased by the second point, that they had found "no evidence" of the appearances of the cadavers "actually having excited" suspicions in either Knox or his assistants. His detractors, though, could note other phrases used by the committee. There were several circumstances, including "the very early period after death" at which the subjects were brought to the rooms, "the absence of external marks of disease," and the "generally abandoned character" of supposed resurrectionists, which should have excited suspicion. Moreover, the committee noted the practice "adopted in Dr. Knox's rooms" to be "very improper in the case of persons bringing bodies which had not been interred."

Asked, presumably, where he had thought the bodies were coming from, Knox told the Committee that "long prior to any dealings with Burke and Hare," he had formed and expressed the opinion "that a considerable supply of subjects for anatomical purposes might be procured by purchase, and without any crime, from the relations or connections of deceased persons in the lowest ranks of society." What follows from this! ridiculed Christopher North, once this response was made public. Did Knox and his assistants really believe "that the poorer inhabitants of Edinburgh were all of them not only willing, but most eager to sell the bodies of their husbands, wives, brothers, and sisters, and sweethearts, and relations in general?" In fact it seems most likely that Knox had convinced himself that the cadavers were not purchased, but stolen, though he could hardly confess this to the committee. As it was, committee members agreed that Knox had acted upon his "preconceived opinion" in a "very incautious manner." He gave "a ready ear to the plausible stories of Burke," delegated the "reception of the subjects" to his assistants and doorkeeper, and instructed them to ask no questions that might "tend to diminish or divert the supply of subjects." Still, they concluded, "it is fair to observe, that perhaps the recent disclosures have made it appear reprehensible to many who would not otherwise have adverted to its possible consequences."

Later writers echoed Scott's views that the committee's investigation was a "whitewashing process," but Knox's students received the report as a triumphant vindication. On April 11 they presented him with a gold vase, accompanied with a letter declaring they "had deeply sympathised with you during the mental sufferings which you must have experienced. . . . That you should now stand acquitted of every imputation affecting your character, must gratify, but cannot surprise us. The public voice has at length exonerated you from charges of which we who know you from the first moment felt the injustice." But by this time Knox lived in a fishbowl, and in *Blackwood's* Christopher North called it incredible, "that his class received him, in consequence of these horrid disclosures, with three cheers." That "savage yell within those blood-stained walls," he went on, "is no more to the voice of the public, than so much squeaking and grunting in a pig-sty during a storm of thunder." Those "who thus disgraced themselves and their human nature were implicated in the charge; and instead of serving to convince any one . . . of their own or their lecturer's innocence, it has had . . . the very opposite effect—exhibiting a ruffian recklessness of general opinion and feeling on a most appalling subject." R. H. Nimmo picked up the theme in another lithograph. A golden cup stands on a pedestal of bone, with images of Burke and Hare murdering one of their victims and their faces just below. "This Cup, originating from and in commemoration of The West Port Murders," reads the caption, "is, as a mark of their great personal regard, and as the expression of their high contempt for Public Feeling, presented to" an image of Knox "by his enthusiastic pupils, session 1828–9." Greville did not think Knox "will be able to regain his original station in Society for a long time, if ever."

There was, however, one place where Knox's connection with the murders was not only discounted, but eliminated entirely: the novel *Murderers of the Close*, which we have already encountered. Neither a gripping novel, nor, certainly, what anyone would call an accurate report, *Murderers of the Close* appears a dreadful piece of hackwork, little known and deservedly so. And yet there may be more to it than meets the eye. The publishers, George Cowie and William Strange, were responsible for many other books, pamphlets, and newspapers, pitched at working-class audiences and supporting radical causes. Robert Seymour, the Dickens illustrator, supplied the woodcuts for *Murderers of the Close*, and he, too, was closely associated with radicals. In 1828 he drew a pro-Benthamite caricature opposing the "Money and Interest" of the proposed King's College, backed by the established elite in church and state, with the "Sense and Science" of University College London, a hotbed of Bentham's supporters. His work on *Murderers of the Close* coincided with his frontispiece for another Cowie and Strange publication, the influential pamphlet *Catholic State Waggon* by Thomas Perronet Thompson. Thompson, part owner of the *Westminster Review*, was a prolific and determined political writer, and the pamphlet juxtaposed intolerant, inflammatory remarks against Catholic emancipation presented in Parliament with reasoned, patriotic arguments in its support. Printed on cheap paper and priced at two pennies, the pamphlet was aimed at working-class readers, who, radical publishers believed, would read political arguments as well as true crime stories. It sold forty thousand copies, vindicating their belief in their audience and more than repaying their investment in Seymour's fee, generally set at 12 shillings per illustration. Seymour continued to produce illustrations for the radicals until his death in 1836.

These and other pamphlets might well have brought Seymour into contact with Henry Warburton and proponents for the proposed Anatomy Act. For whatever else *Murderers of the Close* might have been, it was a clear advocate for the necessity of dissection and the evils inherent in the present system of obtaining bodies. The villains of the piece are always the murderers, William Burke, Helen M'Dougal, and the Hares, never the purchasers. Indeed, the author and illustrator went to great lengths to exonerate the medical profession, even at the risk of interrupting the narrative. Having given an account of the discovery of Madgy Docherty's body, and noting how easy it was to locate victims in a big city—the "wretched outcasts known as abandoned females . . . soldiers' and sailors' wives, beggars, anxious mothers from remote districts"—the author paused to reflect on the condition of modern anatomical practices. "There is no doubt," he wrote, "but that the crimes of the miscreants (Burke and Hare) have arisen from the great difficulty of procuring subjects for anatomical dissection." That should not implicate the medical men who purchase them, though, for such subjects "are absolutely necessary to the best interests of society, and no substitute for them can be found. A course of anatomical dissections forms one of the essential and indispensable requisites in the education of a surgeon," that is, "indispensable to the acquisition of a science so valuable to the world at large, and to which this country is so mainly indebted for its honour and character for humanity."

This is a strong statement, coming in the middle of a thrilling tale by, as we may suppose, a writer of penny dreadfuls. It was unusual, to say the least, for either true or fictional crime narratives to break off the story and insert a disquisition on the donation of bodies for science, but that is exactly what the author of *Murderers of the Close* did. "It is true," he explained, "that in no case can an individual have such ownership of a human body, as to entitle him to do any thing more than subject it to the rites of burial; and though it were otherwise, the dead are surrounded by those who would view the approach of any indecent hand with religious horror." But, he went on, "has not this childish, we may almost say this criminal superstition about dead bodies, occasioned the most atrocious and disgusting crimes? Is not the only remedy that can with safety be recommended at present, the chastising in ourselves, and deprecating in others, those feelings which are instinctive, but which, in a civilized country, must lead to such fatal results? . . . A regard for the welfare of the living has so far already induced many people to allow the bodies of their relations to be dissected privately, for the discovery of the unknown disease which has proved fatal; and good men have been ready, on their death-beds, to request that, after death, their bodies might be delivered over for the advancement of science; thereby conferring a greater benefit on society, than by a legacy of thousands."

And in case any readers could not make the connection between the Select Committee on Anatomy and the Burke and Hare murders, the author made it for them. "That the fearful scenes herein developed have not been acted in this solitary instance alone is more than to be feared from the answer of sir Astley Cooper made to the committee of the house of commons, some time since appointed to enquire into the subject of procuring bodies for anatomical purposes," he noted. "In answer to a question put to him as to the ordinary characters and occupations of the exhumators (resurrectionists), he made this reply: 'They are the lowest dregs of degradation; I do not know how I can describe them better; there is no crime they would not commit; and as to myself, if they would imagine I should make a good subject, they would not have the slighted scruple, *if they could do the thing undiscovered, to make a subject of me!*'" Obviously Burke, M'Dougal, and the Hares, depicted in *Murderers of the Close* as indeed "the lowest dregs of degradation," had proved Sir Astley Cooper's point in the most graphic style imaginable.

The author's main strategy for downplaying the role of the anatomists was to imply that Burke and Hare sold their subjects to many different medical men, thus making it less likely that there could have been collusion or even responsibility on the part of the doctors in question. Margery Docherty's purchaser is referred to merely as "a celebrated surgeon," who had not had a chance to examine her body before the police arrived the next day. He cooperated fully when the sergeant asked if he had any objections to the removal of the body, saying "Certainly I can have none. If, indeed, so monstrous a crime has been committed, I should be guilty of connivance did I not afford every means in my power in dragging the circumstance to light." Hare took Mary Paterson's cadaver to a similarly anonymous "dissecting room, which it was the custom of himself and Burke to supply with subjects." There was no sign in the novel that this was the same surgeon who later purchased Docherty's body. Moreover, this, second surgeon was "startled" on noticing the "extreme freshness of the body, the settled expression of the countenance, the limbs which had not even began [*sic*] to stiffen." He looked suspiciously at Burke and Hare, and at the cadaver, "and exclaimed, 'Why, life has scarcely departed this body—where did ye get it—I suspect all is not as it should be.'" Unlike the rest of the text, this has no counterpart in the Edinburgh publications like Ireland's *West Port Murders*. As we have seen, Knox's name was all over the Edinburgh newspapers. By February it had reached London through the *Gentleman's Magazine*, which summarized the result of Burke's trial and supplied the detail that "All the bodies were sold to Dr. Knox, most of them for ten pounds each." In contrast, *Murderers of the Close* succeeded in exonerating the unnamed surgeon by making him—like everyone else—the murderers' dupe. In the novel, Burke at first did not know how to answer the surgeon when asked about Paterson's body, but Hare, "putting on a bold front, pushed himself before his comrades, and winking his eye, and calling up a ghastly leer, which he meant to be knowing, said to the surgeon, 'Why, this young woman you see, died—yes, she died.'" But how? demanded the surgeon sternly. Well, replied Hare, "her friends *was* poor people, d'ye see, and as they know'd Bill and I was in the trade." "'And who may the friends of the girl be?' enquired the medical man, who still felt some misgivings." But this Hare refused to say, "'No, no master,' said he, shaking his head, 'it will never do to split after that fashion; why, bless ye, 'twould ruin the trade altogether.'" At this point the surgeon gave up his questions, for he knew "that in transactions of this sort these miscreants were obliged to observe silence on such occasion, in order to further their after interest. 'Well, well, I hope its [*sic*] all correct,' said he. 'To be sure it is,' said Burke . . . 'your honour knows us; why we would'nt do what's wrong, by no means; the body's not regular *rose* we *knows*, because it was never buried at all, at all.'" The surgeon, having heard enough, concludes "I believe I may trust you." And the criminals have the last word, at least for the time being: "'Faith! and 'twas a near squeak that,' said Burke, as they closed the door after them; 'bad luck to it, we must mind not to offer the *corpses* when they're too green.'" Perhaps the most telling part of this episode is not the text, but Seymour's accompanying woodcut, for the caption reads "The Surgeon refusing to purchase the body of an apparently murdered Female." Anyone looking only at the illustrations would certainly assume that the surgeon had nobly refused to treat with the murderers (Figure 19).

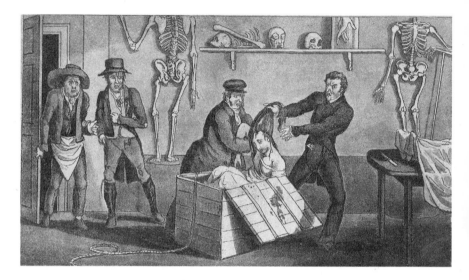

Figure 19. Robert Seymour, "The Surgeon refusing to purchase the body of an apparently murdered Female," from *Murderers of the Close*, reproduced courtesy of the Trustees of the National Library of Scotland. The anonymous author of *Murderers of the Close* hoped to soothe public outrage against the medical profession.

Was the author a medical man himself? Was he a Benthamite? Was the book not really a novel at all, but rather a piece of sensationalist propaganda for Warburton's Anatomy Act, using the murders to sway public opinion in its favor? Certainly Warburton and his associates used the Burke and Hare murders to support their proposed legislation. Their efforts were renewed when the story broke of a copycat crime in London, the murder of a fourteen-year-old Italian vendor, Carlo Ferrari, by the resurrectionists John Bishop and Thomas Williams. "It is totally impossible to describe the impression made upon the feelings of the public in general, since the promulgation of the murder of the Italian boy," reported Pierce Egan, turning again from sporting news to crime. It has "*terrified* the young, alarmed the hitherto bold and strong person, and frightened the aged men and women almost out of their senses: in truth, it has operated like a *panic* upon all ranks of society, from one end of the kingdom to another." Egan, too, cited Sir Astley Cooper on the dreadful character of body snatchers who supplied the medical schools, arguing that Bishop's trade had hardened his conscience, "banished everything like *feeling* from his composition," and so led him on "step by step," in crime, until "*gain* to him superseded every other consideration; and whenever a chance offered to procure him a victim, murder was the quickest way to answer his diabolical purpose." Preventing similar outrages became part of the avowed purpose of the Reformers. "What are the evils against which we are attempting to make provision?" asked Thomas Macaulay in 1832, when the final version of the Anatomy Act was debated in Parliament. "Two especially; that is to say, the practice of burking and bad surgery." No one reading *Murderers of the Close* could miss the point that without parliamentary regulation for anatomy, burking was an ever-present danger to the poor. The *Newgate Calendar* of 1841, the first of the many editions of that publication to include the Burke and Hare case, reemphasized that point. Warburton, according to the *Calendar*'s account, "begged that he should not be understood to treat the feelings of the lower orders with the slightest degree of disrespect by the present enactment." And he begged members of the House of Commons to reflect "that in the case of the late disclosures of the horrid atrocities committed in order to obtain a supply of subjects for dissection in Edinburgh, the lower classes had in all cases been the victims." Much shorter, though only slightly more accurate, than *Murderers of the Close*, the *Newgate Calendar* narrative sealed the connection between the Edinburgh and London burkers and the Anatomy Act. The murders were transmuted, once again, into a cautionary tale, this time of the bad old days before enlightened legislation existed to protect the public. Whether the public needed to be protected from the murderers or from the doctors was a subtlety that the penny dreadfuls did not address.

As *Murderers of the Close* hit the bookseller's shops in London, David Paterson, now permanently identified through the trial publications as "keeper of the museum" for Dr. Knox, was discovering the pitfalls of publicity back in Edinburgh. Like Knox, he was attacked by the press, and Knox's determination to make no public statement left Paterson fully exposed. At the time of the trial he was twenty-three, slightly younger than

Knox had been when caught in the cross fire between Boer and English officers in South Africa. As, in effect, the lowest-ranked person within the dissecting establishment, Paterson found himself the whipping boy, as Knox had once been, in a scandal that was none of his making. "I have been sacrificed in character to some persons in higher life," Paterson wrote indignantly, for within a week of the trial, the *Caledonian Mercury* printed as fact that a "conspicuous witness at the late trial," who had sworn he knew nothing of the murders though he had received Docherty's body, had in fact been intimately involved with Burke and Hare. A respectable teacher of anatomy, according to the *Caledonian Mercury*, had come forward to say that selfsame witness had shown up on his doorstep at 1 A.M. on the morning of November 1, when Docherty had been dead a scant few hours. He had claimed to have a body of a woman to dispose of, for which he asked £15, stating that he had "a desperate gang" in his pay, "through whom he could obtain as many subjects as he wished for." The implication was clear: the body must have been Docherty's, and Paterson must therefore have been Burke and Hare's accomplice, not their dupe.

Paterson, stricken, appealed to Knox, but received no help but the advice to stay silent. Knox made clear his view that it was Paterson who owed him loyalty, not necessarily the other way around: he implied that Paterson "had not always been faithful" to his interests, while offering the tepid reassurance "*No prejudice* shall ever be allowed to enter *my mind* against you, unless your own conduct give rise to it." The price of his continued support was Paterson's continued silence. "I wish to do every thing in my power to prevent your taking wrong steps," Knox wrote; "the public clamour is of course much against you, but all such matters as these subside in a short period, provided the individuals themselves do not adopt false steps." Paterson was induced to remain silent for another week, but by the end of that period, he burst out, he could no longer bear "being held forth to the public as one of the most odious characters in existence." He had acted entirely under Knox's "guidance and direction," and he had understood, he said, that Knox intended "to espouse my cause, and clear my innocence." But he found he had "been shamefully wronged," for Knox had "most cruelly failed to perform" what he had promised. He provided to the *Caledonian Mercury* a long, rather too long, explanation for the rumor concerning the rival anatomist and the cadaver. He had an ongoing relationship with the servant to another anatomist, who had the charge, as did he, to get bodies for his employer. That other "friend of the lecturer" alluded to in the rumor had come to *him* asking for the names of the people who supplied Dr. Knox, and offering £15, some amount of which, Paterson had understood, would be in the form of remuneration, or kickback, to himself. He had never offered that person any of Burke's and Hare's cadavers, but Andrew Lees had, just about the same time, offered him a cadaver, and that was the one he had offered to the lecturer on the night of November 1.

Paterson's account was believable and supported by other evidence: we know that Knox purchased many bodies from a number of different sources, and Lees was arrested on suspicion of stealing a body in December of 1828, that is, while the Burke and Hare investigation was ongoing. We also know that John Lizars and other Surgeon's Square anatomists were desperate enough for cadavers to purchase them from Gow and other resurrectionists within two months of the trial. But it was altogether too much information for the *Caledonian Mercury*, which continued to insinuate Paterson's guilt. And his detailed, circumstantial account of the matter-of-fact way in which anatomists and their employees discussed cadaver procurement— "in a walk along the Bridges," in Paterson's phrase—did neither him, nor the anatomists, any good. By the end of February Paterson had left Knox's employment—as he put it, he was "now no longer a plant in the noxious garden"—and he decided to give a fuller account of his side of the story in the anonymous pamphlet signed by "The Echo of Surgeon's Square." It was addressed to the lord advocate, promising to disclose "the accomplices, secrets, and other facts relative to the late murders." It is likely he hoped to cash in on the craze for everything Burke and Hare, and the idea for the publication may have come from his printer, the rather downmarket publisher Robert Menzies. It is not impossible that the *Caledonian Mercury* had a hand in it as well, as the controversy provided good copy. The result was an embellished version of the testimony Paterson gave the procurator fiscal, written with an eye to his own exculpation and placing the blame squarely on Knox and his assistants.

Fergusson and the other assistants struck back in a savage attack that contrasted their own professional integrity with Paterson's lower-class deceit. They had not been involved in the murder, they said. Instead, they accused Paterson of having been in league with Burke and Hare, and giving false evidence at the trial. He had no business calling himself "Keeper of the Museum belonging to Dr. Knox," a title which belonged to "a gentleman," presumably Frederick John Knox. Paterson was nothing but "a menial servant, hired by the week at 7s, and dismissable at pleasure," a scavenger, a porter, whose mother and sister were employed washing the blood and offal from students' dissecting clothes. "This is the person who presumes to address the Lord Advocate of Scotland!" they wrote. "This is the person who pretends to have had no connexion with Burke and Hare!" The *Caledonian Mercury* sided with the "principal assistants" against Paterson, allowing them to have the last word. They were, after all "young gentlemen," while he was a mere servant. Paterson tried once more to tell his side of the story, this time to Sir Walter Scott. "From what the world has already received from you In the way of delightful entertainment," he wrote, "I am led to think your pen and ability, will be employed in collecting materials for the ground work of a piece on Burke and Hare, but O Sir spare the innocent who has suffered too much already." Paterson offered Scott "if such be your pleasure . . . , sketches of one or two persons, who I dare say will be prominent characters in the above, what, and who they are and what they have been, who have all along been intimately connected with this affair," particularly "the rise and progress of a very public gentleman to his pursuit of glory." But Scott was outraged to receive such a letter from "Dr. Knox's jackall for buying murdered bodies," as he called Paterson. "Did ever one hear the like?" he wrote. "The scoundrel has been the companion and patron of such atrocious murderers and kidnappers and he has the impudence to write to any decent man." He may have assumed that Paterson wanted money in exchange for what Scott derided as his "invaluable collection of anecdotes," but what Paterson really had in mind was redress for having been "calumniated by the very person who did and who still does profit by that dishonourable trade. To save themselves," he wrote, referring to the assistants as well as to Knox, "they endeavoured to turn the blame upon me."

Paterson, "still a respectable inhabitant in Edinburgh" thirty years later, finally found a sympathetic listener in the person of Alexander Leighton, in whose portrait of Knox as self-aggrandizing, despicably cruel to those who deserved better at his hands, we can hear the "echo of Surgeon's Square." Leighton's *Court of Cacus* exonerated "the curator" of the dissecting rooms, as he referred to Paterson, from all blame. Though it was upon him "that the short-lived blind fury of some newspapers of the time fell, with much surprise to himself, and much indignation elsewhere," he was "of all the parties concerned, the most free from blame; nor did any one but himself come forward and assist the authorities in the prosecution." He had even mentioned his suspicions "to his principal," but "that gentleman silenced him at once . . . and so the suspicions passed away." Since Leighton's narrative was, in turn, picked up by later writers, Paterson's "echo" reverberates still.

By the time Leighton's *Court of Cacus* was published, Knox had not lived in Edinburgh for many years. He weathered the scandal, supported by his family and friends, sticking by his determination to say nothing further regarding Burke and Hare. The College of Surgeons dismissed him from his position as conservator of the museum, as he must have expected. Eventually his brother Frederick was appointed as cataloguer, but first he had to acquire some formal credentials as a surgeon, becoming a licentiate of the College of Surgeons in 1831. This would ordinarily have required his producing tickets of his attendance at university medical lectures, and since he does not appear on any official records we do not know how he managed that. It is likely, though, that neither he nor his brother cared much for college regulations. Frederick John continued to maintain his brother's anatomical collection, and in 1836 published a well-regarded book, *The Anatomist's Instructor*, which drew on his extensive experience in preparing specimens. In 1840 he moved with his family to Wellington, New Zealand, where he became its first librarian and was active in scientific circles. He took to signing his name "Frederick John Knox, MD," a title for which, once again, he had no formal medical credentials. But no one in Wellington seemed to know or care, and he and his family flourished.

It is possible that Robert Knox, too, thought of emigrating. His student numbers stayed high for about ten years after the scandal, and he successfully collaborated with former pupils turned friends, most notably William Fergusson. Once the furor had died down, he resumed his presentation of research to the Royal Society of Edinburgh; he resumed, too, his illicit purchases of cadavers throughout Britain. Those ended only when the first Anatomy Act was finally passed in 1832, making available to duly registered anatomy lecturers the cadavers of those who died unclaimed in public institutions. It thus legislated the inequity in the treatment of the dead poor that its proponents recognized and its opposition attacked. But it also reduced the depredations of the body trade from a flood to a trickle. Cadavers became more plentiful; the price of a subject in Edinburgh had dropped to "£1-10 when opened, £2-2 when entire," by the 1840s. There was no longer an incentive to steal them, and certainly no incentive for anatomists to pay for their theft. Most striking, though, was the end of the "anonymous subject," that staple of dissecting establishments for hundreds of years. The Anatomy Act required that the inspectors of anatomy keep records of name, age, date, place, and cause of death for each cadaver. Dissecting material retained a human identity by which it could be traced and accounted for: anatomists could no longer accept late-night parcels and ask no questions. The corpse, while still a commodity, retained its connections to the community from which it had come.

The Anatomy Act further mandated that, once the dissection was completed, the lecturer to whom the cadaver had been assigned was required to provide a coffin and burial for the remains. Leftover bones and viscera could no longer be swept off the dissecting table and dumped in a corner of Surgeon's Square. In that sense the anatomist did not really purchase the corpse; instead, he rented it for the purpose of medical education, with the obligation to return it to its final resting place. For "the bodies which had undergone anatomical examinations in the Edinburgh Schools of Anatomy" after 1832, that resting ground was St. Cuthbert's churchyard near the Castle, and its burial records highlight the post–Anatomy Act shift in treatment of cadavers. Descriptions like "healthy looking female subject" or "young boy" or "stout middle-aged subject" appear in Knox's dissecting notebooks from the 1820s, but the later records from St. Cuthberts reveal names and ages: Elizabeth Shankie, seventy years old, James Shearer, nine years, James Colston, fifty-seven years. Though presumably poor, their remains were invested with the dignity of a name, an appropriate way to honor their service to the living. Illicit sale of cadavers did not altogether disappear, but it became rare as a motive for murder. And not, as Burke's and Hare's victims might attest, a moment too soon.

In putting a stop to the body trade, the Anatomy Act also removed the competitive advantages Knox had derived from his extensive cadaver-procurement network. It is likely that as the number of bodies available to him declined, so did the number of his students. But all the Surgeon's Square anatomists faced the same decline, as new men and new professional specialties emerged in Edinburgh. That may have been the impetus for Knox to apply for university chairs in pathology and physiology in 1837 and 1841. His applications reveal Knox at his most contentious, as he criticized the existing medical professors severely, "adverting . . . to the continual decline of the University," and characterizing his professional opponents as "antique drone," "parasitic vermin crawling on the carcase of genius," and—this last applied to one of his former students—"the worst, the very worst, speaker that has appeared as a Public Lecturer in this City." Knox was not appointed, for Edinburgh was full of talented yet difficult people, and we may wonder if he was surprised by his failure. Though Henry Lonsdale blamed it on political and religious bigotry he cannot avoid mention of Knox's "high sarcastic method."

In fact Lonsdale himself appears to have been personally associated with Knox for only a brief period, though his biography makes it seem as though the two men were friends for decades. He attended Knox's anatomical lectures in 1834, serving as his assistant before leaving to study in London and Paris. He received his MD in 1838 and then left Edinburgh again for two years. By May of 1840 he was back, and he and Knox entered into a partnership to offer anatomical classes at the Argyle Square Medical School. This was less a formal educational institution than a collection of extramural medical lecturers, clustered in one place to facilitate attracting students. But by the 1840s students refused to be attracted, and the partnership lasted only two years. Lonsdale's personal recollections of Knox stem from that fairly brief period of their collaboration, while his practice among the poor of Edinburgh, his authority for the "picture of Edinburgh low life" permeating his account of the Burke and Hare murders, lasted at most five years. In 1845 Lonsdale moved to a hospital position, and, eventually, a wealthy marriage, in Cumberland. Most of his time was devoted to literary and antiquarian pursuits, and it is not clear when, if ever, he saw Knox after leaving Edinburgh.

Knox was heartbroken at the death of his wife and young son in 1842, and it may have influenced his decision to give up the seemingly unending wait for the university chair in anatomy. As it turned out, Alexander Monro did not retire until 1846. He was not replaced by any of the anatomists of Knox's generation, but instead by a new man, John Goodsir, who had been another of Knox's pupils. By that time Knox had moved to London, leaving his family in the charge of his sister Mary, a nephew, and his oldest daughter. "You cannot think what pleasure I have in making you all comfortable," he wrote back home. "I wish you were all here in London, but I know you are all comfortable and happy."

Knox never again obtained a permanent position as medical lecturer. He tried Glasgow, but his notoriety was too great for him to live in peace, while London, where he was less instantly recognizable, was crowded with would-be teachers. The publication of both the *Newgate Calendar* version of Burke and Hare and another popular account of "The Burkers of Edinburgh and London" in the early 1840s meant that Knox's name was once again brought before many of those who would be his patients at a public hospital. His skill as a writer and public lecturer saved him from financial ruin, and he became one of the foremost speakers on popular anatomical subjects. His lectures on race and on artistic anatomy were especially well calculated to appeal to middle-class tastes, and his books on those subjects went through many editions. He was warmly welcomed by like-minded members of the London Ethnological Society, honored for his "earnestness and love of science for its own sake," noted for saying precisely what he thought no matter the consequences. In 1856, he was given the position of pathological anatomist in the recently founded Cancer Hospital in London. He lived in the quiet town of Hackney with his son Edward, maintaining close ties to William Fergusson, by that time a professor of surgery at King's College, London, and surgeon extraordinary to the queen. There is no sign he mellowed—in 1861 he criticized Charles Darwin's *Origin of Species* for leaving "the question precisely where it was left by Goethe, Oken, and Geoffroy St. Hilaire"—but according to Lonsdale, he was an active and sought-after lecturer and dinner guest until his last illness. He had thus made a more graceful recovery from greater scandal than many of his peers. But his anatomical work once he left Edinburgh is negligible. His research agenda, like his most famous sixteen subjects, had died at the hands of Burke and Hare.

Shortly before he died, Lonsdale said, Knox had spoken of writing his life, giving as a reason "that he could explain the terrible events of 1828 better than any other person living." Leighton's *Court of Cacus* had been published one year earlier, and must have given him great pain. It brought up—again—events he may have thought safely thirty years in the past, assigning the blame to anatomical practices which had been the foundation of his scientific career, and calling him, once again, to public attention and public ignominy. His son, Edward Knox, had been born about 1839, long after the "burkers" in Edinburgh and London had met their fates, and it may have been on his account that Knox insisted "he would be able to prove his entire innocence of all and everything pertaining to the West Port atrocities." If Knox did, finally, break his silence and write his version of the story, the manuscript must have been among the ones he burned, for nothing of the kind has come down to us.

And what, we may wonder, could he have told us in any case? It seems evident that Knox knew astonishingly little about the events that turned his life upside down, when his world, and the worlds of Burke, Hare, and their victims, collided at Number 10 Surgeon's Square. He had asked no questions, undertaken no inquiries, devoting himself instead to the scientific research that he believed would secure his reputation. We should grant him his image as a commanding lecturer and superlative dissector, expertly wielding scalpel and saw. But we should also acknowledge how compelling are the caricatures of "Knox the boy who buys the beef," how well they depict the unreflecting negligence of anatomical practices of that era. It must have seemed terribly unfair to Knox—but perhaps not so much to us—that the hundreds of cadavers he studied throughout his lifetime mattered less than sixteen he purchased in the course of one year. A few people today may know of him in connection with the ciliary muscle of the eye, the habits of South African hyenas, or early theories of evolution. But many, many more know him only through his connection to Burke and Hare. Ultimately history, like some evil enchantress in a fairy tale, gave Knox posthumous fame at a price he never would have wanted to pay.

Cast of Characters

IN LEGAL DOCUMENTS, PEOPLE WERE IDENTIFIED BY ALL THE names they were known to have used, as well as all the names that other people used to refer to them. Many sources therefore list all known aliases and nicknames, as well as maiden names of married women. I have included the most frequent variants in the list below.

Perpetrators

William Burke, West Port
Margaret Hare or Laird, Tanner's Close, West Port
William Hare, Tanner's Close, West Port
Helen M'Dougal, West Port

Cadavers

(Approximate chronological order from November 1827 to October 31, 1828)

Donald, died of natural causes in Tanner's Close (Chapter 2)
Joseph, murdered in Tanner's Close (Chapter 3)
Abigail Simpson, murdered in Tanner's Close (Chapter 3)
Englishman from Cheshire, murdered in Tanner's Close (Chapter 4)
Old woman, murdered in Tanner's Close (Chapter 4)
Mary Paterson or Mitchell, murdered in Constantine Burke's house, Canongate (Chapter 5)
Elizabeth Haldane, murdered in Tanner's Close (Chapter 6)
Effy the cinder gatherer, murdered in Tanner's Close (Chapter 7)
Grandmother, murdered in Tanner's Close (Chapter 7)
Grandson, murdered in Tanner's Close (Chapter 7)

Old woman, murdered in Tanner's Close by Hare acting on his own (Chapter 7)

Old woman being taken to the Police Office, murdered in Tanner's Close (Chapter 8)

Margaret or Peggy Haldane, murdered in Brogan's flat (Chapter 6)

Mrs. Hostler, murdered in Brogan's flat (Chapter 8)

Ann M'Dougal, murdered in Brogan's flat (Chapter 8)

James Wilson, known as Daft Jamie, murdered in Tanner's Close (Chapter 9)

Margaret or Margery or Madgy Docherty or Campbell, murdered in Brogan's flat (Chapters 1 and 10)

Anatomists

John Aitken and Thomas Johnstone Aitken, medical lecturers, Surgeon's Square

George Ballingall (1786-1855), professor of surgery, Edinburgh University

George Stewart Campbell, skeleton maker, High School Yards

Lancelot Donelly, doorkeeper and anatomical assistant to John Lizars

William Fergusson (1808–1877), LRCSE, chief assistant to Robert Knox

Thomas Wharton Jones (1808–1891), assistant to Robert Knox

Frederick John Knox, LRCSE (1794–1873), brother of Robert Knox, responsible for his anatomical museum

Robert Knox, MD, FRCSE (1791–1862), anatomical lecturer, head of dissecting establishment at Number 10, Surgeon's Square

Robert Liston, FRCSE (1794–1847), surgeon and lecturer

Alexander Lizars and John Lizars (1791/2–1860), anatomical lecturers, Surgeon's Square

Alexander Miller, assistant to Robert Knox

Alexander Monro *tertius* (1773–1859), professor of anatomy, Edinburgh University

David Paterson, doorkeeper and anatomical assistant to Robert Knox

Granville Sharp Pattison (1791–1851), professor of anatomy, Glasgow University

Thomas Southwood Smith (1788–1861), physician to Jeremy Bentham and proponent of the Anatomy Bill

James Syme, FRCSE (1799–1870), surgeon and lecturer

John William Turner, FRCSE, surgeon and lecturer, Surgeon's Square

Witnesses

Hugh Alston, neighbor of William Burke and Helen M'Dougal

John Brogan, his wife, and son John, friends and neighbors of William Burke

Janet Brown, friend of Mary Paterson and chief witness for her murder

Constantine Burke, brother of William Burke, police scavenger, his wife, Elizabeth Burke or Graham, and their sons, Richard and William

Jean Coghill, friend of Mary Paterson

Ann Conway, neighbor of William Burke and Helen M'Dougal

Ann and James Gray, lodgers with William Burke and Helen M'Dougal

Mary Ann Haldane, daughter of Elizabeth and sister of Margaret Haldane

Janet Law, neighbor of William Burke and Helen M'Dougal

John M'Culloch, porter, Alison's Close

Jean Sutherland, friend of Mary Paterson

Janet Wilson and Janet Downie or Wilson, mother and sister of Daft Jamie (James Wilson)

Isabella Worthington, friend of Mary Paterson

Resurrectionists

John Burnett, medical student, Canongate

George Cameron, Carnegie Street

James Gow, Blackfriars Wynd

James Hewit, Carubber's Close

John Kerr, Skinners Close

Andrew Lees, Scott's Close

John McQuilkan, Drummond Street

John Spouse, Bell's Wynd

Judicial Authorities

Archibald Alison (1792–1867), advocate depute, part of the

prosecution team for the trial of Burke and M'Dougal

David Boyle (1772–1853), lord justice clerk, High Court of Justiciary

John Hope (1794–1858), solicitor general, the immediate supervisor of the procurator fiscal within the Crown Office

Alexander Maconochie, Lord Meadowbank (1777–1861), justice, High Court of Justiciary

Sir Robert Peel (1788–1850), secretary of state for the Home Office, Whitehall, London

Sir William Rae (1769–1842), lord advocate, the Crown's chief legal officer in Scotland, with authority over public prosecution

Archibald Scott, procurator fiscal, responsible for determining whether a crime has been committed and whether probable cause exists to charge an individual

George Tait, sheriff-substitute, the acting sheriff

Defense Attorneys and Private Legal Agents

Henry Cockburn (1779–1854), Faculty of Advocates, senior defense counsel for Helen M'Dougal, prominent Whig

Francis Jeffrey (1773–1850), Faculty of Advocates, prominent Whig, legal counsel for Janet Wilson and Janet (Wilson) Downie

Duncan M'Neill (1793–1874), Faculty of Advocates, part of the defense team for Burke and M'Dougal, later legal counsel for William Hare

Sir James Wellwood Moncreiff (1776–1851), dean of the Faculty of Advocates, senior defense counsel for William Burke, prominent Whig

George Monro, agent for Janet Wilson and Janet (Wilson) Downie in the private prosecution against William Hare

Patrick Robertson (1794–1855), Faculty of Advocates, part of the defense team for Burke and M'Dougal

Erskine Douglas Sandford, legal counsel for Janet Wilson and Janet (Wilson) Downie

Police Establishment

Alexander Black, police surgeon

Alexander Black, junior, acting police surgeon

John Findlay, policeman

John Fisher, criminal officer
George Foulis, policeman
Alexander Moir, policeman
Captain James Steuart, police superintendent
Sergeant John Stuart, criminal officer

Forensic Witnesses

William Pulteney Alison, MD, FRCPE (1790–1859), professor of the Institutes of Medicine, Edinburgh University, additional medical witness for the prosecution of William Burke and Helen M'Dougal

William Brown, FRCSE, medical inspector

Robert Christison, MD, FRCPE (1797–1882), professor of medical jurisprudence, Edinburgh University, medical inspector for the prosecution of William Burke and Helen M'Dougal

David Macbeth Moir (1798–1851), surgeon and writer, medical inspector

William Newbigging, FRCSE (1772–1852), medical inspector for the prosecution of William Burke and Helen M'Dougal

Alexander Watson, FRCSE, medical inspector

$\mathcal{N}otes$

A LL ACCOUNTS OF THE MURDERS TAKE AS THEIR BASIS THE *Trial of William Burke and Helen M'Dougal, before the High Court of Justiciary, at Edinburgh* published by the Edinburgh printer and bookseller Robert Buchanan. The first printing arrived in Buchanan's bookstore on December 31, 1828, though the publication date is generally given as 1829. It provides the most accurate transcript of the trial. By the end of February 1829, the same publisher produced *Supplement to the Trial of William Burke & and Helen M'Dougal,* concerning the legal issues surrounding William Hare, and *Appendix to the Trial of William Burke and Helen M'Dougal.* The *Appendix* is especially valuable, because Buchanan included William Burke's confessions (see Chapter 10) as well as contemporary newspaper articles and pamphlets relating to the murders. The *Trial, Supplement,* and *Appendix* are often found bound together, and they were reprinted in William Roughead, ed., *Burke and Hare.* They are now more widely available on Google Books. Also available on Google Books is *West Port Murders,* originally published in Edinburgh by Thomas Ireland in unbound sections, probably beginning on December 25, 1828, and finishing by mid-January 1829. Much of it reprints articles originally published in newspapers and pamphlets, but Ireland included some original material. It is frequently cited as a source but should be used with caution. One final contemporary source for the trial is the relevant section of David Syme, *Reports of Proceedings in the High Court of Justiciary, from 1826–1829.* Syme's account of the trial is abridged, but he retained more of the original language of the witnesses than Buchanan or Ireland.

The following abbreviations are used in the Notes. See Bibliography for full citations of sources.

Appendix	*Appendix to the Trial of William Burke and Helen M'Dougal*
Burke, Confessions	"Confessions of Burke in the Jail" and "Confessions of Burke" from the *Edinburgh Evening Courant*, published in *Appendix*, 32–44
ECA	Edinburgh City Archives
Edinburgh Room	Edinburgh Room, Edinburgh Central Library
EUL	Edinburgh University Library
GROS	General Registry of Scotland
NAS	National Archives of Scotland
NLS	National Library of Scotland
RCPE	Royal College of Physicians of Edinburgh
RCSE	Royal College of Surgeons of Edinburgh
Select Committee	Great Britain. Parliament. House of Commons. *Report from the Select Committee on the Matter of Obtaining Subjects for Dissections in the Schools of Anatomy.*
Supplement	*Supplement to the Trial of William Burke and Helen M'Dougal*
Trial	*Trial of William Burke and Helen M'Dougal, before the High Court of Justiciary, at Edinburgh*

Introduction. The Burke and Hare Murders

1. *Murder . . . picturesquely horrifying. West Port Murders*, 1–3.

2. medical transplant industry. A recent example involves the remains of the BBC broadcaster Alistair Cooke, illegally harvested by funeral home directors and sold to Biomedical Tissue Services Ltd. See Powell and Segal; Slobodzian. Modern authors who invoke Burke and Hare include Iserson, 342–346; Roach, 49–52; Cheney, 108–111.

2. *An Authentic . . . Views, &c.* Copy of the original numbers of *West Port Murders* held by the Edinburgh Room, 1.

2. *authentic* edition. Advertisement inserted in YRA 637, Edinburgh Room.

2. *dispersed . . . numerous narrow lanes.* Shepherd, 9. Shepherd's description was

adapted from Hugo Arnot's 1780 comparison of the High Street to the head, tail, and sides of a turtle (Arnot, 179).

3. *true authors . . . forbearance.* Cited in Richardson, 131.

5. *marked man . . . walk.* Leighton, *Court of Cacus*, 15.

5. *Unfortunately . . . events.* Lonsdale, 106.

6. introductory essay. Roughead, 1–93. For an appraisal of Roughead's approach to crime narrative, see Sante; Leslie Blake.

7. *Thus the march . . . obscurations. West Port Murders*, 1.

Chapter 1. The Corpus Delicti

9. *petticoat . . . leaving town. Trial*, 49–50. Margaret Docherty was also identified as "Duffie," and this may be closer to her usual pronunciation of her name. "Docherty" could also be written "Daugherty," with the "gh" pronounced as "f," as in "laughter."

11. *one of these . . . communicates to the whole.* Shepherd, 28–29.

12. lawyers attending. Parliament Close, and the Edinburgh law courts, are in the same location on the High Street. The university quadrangle, newly built in the 1820s, is still on South Bridge, now known as Old College. The Royal Infirmary was on Drummond Street, where its imposing stone gates remain, and Surgeon's Square was immediately to the east, farther along the street. A section of the old city wall, known as the Flodden Wall, remains at the corner of Drummond Street and the Pleasance.

12. indicators of poverty . . . Dawson, 340–341.

12. *The Old Town . . . dark.* Kohl, 17.

13. Edinburgh's annual livestock market. Dawson, 351.

14. *the first door . . . highland woman. Trial*, 52–53.

16. *I thought . . . amongst them. Trial*, 74, 79.

16. *were merry . . . dancing. Trial*, 60.

16. *bade me . . . murder here. Trial*, 56, 63.

16. *It was . . . quiet enough now. Trial*, 57.

16. *one of the neatest . . . dwellings of the poor.* North, *Noctes*, 3:235. "Christopher North" was the pseudonym of John Wilson, who was professor of moral philosophy at the University of Edinburgh; his connection to *Blackwood's Magazine* was an open secret.

17. *quantity of straw . . . Doctor. Trial*, 58, 63.

18. *did not wish resurrectionists . . . suited his purpose.* Echo of Surgeon's Square, 7, 20. This pamphlet, published anonymously, has been attributed to David Paterson, though it is likely he collaborated with someone.

18. fifteen-year-old sister. Edwards, 170.

18. *What . . . William.* Syme, 356.

19. *ow'r . . . more. Trial*, 57.

19. *Keep out there . . . hair. Trial*, 75, 86.

20. *I was looking . . . Seven o'clock at night. Trial*, 76–82.

21. *all personal spite. Trial*, 86.

21. *informed them . . . searched. West Port Murders*, 4–5.

22. Sheriff-Substitute. Sheriffs-substitute were officials charged with carrying out the day-to-day responsibilities for law enforcement within a district, or shire. In theory the sheriff in Scottish districts, as elsewhere in Britain, was the chief law-enforcement

officer. The right to appoint sheriffs was held by the Crown, that is, the British government, in effect by the political party in power, and the position was often a sinecure bestowed on the dominant party's political friends. The actual work was delegated to officials known as sheriffs-depute, and though they, too, were expected to be friends of the party in power, they were also expected to have legal training and to conscientiously carry out their responsibilities. Since the district, or shire, under their authority could be extensive, they in turn appointed sheriffs-substitute to act in the Crown's name. George Tait had been involved in law enforcement for many years, writing the manual in use by the Edinburgh police.

22. procurator fiscal. In the Scottish legal system, the procurator fiscal is the official charged with determining whether there is probable cause to prosecute a person for a crime. In contrast to English law, there is neither a coroner's inquest nor a grand jury. Like the district attorney in U.S. courts, the "fisc" is also responsible for putting together the case for the prosecution. It was up to the lord advocate (see below) to decide whether to issue an indictment—a formal charge against a specific individual—and Archibald Scott therefore worked closely with the lord advocate and his staff, collectively known as the Crown Office.

22. lord advocate. The lord advocate is the Crown's chief legal officer in Scotland, the head of the Crown Office. This was a political appointment of the dominant party in Parliament, carrying with it a host of responsibilities designed to keep the current administration in power, including dispensing patronage. But lords advocate also had authority over public prosecution in Scotland, and from the late eighteenth century they were therefore required to have considerable legal experience. All indictments were issued and all criminal cases tried in the name of the lord advocate, though the actual court appearance could be delegated to advocates depute. Sir William Rae had served as sheriff and took an active role in important criminal prosecutions.

22. *had reason . . . follow. Supplement*, 13.

23. penny broadside. *Extraordinary Occurrence, and Supposed Murder, &c* (Edinburgh, November 3, 1828), *The Word on the Street*, NLS.

23. *to dread . . . human life. Supplement*, 12.

23. thirty-six years. November 10, 1828, HH21/8/1, NAS.

23. *of the facts . . . cognisant. Supplement*, 12.

23. High Court. The High Court of Justiciary is the supreme criminal court in Scotland.

24. *Puir folk . . . corpses.* North, *Noctes* 3:236.

24. *to quit . . . assistance.* Egan, *Trial of Bishop*, 6.

Chapter 2. The Anatomy Wars

25. *old pensioner.* Burke, Confessions, 32.

25. *a dirty low . . . few steps. West Port Murders*, 122.

25. *prodigious . . . windows.* North, *Noctes*, 3:235; see Fido, 113–114.

25. *a small . . . dead wall.* North, *Noctes*, 3:235, *West Port Murders*, 122–123.

26. *had an intention . . . Edinburgh.* Burke, Confessions, 32.

26. thriving business. See *Edinburgh and Leith Post Office Annual Directory*, 1832, Nicol Monro, "shoemaker, middle of Portsburgh"; ordinance survey map of Edinburgh, 1849–1853, *Maps of Scotland*, NLS.

26. *sensible . . . respectable.* The phrase is from M'Dougal's attorney, Henry Cockburn, *Memorials*, 430.

26. *proposed that his body . . . dispose of.* Burke, Confessions, 32.

28. *Annual course.* Roughead, 11, gives the date as November 29, 1827, based on Lonsdale, 72. It is not clear where Lonsdale got the date, but we may note that November 29 was a Thursday. If Lonsdale was accurate, Knox's class would have just let out.

28. *referred them . . . Surgeons Square.* Burke, Confessions, 33.

28. "John" and "William." *Trial*, 57.

28. *to know exactly . . . dispose of.* Burke, Confessions, 33, 37.

30. *a lecturer . . . anatomist.* Cited in Grant, 2:389.

30. the reform-minded parliamentary commissioners. Rosner, *Medical Education*, 181.

30. *number of vertebra . . . carotid artery.* These were typical questions asked by the Army Medical Board, cited in Rosner, *Most Beautiful Man*, 36.

31. *from a Professor . . . human body. Regulations . . . for obtaining Diplomas from the Royal College of Surgeons of Edinburgh*, 1828, cited in Rosner, *Medical Education*, 159.

31. Robert Liston. Power; Nicolson, "Syme, James"; Mic Dup 1316, EUL. I am grateful to Michael Barfoot for this reference.

31. John and Alexander Lizars. Lizars; Nicolson, "Lizars, John."

32. *who . . . proud disregard.* Leighton, *Court of Cacus*, 15.

32. John McQuilkan. Precognition against John McQuilkan for the crime of violation of sepulchres, AD14/28/20, NAS; HH21/8/1, NAS. Richardson, 69, argues that London resurrectionists often fell into the trade through association with anatomical lecturers. A precognition is a formal examination of witnesses who were present during a criminal act, to see whether there are sufficient grounds for going to trial.

33. conclusions the Select Committee would reach. Richardson, 108. See also Wise, 32–34.

33. *It is the opinion . . . rites of burial. Select Committee*, 9.

34. *No one can object . . . their remains.* Smith, "Use of the Dead," 51–52.

34. *the bodies of persons . . . without friends. Select Committee*, Appendix, 126–127.

34. *so much latitude . . . friendless poor.* "Article X," *Edinburgh Medical and Surgical Review* 32 (1829): 216.

35. *must be learned . . . discouraging it. Select Committee*, 12.

35. *I would recommend . . . science.* Cited in Richardson, 101. See Belchem, 189–190.

35. *placemen and pensioners . . . cultivated.* Cobbett, *Eleven Lectures*, 17. See also Cobbett, "An Address to the working people."

36. *that children . . . steam vessels. Select Committee*, 107.

36. Irish immigrants. Great Britain, Poor Law Commissioners, *Report on the Sanitary Condition of the Labouring Population of England*, 198.

36. *unfortunate and destitute.* Richardson, 176.

36. *As a child . . . never came out.* Richardson, xvi. For similar responses to racist practices in the United States, see Blakely and Harrington; Abraham.

36. body part harvesting. As portrayed in *Dirty Pretty Things*.

36. *and there was a skull . . . drawn bayonet. Select Committee*, 70.

36. *who had laboured . . . condition.* Cobbett, *Eleven Lectures*, 17.

37. great John Hunter. Moore, 208–215; *Select Committee*, 5.

37. *every public teacher . . . dissections. Select Committee*, 70.

37. Robert Christison. Christison, *Life*, 1:179.

37. *most abhorrent . . . exhumating. Select Committee*, 69.

37. *giving notice . . . firearms.* Syme, 320.

37. *in making his rounds . . . their feelings.* Syme, 315–318.

38. *The people . . . church.* Syme, 319–321.

38. *forty . . . resurrectionmen. Select Committee*, 71–73. Wise, 33–34, and Richardson, 115, have suggested possible identifications of the anonymous resurrectionists who appeared before the Select Committee.

38. *a bad character . . . stealing.* Precognition against Andrew Lees, AD14/31/468, NAS; HH21/8/1, NAS.

38. James Gow. Precognition against James Gow, AD14/30/383, NAS; HH21/8/1, NAS.

38. *When I go . . . wealthier people. Select Committee*, 72. See Richardson, 60.

39. *bodies . . . the poor. Select Committee*, 10.

39. *If we don't . . . sacredness of the grave.* Cobbett, *Eleven Lectures*, 17.

39. every source of supply. Richardson, 59–66.

40. *Lees & Co.* Fergusson, Account book, RCSE.

40. *It was universally known . . . interred. Select Committee*, 54.

41. *no doubt . . . done. Select Committee*, 95.

41. *I myself dissected . . . any other way.* Cited in Johnson.

41. *consist with . . . Dr. Knox. Trial*, 70.

41. *and a rope . . . trunk.* Cited in Johnson.

41. popular demonstrations. Richardson, 87, 90–93, 223–226; Burrell and Gill.

42. *the abolition or restriction . . . great measure removed. Select Committee*, Appendix, 124, 127–128.

42. *With regard . . . supply.* Letter of Sheriff-Substitute George Tait, AD14/29/16, NAS.

42. *that it may . . . dead subjects.* As discussed in letter sent by Sir William Rae to Sir Robert Peel, Edinburgh, November 27, 1828, ADD40339, BL.

43. *risk of the public . . . public authorities.* Letter of John Hope, AD14/29/16, NAS. John Hope was solicitor general for Scotland; that position is part of the Crown Office. The solicitor general has the immediate supervision of the procurator fiscal, and can serve as the deputy of the lord advocate. Like other positions in the Crown Office, the solicitor general was a political appointment requiring considerable experience in the law. Hope had worked closely with Rae for a number of years. See Millar.

43. As Gow later testified. Precognition of James Gow, AD14/29/16, NAS.

44. informants. *Select Committee*, 72.

44. *a number of the inhabitants . . . opportunities occur.* Letter from Archibald Scott, AD14/29/16, NAS.

44. Helen Miller. Precognition of Helen Begbie or Miller, AD14/29/16, NAS.

44. *as he does not approve . . . dead bodies.* Precognition of John Begbie, AD14/29/16, NAS.

44. *that two bodies . . . surface of the earth.* Precognition of James Gow, AD14/29/16, NAS.

46. *medical student . . . resurrectionist.* Precognition of John Lizars, AD14/29/16, NAS. There was a John Burnett registered for the anatomy class at the university in 1825.

46. The four men left. Precognition of James Gow, AD14/29/16, NAS.

46. *which as might be expected . . . opportunity.* Letter from Archibald Scott, AD14/29/16, NAS.

46. *commenced to another grave . . . left in the grave.* Precognition of James Gow, AD14/29/16, NAS.

47. *early on the following morning . . . first buried.* Letter from Archibald Scott, AD14/29/16, NAS.

47. *ascertained . . . natural death.* Precognition of John Lizars, AD14/29/16, NAS.

47. They did not find the cadaver . . . *but was rummaged.* Report of Sheriff-Officer James McKenzie, AD14/29/16, NAS.

49. *I am wholly at a loss . . . implicated.* Letter of John Hope, AD14/29/16, NAS.

49. *having learned . . . subject.* Precognition of John Lizars, AD14/29/16, NAS.

49. *that a search . . . day or two.* Precognition of John Hislop, AD14/29/16, NAS.

50. *in want of a subject.* Precognition of John William Turner, AD14/29/16, NAS.

50. *somewhat disfigured . . . face.* Precognition of George Ballingall, AD14/29/16, NAS.

50. *observed . . . examined privately.* Precognition of John Lizars, AD14/29/16, NAS.

50. *it had been opened . . . abdomen.* Precognition of George Ballingall, AD14/29/16, NAS.

50. corpse of Barbara Rodger. Precognition against James Gow, AD14/30/383, NAS; HH21/8/1, NAS.

51. *Tried in reference . . . spotlessly correct.* Cockburn, *Memorials*, 430.

51. *the incalculable danger . . . becoming greater.* Letter of John Hope, AD14/29/16, NAS.

52. *should of course . . . murder.* Minute books, April 15–17, 1828, RCPE.

52. *getting that . . . subjects.* Burke, Confessions, 44.

Chapter 3. Burking Invented

53. *on her back . . . crime.* Burke, Confessions, 31–44; Sir Walter Scott, cited in *Appendix*, 33–34; see Roughead, 16.

53. *got a small . . . disturbance.* Burke, Confessions, 34; see also Edwards, 86–87.

54. *At every inspiration . . . death. Appendix*, 22.

54. *kept the mouth . . . life went away. Appendix*, 33.

55. *Even . . . space of time. Appendix*, 22.

55. Death by compression. Spitz and Fisher, 336–338.

55. *Have you ever . . . Yes. Trial*, 118–120.

55. Bloodshot eyes. Spitz and Fisher, 336–338.

55. *WHO taught Burke . . . city. Appendix*, 23.

56. *to prevent . . . struggling.* Burke, Confessions, 36.

56. *In what manner . . . chest. Trial*, 118–120.

56. *had once been . . . his wife.* Burke, Confessions, 38–39.

56. *tenderness . . . equal.* Kohl, 92.

56. *they then gave . . . town.* Burke, Confessions, 33, 38. According to Burke, Simpson received a pension from Sir John Hope; if this is correct, they had murdered a pensioner of the Solicitor General.

57. *was in the habit . . . poor.* Great Britain, Poor Law Commissioners, *Report on the Sanitary Condition of the Labouring Population of Scotland,* 155. Hereafter cited as *Sanitary Inquiry.*

57. *a more particular . . . people.* Cited in Rosner, *Medical Education,* 89.

57. *further questions.* This point was made very clear in Burke, Confessions, 31–44.

57. *Either liquid.* Frederick John Knox, 10–11.

57. *never durst . . . resurrection men.* Burke, Confessions, 44.

58. *drab mantle . . . blue spots.* Burke, Confessions, 38.

58. *They often said . . . lamb.* Burke, Confessions, 43.

58. *shots.* Burke, Confessions, 43.

60. At five feet, five inches. November 10, 1828, HH21/8/1, NAS.23.

60. write English. Edwards provides the most detailed and sympathetic analysis of the backgrounds of Burke, the Hares, and M'Dougal; for Burke's family, see 15–16.

60. *natural vivacity.* Cited in Handley, 160.

60. *not at all ferocious . . . his relations.* Cockburn, *Memorials,* 430.

60. *most . . . servant.* Burke, Confessions, 44.

60. Though raised a Catholic. See Edwards, 17–18.

60. Ballina. See Edwards, 18, for a detailed discussion of Burke's hospital experience; for Burke's wife's name, see Edwards, 56.

60. steamboats. Handley, 30.

60. *huddled together . . . lambs.* Cited in Handley, 32.

61. *not merely . . . occupied.* Cited in Handley, 42.

61. *cease forcing themselves . . . take place.* Cited in Handley, 28.

61. *If they are told . . . from them.* Cited in Handley, 40–41.

61. *on a moment's reflection . . . furrows.* Cited in Handley, 45.

62. *It is very hard . . . wage.* Cited in Handley, 51.

62. laborers who tried to join together. Handley, 52–53.

62. *Their output . . . Scotland.* Cited in Handley, 42.

62. *spreading . . . kingdom.* Cited in Handley, 149–150.

62. *Numbers of hand bills . . . starvation.* Cited in Handley, 39.

63. *and are then . . . employment for them.* Cited in Handley, 41.

63. *Irish emigration . . . population.* Cited in Handley, 137.

63. *The means adopted . . . Glasgow.* Cited in Handley, 177.

63. *possession . . . Scotch labourers.* Cited in Handley, 151.

64. The Union Canal . . . stone. "Union Canal."

64. *temporary huts . . . contented and happy.* Cited in Handley, 60–62.

64. *he got no answer.* Burke, Confessions, 44.

64. described in jail records. November 10, 1828, HH21/8/1, NAS.

64. *has lived with . . . ten years. Trial,* 130.

65. *though not legally . . . affection.* Cockburn, *Memorials,* 430.

66. He was five feet, four and three-quarters inches. November 10, 1828, HH21/8/1, NAS.

66. *ferocious . . . liquor. Trial,* xiv. Cited by Edwards, 30.

66. Jail records. November 10, 1828, HH21/8/1, NAS.

67. *provided . . . inhabitants.* Cited in Handley, 179.

67. 10,000 Irish resident. Handley, 89, 109.

67. *small . . . . tradespeople.* Handley, 134–135.

67. *The Irish . . . life.* Cited in Handley, 160.

68. *had a horse . . . fish. Trial,* 96.

68. She was described. November 10, 1828, HH21/8/1. Margaret Hare was named in the list of witnesses for the indictment as "Margaret Laird or Haire or Hare"; presumably Laird was her maiden name. *Trial,* 4.

68. *an epitome . . . with his own. Appendix,* 11.

69. *subletting . . . to repletion.* Bell, *Day and Night,* 12.

69. *better class of houses . . . on demand.* Cited in Handley, 245.

69. *glittering . . . value.* Cited in Handley, 55.

70. whiskey. Observers had been complaining about the deleterious effects of cheap whiskey in Lowland Scotland since the eighteenth century. Deitz, 62–63. In 1877, the standard price for a bottle of whiskey purchased by the "lower classes" was 2 shillings, that is, 24 pence. Approximately ten glasses could be poured per bottle. Great Britain, Parliament, House of Commons, *Reports from Commissioners, Inspectors, and Others,* 69.

70. The population. Handley, 87.

70. *Destroy . . . provide for it.* Bell, *Day and Night,* 34.

70. *Scotch system . . . human existence.* Alison, 1. Hamlin provides an excellent recent analysis of Alison and his impact on sanitary reform, 74–84, 129–141.

71. *attemped to find . . . rule.* Alison, 41.

71. *deficient nourishment . . . water-closets. Sanitary Inquiry,* 156–157.

72. *that their destruction . . . morality.* Kohl, 19–20.

73. *Nature has furnished . . . country. Sanitary Inquiry,* 153.

73. *Edinburgh stands . . . open. Sanitary Inquiry,* 10.

73. *the labour . . . purifying. Sanitary Inquiry,* 10.

73. *and excepting . . . specially paid for. Sanitary Inquiry,* 153.

73. *If any malaria . . . open air. Sanitary Inquiry,* 10.

74. *altogether unfit . . . living men.* Bell, *Blackfriars' Wynd,* 21–22.

74. *Our Irish . . . again.* Scott, 65–66. Spelling is as it appears in the published text.

74. 48 families. Alison, 14.

74. *An old blind woman . . . daughter.* Bell, *Blackfriars' Wynd,* 9–11.

75. *Neighbours . . . attentive. Sanitary Inquiry,* 157.

75. *Very many . . . poor.* Cited in Alison, 15.

75. *a death . . . burial.* Christison, *Life,* 1:311.

75. *not less than 30 . . . small rooms.* Alison, 12.

75. *They could get . . . lodgers.* Burke, Confessions, 43.

76. *a fair specimen . . . endure.* Alison, 14–15.

76. *Female field labourers . . . character.* Alison, 11.

76. *painters . . . needlewomen.* Bell, *Blackfriars' Wynd,* 14.

77. *made it . . . get more.* Burke, Confessions, 42–43.

Chapter 4. Sold to Dr. Knox

79. *an Englishman . . . £10.* Burke, Confessions, 38.

79. *guilty . . . art and part.* AD2/1, NAS.

79. *working on the boats . . . nose.* Burke, Confessions, 38.

81. *of fair complexion . . . blue eyes.* Lonsdale, 4.

82. John Barclay. Lonsdale, 5–6; Grant, 2:390.

82. Professor Monro presided. Graduation is described in Rosner, *Medical Education*, 62–85; Knox's M.D. examination can be found in Minutes and Proceedings of the Medical Faculty 1811–1831, EUL.

82. Knox's first research. Knox, *De viribus stimulantium.*

82. first published article. Knox, "On the relations." See Lonsdale, 7–8.

82. London anatomist John Abernethy. Rae, 8–12, has suggested that Knox sought Abernethy out to improve his knowledge of surgery, and that he returned from Waterloo an accomplished surgeon, but that seems to be unlikely, as I outline below.

83. *as a huge . . . impunity.* Cited in Cantlie, 1:329.

83. usual reaction. Rosner, *Most Beautiful Man,* 72–90. There is no evidence for Knox ever having risen above the rank of hospital assistant, with its rank of ensign and pay of approximately 6 shillings per day.

83. he later wrote up. Lonsdale, 18.

83. *How happy . . . pursuits.* Cited in Lonsdale, 14.

84. *great service . . . presented themselves.* Stockenström, 2:119.

84. *various animals . . . dens.* Knox, "Notice relative to the habits," 383–386. Knox was arguing against William Buckland's theory regarding the presence of prehistoric hyenas in a cave in Kirkdale, Yorkshire. See Rudwick, 41. For a contemporary account of hyenas in South Africa, see Pringle, 135–138. I am grateful to Margaret Lewis for her help with hyena biology.

85. aboriginal skull. Knox, *The Races of Men: A Fragment,* 181; an illustration of the skull is provided in Knox, *The Races of Men: a philosophical enquiry,* 240.

85. Kaffir and Bosjeman. Knox, like other residents in South Africa, was aware that the names used by Europeans were not those the tribes called themselves: see *Fragment,* 155, 159. Pringle, 232–321, provides a detailed and sympathetic account of South Africa's indigenous peoples.

85. *five enchanting volumes. . . inevitable.* Knox, *Fragment,* 310–312.

86. *From the earliest . . . to do so.* Knox, *Fragment,* 149. Some modern writers, embarrassed by Knox's racism, have implied that he was forced into writing popular anatomical works to earn a living in the wake of the Burke and Hare scandal. See Roger Smith, 399. However, Knox himself was proud of his ideas on race and dated them to his first trip to London in 1817. His research on the Xhosa and Khoisan was first published in the *Memoirs* of the Wernerian Society in 1823. Lonsdale, 24.

86. *The theory . . . Boer origin.* Stockenström, 1:79. For more discussion of Stockenström's relations with the Xhosa, see Pringle, 100, 218–220.

86. *enlightened . . . command.* Stockenström, 1:219.

86. *We had possessed ourselves . . . mitigate their sufferings.* Stockenström, 1:79.

87. *real founder . . . racism.* Curtin, 377.

87. *Race . . . depend on it.* Knox, *Fragment*, 7.

87. *all races . . . ability.* Knox, *Fragment*, 141.

87. *must be forced . . . must leave.* Knox, *Fragment*, 253.

87. *Zoological history.* Knox, *Fragment*, 9. Broca is discussed in Gould.

87. *instinctual . . . scheme.* Knox, *Fragment*, 60.

87. *in the midst . . . striking.* Knox, *Fragment*, 30–31.

87. *the interior organs . . . to vary.* Knox, *Fragment*, 152–153.

87. modern scholars. Horsman, 406.

87. *Call them Species . . . everything.* Knox, *Fragment*, 9–10. For contemporary distinctions among hyenas, see Buffon, 2:117–125.

88. many of the writers. The literature on Knox and racial thought is extensive. In addition to Curtin and Horsman, cited above, see Desmond; Rich; Stocking; Odom.

88. proper credit. Knox, *Fragment*, 8.

88. proslavery advocates. See, for example, L S M, "Diversity of the Races"; "Knox on the Celtic Race."

88. *Journal of Anthropology.* C. Carter Blake, 332–338.

88. *one of . . . anthropologists.* Hunt, lviii.

88. "Kaffir" cranium. Knox, *Fragment*, 181; see Bank. Paul Turnbull has pointed to the use made of Aboriginal Australian anatomy by Alexander Monro *tertius.*

88. African peoples. Knox, *Fragment*, 179.

88. He had first formulated. Knox, *Fragment*, 93–97, 247.

88. Irish question . . . Austrian empire. Knox, *Fragment*, 26, 200, 93, 45.

88. *Each race . . . truth.* Knox, *Fragment*, 8.

88. *imbecility . . . qualification.* Knox, *Fragment*, 252.

88. Lord Charles Henry Somerset. Pringle, 184–199; Davenport.

89. *an infatuated . . . suggest.* Stockenström, 1:129, 162.

89. *That Captain Stockenström's . . . him.* Stockenström, 1:165; Theal, 29:190. See Hillman on the rank-sensitive practices of recent U.S. military courts.

89. *looked on . . . invective.* Hunt, lviii.

89. *chief primary tool . . . placarded.* Stockenström, 1:136; Theal, 29:190.

89. modern biographers. See Rae, 19–21.

90. drinking and fighting. McGrigor, 194–196; Rosner, *Most Beautiful Man*, 87, 117–122.

90. *Of the character . . . here speak.* Knox, *Fragment*, 252.

90. subsequent sharp condemnation. See Richards, "Political Anatomy," 384; and Richards, "'Moral Anatomy'."

90. *the great school . . . science.* Lonsdale, 18.

90. Students and physicians. Cross; Hannaway and LaBerge.

90. *the discoverer . . . branch of knowledge.* Knox, *Great Artists*, 37.

90. *laid it down . . . science.* Knox, *Great Artists*, 37–38, 51.

91. *intimate with both.* Knox, *Fragment*, 296.

91. *transcendental . . . function.* Knox, *Great Artists*, 105–106.

91. method for formulating laws. Knox, *Great Artists*, 62–65.

92. *When studied by the surgeon . . . universe.* Knox, *Races of Men: A philosophical enquiry*, 426.

92. *held in the most . . . medical students.* Knox, *Great Artists*, 20–21.

92. *inconsiderately . . . inferior rank.* Lonsdale, 36.

92. *hardly presentable.* Bridie, 47.

92. his sister. "Extensive Sale, by Auction, of Rich Silkes, Satins, Velvets, &c," September 16, 1826, *Scotsman*.

93. affectionate husband. Taylor.

93. *Towards . . . spirits, &c.* Cited in Lonsdale, 37.

93. *of the whole labour . . . co-partnery.* Cited in Lonsdale, 44.

93. *the causes . . . spine.* Knox, *A probationary essay.*

93. beauty of the spinal column. Knox, *A Manual of Artistic Anatomy*, 33.

94. three hundred students per year. Lonsdale, 130.

94. £800 in a single year. Fergusson, Account book, outlay for 1829–1830, RCSE.

94. Frederick Knox. Frederick John Knox, 41; Frederick Knox has been discussed in Kaufman; and Beasley.

94. "writer to the signet." Under the British legal system, there are two broad categories of attorneys. The first are trial lawyers, called barristers in England and advocates in Scotland. The second are, to put it plainly, lawyers who do everything else, including preparing cases to go to trial. These are called solicitors in England, and writers to the signet in Scotland. Their respective professional bodies in Scotland are the Faculty of Advocates and the Society of Writers to His/Her Majesty's Signet.

94. *was a great concern . . . otherwise.* Lonsdale, 213.

94. £195 per year. See *Appendix*, 31.

94. *such as . . . class-room.* Cited in *Appendix*, 31.

94. Friedrich Tiedemann. Tiedemann; Scarpa; Sue; Béclard; Cloquet. Knox worked with the engraver Edward Mitchell on all these books.

95. *want of candour . . . characters.* Lonsdale, 233.

95. *Pictorial-Anatomy School . . . nature.* Cited in Lonsdale, 153.

95. Lizars brothers. Lonsdale, 70–71; Fergusson, Account book, 1832, RCSE.

95. *which treats . . . ignorant.* Béclard, iv.

95. *esteemed . . . mechanical.* Knox, *Races of Men: a philosophical enquiry*, 429.

96. *He came to me . . . men of science are.* Audubon, 305, 329, 325.

97. *Left arm . . . Tendon.* Knox, Anatomical and Pathological Appearances, EUL; Gray, 853. The notebook was first described in Ross and Taylor.

97. *An original type . . . structures.* Knox, "Hermaphroditism," 477.

97. *generally dropsical . . . distinct.* Knox, "Anatomical and Pathological Appearances," EUL.

97. *the marrow . . . serum.* Horner, 37.

97. *Taken . . . inflamed.* Museum General Catalogue, 2: no. 1121, RCSE; Knox, "On the tendon," 404; Stanley.

99. *The appearances . . . allude.* Knox, "On the tendon," 404.

Chapter 5. Based on a True Story

100. *much given to drink.* AD2/1/3, NAS.

100. *Drunk . . . crowd.* HH21/6/7, NAS.

100. *fell in with the girl Paterson . . . same manner.* Burke, Confessions, 35.

100. *taken down . . . own words. West Port Murders*, 129.

101. *for protection. Low Life*, 125.

101. *girl . . . intelligence. West Port Murders*, 126.

101. *two pence halfpenny.* Burke, Confessions, 38. Burke used the same phrase for a later victim, so we cannot say how accurate his memory was on this point.

101. *This they called . . . to them. Low Life*, 30.

101. a glass of rum. AD2/1/3, NAS.

101. *always . . . comfortable for life. West Port Murders*, 126.

102. *of tea, bread . . . M'Dougal. West Port Murders*, 131.

102. *with distinctness . . . truth. West Port Murders*, 126.

102. William Swanston . . . *best authority. West Port Murders*, endmatter; CS181/6822, NAS.

103. wife of John Clark. AD2/1/3, NAS. Mistakes in names are very common among both contemporary and later sources dealing with the murders.

103. *How the hell . . . to-morrow. West Port Murders*, 131.

103. *in the same manner.* Burke, Confessions, 38.

103. Constantine Burke knew perfectly well. AD2/1/3, NAS.

104. *more bold . . . like to another.* Burke, Confessions, 38–39.

104. Alexander Miller. AD2/1/3, NAS.

105. *he thought . . . recover her.* ADD40339, BL. This account of Fergusson's comment comes from a letter of Sir Robert Peel to Sir William Rae, commenting on Hare's deposition. The deposition itself is no longer among Peel's papers.

105. *the beautiful symmetry . . . body.* Echo of Surgeon's Square, 6.

105. *pair of scissors . . . body and limbs.* Burke, Confessions, 39.

105. According to David Paterson . . . *purchase subjects.* Echo of Surgeon's Square, 8.

106. *infamous . . . noted brothel.* "Police Court," April 5, 1828, July 5, 1828, *Scotsman.*

106. *The first victim . . . twenty-one.* Sharpe, Preface, vii.

107. *numbers of the unfortunate females . . . Halkerston's wynd. Appendix*, 5.

107. *a young girl . . . the old abuse.* Leighton, *Court of Cacus*, 164.

107. *Bonny Mary Paterson . . . death's door.* Lonsdale, 102.

107. *wishing for the best . . . Paterson's remains.* Lonsdale, 101.

107. *girls of about eighteen . . . daughters of joy.* Roughead, 24.

108. *J. Oliphant . . . in the text.* Roughead, 21.

108. *art students . . . Rokeby Venus.* Rae, 74. There is no evidence that Knox taught art students while in Edinburgh.

108. *a pupil . . . anatomist.* Lonsdale, 101.

108. *such mere males . . . acquaintance with her.* Roughead, 30. See Edwards, 89.

108. *Intensely aristocratic . . . eyebrows.* Chambers, 7–8.

109. Sharpe's research. Cadell.

109. Stevenson. YRA 637, Edinburgh Room.

109. *any case . . . lover.* Chambers, 8.

109. *portraits . . . to destruction.* Sharpe, *The Whore's Rhetorick*; see Garside, liii.

109. *scandalous anecdote . . . sexual order.* Masson, 360, 369.

110. Hugh Alston. "Edinburgh Murder Dens," *Weekly Scotsman*, July 19, 1902, clipping inserted in L.C. Folio 62, NLS.

110. *consisting . . . nine lasts.* William Archibald, inventory of John Brogan's House West Port, inserted into Ry III No. 6, NLS.

110. *the two men . . . we cannot vouch.* YRA 637, Edinburgh Room.

111. interested in the other victims . . . the course of the week. This chronology is based on the edition of Ireland's *West Port Murders* held in the Edinburgh Room, and on Sharpe's correspondence and scrapbook, YRA 637, Edinburgh Room.

111. *dreadful proof . . . dissection.* Sharpe, Preface, v–vi.

112. *Some sort of explanation . . . narrative. Murderers of the Close*, iii–iv.

112. *destitute and houseless . . . I'll warrant. Murderers of the Close*, 58–63.

113. *the cold blooded indifference . . . dropped. Murderers of the Close*, 43.

113. Social reformers. The most authoritative source for Edinburgh is Tait; colorful though less reliable information can be found in *Low Life in Victorian Edinburgh.* See also Neild. According to Lonsdale, 370, the apparently inexhaustible public interest in "deep depravity" later led Robert Knox to publish a compilation work on *The Greatest of Our Social Evils: Prostitution, as it now exists in London, Liverpool, Manchester, Glasgow, Edinburgh, and Dublin.* There is no hint of the author's personal experience in it, for it was published anonymously and drew extensively from British and French writers, including Tait, but Lonsdale, on examining it, "unhesitatingly declared" that it was written by Knox.

113. *In Edina town . . . knife.* Broadside, "A Timely Hint to Anatomical Practitioners and their Associates—the Resurrectionists," *The Word on the Street*, NLS.

114. artist's model. For example, see the newspaper clipping with handwritten attribution to "Ladies own Journal Oct 27 1866," bound in Ry III no. 6, NLS.

114. In Robert Wise's 1945 . . . *Wednesdays. The Body Snatcher*, Thomas, 28–29. See the review of *Doctor and the Devils*, Canby, C8.

114. *Jessie Paterson . . . Oliphant.* Drawing pasted into *Wretch's Illustrations*, Edinburgh Room.

115. John Oliphant. *Edinburgh and Leith Post Office Annual Directory*, 1831–1832, lists "Oliphant, John, 14 Waterloo Place"; Harris and Halsby, 173. I am grateful to James Hogg at the Edinburgh Room for these references. John Oliphant may have been related to the painter and designer Francis Wilson Oliphant, and he may have spent some time in Newcastle in the 1840s. The Tyne and Wear Museum Collections on-line version shows John Oliphant's *Portrait of William Wailes* on its website, http://www.imagine.org.uk/. His *Cottages by a Shack*, 1847, is displayed on Artnet, http://www.artnet.com/artist/680404/john-oliphant.html.

115. *The unfortunate girl . . . thus exposed.* Bound into Ry III no. 6, NLS.

115. *lithographed studies . . . printsellers.* July 2, 1859, *Scotsman.*

116. *irregular in her habits . . . represented. West Port Murders*, 131.

116. *a Girl of the Town . . . residence.* GD1/353/5, NAS.

116. *one of the creatures . . . beauty.* Scott, *Letters*, 72.

116. *residing . . . Worthington.* AD2/1/3, NAS.

116. *Mary Paterson . . . Mason.* September 18, 1826, SL237/3/5, ECA.

116. *seal-engraver . . . Majesty. Edinburgh and Leith Post Office Annual Directory*, 1826–1827.

116. *4 months . . . sew and wash.* September 18, 1826, SL237/3/5, ECA.

117. *between the . . . prostitution.* Tait, 1–2.

118. *No reliance . . . month.* Tait, 51–52.

118. *Most were single . . . orphan.* Walkowitz, 19. There is an extensive scholarly literature on nineteenth-century prostitution. See Mahood; McHugh; Luddy; Cohen.

119. *well educated . . . situation. West Port Murders,* 131–132; January 21, 1828, SL237/3/5, ECA.

119. *desirous . . . to go.* April 8, 1828, SL237/3/5, ECA.

120. *represented . . . appeared. West Port Murders,* 131.

121. *while a servant . . . there.* November 6, 1826, SL237/3/5, ECA.

121. *from night . . . appearance.* Tait, 13.

122. March 15, 1828. LHB1/125/24, EUL.

122. Mary Mitchell. December 28, 1827, January 3, 1828, LHB1/125/24, EUL.

123. *fraudulently obtained.* AD 9/2, NAS.

124. *conviction . . . virtuous part of society. Supplement,* 5.

Chapter 6. *The Dangerous Classes*

126. *stout old woman . . . in front.* Burke, Confessions, 34.

126. *a dissipated character . . . neighbourhood.* She was reported to have a daughter married to a tinsmith on the High Street, but if so the daughter never came forward. *West Port Murders,* 192.

126. *nothing farther . . . drinking.* Burke, Confessions, 41–42.

126. fictional re-creations. Leighton, *Court of Cacus,* 122–131. Roughead, 22, repeats the story and refers to "inquiries made by Leighton," but comparison with extant sources shows that Leighton's account of the Haldanes is fiction based loosely on *West Port Murders.*

127. *with her face . . . £8 got for her.* Burke, Confessions, 41–42.

127. *a woman . . . dissolute life. West Port Murders,* 192.

127. *vagrancy . . . infesting the New Town.* HH21/6/5, NAS. In 1828, Edinburgh had two main facilities for offenders, the Bridewell and the New Jail. Generally speaking, the Bridewell was for detention, while the New Jail was for convicts, but prisoners could wind up in either building. In both facilities, men and women were separated, as were debtors, minor offenders, and felons. Prisoners awaiting hearings could also be held at the Police Office on the High Street.

127. *the dangerous classes . . . swell its number.* Symons, *Tactics,* 1.

127. *Newgate Calendar.* Newgate Calendar, http://www.exclassics.com/newgate/ngintro.htm; Horne, xxxi.

127. *crimes of passion . . . all they know.* Symons, *Tactics,* 15–17. See Jones, for an extended discussion of the definition of vagrant as criminal, 178–209.

128. *to establish . . . peace and good order.* Cited in McGowan, 96. See Barrie, 92–140.

128. *efficient.* May 17, 1828, ED9/2/2, ECA. The superintendent's name also appears in contemporary documents as Stuart or Stewart.

128. *great object . . . Crime.* List, *Instructions to Constables,* 18. See also the updates in List, *Copy of General Orders.* List's two publications echo *Instructions, Orders, Regulations, and Bye-Laws, given, made, and passed, by the Commissioners of Police for the City of Edinburgh.* See McGowan, 243–245.

128. Captain Steuart's force. McGowan, 245.

129. *to apprehend persons . . . of doing so.* List, *Instructions to Constables*, 18.

129. *were to be civil . . . duty.* Instructions, Orders, Regulations, 6. See List, *Instructions to Constables*, 29.

129. Injuries in the line of duty. McGowan, 264; January 14, 1828, ED9/1/6, ECA.

129. *exert the utmost care . . . a crime.* List, *Copy of General Orders*, 8–16. For examples of this in practice, see McLevy; and McLevy's fictional counterpart, McGovan.

130. clerks of the Police Establishment. McGowan, 252–253; February 19, 1828, ED9/1/6, ECA.

130. One quarter of these. For an excellent survey of the range of felonies in Edinburgh, see Kilday; a provocative discussion of women and crime in 1828 can be found in Symonds.

131. Mary Ann Haldane. HH21/8/1, NAS.

131. *What do you do . . . What we can.* Symons, *Arts and Artisans*, 117.

131. *carrying something . . . very bad characters.* Precognition against Mary Ann Haldane for the crime of theft, AD14/27/17, NAS. Sergeant John Stuart's surname also appears in the records as "Stewart." He was no relation to the superintendent, James Steuart.

132. verdict of not proven. Syme, 180.

133. Finlayson was found guilty. Syme, 231.

133. *unanimously guilty.* Syme, 261–262; Register of Criminal Prisoners, HH21/8/1, NAS.

134. *lagged . . . starve. Low Life*, 11.

134. *one of the most appalling . . . released.* "Police Court," April 5, 1828, *Scotsman*.

134. *In no other city . . . hat-binders.* Tait, 146.

134. *the supply of labourers . . . day.* Tait, 150.

135. *A dozen . . . no employment.* Cited in Symons, *Arts and Artisans*, 118.

135. *may, and should . . . occupation.* List, *Instructions to Constables*, 30.

135. *clearing the town . . . subsistence.* "Police Court," April 5, 1828, *Scotsman*.

135. *Anxious to encourage . . . cumber the streets.* "Police Court," February 18, 1829, *Scotsman*.

136. *We cannot . . . prisoners of a morning. Low Life*, 17–19.

136. fiddlers on Saturday night. *Low Life*, 51.

136. *Day by day . . . natural guardians.* Cited in Syme, 16.

137. William Campbell. Syme, 247–248; Precognition against Elizabeth Kelly, William Kelly . . . William Campbell, AD14/27/5, NAS.

137. William Kelly. Precognition against Andrew Campbell, William Kelly, AD14/28/28, NAS.

137. Ghost of Christmas Present. Dickens, *A Christmas Carol*, 38.

137. *the Practicability . . . any effect.* Cited in McGowan, 258. See GD31/557, NAS. Aspects of the proposed House of Refuge were revived among later reform efforts. See Wigham.

138. *sad enough . . . the world began. Low Life*, 13–14.

138. the Edinburgh police. June 12, 1827, HH21/6/7, NAS. See McGowan, 257.

138. *they must steal . . . honest industry.* Cited in Symons, *Tactics*, 16.

139. thousands of pounds estimated. See *Low Life*, 119, for a mid-century attempt to estimate the value of property loss due to theft.

139. *her door . . . carried away.* Precognition against Thomas Nesbit and Agnes Brown, AD/14/29/11, NAS.

139. respectable side. *Low Life*, 42.

139. *cohabitated together . . . purchased them.* Precognition against Thomas Nesbit and Agnes Brown, AD/14/29/11, NAS.

141. prisoners in jail. HH21/6/5, NAS.

141. Catherine Douglas. Precognition against John Stuart, AD14/30/282, NAS.

143. Policemen were dismissed. See Ruthven-Murray.

143. *was likely . . . of trifling value.* Precognition against John Stuart, AD14/30/282, NAS; John Stuart, "Memorial to the Police Commissioners," July 12, 1830, and "Regulations for the Edinburgh Police Office," April 2, 1830, ED9/1/6, ECA.

146. Peggy Haldane. HH21/6/5, NAS.

Chapter 7. Anonymous Subjects

147. *She was in the habit . . . grandmother.* Burke, Confessions, 39.

148. *almost charitably . . . face. West Port Murders*, 193–194.

148. a most unlikely story. This critique of Leighton is from Edwards, 94–99.

148. *of a peculiarly . . . description. West Port Murders*, 193.

148. *as he was afraid . . . for £8.* Burke, Confessions, 42.

149. *A knowledge . . . rooms.* Knox, *The Edinburgh Dissector*, 1.

150. *full and complete . . . details.* Notice inserted into Fergusson, Account book, RCPE.

150. *actually engaged . . . body. Regulations to be observed by Candidates.*

150. four hundred students. "Report of the Committee of Investigation as to the Dealings of Dr. Knox with the West Port Murderers," printed in Roughead, 278.

151. *The basis . . . another.* Thomas Southwood Smith, 2–3.

151. *Naming parts first . . . lie within.* Cited in Rosner, *Medical Education*, 95–96.

151. *not more . . . manner.* Thomas Southwood Smith, 14.

152. *All incisions . . . living.* Liston, xi, 2.

152. *The ultimate benefit . . . estimated.* Averill, xv.

152. *The infliction . . . criminal.* Liston, xi.

152. *have been much exaggerated . . . explanations.* Averill, 213–214.

152. *inconvenient complaint . . . pernicious.* Thomas Southwood Smith, 15.

153. *A remarkable Tumour . . . taken.* Knox, "Anatomical and Pathological Appearances," EUL.

153. *The situation . . . aneurism. General Catalogue,* 1: no. 1082, RCSE.

153. *been performed . . . success.* Averill, 37.

153. Slightly over half. Henry Hollingsworth Smith, 37, 329–330.

153. fatal mistake. Thomas Southwood Smith, 12.

153. *The dissection . . . attempted. General Catalogue,* 1: no. 1082, RCSE.

153. Autopsies. Testimony of Benjamin Brodie, *Select Committee*, 26, Appendix 124.

154. *by reasoning with the poor . . . acquiesce in it.* Testimony of Thomas Southwood Smith, *Select Committee*, 86.

154. *as the thing was known . . . bodies themselves.* Testimony of Granville Sharp

Patisson, *Select Committee*, 84. The Irish surgeon was Crompton, surgeon general for Ireland.

155. *these matters . . . possible.* Robert Knox, letter to the *Caledonian Mercury*, Edinburgh, March 17, 1829, cited in Rae, 98–99.

155. anatomy to be dignified. See Sappol, 44–73.

155. *secrecy and mystery. Select Committee*, 86.

155. Knox began to get ready. Fergusson, Account book, RCSE.

155. distanced the cadaver. For dissection as ritual, see Sappol, 74–97; on dehumanizing language used by those who work with cadavers, see Ratner; Flood.

155. stole fingers. Frederick John Knox, 3–6.

156. *the perfect . . . entire skeleton.* Frederick John Knox, 41–43.

156. articulated skeleton. Robert Knox, *Edinburgh Dissector*, 2.

156. skeleton maker. Fergusson, Account book, RCSE.

156. *from a set of bones . . . texture.* Robert Knox, *Edinburgh Dissector*, 2.

156. *natural skeleton . . . posteriorly.* Robert Knox, *Edinburgh Dissector*, 17.

157. *pieces of cork, putty &c.* Robert Knox, *Edinburgh Dissector*, 9.

157. *the fresh bones . . . room.* Robert Knox, *Edinburgh Dissector*, 2.

157. *composed of an assemblage . . . spine.* Robert Knox, *Edinburgh Dissector*, 23–24.

157. *forms at once . . . numerous.* Robert Knox, *Edinburgh Dissector*, 84.

158. *we shall run . . . without one.* Robert Knox, *Edinburgh Dissector*, 90.

158. *upper extremities . . . man.* Robert Knox, *Edinburgh Dissector*, 117.

158. *in the highest . . . instructive.* Lonsdale, 126–128.

158. *a subject . . . memory. Select Committee*, Appendix, 128. According to his account books, Robert Knox purchased between twenty to twenty-five cadavers each December; assuming he followed this system of rotation, he would have been able to accommodate thirty to thirty-five students in his practical dissecting classes.

159. *Thus the student . . . locomotion.* Robert Knox, *Edinburgh Dissector*, 2.

159. *bad effects . . . bad smell.* Shaw, xvi.

159. *so loose . . . fit for use.* Horner, 17–18.

160. *very putrid . . . bound over it.* Horner, 39–40; see also Parsons, 18; Thomas Southwood Smith, 92. See Turgenev's *Fathers and Sons*, 186–196.

160. The first group . . . subjects. Robert Knox, *Edinburgh Dissector*, 461.

161. *should almost uniformly . . . dissections.* Robert Knox, *Edinburgh Dissector*, 180.

161. *slashing away . . . skeleton?* Lonsdale, 160.

161. *thoracic . . . body.* Robert Knox, *Edinburgh Dissector*, 195.

162. *All this will require . . . turned.* Robert Knox, *Edinburgh Dissector*, 287.

163. *the dissection of the Thorax . . . muscles.* Robert Knox, *Edinburgh Dissector*, 244–247.

163. *cut through . . . interior.* Robert Knox, *Edinburgh Dissector*, 251.

163. organ in situ. Robert Knox, *Edinburgh Dissector*, 280.

164. *form but one . . . stretch.* Robert Knox, *Edinburgh Dissector*, 340.

164. *display . . . time.* Robert Knox, *Edinburgh Dissector*, 356–358.

164. *stomach . . . branches.* Robert Knox, *Edinburgh Dissector*, 391.

165. *put as in the situation . . . hooks.* Robert Knox, *Edinburgh Dissector*, 415.

165. *with which the student . . . studies.* Robert Knox, *Edinburgh Dissector*, 461.

165. *Having removed . . . advantage.* Robert Knox, *Edinburgh Dissector*, 465.

165. *well acquainted with . . . anatomy.* Robert Knox, *Edinburgh Dissector*, 506.

165. *with these . . . accomplish.* Robert Knox, *Edinburgh Dissector*, 533.

165. *There cannot be . . . comfort.* Fergusson, *Practical Surgery*, 24–31. See also Liston, 2.

167. *It is not . . . light from dark. John Bull*, January 5, 1829.

167. *assemblage . . . bone.* Henderson, Collard, and Johnston, 940–941. I am grateful to John Lawson, City of Edinburgh Council Archaeology Service, for his assistance.

Chapter 8. The Criminal Mind

168. *Let the woman . . . visited them sooner.* Burke, Confessions, 40.

168. security for Brogan's rent. William Burke to William Archibald, Edinburgh, May 30, 1828, 594, 2222, NLS.

169. *they could not trust . . . trunks there.* Burke, Confessions, 42.

170. *assaulting . . . a woman.* HH21/6/7, NAS.

170. *First ae drunk . . . third.* North, *Noctes*, 3:230.

170. hoping to be caught. Edwards, 107.

170. true and fictional crime. DeQuincy, 10; Peterson, 3–8. See also Robert Morrison's introduction to DeQuincey (vii–x); *The trial of Katherine Nairn*; *The trial of Miss Broderick*.

171. *You know my forte . . . more freely.* Egan, *Recollections*, 27–32.

172. theory of phrenology. See Cooter; Tomlinson, 97–114.

174. *correspondence between . . . brain.* Macnish, *Introduction to Phrenology*, 2–4.

174. *the true . . . mind.* Combe, *A System of Phrenology*, 41. On Combe, see Cooter, 101–133; van Wyhe, 52–56.

175. *heart . . . wicked.* Macnish, *Confessions*, 5.

175. Dr. Jekyll. Stevenson, *Strange Case of Dr. Jekyll*; McCracken-Flesher.

175. *the effect . . . cultivate the good.* Combe, "Phrenological Observations," 94; Combe, appendix to Haggart, 159.

175. *I gave only . . . truly affecting.* Haggart, 88–91; "Execution. A full and particular account of the execution of David Haggart," *The Word on the Street*, NLS. The precognitions for David Haggart's many offenses can be found at AD14/20/11, AD14/20/122, AD14/20/182, AD14/21/248, NAS.

176. *in a wish . . . bestowed.* Haggart, v–viii.

176. *drawn from . . . career.* Combe, appendix to Haggart, 159.

177. *have arisen . . . amiss.* Haggart, 159–169.

178. Scholars have noted. Cooter, 101–119.

178. *so closely cropped . . . manifestations.* Combe, "Phrenological Observations."

181. *Merely telling us . . . simulation.* Printed in *West Port Murders*, 268–269.

182. *An ordinary person . . . murderers.* North, Review, 683; for similar views see Hazlitt, "Burke and the Edinburgh Phrenologists."

182. *It is altogether . . . profligate courses.* Printed in *West Port Murders*, 269–272; *Appendix*, 49.

183. *one of the most . . . received. Edinburgh Literary Journal* 1 (July 11, 1829): 11; Combe was involved in many running controversies with Edinburgh intellectuals, including William Hamilton, professor of civil history, and Stone was one of Hamilton's students. See Ryan.

183. *correspond . . . brute creation.* Stone, 27.

184. *The wild cry . . . subside.* Combe, "Phrenological Observations," 94–96.
186. *at the first murder . . . routine!* Egan, *Trial of Bishop*, 7.

Chapter 9. Crime Scene: Edinburgh

187. *had been for some time watched . . . exciting suspicion. West Port Murders*, 135.
187. *imbecile . . . always clean. West Port Murders*, 132–133.
189. *as a lamb to the slaughter . . . quarrel about them.* Burke, Confessions, 41.
189. Jamie's green waistcoat. AD2/1/3, NAS.
189. The clothes were noticed. *West Port Murders*, 137.
190. *the only light . . . seen before.* Precognition of David Paterson, JC29/24, NAS. The precognitions taken in preparation for the case, from Paterson and from Hare, were sealed on January 26, 1829, and opened only in November 1990.
190. *This is the body . . . perfect health.* Precognition of David Paterson, JC29/24, NAS.
190. *scientific individuals . . . penny. Laconic Narrative*, 11.
191. *the Cranium. . . upon his breast.* Precognition of David Paterson, JC29/24, NAS.
191. *peculiarly formed. West Port Murders*, 133.
191. *twisted or diseased . . . swear that it was.* Precognition of David Paterson, JC29/24, NAS.
191. never forgetting the face. Gordon-Taylor, 13.
191. he believed it was Jamie. AD2/1/3, NAS.
192. *seemed doubly anxious . . . facts.* Echo of Surgeon's Square, 17.
192. *make anxious enquiries . . . preserved them all.* Precognition of David Paterson, JC29/24, NAS.
192. Evans had no suspicion. AD2/1/3, NAS.
192. *Having been connected . . . applies.* Fergusson, *Probationary Essay*, 2.
193. *of whose dissecting room . . . possessed.* Cited in Rae, 158.
193. careful record keeping. Fergusson, Account book, RCSE.
193. *Tyro . . . given.* Echo of Surgeon's Square, 14.
193. *impatience and impetuosity . . . colour.* Cited in Roughead, 389–390.
194. Robert Christison. Christison, *Life;* White. For the subsequent history of Scottish forensics, see Crowther and White. Recent scholarly works on the history of forensic science include Bertomeu-Sanchez and Nieto-Galan; Mohr; Asher, Goodheart, and Rogers.
195. *the highest authority . . . produce.* Cited in Syme, 127.
195. John Hope. Millar.
195. *clear and settled law . . . proof.* Syme, 300.
196. restrictions on interrogation. I am grateful to Roger Davidson for this information. See Davidson, 508.
196. *furnishes good tests . . . evidence.* Christison, *Suggestions,* 8.
196. *The Procurators-fiscal . . . medical evidence.* Christison *Suggestions,* 6.
196. *with a view to discover . . . preserved for analysis.* Christison, *Suggestions,* 12.
197. *examination and dissection . . . inadmissable.* Christison, *Suggestions,* 9–12.
197. *lying on the floor . . . he was dying.* Precognition of Alexander Black against James Gow, AD14/31/438, NAS.

199. *wickedly culpably . . . mortally wounded.* Precognition against John Gray, JC26/522, NAS.

199. *not neglecting the back . . . the nape of the neck.* Christison, *Suggestions,* 14–15.

200. *We could discover . . . substance.* Precognition against John Gray, JC26/522, NAS. Moir was also a writer in the *Blackwood's* circle; he published under the pen name Delta.

201. *in cases of suspected death . . . chest, back, and arms.* Christison, *Suggestions,* 30–31.

202. *Grannie . . . stronger than water.* Syme, 153–157; Precognition against Catherine Graham, AD14/27/41, NAS.

203. *Murder, Murder . . . spilt on the floor.* Precognition against Euphemia Lawson and Hugh McMillan, AD14/27/14, NAS; Syme, 288–295.

205. Alexander Black junior. He was probably planning to follow in his father's footsteps, for in the summer of 1829 he attended Robert Christison's course on medical jurisprudence. General and medical matriculation albums, vol. 23, 1828–1829, EUL.

205. *Someone . . .* not guilty. Precognition against Euphemia Lawson and Hugh McMillan, AD14/27/14, NAS; Syme, 288–295.

206. *considerable period . . . much decayed.* Christison, *Suggestions,* 8.

207. *found the body of a man . . . prisoner's head.* Precognition against Charles MacMahon and Margaret MacMahon, AD14/27/51, NAS; Syme, 281–287.

211. *before it is undressed . . . removal of it.* Christison, *Suggestions,* 7.

211. *but I canna help . . . ain atonies.* North, *Noctes,* 3:241.

Chapter 10. Day in Court

212. *whose hands . . . crimes. West Port Murders,* 247.

213. *to remain . . . victims also. Appendix,* 59.

213. *year's impunity . . . been. West Port Murders,* 204.

214. *not allowing . . . mystery. Appendix,* 60.

214. *a very distinct manner. West Port Murders,* 50.

214. *'But Nanny . . . police office. Murderers of the Close,* 25.

214. *Books . . . cause.* John Stevenson to Charles Kirkpatrick Sharpe, YRA 637, Edinburgh Room.

214. *from the great . . . matter.* January 12, 1829, ED9/1/6, ECA.

214. *You are the only . . . lodgings.* Ann Gray to Charles Kirkpatrick Sharpe, YRA 637, Edinburgh Room.

215. *Sensible . . . himself.* Cited in Fry.

215. Rae's sympathy for reform. See Fry; Rae's attitude to reform in relation to the Whig opposition is well illustrated in the set of articles on "Nomination of Scottish Juries."

215. *Mysie . . . Duffey.* GD 1/353/3, NAS.

215. Burke's and M'Dougal's. Printed in *Trial,* 124–125.

216. *of any consequence . . . nose. Trial,* 118–119.

216. *about a pint . . . during life.* Christison, "Cases and Observations," 239–240.

217. *but he cannot . . . intoxication. Trial,* 127–130.

218. *At eleven . . . suspected.* Christison, "Cases and Observations," 241–242. In the Ted Binion case, a modern example of "burking" that became the basis for the *CSI* television episode "Burked," the hyoid was likewise found intact. King, 72.

218. *probable . . . nothing more. Trial,* 123–124.

218. *that a conviction . . . human life. Appendix,* 11–12.

219. *the particular murder . . . vengeance. Edinburgh Observer,* cited in *West Port Murders,* 156.

219. *glad . . . I suppose. Murderers of the Close,* 42.

219. arrest warrants. GD 1/353/3, NAS.

219. *The infernal . . . ruined. Murderers of the Close,* 44–45.

220. *painful duty . . . bar. Trial,* 134–135. See Edwards, 155–157.

220. James Moncreiff . . . Henry Cockburn Mackay; Miller; for the political context, see Edwards, 138–230.

221. *that they might acquire . . . disapprobation.* Syme, 296–299.

223. *No trial . . . black eyes. West Port Murders,* 9–11.

224. *I am against . . . prejudice. Trial,* 19.

225. *a large window . . . personage. West Port Murders,* 102–104.

226. *he had . . . doctors.* Syme, 362; *Trial,* 88–89.

226. *It was Nelly M'Dougal . . . breath. Trial,* 88–96.

226. *and said . . . before. Trial,* 111–118; Syme, 368.

226. *Have you been connected . . . Yes. Trial,* 96–110.

227. *a monster . . . absurd. Trial,* 182.

228. *particular attention . . . eyes. Trial,* 79–80, 149.

229. *by raising . . . grave.* Burke, Confessions, 35.

229. *which necessarily . . . suspicion of having them. Trial,* 173–176.

230. *In view of which . . . protection. West Port Murders,* 102.

230. *of a blacker . . . doom. Trial,* 198–200.

230. *that your verdict . . . doubts. Trial,* 195.

231. *The jury might . . . Life another.* North, *Noctes,* 3:237.

231. *The jury . . . years. Trial,* 195.

231. *The citizens . . . descended. West Port Murders,* 107–111.

232. *her attachment . . . strong.* Cited in *Trial,* 16.

232. *in terms of . . . need it. West Port Murders,* 115, 208.

232. *gad . . . described.* Scott, *Guy Mannering,* 416.

232. *condemned cell . . . undergo. West Port Murders,* 110, 115, 211.

233. *after a very full . . . confessed. Appendix,* 32.

233. *Whatever is interesting . . . put to him. West Port Murders,* 213–216.

234. *regarding the crimes . . . truth. West Port Murders,* 212–214; *Appendix,* 37.

235. *that docter . . . them done.* Burke, Confessions, 44.

235. *particularly anxious . . . deaths. West Port Murders,* 114.

236. *The sacrifice . . . justice. Appendix,* 20–23.

236. *the most anxious . . . excluded. Appendix,* 9–13.

237. *Hare's wife . . . penitence. Appendix,* 55–56.

237. *interrogated . . . no more. Appendix,* 6; JC29/24, NAS.

238. This case. See Roughead, 68–75.

238. *wisdom . . . disgrace. Supplement,* 60.

238. *Good bye . . . miserable life. Appendix,* 53–56.

240. *Hare's sister . . . arrived.* "Hare's Sister," in Burke and Hare Ephemera, RCPE.

240. *The time . . . thousand. West Port Murders,* 210, 223–230.

241. *last moments . . . execution.* Mic Dup 1316, EUL.

242. *respectful . . . one side. West Port Murders,* 234–240.

243. *It was commenced . . . strangulation. West Port Murders,* 253–258.

244. *in order . . . crimes. Trial,* 199.

244. *This is written . . . 1829.* Mic Dup 1316, EUL.

Chapter 11. *All That Remains*

245. *obstacles . . . Great Britain.* Cited in Rae, 63.

245. *of the enfeebled action . . . grave.* Lonsdale, 293–294.

246. *he had procured . . . been interred. Trial,* 67–68.

246. *The Lecturer . . . great advantage. Noxiana,* figure 2.

246. *the present . . . call him hither. Wretch's Illustrations,* figure 3.

247. *ill-founded . . . very bottom.* Cited in *Appendix,* 6.

247. *kept silence . . . sound about it.* Dk.6.20/123, EUL.

247. *the disclosures . . . science.* Cited in Rae, 98–99.

248. baptismal record. Old parish registers, GROS.

248. *evidently laboured . . . if they can.* Alexander (Lesassier) Hamilton Collection, January 9, 1829, box 14, folder 86, RCPE.

248. *popular prejudice . . . I have been.* Cited in Rae, 98.

249. *expressed . . . those crimes.* Burke and Hare Ephemera, RCPE.

249. *on some dissections . . . Humanity.* Scott, *Journal,* 565–566.

249. *I believe . . . whole place.* Dk.6.20/123, EUL.

249. *these proceedings . . . deponed by Hare.* ADD40339, BL.

250. *occurred to Hare . . . knew.* Burke, Confessions, 36.

250. *docter Knox . . . person,* Burke, Confessions, 44.

251. *conceal . . . facts can be.* ADD40339, BL.

251. *asked no questions . . . sixteen in whole.* Burke, Confessions, 32–44.

251. *Men, women . . . had died.* Burke and Hare Ephemera Collection, RCPE.

252. *man . . . rabble.* Lonsdale, 109.

252. *You ask me . . . plant.* Dk.6.20/123, EUL.

253. *Dedicated . . . obnoxious Session.* Burke and Hare Ephemera, RCPE.

253. *Here you have . . . ha'penny.* Mic Dup 1316, EUL.

253. *popular tumult . . . 'propriety.'* February 14, 1829, March 4, 1829, *Scotsman.*

254. *a few persons . . . character.* "Robert Knox to the *Caledonian Mercury,*" printed in Roughead, 276.

254. *to sit . . . boat.* Scott, *Journal,* 571–572.

254. *no evidence . . . ranks of society.* "Report of the Committee of Investigation as to the Dealings of Dr. Knox with the West Port Murderers," printed in Roughead, 277–279.

255. *that the poorer inhabitants . . . in general?* North, *Noctes,* 3:238.

255. *preconceived opinion . . . possible consequences.* Cited in Roughead, 278–279.

255. *whitewashing process.* Leighton, *Court of Cacus,* 228; Roughead, 85.

255. *had deeply sympathised . . . injustice.* Cited in Lonsdale, 115.

255. *that his class . . . subject.* North, *Noctes,* 3:240.

256. *This Cup . . . session 1828–9. Noxiana,* figure 3.

256. *will be able . . . if ever.* Dk.6.20/123, EUL.

256. Bentham's supporters. Robert Seymour, *Kings College versus London University or which is the weightiest*, 1828, Bentham Project, University College London, http://www.victorianweb.org/history/education/ulondon/13.html. On Seymour, see Cohen, 39–50.

256. *Catholic State Waggon.* Thompson; Turner. On Cowie and Strange as well as Seymour's fee, see Hollis, 3, 132.

257. illustrations for the radicals. See "Sketches of Society"; George, plates 82, 88, 89, 94, 96.

257. *wretched outcasts . . . subject of me. Murderers of the Close*, 43–45. See *Select Committee*, 18.

258. *a celebrated surgeon . . . to light. Murderers of the Close*, 19, 36.

259. *dissecting room . . . it should be. Murderers of the Close*, 65.

259. *All the bodies . . . each. Gentleman's Magazine* 145 (February 1829): 169.

259. *putting on . . . Female. Murderers of the Close*, 65–66.

260. *It is totally . . . diabolical purpose.* Egan, *Trial of Bishop*; Wise.

261. *What are the evils . . . surgery.* Macaulay, 8:77.

261. *begged . . . victims.* "William Burke," in *The Newgate Calendar*, http://www.exclassics.com/newgate/ng601.htm.

262. *I have been . . . life.* 3908/183–184, Walter Scott Collection, NLS.

262. *conspicuous witness . . . Bridges.* Cited in *Appendix*, 25–31.

263. *now no longer . . . garden.* 3908/183–184, Walter Scott Collection, NLS.

263. *the accomplices . . . murders.* Echo of Surgeon's Square.

263. *Keeper of the Museum . . . young gentlemen.* Cited in *Appendix*, 31.

264. *From what . . . pursuit of glory.* 3908/183–184, Walter Scott Collection, NLS.

264. *Dr. Knox's jackall . . . anecdotes.* Scott, *Journal*, 608–609.

264. *calumniated . . . upon me.* 3908/183–184, Walter Scott Collection, NLS.

264. *still a respectable . . . passed away.* Leighton, *Court of Cacus*, 227–228.

265. Frederick John. Beasley. In 1847 Robert Knox was involved in a quarrel with the Royal College of Surgeons over his disregarding their regulations when providing certificates of attendance for students. See Taylor; Rae, 135–146.

265. price of a subject. Dr. Wood to Henry Lonsdale, June 8, 1843, MH 3, NAS; MH1/7/, NAS. Inmates of institutions could state that they did not want their bodies to be dissected after death, even if they had no families. In Scotland, at least, their wishes appear to have been respected. I am grateful to Anne Crowther for calling this to my attention.

266. *the bodies which had undergone.* CH/715/259/22, 23, 67, NAS.

267. *adverting . . . in this City.* Knox, *Letter.* The copy held by the Royal College of Surgeons of Edinburgh has penciled notations filling in the names of the people Knox referred to in the pamphlet.

267. *high sarcastic method.* Lonsdale, 246.

267. *picture . . . life.* Lonsdale, xiv; Goodwin.

267. *You cannot think . . . happy.* Cited in Lonsdale, 377.

268. "The Burkers." *Wilson's Remarkable Trials*, 417–431.

268. *earnestness . . . sake.* Blake, 334.

268. *the question . . . St. Hilaire.* Lonsdale, 386.

268. *that he could explain . . . atrocities.* Lonsdale, 394.

Selected Bibliography

MANUSCRIPTS AND ARCHIVES

British Library
ADD40339. Robert Peel Correspondence and Papers.

Edinburgh City Archives
Edinburgh Police Commissioners:
ED9/1/6. General Commissioners Minute Book, October 15, 1827–June 23, 1832.
ED9/2/2. Police Commissioners Committee Minute Book, April 5, 1827–April 12, 1839.
Magdalene Asylum:
SL 237/1/3. Magdalene Asylum Minutes, 1825–1838.
SL 237/3/4. Committee Minute Book, 1812–1823.
SL 237/3/5. Minute Book of Subcommittee, 1823–1834.

Edinburgh Room, Edinburgh Central Library
Wretch's Illustrations of Shakespeare. Edinburgh: R. H. Nimmo, 1829. Illustrations and ephemera pasted into volume.
YRA 637. Charles Kirkpatrick Sharpe Collection.

Edinburgh University Library
Dk.6.20/123. Greville, Robert, to William Jardine. Edinburgh, February 12, 1829.
Knox, Robert. "Anatomical and Pathological Appearances met with in the Dissecting Rooms during the Winter Session of 1827.8."

LHB1/125/24. Lothian Regional Health Board Archives. Royal Infirmary. General Register of Patients August 20, 1827, to June 9, 1830.

Matriculation Albums, General and Medical.

Mic Dup 1316. Monro, Alexander, *tertius.* "Memorial to Burke and Hare the West Port Murderers." 1828.

Minutes and Proceedings of the Medical Faculty, 1811–1831.

General Register Office for Scotland

Old Parish Registers.

National Archives of Scotland

AD2/1/3. Printed indictment, with notes, of William Burke and Helen M'Dougal. These notes are handwritten and summarize in a few words the main point of the witnesses' testimony as it pertains to the prosecution's case.

AD9/2. Crown Counsel Procedure Books, 1828–1831.

AD14. Crown Office Precognitions, 1800–1900.

CH/715/259/22, 23, 67. Accounts of the burying ground of St. Cuthberts for coffins furnished and interment, to the inspector and manager for the Edinburgh schools of anatomy.

CS181/6822. Legal process of William Swanston against Thomas Ireland.

GD1/353/3–5. Petitions for arrest warrants for William Burke, Helen M'Dougal, and William and Margaret Hare for the murders of Margaret Docherty or Campbell, James Wilson, and Mary Paterson.

GD31/557. *Report of a Committee of Police concerning the proposed establishment of a house of refuge for delinquent youths in Edinburgh.* 1824.

HH21/6/5. Edinburgh (Calton) Bridewell (Jail), 1824–1835.

HH21/6/7. Account of prisoners confined in Edinburgh Bridewell (Jail), May 29, 1827, to August 4, 1828.

HH21/8/1. Register of Criminal Prisoners, Edinburgh Lock Up.

JC26/522. High Court of Justiciary Processes.

JC29/24. Advocation, suspension and liberation, William Hare v Janet Wilson senior and junior.

MH1/7. Register of the inspector of anatomy for Scotland. Edinburgh. October 1842–1853.

MH3. Letter Book, inspector of anatomy for Scotland.

National Library of Scotland

Digital collections:

Maps of Scotland. http://www.nls.uk/maps/index.html .

The Word on the Street. http://www.nls.uk/broadsides/index.html.

Manuscripts and ephemera:

L.C. Folio 62. *Wretch's Illustrations of Shakespeare.* Edinburgh: R. H. Nimmo, 1829. Illustrations and ephemera pasted into volumes.

Ry III No. 6. *Wretch's Illustrations of Shakespeare.* Edinburgh: R. H. Nimmo, 1829. Illustrations and ephemera pasted into volumes.

Walter Scott Collection.

Royal College of Physicians of Edinburgh

Burke and Hare Ephemera.

Alexander (Lesassier) Hamilton Collection.

Minute books 1823–1834. Typescript 2696–2707.

Royal College of Surgeons of Edinburgh

Fergusson, William. Account book of anatomy class of Robert Knox. Edinburgh. 1829–1832. Photocopy.

Museum, *General Catalogue.* 2 vols.

Signet Library

William Roughead Collection.

PUBLISHED WORKS

Abraham, Laurie. *Mama Might Be Better Off Dead.* Chicago: University of Chicago Press, 1993.

Alison, William Pulteney. *Observations on the Management of the Poor in Scotland.* Edinburgh: William Blackwood and Sons, 1840.

Appendix to the Trial of William Burke and Helen M'Dougal. Edinburgh: Robert Buchanan, 1829.

Arnot, Hugo. *The History of Edinburgh, from the Earliest Accounts, to the Year 1780.* Edinburgh: Thomas Turnbull, 1816.

Asher, Robert, Lawrence B. Goodheart, and Alan Rogers, eds. *Murder on Trial: 1620–2002.* Albany: SUNY Press, 2005.

Audubon, John James. *The 1826 Journal of John James Audubon*. Edited by Alice Ford. New York: Abbeville Press, 1967.

Averill, Charles. *A Short Treatise on Operative Surgery, describing the principal operations . . . on the dead body*. Philadelphia: Carey and Lea, 1823.

Bank, Andrew. "Of 'Native Skulls' and 'Noble Caucasians': Phrenology in Colonial South Africa." *Journal of Southern African Studies* 22 (1996): 387–403.

Barrie, David. *Police in the Age of Improvement: Police Development and the Civic Tradition in Scotland, 1775–1865*. Devon: Willan Publishing, 2008.

Bass, William, and Jon Jefferson. *Death's Acre*. New York: Penguin, 2003.

Beasley, A. W. "The Other Brother: A Brief Account of the Life and Times of Frederick John Knox LRCSEd." *Journal of the Royal College of Surgeons of Edinburgh* 46 (2001): 119–123.

Béclard, Pierre Augustin. *Elements of General Anatomy*. Translated by Robert Knox. Edinburgh: MacLachlan and Stewart, 1830.

Belchem, John. *Orator Hunt: Henry Hunt and English Working-Class Radicalism*. Oxford: Oxford University Press, 1985.

Bell, George. *Blackfriars' Wynd Analyzed*. Edinburgh: Johnstone and Hunter, 1840.

———. *Day and Night in the Wynds of Edinburgh*. Edinburgh: Johnstone and Hunter, 1849.

Bell, John. *Letters on Professional Character and Manners*. Edinburgh: John Muir, 1810.

Bertomeu-Sanchez, José Ramon, and Agusti Nieto-Galan, eds. *Chemistry, Medicine, and Crime: Mateu J. B. Orfila (1787–1853) and His Times*. Sagamore Beach, Mass.: Science History Publications, 2006.

Blake, C. Carter. "The Life of Dr. Knox." *Journal of Anthropology* 1 (1871): 332–338.

Blake, Leslie William. "Roughead, William (1870–1952)." *Dictionary of National Biography*. Oxford: Oxford University Press, 2004. http://www.oxforddnb.com/view/article/49504.

Blakely, Robert L., and Judith M. Harrington. *Bones in the Basement: Postmortem Racism in Nineteenth-Century Medical Training*. Washington, D.C.: Smithsonian Institution Press, 1997.

Blood Work. Directed by Clint Eastwood. 2002. Warner Studios, 2004. DVD.

The Body Snatcher. Directed by Robert Wise. 1945. Turner Home Entertainment, 2005. DVD.

Bridie, James [Osborne Henry Mavor]. *The Anatomist.* London: Constable, 1979.

Buffon, Georges Louis Leclerc. *A Natural History of the Globe: Of Man, of Beasts, Birds, Fishes, Reptiles, Insects, and Plants.* 2 vols. London: Grey and Bowen, 1831.

"Burked." In *CSI: The Complete Second Season.* 2000. Paramount, 2003. DVD.

Burney, Ian. *Bodies of Evidence: Medicine and the Politics of the English Inquest, 1830–1926.* Baltimore: Johns Hopkins University Press, 2000.

Burrell, Sean, and Geoffrey Gill. "The Liverpool Cholera Epidemic of 1832 and Anatomical Dissection: Medical Mistrust and Civil Unrest." *Journal of the History of Medicine and Allied Sciences* 60 (2005): 478–495.

Cadell, Patrick. "Sharpe, Charles Kirkpatrick (1781–1851)." *Dictionary of National Biography.* Oxford: Oxford University Press, 2004. http://www.oxforddnb.com/view/article/25225.

Cage, R. A. *The Scottish Poor Law 1745–1845.* Edinburgh: Scottish Academic Press, 1981.

Canby, Vincent. "Film: Body-Snatching in 'Doctor and the Devils.'" *New York Times*, October 4, 1985, C8.

Cantlie, Neil. *A History of the Army Medical Department.* 2 vols. London: Churchill Livingstone, 1974.

Chambers, Robert. *The Letters of Sir Walter Scott and Charles Kirkpatrick Sharpe to Robert Chambers, 1821–45.* Edinburgh: W. and R. Chambers, 1904.

Cheney, Annie. *Body Brokers: Inside America's Underground Trade in Human Remains.* New York: Random House, 2007.

Christison, Robert. "Cases and Observations in Medical Jurisprudence." *Edinburgh Medical and Surgical Journal* 31 (1829): 236–250.

———. *Life of Sir Robert Christison, Bart.* 2 vols. Edinburgh: W. Blackwood and Sons, 1886.

———. *Suggestions for the medico-legal examination of dead bodies.* Edinburgh: Alexander Smellie, 1839.

Cloquet, Hippolyte. *A System of Human Anatomy.* Translated by Robert Knox. Edinburgh: MacLachlan and Stewart, 1828.

Cobbett, William. "An Address to the working people, on the new Dead body Bill." In *Thirteen Sermons*, 243–276. New York: J. Doyle, 1834.

————. *Eleven Lectures*. London: W. Strange, 1830.

Cockburn, Henry. *Circuit Journeys by the Late Lord Cockburn*. 1888. Reprint, Edinburgh: Mercat Press, 1975.

————. *Memorials of Our Time*. Edinburgh: Adam and Charles Black, 1856.

Cohen, Jane R. *Charles Dickens and His Original Illustrators*. Columbus: Ohio State University Press, 1980.

Combe, George. "Phrenological Observations on the Cerebral Development of William Burk." In *Illustrations of Phrenology*, edited by George Henry Calvert, 70–97. Edinburgh: W. and J. Neal, 1832.

————. *A System of Phrenology*. New York: Harper and Brothers, 1860.

Cooter, Roger. *The Cultural Meaning of Popular Science: Phrenology and the Organization of Consent in Nineteenth-Century Britain*. New York: Cambridge University Press, 1984.

"Corpse-Selling Case Outrages Colombians: Police Say Homeless Slain to Get Bodies for Medical School." DaveMarcus.com. http://davemarcus.com.

Cox, Catherine. "Women and Business in Eighteenth-Century Dublin: A Case Study, 1750–1800." In *Women and Paid Work, 1500–1930*, edited by Bernadette Whelan, 30–43. Dublin: Four Courts Press, 2000.

Cross, John. *Sketches of the Medical Schools of Paris*. London: J. Callow, 1815.

Crowther, M. Anne, and Brenda White. *On Soul and Conscience: The Medical Expert and Crime*. Aberdeen: Aberdeen University Press, 1988.

Curtin, Philip. *The Image of Africa: British Ideas and Action, 1780–1850*. Madison: University of Wisconsin Press, 1964.

Davenport, T. R. H. "Somerset, Lord Charles Henry (1767–1831)." Revised by K. S. Hunt. *Dictionary of National Biography*. Oxford: Oxford University Press, 2004. http://www.oxforddnb.com/view/article/37992.

Davidson, Roger. "'The Sexual State': Sexuality and Scottish Governance, 1950–1980." *Journal of the History of Sexuality* 13 (2004): 500–521.

Dawson, James Hooper. *An Abridged Statistical History of Scotland*. Edinburgh: W. H. Lizars, 1853.

Defoe, Daniel. *The Fortunes and Misfortunes of the Famous Moll Flanders*. New York: Penguin, 1989.

DeQuincey, Thomas. *On Murder*. Introduction by Robert Morrison. Oxford: Oxford University Press, 2006.

Desmond, Adrian. *The Politics of Evolution: Morphology, Medicine, and Reform in Radical London.* Chicago: University of Chicago Press, 1992.

Dickens, Charles. *A Christmas Carol and Other Christmas Writings.* London: Penguin, 2003.

———. *Oliver Twist.* London: Penguin, 2002.

———. *The Pickwick Papers.* London: Penguin, 2000.

Dietz, Vivien E. "The Politics of Whisky: Scottish Distillers, the Excise, and the Pittite State." *Journal of British Studies* 36 (1997): 35–69.

Dirty Pretty Things. Directed by Stephen Frears. 1993. Miramax, 2004. DVD.

The Doctor and the Devils. Directed by Freddie Francis. 1985. Twentieth Century Fox, 2005. DVD.

Echo of Surgeon's Square. *Letter to the Lord advocate, disclosing the accomplices, secrets, and other facts relative to the late murders.* Edinburgh: R. Menzies, 1829.

Edinburgh and Leith Post Office Annual Directories, 1825–1870.

Edwards, Owen Dudley. *Burke & Hare.* Edinburgh: Mercat Press, 1993.

Egan, Pierce. *Pierce Egan's Account of the Trial of Bishop, Williams, and May for Murder.* London: Sherwood, 1831.

———. *Pierce Egan's Account of the Trial of John Thurtell and Joseph Hunt.* London: Knight and Lacey, 1824.

———. *Recollections of John Thurtell.* London: Knight and Lacey, 1824.

Ellis, George Viner. *Illustrations of Dissections.* 2 vols. New York: William Wood, 1882.

Fergusson, William. *A Probationary Essay on the Arch of the Aorta.* Edinburgh: P. Neill, 1820.

———. *A System of Practical Surgery.* Philadelphia: Lea and Blanchard, 1843.

Fido, Martin. *Bodysnatchers: A History of the Resurrectionists, 1742–1832.* London: Weidenfeld and Nicolson, 1922.

Flood, David. "Organ Procurement: Urban Legends and Other Tales from the Dark Side of Organ Transplantation." October 29, 2007, paper presented at the College of Physicians of Philadelphia.

Forbes, Thomas Rogers. *Surgeons at the Bailey: English Forensic Medicine to 1878.* New Haven: Yale University Press, 1985.

Fry, Michael. "Rae, Sir William, Third Baronet (1769–1842)." *Dictionary of National Biography*. Oxford: Oxford University Press, 2004. http://www.oxforddnb.com/view/article/23005.

Garside, Peter. Introduction. *The Private Memoirs and Confessions of a Justi-fied Sinner*, by James Hogg, xi–xcix. Edinburgh: Edinburgh University Press, 2002.

George, Dorothy. *English Political Caricature, 1793–1832*. Oxford: Claren-don Press, 1959.

Goodwin, Gordon. "Lonsdale, Henry (1816–1876)." Revised by Patrick Wallis. *Dictionary of National Biography*. Oxford: Oxford University Press, 2004. http://www.oxforddnb.com/view/article/16999.

Gordon-Taylor, Gordon. "Sir William Fergusson, Bt. FRCS. FRS (1808–1877)." *Medical History* 5 (1961): 1–14.

Gould, Stephen Jay. *The Mismeasure of Man*. New York: W. W. Norton, 1996.

Grant, Alexander. *The Story of the University of Edinburgh During Its First Three Hundred Years*. 2 vols. London: Longmans, Green, 1884.

Gray, Henry. *Gray's Anatomy: The Anatomical Basis of Clinical Practice*. New York: Elsevier Churchill Livingstone, 2005.

Great Britain. Parliament. House of Commons. *Report from the Select Com-mittee on the Matter of Obtaining Subjects for Dissections in the Schools of Anatomy*. Session 1828, 568. Volume 7.

———. *Reports from Commissioners, Inspectors, and Others: Grocers' Licenses, Scotland*. Session 1878. Volume 26.

Great Britain. Poor Law Commissioners. *Report on the Sanitary Condition of the Labouring Population of England*. London: W. Clowes and Sons, 1842.

———. *Report on the Sanitary Condition of the Labouring Population of Scot-land*. London: W. Clowes and Sons, 1842.

The Greatest of our Social Evils, Prostitution, as it now exists in London, Liv-erpool, Manchester, Glasgow, Edinburgh, and Dublin. London: H. Bail-liere, 1857.

Haggart, David. *The Life of David Haggart*. Edinburgh: W. and C. Tait, 1821.

Hamlin, Christopher. *Public Health and Social Justice in the Age of Chadwick: Britain, 1800–1854*. Cambridge: Cambridge University Press, 1998.

Handley, James Edmund. *The Irish in Scotland, 1798–1845*. Cork: Cork University Press, 1945.

Hannaway, Caroline, and Ann LaBerge. *Constructing Paris Medicine.* Amsterdam: Rodopi, 1998.

Harris, Paul, and Julian Halsby. *The Dictionary of Scottish Painters, 1600 to the Present.* Edinburgh: Canongate, 2001.

Hazlitt, William. "Burke and the Edinburgh Phrenologists." In *New Writings by William Hazlitt,* edited by P. P. Howe, 116–122. New York: Dial Press, 1925.

———. "The Late Murders." In *New Writings by William Hazlitt,* edited by P. P. Howe, 100–104. New York: Dial Press, 1925.

Henderson, David, Mark Collard, and Daniel A. Johnston. "Archaelogical Evidence for Eighteenth-Century Medical Practice in the Old Town of Edinburgh: Excavations at 13 Infirmary Street and Surgeon's Square." *Proceedings of the Society of Antiquities of Scotland* 126: (1996): 929–941.

Hillman, Elizabeth. *Defending America: Military Culture and the Cold War Court-Martial.* Princeton: Princeton University Press, 2005.

Hollis, Patricia. *The Pauper Press: A Study in Working-Class Radicalism of the 1830s.* Oxford: Oxford University Press, 1970.

Horne, Philip. Introduction. *Oliver Twist,* by Charles Dickens, xxii–xxxv. London: Penguin, 2002.

Horner, William. *The United States Dissector, or Lessons in Practical Anatomy.* Philadelphia: Lea and Blanchard, 1846.

Horsman, Reginald. "Origins of Racial Anglo-Saxonism in Great Britain Before 1850." *Journal of the History of Ideas* 37 (1976): 387–410.

Hunt, James. "President's Address." *Journal of the Anthropological Society of London* 5 (1867): xliv–lxxi.

Instructions, Orders, Regulations, and Bye-Laws, given, made, and passed, by the Commissioners of Police for the City of Edinburgh, July 1822.

Iserson, Kenneth. *Death to Dust: What Happens to Dead Bodies?* Tucson: Galen Press, 1987.

Johnson, A. "My Friend Dr. Knox: A Pupil Writes About the Anatomist." *The Surgeon* 3.6 (2005). http://www.thesurgeon.net/site.

Jones, David. *Crime, Protest, Community, and Police in Nineteenth-Century Britain.* London: Routledge and Kegan Paul, 1982.

Kaufman, M. H. "Frederick Knox, Younger Brother and Assistant of Dr. Robert Knox: His Contribution to 'Knox's Catalogues.'" *Journal of the Royal College of Surgeons of Edinburgh* 46 (2001): 44–56.

Kilday, Anne-Marie. *Women and Violent Crime in Enlightenment Scotland.* Suffolk: Royal Historical Society, 2007.

King, Gary. *An Early Grave.* New York: St. Martin's, 2001.

Knox, Frederick John. *The Anatomist's Instructor and Museum Companion.* Edinburgh: Adam and Charles Black, 1836.

"Knox on the Celtic Race." *Anthropological Review* 6 (1868): 175–191.

Knox, Robert. *De viribus stimulantium et narcoticorum in corpore sano.* Edinburgh: J. Ballantyne, 1814.

———. *The Edinburgh Dissector; or, system of practical anatomy for the use of students in the dissecting room.* Edinburgh: P. Rickard, 1837.

———. *Great Artists and Great Anatomists.* London: J. Van Voorst, 1852.

———. "Hermaphroditism: a memoir read to the Royal Society of Edinburgh in 1827 and 1828." *London Medical Gazette,* June 30, 1848.

———. *Letter to the Right Honourable The Lord Provost and Council of the City of Edinburgh.* Edinburgh, 1837.

———. *A Manual of Artistic Anatomy.* London: Henry Renshaw, 1852.

———. "Notice relative to the habits of the hyaena of Southern Africa." *Memoirs of the Wernerian Natural History Society* 4 (1823): 383–385.

———. "On the relations subsisting between the time of day and various functions of the human body." *Edinburgh Medical and Surgical Review* 11 (1815): 52–65, 164–167.

———. "On the tendon of the biceps flexor cubiti." *London Medical Gazette,* March 8, 1828, 404.

———. *Plates on the Arteries of the Human Body, after Frederic Tiedemann.* Engraved by Edward Mitchell, under the superintendency of Thomas Wharton Jones. Edinburgh: MacLachlan and Stewart, 1829.

———. *A probationary essay, on the causes and treatment of lateral curvature of the human spine.* Edinburgh: Neill, 1825.

———. *The Races of Men: A Fragment.* Philadelphia: Lea and Blanchard, 1850.

———. *The Races of Men: A philosophical Enquiry into the Influence of Race over the Destinies of Nations.* London: H. Renshaw, 1862.

Kohl, Johann Georg. *Ireland, Scotland, and England.* London: Chapman and Hall, 1844.

Laconic Narrative of the Life and Death or [sic] *James Wilson, known by the name of Daft Jamie.* Edinburgh: W. Smith, 1829.

Leighton, Alexander. *The Court of Cacus; or, The Story of Burke and Hare.* Edinburgh: W. P. Nimmo, 1861.

————. "Mrs. Corbet's Amputated Toe." In *Mysterious Legends of Edinburgh*, 30–56. Edinburgh: W. P. Nimmo, 1864.

Levitt, Ian, and Christopher Smout. *The State of the Scottish Working Class in 1843.* Edinburgh: Scottish Academic Press, 1979.

List, Alfred John. *Copy of General Orders Issued to Constables.* Edinburgh: Thomas Allan, 1843.

————. *Instructions to Constables within the County of Edinburgh, for their guidance in matters of police.* Edinburgh: Thomas Allan, 1840.

Liston, Robert. *Practical Surgery.* Edited by George W. Norris. Philadelphia: Thomas, Cowperthwait, 1842.

Lizars, John. *A System of Anatomical Plates of the Human Body.* 12 vols. Edinburgh: W. H. Lizars, 1822–1826.

Lonsdale, Henry. *A sketch of the life and writings of Robert Knox the Anatomist.* London: Macmillan, 1870.

Low Life in Victorian Edinburgh. Edinburgh: Paul Harris Publishing, 1980. Reprint of *An Inquiry into Destitution, Prostitution and Crime in Edinburgh, by a Medical Gentleman.* Edinburgh: James G. Bertram, 1851.

L.S.M. "Diversity of the Races: Its Bearing upon Negro Slavery." *Southern Quarterly Review* (1851): 392.

Luddy, Maria. *Prostitution and Irish Society, 1800–1940.* New York: Cambridge University Press, 2008.

Macaulay, Thomas. *The Works of Lord Macaulay Complete.* Edited by Lady Trevelyan. 8 vols. New York: Longmans, Green, 1897.

MacDonald, Helen. *Human Remains: Dissection and Its Histories.* New Haven: Yale University Press, 2005.

Mackay, A. J. G. "Moncreiff, Sir James Wellwood, Ninth Baronet, Lord Moncreiff (1776–1851)." Revised by Michael Fry. *Dictionary of National Biography.* Oxford: Oxford University Press, 2004. http://www.oxforddnb.com/view/article/18948.

Macnish, Robert. *Confessions of an Unexecuted Femicide.* Glasgow: W. R. M'Phun, 1827.

————. *An Introduction to Phrenology.* Glasgow: John Reid, 1836.

Mahood, Linda. *The Magdalenes: Prostitution in the Nineteenth Century.* New York: Routledge, 1990.

————. *Policing Gender, Class and Family: Britain, 1850–1940*. Edmonton: University of Alberta Press, 1995.

Masson, David. *Edinburgh Sketches and Memories*. Edinburgh: Adam and Charles Black, 1892.

McCracken-Flesher, Caroline. "Burking the Scottish Body: Robert Louis Stevenson and the Resurrection Men." In *Robert Louis Stevenson, Writer of Boundaries*, edited by Richard Ambrosini and Richard Dury, 133–144. Madison: University of Wisconsin Press, 2008.

McGovan, James [William Honeyman]. *The McGovan Casebook*. Edinburgh: Mercat Press, 2003.

McGowan, John. "The Emergence of Modern Civil Police in Scotland: A Case Study of the Police and Systems of Police in Edinburghshire 1800–1822." Ph.D. dissertation, Open University, 1996.

McGrigor, James. *The Autobiography and Services of Sir James McGrigor, Bart.* London: Longman, Green, Longman, and Roberts, 1861.

McHugh, Paul. *Prostitution and Victorian Social Reform*. New York: St. Martin's Press, 1980.

McLevy, James. *The Casebook of a Victorian Detective*. Edited by George Scott-Moncrieff. Edinburgh: Canongate, 1975.

Millar, Gordon F. "Hope, John (1794–1858)." *Dictionary of National Biography*. Oxford: Oxford University Press, 2004. http://www.oxforddnb.com/view/article/13733.

Miller, Karl. "Cockburn, Henry, Lord Cockburn (1779–1854)." *Dictionary of National Biography*. Oxford: Oxford University Press, 2004. http://www.oxforddnb.com/view/article/5771.

Mitchison, Rosalind. *The Old Poor Law in Scotland*. Edinburgh: Edinburgh University Press, 2001.

Mohr, James. *Doctors and the Law*. Baltimore: Johns Hopkins University Press, 1996.

Moore, Wendy. *The Knife Man: The Extraodinary Life and Times of John Hunter, Father of Modern Surgery*. New York: Broadway Books, 2005.

Murderers of the Close. London: Cowie and Strange, 1829.

Newgate Calendar. The Ex-Classics Web Site. http://www.exclassics.com/newgate/ngintro.htm.

Nicolson, Malcolm. "Lizars, John (1791/2–1860)." *Dictionary of National Biography*. Oxford: Oxford University Press, 2004. http://www.oxforddnb.com/view/article/16814.

———. "Syme, James (1799–1870)." *Dictionary of National Biography*. Oxford: Oxford University Press, 2004. http://www.oxforddnb.com/view/article/26876 .

Nield, Keith, ed. *Prostitution in the Victorian Age: Debates on the Issue from Nineteenth Century Critical Journals*. Westmead, England: Gregg International Publishers, 1973.

"Nomination of Scottish Juries." *Edinburgh Review* 36 (1821–1822): 174–219; 38 (1823): 226–234.

North, Christopher [John Wilson]. *Noctes Ambrosianae*. 5 vols. New York: W. J. Widdleton, 1880.

———. "Review of Phrenological Observations on the Cerebral Development of David Haggart." *Blackwood's Edinburgh Magazine* 10 (1821): 682–691.

Noxiana. Edinburgh: R. H. Nimmo, 1829.

Odom, Herbert. "Generalizations on Race in Nineteenth-Century Physical Anthropology." *Isis* 58 (1967): 4–18.

Palmer, Stanley H. *Police and Protest in England and Ireland, 1780–1850*. Cambridge: Cambridge University Press, 1988.

Parsons, Usher. *Directions for making Anatomical Preparations*. Philadelphia: Carey and Lea, 1831.

Patrizio, Andrew, and Dawn Kemp, eds. *Anatomy Acts: How We Come to Know Ourselves*. Edinburgh: Birlinn, 2006.

Peterson, Spero. Foreword. *The Counterfeit Lady Unveiled*, 3–8. New York: Doubleday, 1961.

Powell, Michael, and David Segal. "In New York, a Grisly Traffic in Body Parts." *Washington Post*, January 28, 2006, A03. http://www.washingtonpost.com/wp-dyn/content/article/2006/01/27/AR2006012701569.html.

Power, D'A. "Liston, Robert (1794–1847)." Revised by Jean Loudon. *Dictionary of National Biography*. Oxford: Oxford University Press, 2004. http://www.oxforddnb.com/view/article/16772.

Pringle, Thomas. *Narrative of a Residence in South Africa*. 1835. Reprint, Cape Town: C. Struik, 1966.

Rae, Isobel. *Knox the Anatomist*. Springfield, Ill.: Charles C. Thomas, 1965.

Rankin, Ian, *Fleshmarket Close*. London: Orion, 2005.

Ratner, Lizzy. "The Doctor Stories," review of *Final Exam: A Surgeon's*

Reflections on Mortality, by Pauline Chen. *Nation*, 11 June 2007. http://www.thenation.com/doc/20070611/ratner.

Reekiana: Minor Antiquities of Edinburgh. Edinburgh: William and Robert Chambers, 1833.

Regulations to be observed by Candidates, previous to their being taken upon trials for obtaining Diplomas from the Royal College of Surgeons of Edinburgh. Edinburgh: Walker and Greig, 1828.

Reid, J. C. *Bucks and Bruisers: Pierce Egan and Regency England*. London: Routledge and Kegan Paul, 1971.

Rich, Paul. *Race and Empire in British Politics*. Cambridge: Cambridge University Press, 1986.

Richards, Evelleen. "The 'Moral Anatomy' of Robert Knox: The Interplay Between Biological and Social Thought in Victorian Scientific Naturalism." *Journal of the History of Biology* 22 (1989): 373–436.

———. "A Political Anatomy of Monsters, Hopeful and Otherwise: Teratogeny, Transcendentalism, and Evolutionary Theorizing." *Isis* 85 (1994): 377–411.

Richardson, Ruth. *Death, Dissection, and the Destitute*. Chicago: University of Chicago Press, 1987.

Roach, Mary. *Stiff: The Curious Lives of Human Cadavers*. New York: W. W. Norton, 2003.

Rosner, Lisa. *Medical Education in the Age of Improvement: Edinburgh Students and Apprentices, 1760–1826*. Edinburgh: Edinburgh University Press, 1991.

———. *The Most Beautiful Man in Existence: The Scandalous Life of Alexander Lesassier*. Philadelphia: University of Pennsylvania Press, 1999.

Ross, James A., and Hugh W. Y. Taylor. "Robert Knox's Catalogue." *Journal of the History of Medicine and Allied Sciences* 10 (1955): 269–276.

Roughead, William, ed. *Burke and Hare*. London: William Hodge, 1920.

Rudwick, Martin. *Scenes from Deep Time: Early Pictorial Representations of the Prehistoric World*. Chicago: University of Chicago Press, 1992.

Ruthven-Murray, Peter, ed. *The Edinburgh Police Register, 1815–1859*. Edinburgh: Scottish Genealogy Society, 1991.

Ryan, A. "Hamilton, Sir William Stirling, Baronet (1788–1856)." *Dictionary of National Biography*. Oxford: Oxford University Press, 2004. http://www.oxforddnb.com/view/article/12144.

Sales, Roger. "Pierce Egan and the Representation of London." In *Review-*

ing Romanticism, edited by Philip Martin and Robin Jarvis, 154–169. New York: St. Martin's Press, 1992.

Sante, Luc. Introduction. *Classic Crimes*, by William Roughead, vii–xii. New York: New York Review of Books, 2000.

Sappol, Michael. *A Traffic of Dead Bodies: Anatomy and Embodied Social Identity in Nineteenth-Century America*. Princeton: Princeton University Press, 2002.

Scarpa, Antonio. *Engravings of the cardiac nerves*. Translated by Robert Knox. Edinburgh: MacLachlan and Stewart, 1832.

Scotsman (The). Digital Archive, http://archive.scotsman.com/.

Scott, Walter. *Guy Mannering*. New York: Century, 1910.

———. *The Heart of Midlothian*. New York: George Routledge and Sons, 1878.

———. *The Journal of Sir Walter Scott*. Edited by W. E. K. Anderson. Edinburgh: Canongate Classics, 1998.

———. *The Letters of Sir Walter Scott, 1828–1831*. Edited by H. J. C. Grierson. London: Constable, 1936.

Seymour, Robert. *Kings College versus London University or which is the weightiest*. 1828. Bentham Project. University College London. http://www.victorianweb.org/history/education/ulondon/13.html.

Sharpe, Charles Kirkpatrick. Preface. *Trial of William Burke and Helen M'Dougal*, v–xii. Edinburgh: Robert Buchanan, 1829.

———. *The Whore's Rhetorick*. Edited by James Maidment. Edinburgh: Stevenson, 1836.

Shaw, John. *A Manual for the Student of Anatomy*. Troy, N.Y.: J. Disturnell, 1825.

Shepherd, Thomas. *Modern Athens: Displayed in a Series of Views; or, Edinburgh in the Nineteenth Century*. London: Jones, 1831.

"Sketches of Society." *London Literary Gazette*, November 7, 1835.

Slobodzian, Joseph. "Funeral Directors Who Sold Body Parts Sentenced." *Philadelphia Inquirer*, October 23, 2008. http://www.philly.com/philly/news/local/32761044.html.

Smith, Henry Hollingsworth. *A System of Operative Surgery*. Philadelphia: Lippincott, Grambo, 1852.

Smith, Roger. *The Norton History of the Human Sciences*. New York: W. W. Norton, 1997.

Smith, Thomas Southwood. *Use of the Dead to the Living*. London:

Baldwin and Cradock, 1828. First published in *Westminster Review* 2 (1824): 59–97.

Spitz, Werner, and Russell Fisher, eds. *Medicolegal Investigation of Death*. Springfield, Ill.: Charles Thomas, 1980.

Stanley, Edward. "Observations relative to the rupture of the tendon of the biceps." *London Medical Gazette*, December 6, 1828, 12–14.

Stevenson, Robert Louis. "The Body Snatcher." *Pall Mall Christmas Extra*, No. 13. London, 1884.

———. *The Strange Case of Dr. Jekyll and Mr. Hyde*. New York: Viking, 1999.

Stockenström, Andries. *The Autobiography of the Late Sir Andries Stockenstrom, Bart*. 2 vols. Cape Town: J. C. Juta, 1887.

Stocking, George W., Jr. "What's in a Name? The Origins of the Royal Anthropological Institute (1837–71)." *Man*, new series, 6 (1971): 369–390.

Stone, Thomas. *On the Phrenological Development of Burke, Hare, and Other Atrocious Murderers*. Edinburgh: Robert Buchanan, 1829.

Sue, Jean Joseph. *The Anatomy of the Bones of the Human Body*. Edited by Robert Knox. Edinburgh: MacLachlan and Stewart, 1829.

Supplement to the Trial of William Burke and Helen M'Dougal, containing the Whole Legal Proceedings against William Hare. Edinburgh: Robert Buchanan, 1829.

Syme, David. *Reports of Proceedings in the High Court of Justiciary, from 1826–1829*. Edinburgh: Thomas Clark, 1829.

Symonds, Deborah. *Notorious Murders, Black Lanterns, and Moveable Goods*. Akron, Ohio: University of Akron Press, 2006.

Symons, Jeliger. *Arts and Artisans at Home and Abroad*. Edinburgh: William Tait, 1839.

———. *Tactics for the Times: As regards the condition and treatment of the dangerous classes*.1849. Reprint, New York: Garland, 1984.

Tait, William. *Magdalenism: An Inquiry into the Extent, Causes, and Consequences, of Prostitution in Edinburgh*. Edinburgh: P. Rickard, 1842.

Taylor, Clare L. "Knox, Robert (1791–1862)." *Dictionary of National Biography*. Oxford: Oxford University Press, 2004. http://www.oxforddnb.com/view/article/15787.

Theal, George McCall, ed. *Records of the Cape Colony December 1826*. Cape Town: Government of Cape Colony, 1905.

Thomas, Dylan. *The Doctor and the Devils and Other Scripts*. New York: New Directions, 1970.

Thompson, Thomas Perronet. *Catholic State Waggon*. London: Cowie and Strange, 1829.

Tiedemann, Friedrich. *Plates of the arteries of the human body*. Translated by Robert Knox and Thomas Wharton Jones. Edinburgh: MacLachlan and Stewart, 1831.

Tomlinson, Stephen. *Head Masters: Phrenology, Secular Education, and Nineteenth-Century Social Thought*. Tuscaloosa: University of Alabama Press, 2005.

The trial of Katherine Nairn and Patrick Ogilvie for the crime of incest and murder. Edinburgh: Auld and Smellie, 1765.

The trial of Miss Broderick, for the wilful murder of George Errington, esq. Edinburgh: J. Robertson, 1794.

Trial of William Burke and Helen M'Dougal, before the High Court of Justiciary, at Edinburgh. Edinburgh: Robert Buchanan, 1829.

Turgenev, Ivan. *Fathers and Sons*. Oxford: Oxford University Press, 1998.

Turnbull, Paul. "British Anatomists, Phrenologists and the Construction of the Aboriginal Race, c. 1790-1830." *History Compass* 5 (2007): 26–50.

Turner, Michael J. "Thompson, Thomas Perronet (1783–1869)." *Dictionary of National Biography*. Oxford: Oxford University Press, 2004. http://www.oxforddnb.com/view/article/27280.

Tyne and Wear Museum Collections. http://www.imagine.org.uk.

"Union Canal." Seagull Trust. http://www.seagulltrust.org.uk/html/canal_history.html.

van Wyhe, John. *Phrenology and the Origins of Victorian Scientific Naturalism*. Aldershot: Ashgate, 2004.

Walkowitz, Judith. *Prostitution and Victorian Society: Women, Class, and the State*. New York: Cambridge University Press, 1980.

Watson, Alexander. *A medico-legal treatise on homicide by external violence*. Edinburgh: MacLachlan Stewart, 1841.

West Port Murders. Edinburgh: Thomas Ireland, 1829.

White, Brenda M. "Christison, Sir Robert, First Baronet (1797–1882)." *Dictionary of National Biography*. Oxford: Oxford University Press, 2004. http://www.oxforddnb.com/view/article/5370.

Wigham, John. *Letter to the Citizens of Edinburgh on the Expediency of*

Establishing a House of Refuge for Juvenile Offenders. Edinburgh: Bell and Bradfute, 1832.

Wilson's Remarkable Trials. London: G. Berger, 1841.

Wise, Sarah. *The Italian Boy: A Tale of Murder and Body Snatching in 1830s London*. London: Macmillan, 2005.

Wretch's Illustrations of Shakespeare. Edinburgh: R. H. Nimmo, 1829.

Index

Acknowledgments

THE HELP AND ENCOURAGEMENT I RECEIVED FROM FRIENDS and colleagues made writing this book a delight. I would like to thank all the people who assisted and encouraged my research in Scotland: Michael Barfoot, Adam Budd, Gayle Davis, and Steve Sturdy, Edinburgh University; Andrew Connell, Dawn Kemp, and Marianne Smith, Royal College of Surgeons of Edinburgh; Iain Milne, Royal College of Physicians of Edinburgh; Rosemary Elliot and Malcolm Nicolson, Glasgow University. I'd also like to thank Richard Hunter and the staff of the Edinburgh City Archives, John Lawson, City of Edinburgh Council, and Victoria Endean, The Signet Library, as well as the curators and staff at the National Library of Scotland, the Edinburgh Room of the Edinburgh Central Library, the Edinburgh University Library, the National Archives of Scotland, and the General Register Office for Scotland. Thank you all for making Scotland a paradise for historians.

Closer to home, I would like to thank Anna Dhody, Robert Hicks, and the library staff of the College of Physicians of Philadelphia; Stacey Peebles, Pennsylvania Hospital Historical Collections; John Pollack, Rare Book and Manuscript Library, University of Pennsylvania. I would also like to thank the Historical Collections of the New York Academy of Medicine Library and the Research Collection, New York Public Library. Many thanks to Susan Bucikowski and the Interlibrary Loan department at Stockton College, and to David Pinto, Director of the Stockton Library, for his continued support of this vital research tool.

I have benefited from the enthusiastic and penetrating feedback Burke and Hare seems to inspire. Special thanks to the organizers and participants of the History of Medicine Seminar, Johns Hopkins University, the

Edinburgh History of Medicine Group, Royal College of Physicians of Edinburgh, the Regional Forum for the History of Scottish Medicine, Glasgow University, and the Lees Seminar, Rutgers University–Camden. I would also like to thank Mary Fissell, Johns Hopkins University, and the anonymous reviewer for the University of Pennsylvania Press. As always, Penn Press is a delight to work with. Many thanks to Jerry Singerman, for his continued support for the dark side of medical history, and to Stephanie Brown, Sandra Haviland, John Hubbard, Yumeko Kawano, Robert Milks, Noreen O'Connor-Abel, and Ellen Trachtenberg.

Thank you to all my friends and colleagues who read, commented on, or listened to me talk about this book: Eithne and William Bearden, Robert Gregg, Michael Hayse, Rodger Jackson, Bill Lubenow, Michelle McDonald, Linda Merians, Sharon Musher, Robert Nichols, Maryann McLoughlin, Kate Ogden, Beth Olsen, Tom Papademetriou, and Laura Zucconi. And thank you to the friends and family in Great Britain who always make my trips a pleasure: Shelley and Ron Debate, Helen Dingwall, John and Elizabeth Grant, Jane Kellett, Tony Kennedy, and Jane Rendall.

Finally, heartfelt thanks to John Theibault, Alice Theibault, Monica Theibault, Lillian Rosner, and Henry Rosner. I couldn't have done it without you.